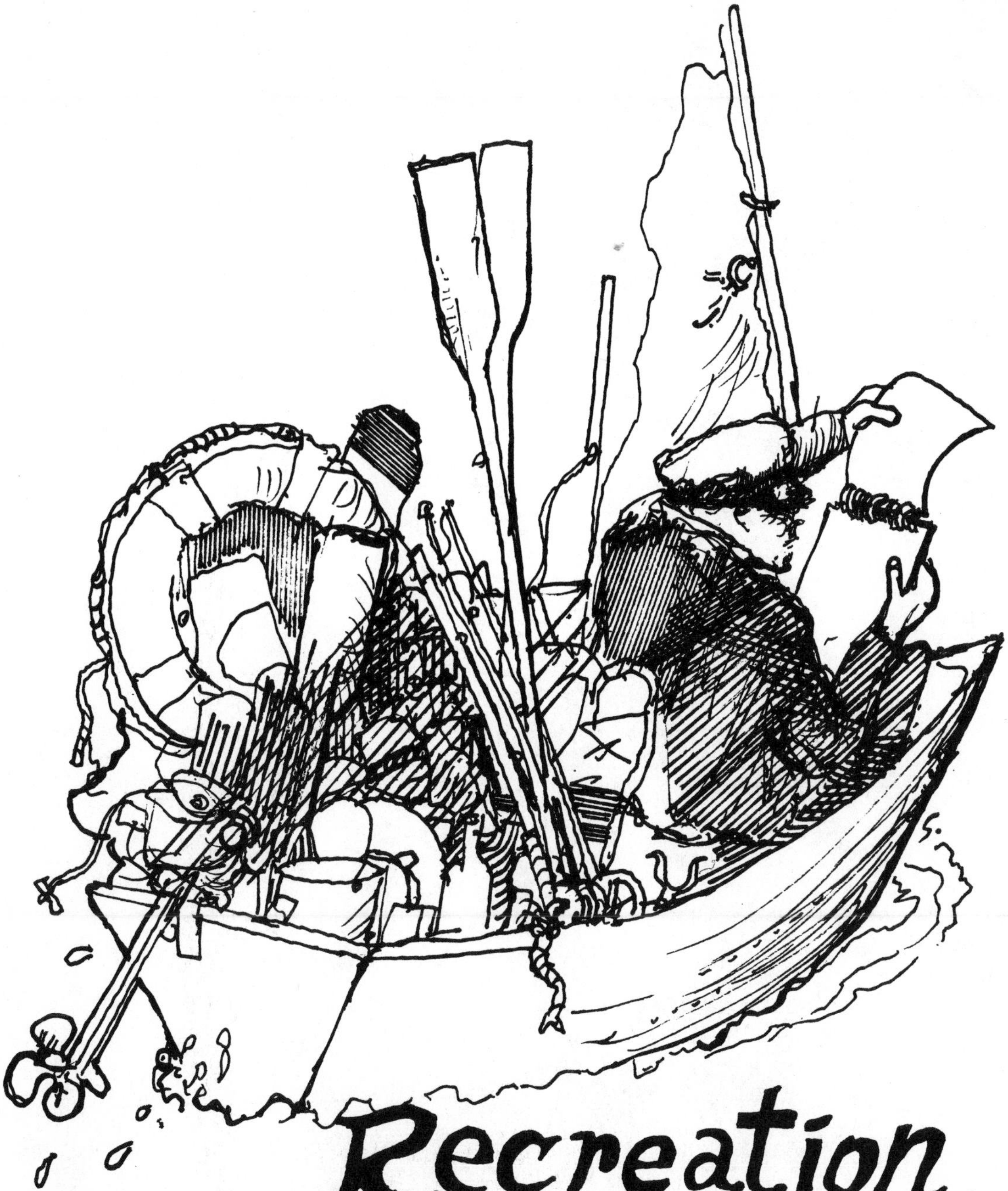

Recreation Lakes of Central California

by D.J. Dirksen

SAIL SALES
P. O. Box 1028
Aptos, California 95003
Phone: 408-662-2456

Rowing with
a six handicap
Snyder 79

1ST EDITION - 1978

2ND EDITION - 1979

3RD EDITION - 1980

Published by: SAIL SALES
P. O. BOX 1028
APTOS, CALIF. 95003
PHONE: 408-662-2456

ACKNOWLEDGMENTS

TO DAN SNYDER,

THE ARTISTIC GENIUS WHO HAS STUDIED IN THE SOUTH OF FRANCE AND WHO IS NOW DOING OUR DRAWINGS IN THE SOUTH OF DAVIS,

OUR SPECIAL THANKS.

away from Civilization!
SNYDER

We are extremely grateful to all the people who took the time to fill out our questionnaires, send brochures and letters and answer our never-ending phone calls. The U. S. Forest Service, California State Park System and all City and County Park Services were very helpful as well as all the private individuals involved with the Recreation Lakes.

snyder

TO: SAIL SALES
P. O. BOX 1028
APTOS, CA. 95003

ORDER BLANK

SEND RECREATION LAKES OF CENTRAL CALIFORNIA

$ 5.95	Book
.39	Sales Tax
.66	Postage
$ 7.00	Check Enclosed

Name : ______________________________

Address: ______________________________

SCOTTIES
APTOS
Snyder

FAVORITE QUOTES

Government Agencies:	"Please hold. I'll transfer your call."
Kay's Resort:	"This *!##* Questionnaire."
Diablo Sailing Club:	"Whatever happened to that book on Lakes?"

The Understanding Printers with our appreciation - Delta Lithograph Company

Neil Wilkinson:	"It is all taken care of."
Les Spencer:	"Don't panic!"
E. M. Kupfer:	"Some of our books have gone to the Moon." . . . this may go in the other direction.

Private Thoughts of Special People

G. Ferrabee:	"Why in the world are you doing this now?"
Renée Reeves:	"You hired me to learn the business......but aren't I really running the business?"
Greg, Trevor and Jake Dirksen:	"But . . . . "

Thank you for the support!

Carol Munro - Marina Recreation Association - Last seen recruiting members in Palm Springs!?

Norm Phillips - Columnist - Last seen looking for Aptos!?

Bob Reeves - Last seen "getting the books out"!

INTRODUCTION

As we go into our Third Edition of "RECREATION LAKES OF CENTRAL CALIFORNIA", we are happy to report our book has been a huge success and is helping to fill a need of all people who enjoy outdoor recreation.

For many years, we have been enthusiastic boaters and campers. Like most people, we returned year after year to our favorite spots for boating and fishing. From being in the recreation business, we began to realize that few people venture out to try new Lakes in new areas simply because they don't know they exist or don't know what might await them in the way of facilities.

This Guide was put together to stir your imagination and perhaps help you to understand what surprises may be in store at Recreation Lakes in Central California. We visited all of them and that alone makes the effort worthwhile.

These Lakes were chosen with the boat owner in mind, and the information is as accurate and up-to-date as we could possibly make it. Fees are subject to change, and Management at many of the Lakes are continuing to add campsites and other recreational facilities. We will continue to search for the perfect guidebook and will welcome all comments, criticisms or tidbits of information you can offer so that our future Editions will be more helpful.

Diane and Jim Dirksen
Sail Sales Publishing
P. O. Box 1028
Aptos, California 95003
Phone: 408-662-2456

Recreation Lakes Of Central California

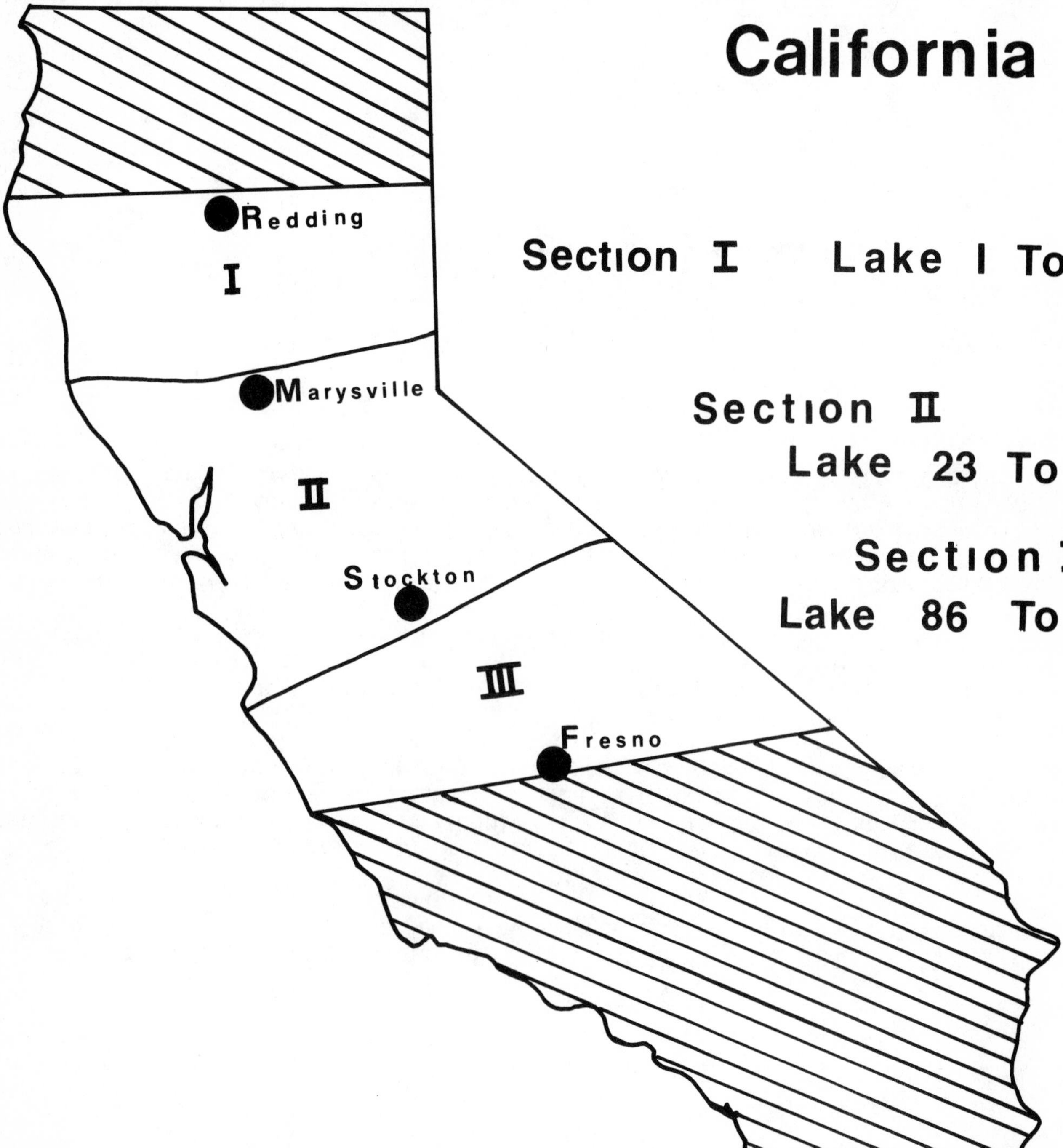
Redding
I
Marysville
II
Stockton
III
Fresno

Section I Lake 1 To 22

Section II
Lake 23 To 85

Section III
Lake 86 To 112

INDEX - ALPHABETICAL ORDER

(PAGES ARE SHOWN BY NUMBER OF LAKE)

WILDERNESS AREAS

There are 24 Wilderness Areas in the California Region of the U. S. Forest Service.

A Wilderness Permit is required to enter these areas and there are regulations governing access. These Permits are issued at Ranger Stations or Forest Service Offices near your point of entry.

The following list relates to the Areas contained in this book:

EL DORADO NATIONAL FOREST

Main Office
100 Forni Road
Placerville 95667
Phone: 916-622-5061

Amador Ranger District
P. O. Box 1327
Jackson 95642
Phone: 209-223-1623

Georgetown Ranger District
Georgetown 95634
Phone: 916-333-4312

Placerville Nursery
2375 Fruitridge Rd.
Camino 95709
Phone: 916-622-9600 or 9601

Pacific Ranger District
Pollock Pines 95726
Phone: 916-644-2348

Placerville Ranger District
3491 Carson Court
Camino 95667
Phone: 916-644-2324

LAKE TAHOE BASIN MANAGEMENT UNIT (Covers parts of El Dorado, Tahoe and Toiyabe National Forests)

Main Office
P. O. Box 8465
1052 Tata Lane
South Lake Tahoe 95705
Phone: 916-541-1130

Tahoe Visitor Center
Camp Richardson
Phone: 916-541-0209 (Closed in Winter)

TAHOE NATIONAL FOREST

Main Office
Highway 49
Nevada City 95959
Phone: 916-265-4531

Downieville Ranger District
Downieville 95936
Phone: 916-289-3232

Foresthill Ranger District
Foresthill 95631
Phone: 916-367-2224

Nevada City Ranger District
110 N. Pine St.
Nevada City 95959
Phone: 916-273-1371

Sierraville Ranger District
Sierraville 96126
Phone: 916-994-3401

Truckee Ranger District
Truckee 95734
Phone: 916-587-3558

MENDOCINO NATIONAL FOREST

Main Office
420 E. Laurel St.
Willows 95988
Phone: 916-934-3316

Corning Ranger District
1120 Solano St.
Corning 96021
Phone: 916-824-5196

Covelo Ranger District
Route 1, Box 62-C
Covelo 95428
Phone: 707-983-2941

Stonyford Ranger District
La Doga Road
Stonyford 95979
Phone: 916-963-3128

Upper Lake Ranger District
P. O. Box 96
Upper Lake 95485
Phone: 707-275-2361

Chico Tree Improvement
Nimshew Stage Box 29A
Chico 95926
Phone: 916-342-0408

. . . Continued . . .

SHASTA-TRINITY NATIONAL FOREST

Main Office
1615 Continental St.
Redding 96001
Phone: 916-246-5222

McCloud Ranger District
Drawer I
McCloud 96057
Phone: 916-964-2184 or 2185

Sacramento Ranger District
204 West Alma
Mt. Shasta 96067
Phone: 916-926-4596

Shasta Lake Ranger District
6543 Holiday Rd.
Redding 96001
Phone: 916-275-1587

Weaverville Ranger District
P. O. Box T
Weaverville 96093
Phone: 916-623-2131 or 2121

SIERRA NATIONAL FOREST

Main Office
Federal Building
1130 "O" St.
Fresno 93721
Phone: 209-487-5155

Bass Lake Ranger District
P. O. Box 366
Oakhurst 93644
Phone: 209-683-4665

Pineridge Ranger District
P. O. Box 306
Shaver Lake 93664
Phone: 209-841-3311

LASSEN NATIONAL FOREST

Main Office
707 Nevada St.
Susanville 96130
Phone: 916-257-2151

Almanor Ranger District
P. O. Box 586
Chester 96020
Phone: 916-258-2141

Eagle Lake Ranger District
2545 River St.
Susanville 96130
Phone: 916-257-2595 or 2161

PLUMAS NATIONAL FOREST

Main Office
159 Lawrence St.
Quincy 95971
Phone: 916-283-2050

Beckwourth Ranger District
P. O. Box 7
Blairsden 96103
Phone: 916-836-2575

La Porte Ranger District
P. O. Box F
Challenge 95925
Phone: 916-675-2462

Oroville Ranger District
875 Mitchell Ave.
Oroville 95965
Phone: 916-534-6500

Quincy Ranger District
P. O. Box 69
Quincy 95971
Phone: 916-283-0555

Greenville Ranger District
P. O. Box 329
Greenville 95947
Phone: 916-284-7126

STANISLAUS NATIONAL FOREST

Main Office
175 S. Fairview Lane
Sonora 95370
Phone: 209-532-3671

Calaveras Ranger District
P. O. Box 48
Arnold 95223
Phone: 209-795-1381

Groveland Ranger District
Drawer I
Groveland 95321
Phone: 209-962-7824

Mi-Wuk Ranger District
P. O. Box 100
Mi-Wuk Village 95346
Phone: 209-586-3234

Summit Ranger District
Pinecrest Ranger Station
Star Route, Box 1295
Sonora 95370
Phone: 209-965-3434

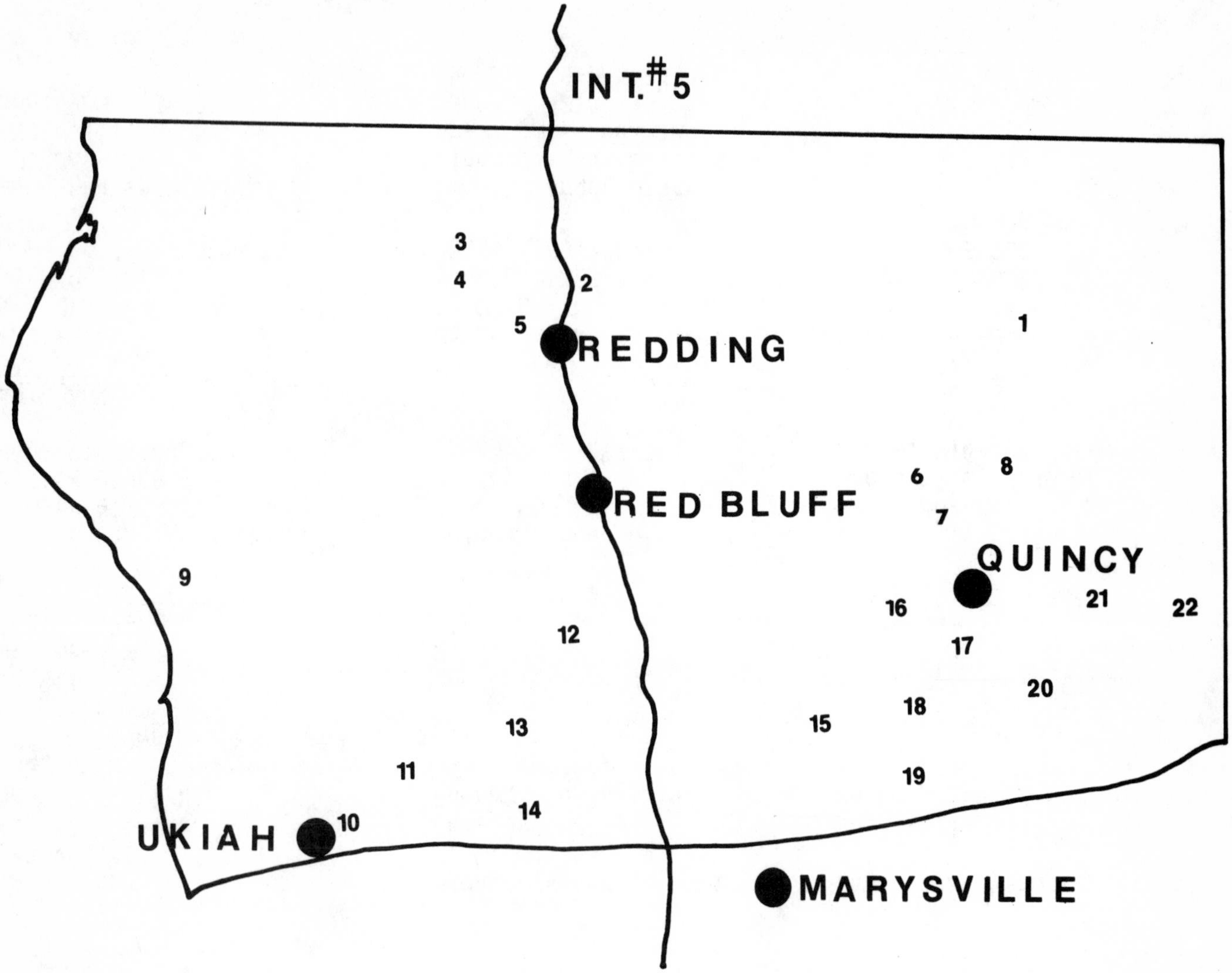
INT.#5
3
4
2
5
REDDING
1
6
8
RED BLUFF
7
QUINCY
9
16
21
22
12
17
20
18
13
15
11
19
14
UKIAH
10
MARYSVILLE

* Numbers As Shown Represent Lakes In Numerical Order In Book.

SECTION I

SECTION I

1. EAGLE LAKE
2. LAKE SHASTA
3. TRINITY LAKE
4. LEWISTON LAKE
5. WHISKEYTOWN LAKE
6. LAKE ALMANOR
7. ROUND VALLEY RESERVOIR
8. ANTELOPE LAKE
9. BENBOW LAKE
10. LAKE MENDOCINO
11. LAKE PILLSBURY
12. BLACK BUTTE LAKE
13. STONY GORGE RESERVOIR
14. EAST PARK RESERVOIR
15 LAKE OROVILLE
16. BUCKS LAKE
17. LITTLE GRASS VALLEY RESERVOIR
18. SLY CREEK AND LOST CREEK RESERVOIRS
19. BULLARDS BAR RESERVOIR
20. GOLD LAKE
21. LAKE DAVIS
22. FRENCHMAN LAKE

EAGLE LAKE

Eagle Lake, the second largest natural Lake in California, is 16 miles long and 5,100 feet in elevation. Eagle Lake Trout, found nowhere else in the world, average 2-3 pounds. Four U. S. Forest Service campgrounds are on the South Shore from Christie Point to Gallatin Beach and offer 486 sites for tents, R.V.s and trailers. Ice caves and a spine of lava rock can be found near Spaulding's Resort which has cabins, launch ramp, restaurant and camping. The Bureau of Land Management operates 20 sites on the North Shore at Eagle Lake Campground. There are no restrictions for boaters, boat camping, swimming or water-skiing. Nice beaches and good boating facilities make this Lake an ideal vacation area.

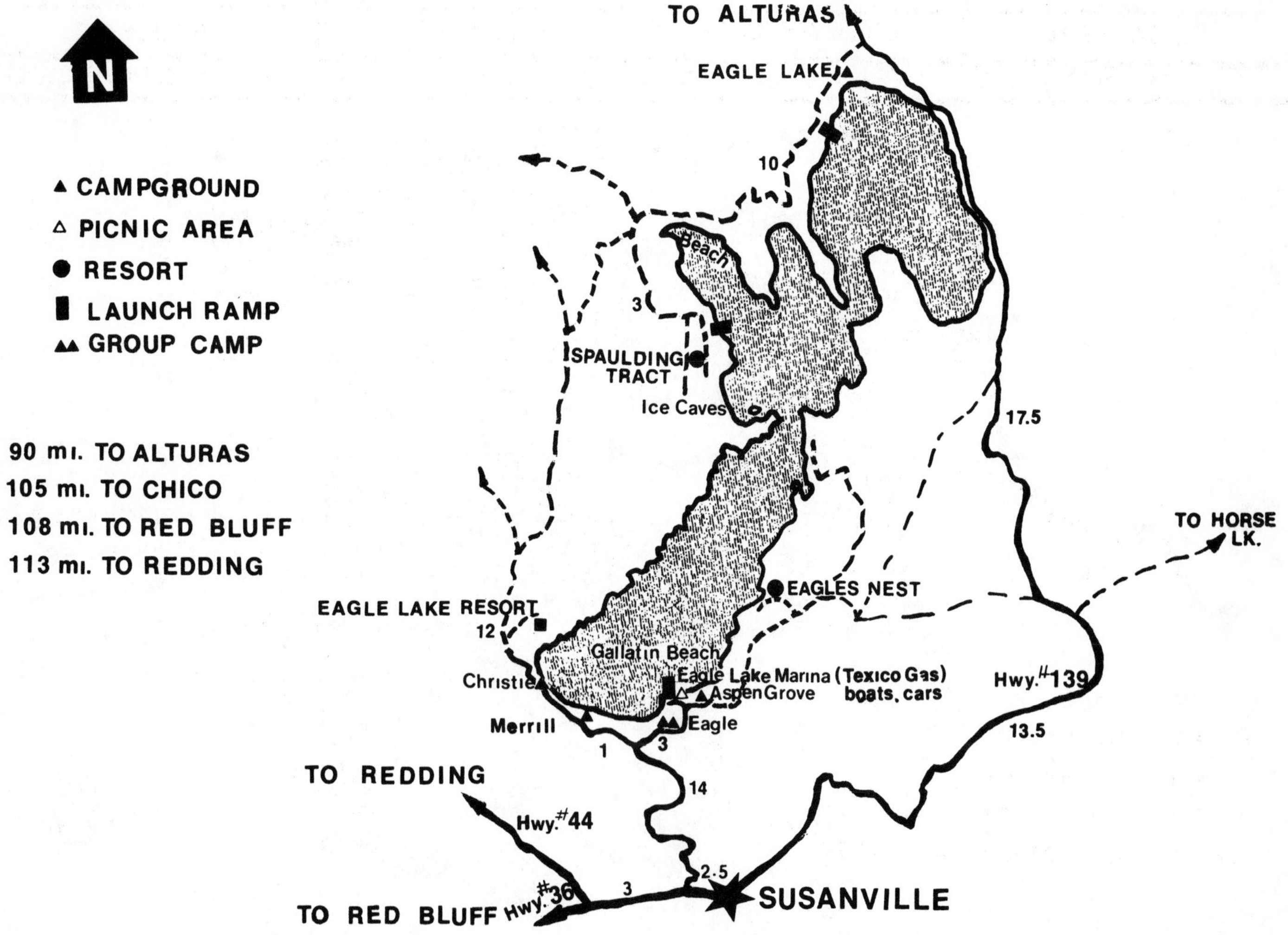
TO ALTURAS
EAGLE LAKE
N
▲ CAMPGROUND
△ PICNIC AREA
● RESORT
▮ LAUNCH RAMP
▲▲ GROUP CAMP
90 mi. TO ALTURAS
105 mi. TO CHICO
108 mi. TO RED BLUFF
113 mi. TO REDDING
10
Beach
3
SPAULDING TRACT
Ice Caves
17.5
TO HORSE LK.
EAGLES NEST
EAGLE LAKE RESORT
12
Gallatin Beach
Christie
Eagle Lake Marina (Texico Gas) boats, cars
AspenGrove
Eagle
Merrill
1
3
Hwy. #139
13.5
TO REDDING
14
Hwy. #44
2.5
3
TO RED BLUFF Hwy. #36
SUSANVILLE

INFORMATION: U. S. Forest Service, Susanville 96130

CAMPING	BOATING	RECREATION	RESORTS
486 Developed Sites for Tents, R.V.s and Trailers - USFS	All Boating Allowed	Trout Fishing	Cabins
20 Developed Sites Bureau of Land Management	Launch Ramps	Swimming	Snack Bar
Fee: $3 a Day	Boat & Motor Rentals	Picnicking	Ice
	Supplies	Hiking	Grocery Store
	Full Service Marina		Laundromat
	Boat Storage		Showers

Lake Shasta, at 1,065 feet elevation, is made up of four main arms: Sacramento River, McCloud River, Squaw Creek and Pit River. This Lake is 35 miles long with 370 shoreline miles (more than San Francisco Bay, which has 276 shoreline miles). The maximum depth is 515 feet. Camping is allowed along the shoreline except in designated restricted areas, and boat camping is also permitted, but campfire permits are required. Houseboating on the Lake is excellent and very popular, as is waterskiing. The shoreline is often steep and covered with tall pine trees. There are several interesting attractions, including the Buly Hill Mine Tour. You can take a ferry to Lake Shasta Caverns, the largest in California. Shasta Dam is the second largest concrete dam in the United States, surpassed only by Grand Coulee in size, or Hoover Dam in height. It is higher than the Washington Monument and its spillway is three times the height of Niagara Falls. It is brilliantly lighted at night and is quite a spectacular sight. Tours of the Dam and Powerhouse, displays and films are available daily at the Visitor's Center next to the Dam. The Lake water drops an average of 53 feet by Fall. The winds are variable and boating is good.

. . . Continued . . .

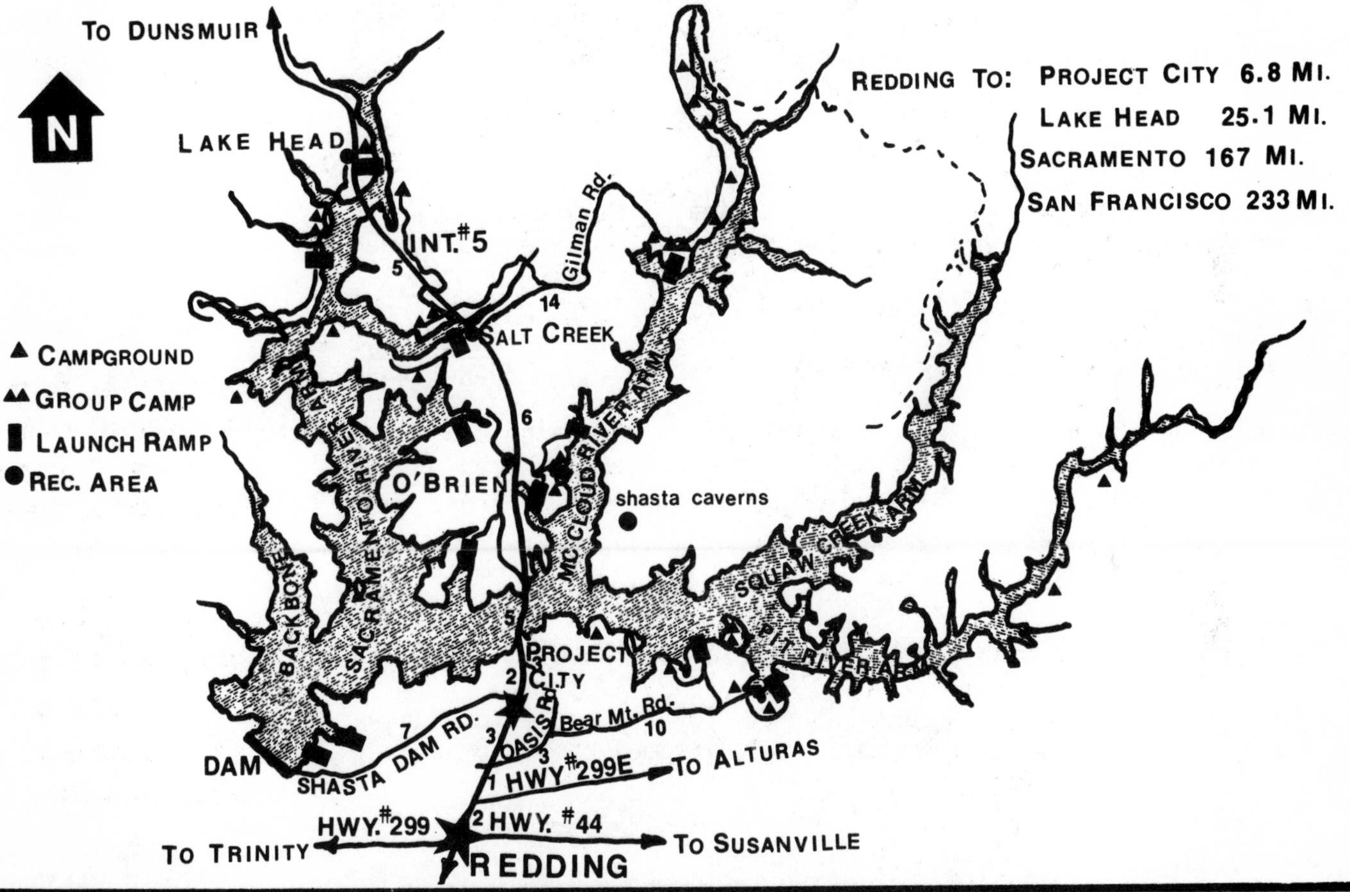
To Dunsmuir
N
Redding To: Project City 6.8 Mi.
Lake Head 25.1 Mi.
Sacramento 167 Mi.
San Francisco 233 Mi.
Lake Head
Int.#5
Gilman Rd.
Salt Creek
Campground
Group Camp
Launch Ramp
Rec. Area
O'Brien
shasta caverns
Sacramento River Arm
McCloud River Arm
Squaw Creek Arm
Pit River Arm
Backbone Arm
Project City
Oasis Rd.
Bear Mt. Rd.
Shasta Dam Rd.
Dam
Hwy #299E
To Alturas
Hwy #299
Hwy. #44
To Trinity
To Susanville
Redding

INFORMATION: District Ranger, 6543 Holiday Rd., Redding 96001, Ph. 916-275-1587

CAMPING	BOATING	RECREATION	RESORTS
445 Developed Sites for Tents, R.V.s and Trailers - USFS Fee: $1 to $3 a Day 108 Boat Access Camps 200 Capacity Group Camp 279 Private Campsites	All Boating Allowed Rentals Available: Houseboats, Ski Boats, Fishing Boats, Jet Skis Launch Ramps Marinas Supplies	Fishing Hiking Picnicking Swimming Tours	Motels & Cabins Trailer Parks Snack Bars Restaurants Markets Laundromats

. . . Continued . . .

Approximate Mileage from Interstate 5 at Oasis Road	Camping Facilities - U. S. Forest Service
	Pit River Arm
11 Miles Northeast	Rocky Ridge - 10 campsites (tents only), water, toilets, boat access also. Fee $1.
11 Miles Northeast	Jones Valley - 27 campsites (tents/trailers), water, toilets, boat access also. Fee $2.
13 Miles Northeast	Mariner's Point - 8 campsites (tents only), water, toilets, boat access and vehicle access.
Approximate Mileage from Interstate 5 at O'Brien	McCloud River Arm
1 Mile East	Bailey Cove - 25 campsites (20 tents only, 5 trailers/tents), water, toilets. Fee $3. Launch ramp.
2 Miles East	Wintoon - 11 campsites (tents only), toilets.
From Interstate 5 at Gilman Road	
9 Miles East	Hirz Bay - 48 campsites (tents/trailers), water, toilets. Fee $3. Launch ramp, amphitheater. Reservations through your local Ticketron Outlet or write: Ticketron, P.O.Box 26430, San Francisco
10 Miles East	Dekkas Rock - 12 campsites (tents only), water, toilets. Fee $2.
11 Miles East	Moore Creek - 10 campsites (tents only), water, toilets. Fee $2.
13 Miles East	Jennings Creek - 8 campsites (tents only), water, toilets, boat access and walk-in. Fee $1.
15 Miles East	Ellery Creek - 19 campsites (9 tents only, 10 tents/trailers), water, toilets. Fee $2.
16 Miles East	Pine Point - 13 campsites (6 tents only, 7 tents/trailers), water, toilets. Fee $2.
17 Miles East	McCloud Bridge - 19 campsites (9 tents only, 9 tents/trailers), water, toilets. Fee $2.
18 Miles East	Point McCloud - Undeveloped Camping Only - Access by Gravel Road.
	Group Camp
9 Miles East	Hirz Bay Group Camp - Camp #1: Minimum Capacity - 25, Maximum Capacity - 150. Fee $20 a day. Camp #2: Minimum Capacity - 15, Maximum Capacity - 50. Fee $10 a day. Tents or Trailers. Water, toilets. Reservations through your local Ticketron Outlet or write: Ticketron, P. O. Box 26430, San Francisco 94120.

. . . Continued . . .

Approximate Mileage from Interstate 5 at Salt Creek	Sacramento River Arm
0 Miles	Upper Salt Creek - 44 campsites (tents only), water, toilets. Fee $2. Improved sandy beach.
1 Mile South	Lower Salt Creek - 12 campsites (tents only), water, toilets, launch ramp. Fee $1.
0.5 Mile West	Nelson Point - 8 campsites (tents only), water, toilets. Fee $2.
1 Mile West	Oak Grove - 43 campsites (trailers/tents), water, toilets. Fee $3.
3 Miles Northeast	Gregory Creek - 18 campsites (trailers), water, toilets. Fee $3.
Approximate Mileage from Interstate 5 at Lakehead	
1.7 Miles South	Antlers - 59 campsites (tents/trailers), water, toilets. Fee $3. Amphitheater, launch ramp, adjacent to Resort with full facilities. Reservations through your local Ticketron Outlet or write: Ticketron, P. O. Box 26430, San Francisco 94120.
2.5 Miles South	Lakeshore - 36 campsites (18 tents only, 18 trailers/tents), water, toilets. Fee $3. Adjacent to Resort with full facilities.
7.6 Miles South	Old Man - 10 campsites (tents only), water, toilets, boat access. Fee $2.

Boat Access Camping

Pit River Arm

Rend Island - 18 campsites, toilets, water.

Stein Creek - 5 campsites, toilets.

Arbuckle Flat - 11 campsites, toilets.

Sacramento River Arm

Slaughterhouse Island - 13 campsites, toilets, water.

Gooseneck Cove - 10 campsites, toilets, water.

Salt Creek Point - 7 campsites, toilets.

Between McCloud River and Squaw Creek

Allie Cove - 4 campsites, toilets, water.

Ski Island - 29 campsites, toilets, water, amphitheater.

McCloud River Arm

Greens Creek - 11 campsites, toilets, water.

. . . Continued . . .

. . . Continued . . .

Public Launch Ramps - No Fee

Pit River Arm - Jones Valley Ramp - 11 Miles Northeast on Oasis Road.

Packers Bay Launch Ramp - 2 Miles Southwest of O'Brien.

McCloud River Arm - Bailey Cove Ramp - 1 Mile East of O'Brien, 17.5 Miles North of Redding.

Hirz Bay Ramp - 9 Miles East of Gilman Road, 28 Miles North of Redding.

Sacramento River Arm - Centimudi Launch Ramp - 1 Mile East of Dam.

Antlers Ramp - 23.3 Miles North of Redding.

Private Resorts and Facilities

Bridge Bay - at South Interstate 5 Crossing - Bridge Bay Resort.

Jones Valley - at Pit River - Jones Valley Resort & Marina, Silverthorn Bay Resort.

Lakehead - at North Interstate Crossing - Antlers Resort, Antlers Trailer Resort, Lakehead Campground, Lakeshore Villa Trailer Park, Riverview Resort.

O'Brien - at McCloud River - Aqua Cruisers, Lakeview Resort, Lake Shasta Caverns Tour, Shasta Flowtels, Shasta Marina.

Project City - Central Valley - off South Interstate 5 - B & B Bait, Digger Bay Marina.

Salt Creek - North Sacramento River Inlet - Holiday Flotels, Salt Creek Lodge & Marina, Cascade Cove Resort, Nelson Point Cabins, Solus Campground.

Sugarloaf - North Sacramento River - Sugarloaf Beach & Marina, Sugarloaf Cottages, Tsadi Resort, Westaire Floatels.

Wonderland - Mountain Gate - Fawndale Lodge, Fawndale Oaks R.V. Park, Wonderland Mobile Home Park.

For Further Information Contact:

Shasta Dam Chamber of Commerce
5109 Shasta Dam Blvd.
Central Valley, California 96019
Phone: 916-275-1587

TRINITY LAKE

Trinity Lake is at 2,300 feet elevation, 22 miles long with a shoreline of 145 miles. There are complete boating facilities including boat camping. The area has very rugged terrain with large pine trees on the edge of the shoreline. The water is good for swimming with the temperature about 65 to 70 degrees in the summer. Many resorts and campgrounds are on the west shore of the Lake. There are a total of 519 campsites and 35 boat access camps as well as a 55 person group camp. The Primitive Area behind the Lake on the west side is good for hiking and backpacking, but a Wilderness Permit is required. There is an airport at Trinity Center and another one at Weaverville. The Scott Museum at Trinity Center displays artifacts of California history.

. . . Continued . . .

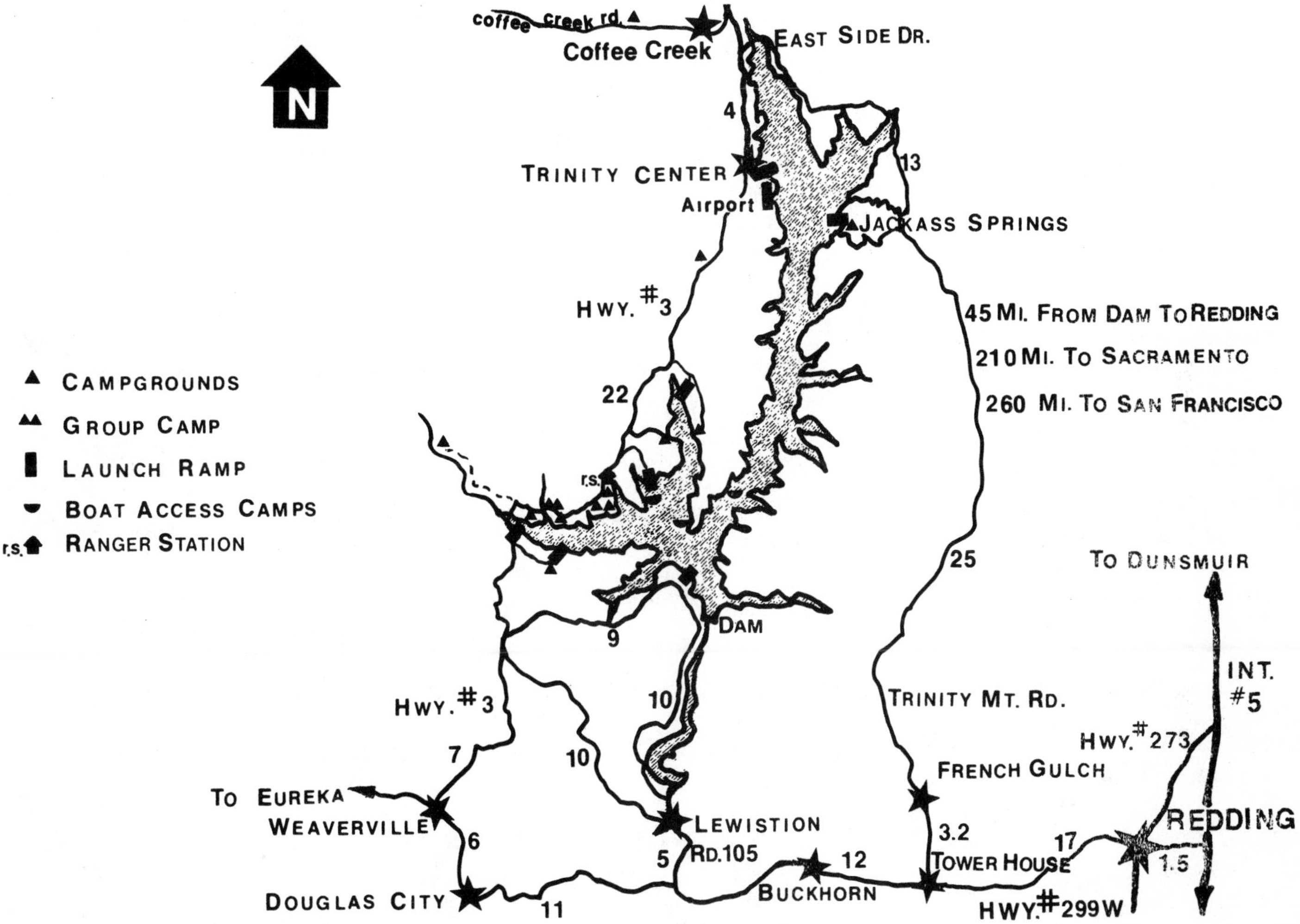
coffee creek rd.
Coffee Creek
East Side Dr.
N
4
Trinity Center
13
Airport
Jackass Springs
Hwy. #3
45 Mi. From Dam To Redding
210 Mi. To Sacramento
260 Mi. To San Francisco
22
Campgrounds
Group Camp
Launch Ramp
Boat Access Camps
r.s.
r.s. Ranger Station
25
To Dunsmuir
Dam
9
Int. #5
Hwy. #3
10
Trinity Mt. Rd.
Hwy. #273
7
10
French Gulch
To Eureka
Weaverville
Lewistion
Redding
3.2
6
5
Rd.105
12
Tower House
17
1.5
Douglas City
Buckhorn
11
Hwy. #299W

INFORMATION: District Ranger, U.S. Forest Service, Weaverville, Ph. 916-623-2121

CAMPING	BOATING	RECREATION	RESORTS
519 Developed Sites for Tents, R.V.s and Trailers	All Boating Allowed	Swimming	Motels & Cabins
35 Boat Access Sites	Houseboat Rentals	Picnicking	Trailer Parks
55 People Group Camp	Fishing Boat Rentals	Hiking	Snack Bars
Fee: $2 to $3 per day	5 Launch Ramps	Backpacking	Restaurants
		Fishing	Supermarket
		Horseback Riding	Laundromat

TRINITY LAKE

. . . Continued . . .

Mileage from Weaverville North	Camping Facilities from Dam West to Jackass Spring, N. E. Shore U. S. Forest Service
12	Tannery Gulch - 87 campsites (49 tents only, 38 trailers/tents), water, toilets, swimming beach, launch ramp, amphitheater.
14	Stony Point - 22 campsites (tents only), water, toilets.
15	Fawn Camp - 60 campsites, water, toilets.
17	Bridge Camp - 10 campsites, water, toilets, horse corral, Primitive Area Trailhead.
17	Bushytail - 40 campsites, water, toilets.
18	Minersville - 30 campsites (28 tents only, 2 trailers/tents), water, toilets, low water launch ramp.
19	Clark Springs - 30 campsites (26 tents only, 4 trailers/tents), water, toilets, 7 picnic units with grills, swimming beach.
20	Hayward Flat - 108 campsites (75 tents only, 33 trailers/tents), water, toilets, swimming beach.
25	Alpine View - 66 campsites (41 tents only, 25 trailers/tents), water, toilets, Bowerman launch ramp, trails.
28	Preacher Meadow - 45 campsites (12 tents only, 33 trailers/tents), water, toilets.
35 Miles to Carroll Bridge, then 17 miles on Blue Mtn. Road.	Jackass Spring - 21 campsites (1 tent only, 20 trailers/tents), water, toilets.

Group Camp

14.5	Stony Creek - 10 campsites (tents only), 55 people capacity, water, toilets. Reservations through your local Ticketron outlet or write: Ticketron, P. O. Box 26430, San Francisco 94120.

Boat Access Camping

Captains Point - 3 campsites, toilets.

Mariners Roost - 7 campsites, toilets.

Ridgeville - 22 campsites, toilets.

Ridgeville Island - 3 campsites, toilets.

. . . Continued . . .

Picnicking Units

Mileage from Weaverville North	
12.6	Tanbark - 7 picnic units, water, toilets.
13.2	Stuart Fork - 4 picnic units, water, toilets, boat launching.
13.7	Kokanee - 7 picnic units, water, toilets.
30	Trinity Center - 3 picnic units, water, toilets.

Launch Ramps

2 Miles North of Dam	Fairview Marina - boat launching, toilets.
12	Tannery Gulch - water, toilets, trails, amphitheater, trailer spaces, 87 campsites.
12.9	Stuart Fork Ramp - 4 picnic units, water, toilets.
17	Cedar Stock Resort & Marina - Store, Gas, Cabins, Restaurant.
18	Minersville - low water ramp adjacent to Minersville Campground.
23	Estrellita Marina - Store, Gas.
26	Bowerman Ramp - water, toilets.
29	Trinity Center Marina - Numerous commercial facilities.

Some Privately Owned Resorts

Trinity Alps Resort - 15 miles North on Highway 3, 1 mile left on Trinity Alps Road - the oldest resort in Trinity with delightful accommodations in completely equipped rustic housekeeping cabins situated along Stuarts Fork River, excellent restaurant with home cooking, full vacation facilities, ideal family Resort.

Cedar Stock Resort & Marina - About 17 miles North on Highway 3 - housekeeping cabins, restaurant, lounge, store, plus full service Marina, houseboat rentals for 6-8 people or 10 people super deluxe models.

Seymour's Ranch - 42 miles North on Highway 3, 8 miles North of Trinity Center - fully equipped housekeeping cabins for parties from 2 to 6, private stream fed pond with sandy beach.

Coffee Creek Ranch - 13 miles Northwest of Trinity Center on Coffee Creek Road - Full American Plan cabins, some with fireplaces, restaurant, swimming pool, weekly steak fry, full vacation facilities, horseback riding, stream fishing on Coffee Creek which runs through Ranch.

There are numerous other private Resorts, trailer parks, houseboat rentals and Marinas offering excellent vacation facilities. For a complete list, write Trinity County Chamber of Commerce, P. O. Box 517, Weaverville 96093.

LEWISTON LAKE

Lewiston Lake, at 2,000 feet elevation is the Forebay of Trinity Lake. The water is very cold all year as it comes from the bottom of Trinity Dam. Since the water is constantly moving, this Lake is primarily used for fishing. There are four campground facilities and several private resorts on the County Road No. 105 that goes along the Lake. Mary Smith Campground has 18 units for tent camping, toilets and water, and is 2.1 miles from Lewiston. Copper Gulch Campground has 11 units for tent camping, toilets and water. It is 4.2 miles from Lewiston. Tunnel Rock Campground has 6 units for tent camping, toilets and water and is 7.2 miles from Lewiston. Ackerman Campground has 65 units, 30 for tents only and 35 for trailers or tents. It has toilets and water and is 8.1 miles from Lewiston. These four campgrounds are run by the U. S. Forest Service. Private Resorts include Lakeview Terrace which has housekeeping cabins, a trailer park, swimming pool and laundry. Pine Cove Marina and Trailer Park has a launch ramp, rental boats, gas and store.

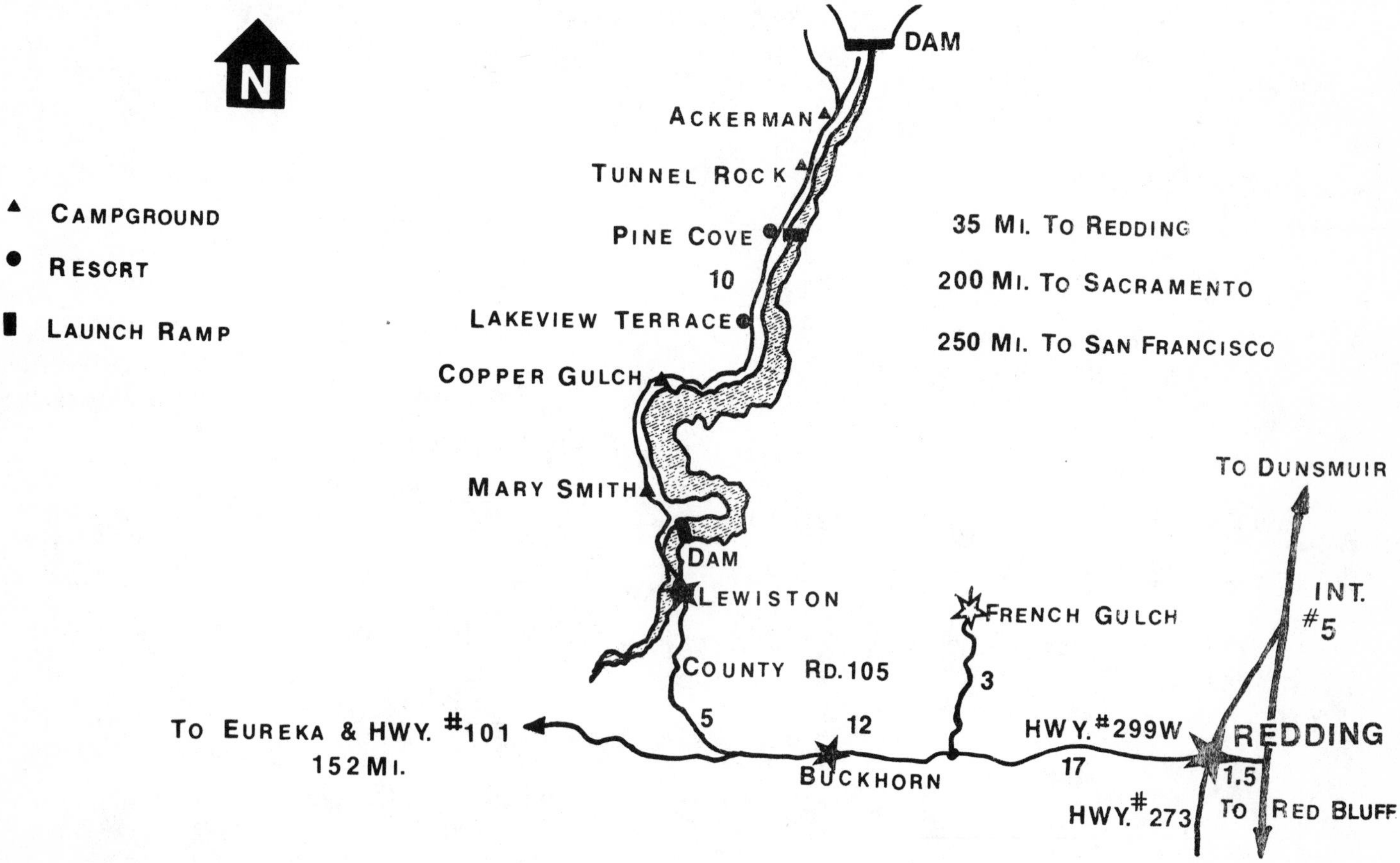
N
DAM
ACKERMAN
TUNNEL ROCK
CAMPGROUND
RESORT
LAUNCH RAMP
PINE COVE
10
LAKEVIEW TERRACE
COPPER GULCH
35 MI. TO REDDING
200 MI. TO SACRAMENTO
250 MI. TO SAN FRANCISCO
MARY SMITH
DAM
LEWISTON
TO DUNSMUIR
INT. #5
FRENCH GULCH
COUNTY RD.105
3
5
12
TO EUREKA & HWY. #101
152 MI.
BUCKHORN
HWY. #299W
17
REDDING
1.5
HWY. #273
TO RED BLUFF

INFORMATION: District Ranger, U.S. Forest Service, Weaverville, Ph. 916-623-2121

CAMPING	BOATING	RECREATION	RESORTS
100 Developed Sites for Tents, R.V.s and Trailers Fee: $2 a Day	Fishing Boats 10 MPH Speed Limit Rentals per Day: 12 ft. boat - $17 14 ft. boat - $21 Pontoon Boat - $25	Trout Fishing Picnicking Hiking	Motels & Cabins Trailer Parks Restaurants Snack Bars

WHISKEYTOWN LAKE

Whiskeytown Lake, at 1,209 feet elevation, has 36 miles of shoreline and a maximum depth of 264 feet. On the south side of the Lake, Brandy Creek has two access roads. The first one is for the swim beach, snack bar and picnic area. The second one is for 37 self-contained campsites with a dump station, marina supplies, slips, boat rentals and ramp. Beyond Brandy Creek is Dry Creek Group Campground, tent camping only, for 160 people maximum, reservations required. North of the Lake on Highway 299W is Oak Bottom Campground, with 105 tent sites and 50 R.V. sites, and a dump station. A Ranger Station, boat rentals, slips, launch ramp, marina supplies, camper store, swim beach, snack bar and picnic area are also there. Whiskey Creek, to the right of Highway 299W, has a launch ramp and picnic area. A store and post office are on this road. Also on the east side of the Whiskey Creek area is a 3-site group picnic area, reservations required. The Bald Eagle, one of the protected endangered species, is found in this area.

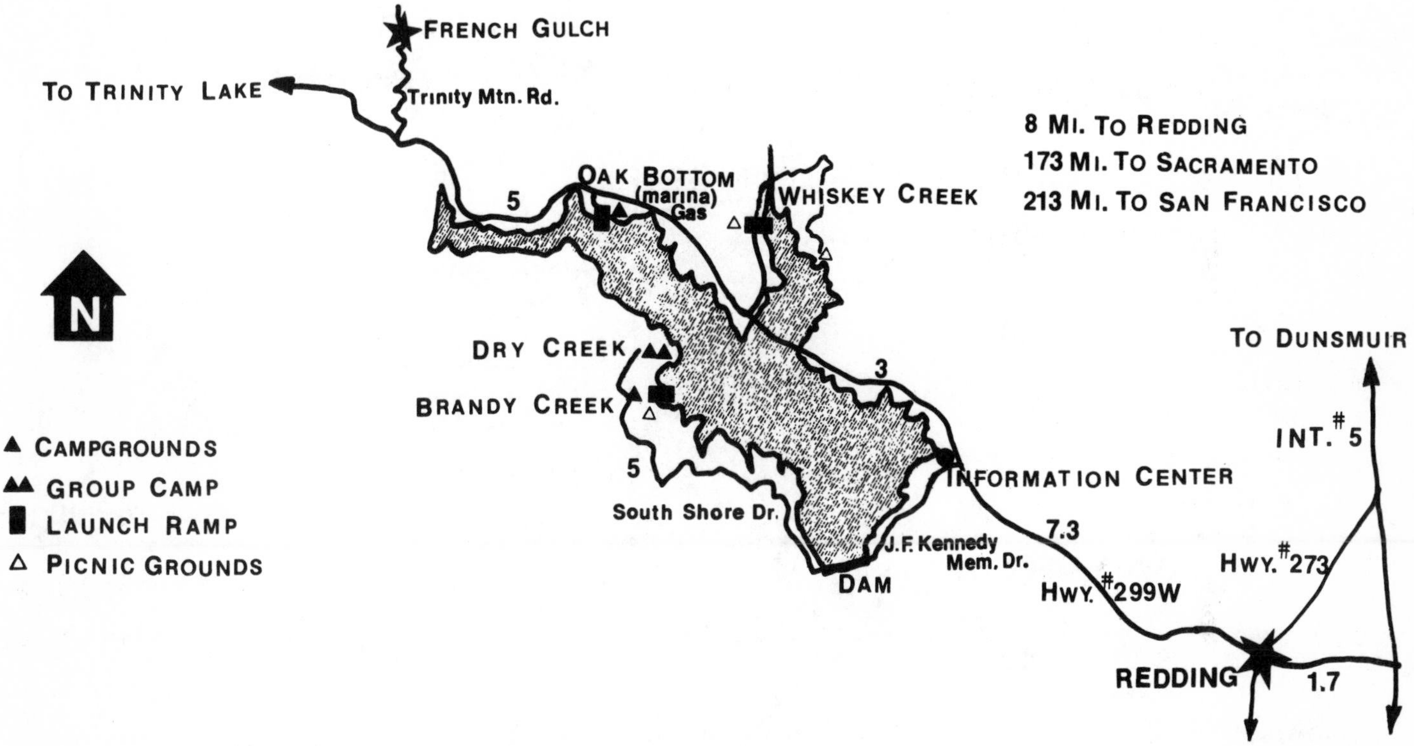

FRENCH GULCH
TO TRINITY LAKE
Trinity Mtn. Rd.
8 MI. TO REDDING
173 MI. TO SACRAMENTO
213 MI. TO SAN FRANCISCO
OAK BOTTOM
(marina)
Gas
WHISKEY CREEK
5
N
DRY CREEK
BRANDY CREEK
3
TO DUNSMUIR
INT. #5
CAMPGROUNDS
GROUP CAMP
LAUNCH RAMP
PICNIC GROUNDS
5
INFORMATION CENTER
South Shore Dr.
7.3
J.F. Kennedy
Mem. Dr.
DAM
HWY. #299W
HWY. #273
REDDING
1.7

INFORMATION: Superintendent, P.O. Box 188, Whiskeytown 96095, Ph. 916-241-6584

CAMPING	BOATING	RECREATION	RESORTS
105 Developed Sites for Tents 87 Sites for R.V.s and Trailers Fee: $3 a Day Reservations Required at the 160 person Group Campground.	All Boating Allowed but Motors must meet California Noise Level Laws Rental Boats 3 Launch Ramps Marinas No overnight house-boating.	Fishing Swimming Hiking Picnicking Reservations Required at the Group Picnic Area.	Snack Bar Grocery Store Motels - 10 Miles

The name, Almanor, was derived from parts of the names of three daughters of the Controller of Great Western Power Company. The Dam was built in 1914. The Lake is 13 miles long and 6 miles wide and is one of the largest man-made lakes in California. Lake Almanor is a full facility Lake, and all types of boating are permitted. Winds are usually from the West, but caution is advised as gusty winds can come up very suddenly. The water fluctuates and some ramps may not be used in the Fall as the water drops about 30 feet. Butt Valley Reservoir is 3 miles Southwest of Almanor by dirt road and has 67 campsites.

. . . Continued . . .

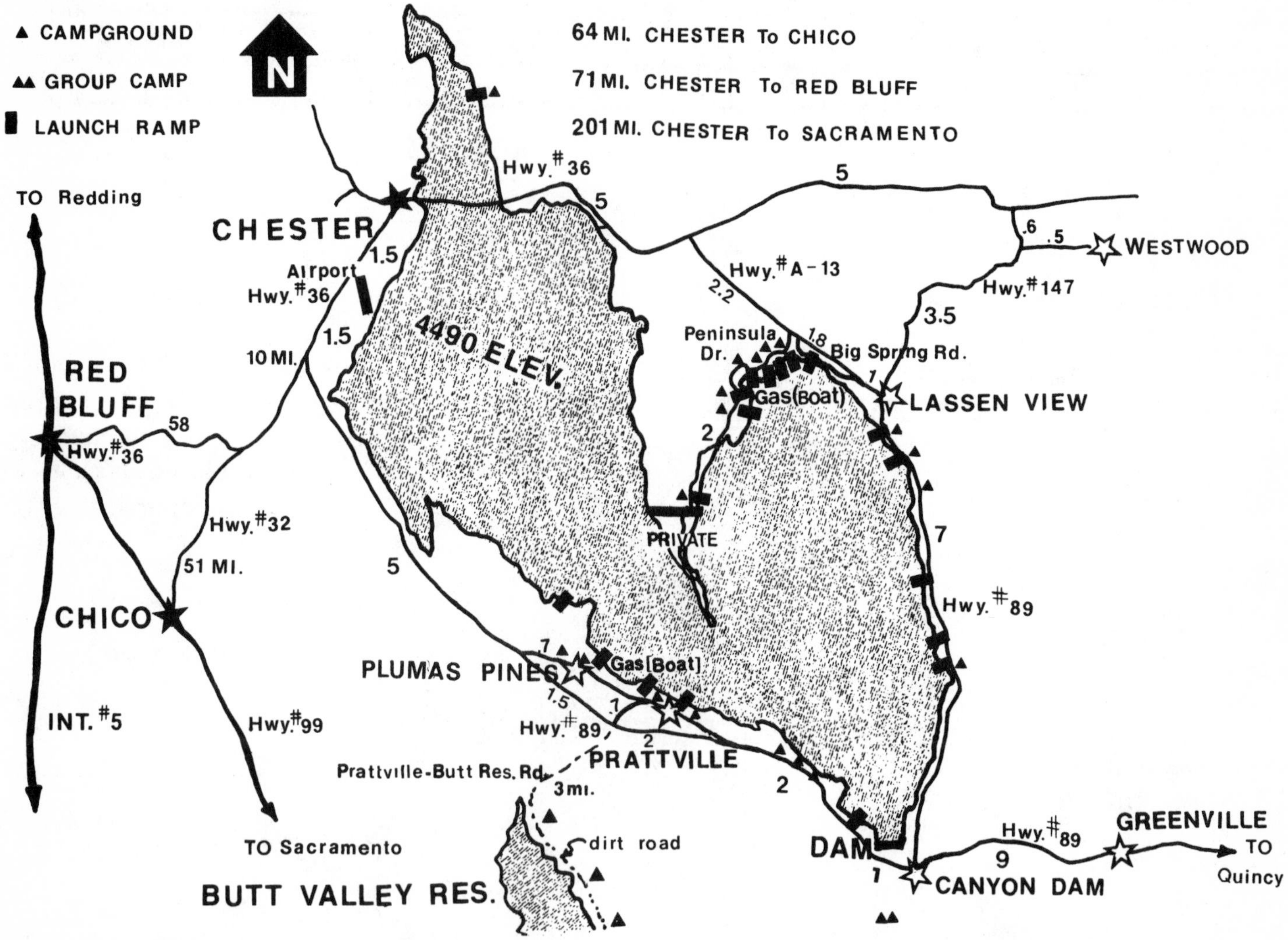
▲ CAMPGROUND
▲▲ GROUP CAMP
▮ LAUNCH RAMP
N
64 MI. CHESTER To CHICO
71 MI. CHESTER To RED BLUFF
201 MI. CHESTER To SACRAMENTO
TO Redding
CHESTER
Airport
Hwy. #36
1.5
10 MI.
RED BLUFF
58
Hwy. #36
Hwy. #32
51 MI.
CHICO
INT. #5
Hwy #99
TO Sacramento
4490 ELEV.
5
PLUMAS PINES
Gas(Boat)
Hwy. #89
PRATTVILLE
Prattville-Butt Res. Rd.
3 mi.
dirt road
BUTT VALLEY RES.
DAM
CANYON DAM
9
GREENVILLE
TO Quincy
PRIVATE
7
Hwy. #89
LASSEN VIEW
Peninsula Dr.
Big Spring Rd.
Hwy. #A-13
2.2
1.8
3.5
Hwy. #147
WESTWOOD
.6
.5

INFORMATION: P. G. & E., 350 Salem St., Chico 95926, Ph. 916-343-5521			
CAMPING	**BOATING**	**RECREATION**	**RESORTS**
105 Developed Sites for Tents, R.V.s, Trailers - P.G.E. 102 Developed Sites for Tents, R.V.s, Trailers - USFS 40 People Group Camp 67 Developed Sites at Butt Valley Reservoir.	All Boating Allowed 19 Launch Ramps Full Service Marinas	Fishing Swimming Hiking Picnicking	Motels & Cabins Trailer Parks Snack Bars Restaurants

Approximate Mileage from Dam on Highway 89	Camping Facilities - P. G. & E.
0.1 Mile East	Skinner Flat Group Camp - Maximum Capacity - 40 people. Water, toilets, multi-purpose utility building with cook area, grill, regrigeration, showers and 5 bunk houses, swimming beach and picnic area. Reservations only. Write: P. G. & E., 350 Salem Street, Chico 95926, Phone 916-343-5521.
1.5 Miles Northwest	Fox Farm - 43 campsites, water, toilets.
1.5 Miles Northwest	Mountain View - 20 campsites, handicapped facilities, water, toilets.
1.5 Miles Northwest	Rocky Point - 17 campsites, water, toilets.
4 Miles North from Chester via Feather River Road.	Last Chance Creek - 25 campsites, water, toilets.
2.5 Miles Northwest of Dam	Almanor Campground - U. S. Forest Service 102 campsites (57 tents only, 45 trailers/tents), water, toilets, handicapped facilities. Fee: $2 a Day.

Some Privately Owned Resorts

Northshore Campground - at Chester Causeway.

Harbor Lites Resort - 300 Peninsula Drive - R. V. Sites, Cabins. Marina.

Knotty Pine Resort - 430 Peninsula Drive - Cabins, Marina, Boat Rentals, Snack Bar, Store.

Little Norway Resort - 432 Peninsula Drive - Excellent facilities, Marina, Campsites, Cabins, Store, Snack Bar, Boat Rentals: Ski Boats, Sailboats, Hobie Cats, and Mopeds.

The Boat Dock - 440 Peninsula Drive - Cabins, Dockage.

Big Cove Resort - 442 Peninsula Drive - Campsites, Chalet for up to 8 people, Ramp, Boat Rentals, Store.

Moonspinners Cove Resort - 508 Peninsula Drive - Campsites, Cabins.

Kokanee Resort - End of Peninsula Drive before gate to private homes - Campsites, R.V.s, Chalets, Cabins, Marina, Boat Rentals, Store.

. . . Continued . . .

Lassen View Resort - on Highway 147 - Campsites, R.V.s, Cabins, Marina, Boat Rentals, Store.

Lake Haven Resort - on Highway 147 - Cabins, R.V. Sites, Marina.

Dorado Inn - on Highway 147 - Campsites, Cabins, Marina, Boat Rentals.

Crawfords Lakeside Resort - on Highway 147 - Motel, Housekeeping Cabins, Marina, Boat Rentals.

Camp Prattville - on Highway 89 in Prattville - Campsites, R.V.s, Restaurant, Marina.

Plumas Pines Resort - on Highway 89 near Prattville - Motel, Cabins, R.V. Sites, Restaurant, Marina, Store.

Almanor Inn - on Highway 89 near Plumas Pines - Motel, Cabins, Restaurant, Marina.

Paul Bunyan Trailer Resort - on Peninsula Drive

Big Springs Trailer Park - on Big Springs Road

Vagabond Trailer Park - on Highway 147

Lake Cove Trailer Lodge & Marina - on Highway 147

Snyder

ROUND VALLEY RESERVOIR

Round Valley is at 4,600 feet elevation, three miles South of Greenville. Boating is allowed with a maximum of 7-1/2 HP motors. You can launch small boats anywhere from the road along the shore. The U. S. Forest Service operates a picnic area with 16 sites, water and toilets. Frank's Campground at Round Valley Lake Resort has 50 campsites for tents or trailers, located under tall pine trees. Call Frank Rahn at 916-284-7530 for information. The launching ramp is rocked but not very steep. Swimming is not allowed but there is good fishing for bass, perch and catfish.

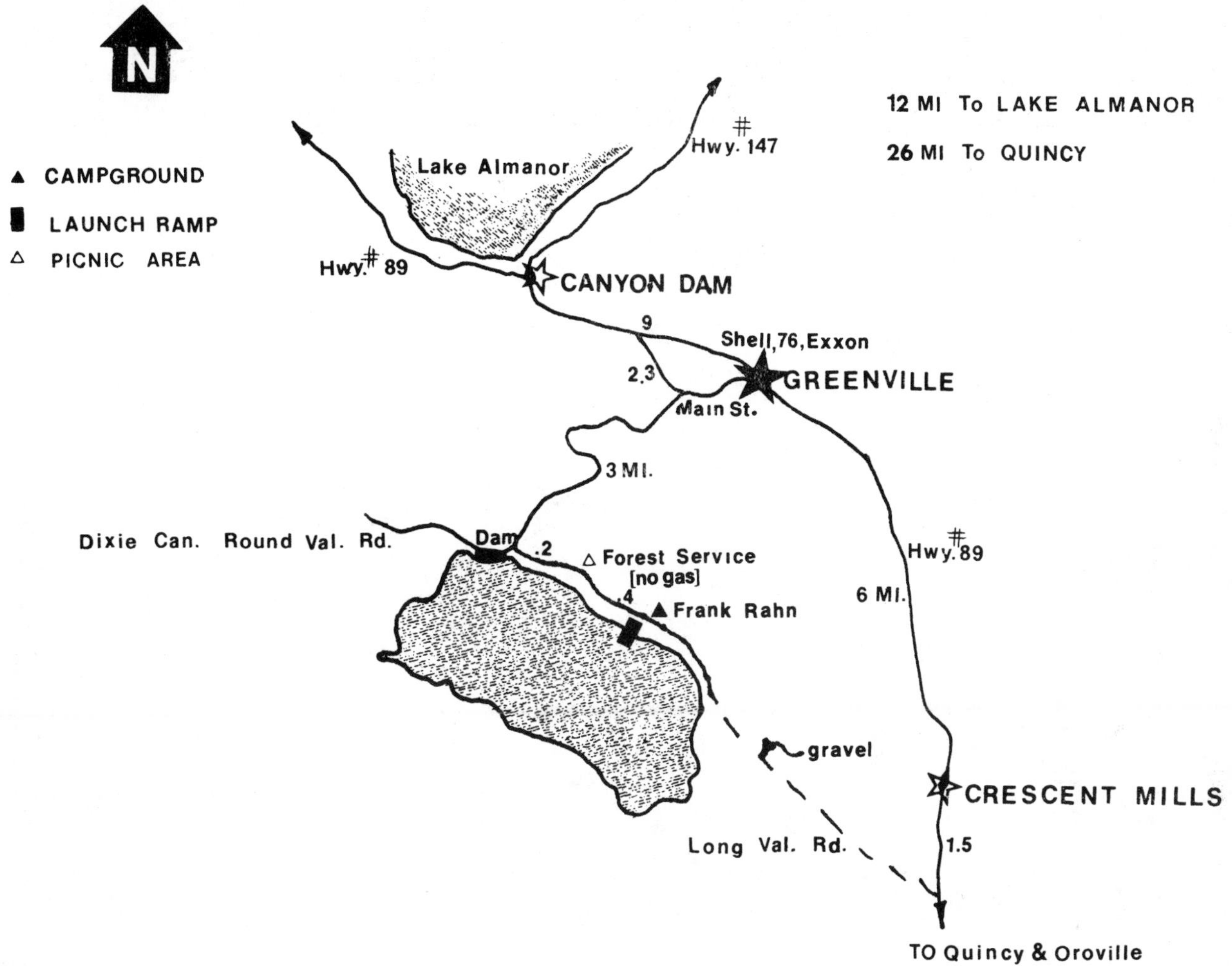

N
12 MI To LAKE ALMANOR
26 MI To QUINCY
CAMPGROUND
LAUNCH RAMP
PICNIC AREA
Lake Almanor
Hwy. # 147
Hwy # 89
CANYON DAM
9
Shell,76,Exxon
2.3
GREENVILLE
Main St.
3 MI.
Dixie Can. Round Val. Rd.
Dam
.2
Forest Service
[no gas]
.4
Frank Rahn
Hwy. # 89
6 MI.
gravel
CRESCENT MILLS
Long Val. Rd.
1.5
TO Quincy & Oroville

INFORMATION: U. S. Forest Service, Greenville 95947 (Information only)

CAMPING	BOATING	RECREATION	RESORTS
Round Valley Lake Resort 50 Developed Sites for Tents, R.V.s and Trailers Fee: $4 a Day	All Boating Allowed to 7-1/2 HP Motors Rocked Launch Ramp Rentals: Rowboats - $7 a Day Motorboats - $14 a Day	Fishing Hiking Picnicking No Swimming	Showers

ANTELOPE LAKE

Antelope Lake is located at 5,002 feet in elevation with 930 surface acres and 15 miles of shoreline. An excellent road into this Lake allows easy access for campers, motorhomes and boats, and is open from May through October. The U. S. Forest Service operates a total of 211 sites located at Boulder Creek, Lone Park and Long Point campgrounds with tables, stoves, water, and toilets. Trout are stocked in the Lake, and you can watch beavers building dams along Little Antelope Creek. Many sandy protected coves and islands on the Lake offer quiet resting spots in a lovely mountain setting with tall pine and fir trees.

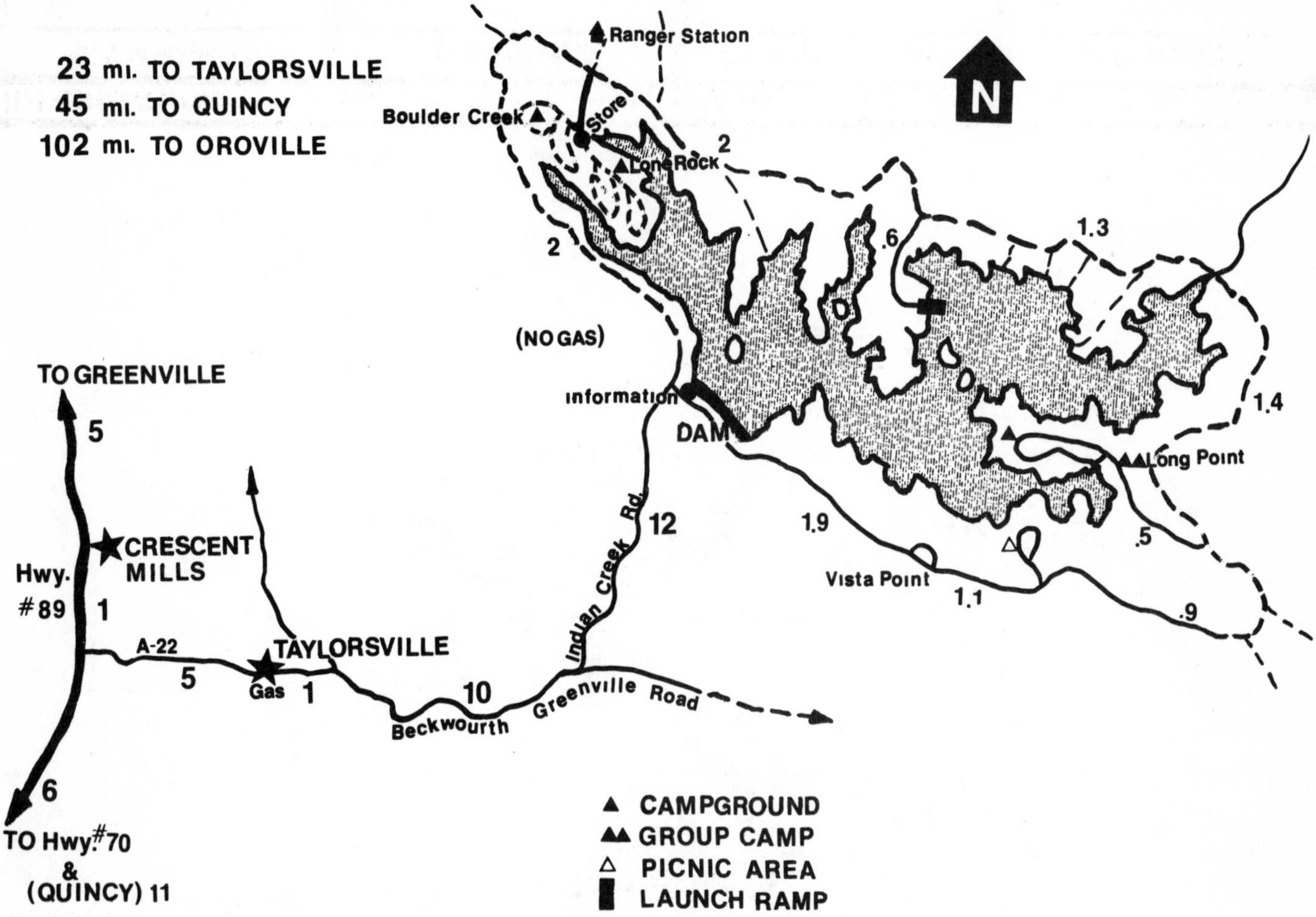
23 mi. TO TAYLORSVILLE
45 mi. TO QUINCY
102 mi. TO OROVILLE
Ranger Station
N
Boulder Creek
Store
Lone Rock
2
2
.6
1.3
(NO GAS)
TO GREENVILLE
5
information
DAM
1.4
Long Point
12
1.9
.5
CRESCENT MILLS
Hwy. #89
1
Vista Point
1.1
.9
A-22
TAYLORSVILLE
5
Gas
1
10
Indian Creek Rd.
Beckwourth Greenville Road
6
TO Hwy.#70 & (QUINCY) 11
CAMPGROUND
GROUP CAMP
PICNIC AREA
LAUNCH RAMP

INFORMATION: Plumas National Forest, P.O. Box 1500, Quincy 95971, Ph. 916-283-2050

CAMPING	BOATING	RECREATION	RESORTS
211 Developed Sites for Tents, R.V.s and Trailers No Hookups	All Boating Allowed Launch Ramp	Swimming Fishing Hiking Nature Trails	Store - Limited Supplies Amphitheater No Gas Available

<u>BENBOW LAKE STATE RECREATION AREA</u>

Benbow is a small Lake located off Highway 101 in the Redwood country. It is actually a Dam of the Eel River from Spring through August. Motorboats are not allowed so it is a good Lake for small sailboats and rowboats. There are 76 campsites for tents and trailers developed by the California State Park System with water and toilets. The fee for camping is $5 a day. There is a launch ramp and 35 picnic units. The Day Use only Fee at the Lake is $2. The Lake is adjacent to the Hotel Benbow, a lovely old building with rooms and a restaurant.

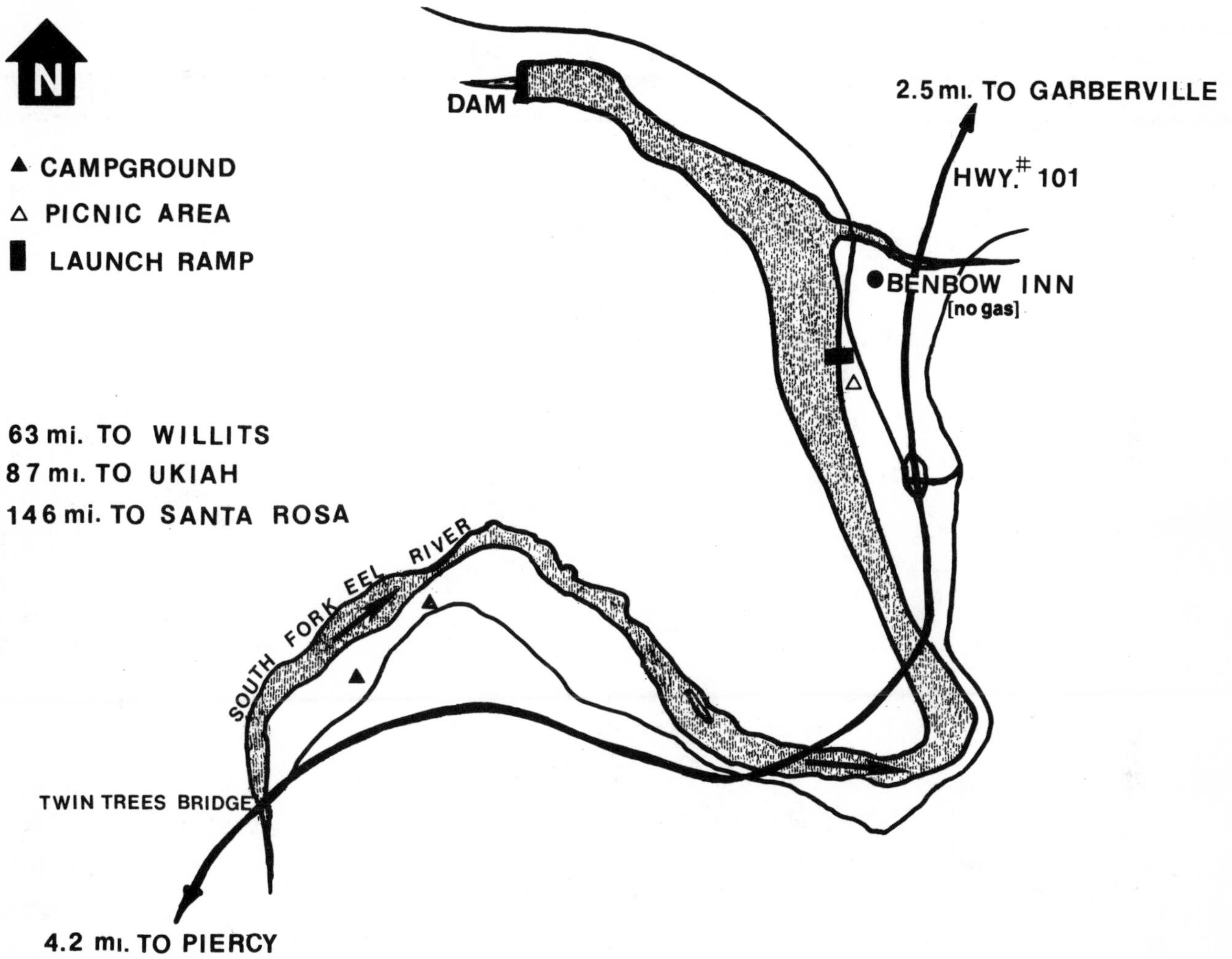
N
▲ CAMPGROUND
△ PICNIC AREA
LAUNCH RAMP
DAM
2.5 mi. TO GARBERVILLE
HWY.# 101
BENBOW INN
[no gas]
63 mi. TO WILLITS
87 mi. TO UKIAH
146 mi. TO SANTA ROSA
SOUTH FORK EEL RIVER
TWIN TREES BRIDGE
4.2 mi. TO PIERCY

INFORMATION: District Ranger, Richardson Grove State Park, Garberville 95440

CAMPING	BOATING	RECREATION	RESORTS
76 Developed Sites for Tents, R.V.s and Trailers Fee: $5 a Day	Motorboats are <u>Not</u> Allowed Launch Ramp	Swimming Fishing Picnicking Hiking Day Use Fee: $2	Hotel Restaurant

LAKE MENDOCINO

Lake Mendocino is the result of the construction, in 1958, of Coyote Dam. The project cost about $17,000,000. The Lake covers 1700 acres and is about 3 miles long. It is operated by the San Francisco District of the Army Corps of Engineers with the water coming from Lake Pillsbury via the Russian River and the Eel River. There are a total of 321 campsites for tents and trailers and handicapped facilities. Some of the sites are at water's edge and some in the wooded hills surrounding the Lake. Water, toilets and showers are located throughout the campgrounds. 4 Group Campgrounds are available, and 7 Group picnic areas with a massive stone barbecue pit. Reservations for Group Sites can be made through the Park Manager. Many well-kept grassy picnic areas provide tables and barbecue pits. Rental boats are available at the Marina concession, and a protected swimming beach is at the North end of the Lake. There are amphitheaters and a delightful Pomo Indian Gathering in July.

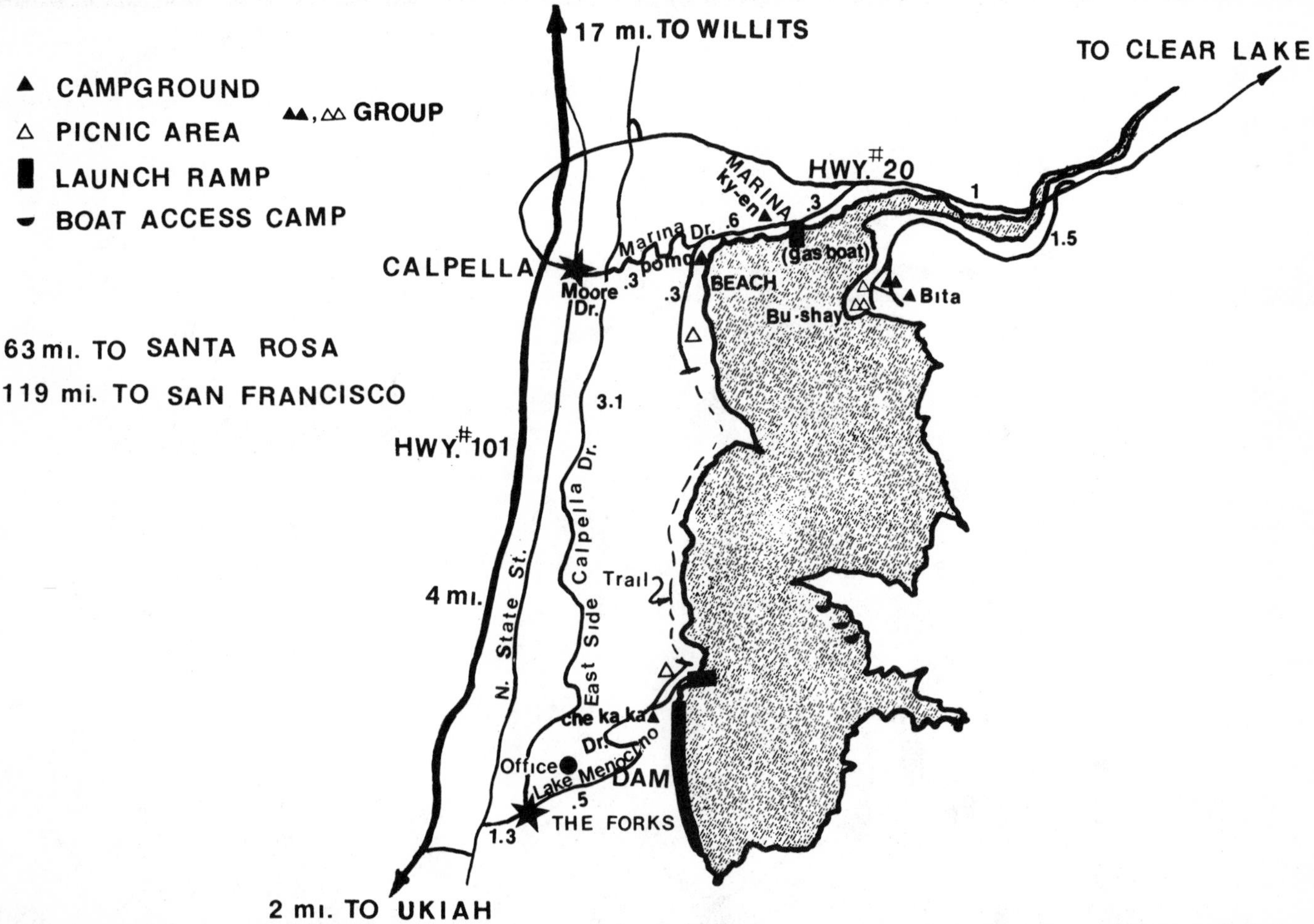
17 mi. TO WILLITS
TO CLEAR LAKE
CAMPGROUND
PICNIC AREA
GROUP
LAUNCH RAMP
BOAT ACCESS CAMP
HWY. #20
MARINA
ky-en
Marina Dr.
pomo
CALPELLA
Moore Dr.
BEACH
(gas boat)
Bita
Bu-shay
63 mi. TO SANTA ROSA
119 mi. TO SAN FRANCISCO
3.1
HWY. #101
East Side Calpella Dr.
N. State St.
Trail
4 mi.
che ka ka
Lake Mendocino Dr.
Office
DAM
THE FORKS
1.3
2 mi. TO UKIAH

INFORMATION: Park Manager, 1160 Lake Mendocino Dr., Ukiah, Ph. 707-462-7581

CAMPING	BOATING	RECREATION	RESORTS
321 Developed Sites for Tents, R.V.s and Trailers No Fee at Che ka ka $3 a Day at other sites 4 Group Campgrounds	All Boating Allowed 2 Launch Ramps 2 Boat Docks Boat Rentals Marina	Swimming Fishing Hiking Picnicking	Store

LAKE PILLSBURY

Lake Pillsbury is a man-made reservoir on the upper reaches of the Eel River and is an excellent Lake for sailing. Its waters are used for the Potter Valley Powerhouse and irrigation as well as maintaining the Russian River flow. Roads go only about half way around the Lake so much of the shore area can only be reached by boat or on foot. The U. S. Forest Service operates 3 campgrounds. Pogie Point has 49 campsites (41 tents only, 8 tents/trailers), water and toilets. Sunset has 54 sites (30 tents only, 24 tents/trailers), water and toilets. There are 12 sites for tents/trailers at Oak Flat Campground with toilets. Squaw Creek has 5 picnic units. There are 3 Resorts located at the North Shore, Bogner's Pillsbury Pines Resort, Phone: 707-743-1573, Lake Pillsbury Resort, Phone: 707-743-1581, and Soda Creek Camp, Phone: 707-743-1593, all with cabins and campsites.

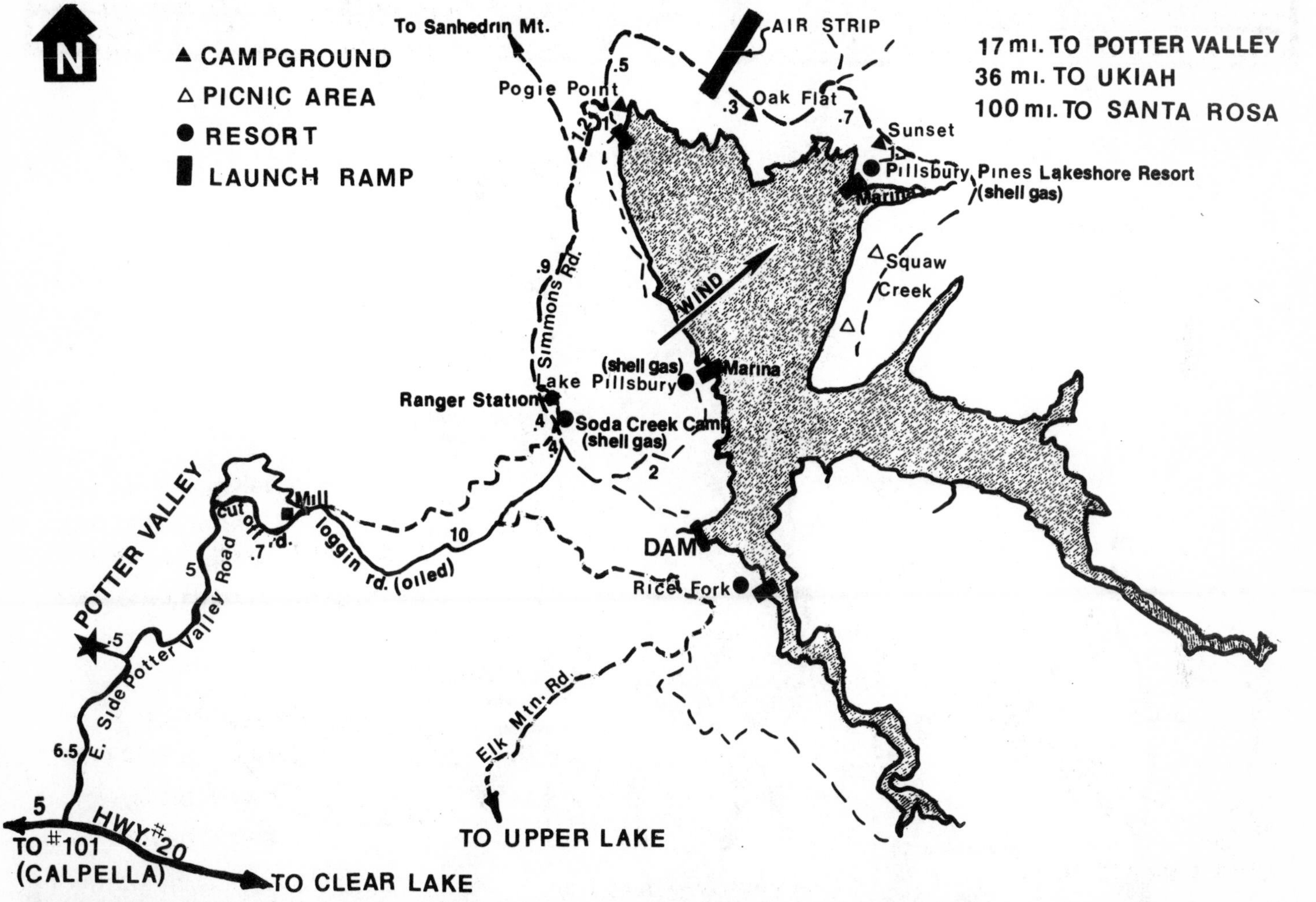
N
▲ CAMPGROUND
△ PICNIC AREA
● RESORT
▮ LAUNCH RAMP
To Sanhedrin Mt.
AIR STRIP
17 mi. TO POTTER VALLEY
36 mi. TO UKIAH
100 mi. TO SANTA ROSA
Pogie Point
Oak Flat
Sunset
Pillsbury Pines Lakeshore Resort
(shell gas)
Marina
Squaw
Creek
WIND
Simmons Rd.
(shell gas)
Lake Pillsbury
Marina
Ranger Station
Soda Creek Camp
(shell gas)
Mill
cut off rd.
loggin rd. (oiled)
DAM
Rice Fork
POTTER VALLEY
E. Side Potter Valley Road
Elk Mtn. Rd.
TO UPPER LAKE
HWY. #20
TO #101
(CALPELLA)
TO CLEAR LAKE

INFORMATION: U.S. Forest Service, P. O. Box 96, Upper Lake 95485, Ph. 707-743-1582

CAMPING	BOATING	RECREATION	RESORTS
115 Developed Sites for Tents, R.V.s and Trailers Fee: $3 a Day No Fee at Oak Flat Campground Additional Sites at 3 Private Resorts. Fee: $3 - $4 a Day	All Boating Allowed Launch Ramps Rentals Available: Canoes, Motorboats, Pontoon Boats Marina Supplies	Fishing Swimming Hiking Picnicking Motor Bike Trails	Cabins Snack Bars Restaurant Grocery Stores Movies

BLACK BUTTE LAKE

Black Butte Lake is about 7 miles long and has a shoreline of 40 miles. Water is used for irrigation of agricultural lands and flood control and is maintained by the Army Corps of Engineers. The water level of the Lake can change rapidly and boaters are cautioned of possible hazards. Five recreational facilities serve the Lake and 100 plus campsites with water and toilets are located at Buckhorn and Orland Buttes, all on a first come, first serve basis. Both these locations have a launch ramp as well as one at Eagle Pass. Orland Buttes has a Group Use Area by reservation. Fishing is permitted all year although it is best in early Spring and Summer for Bass, Catfish and especially Crappie.

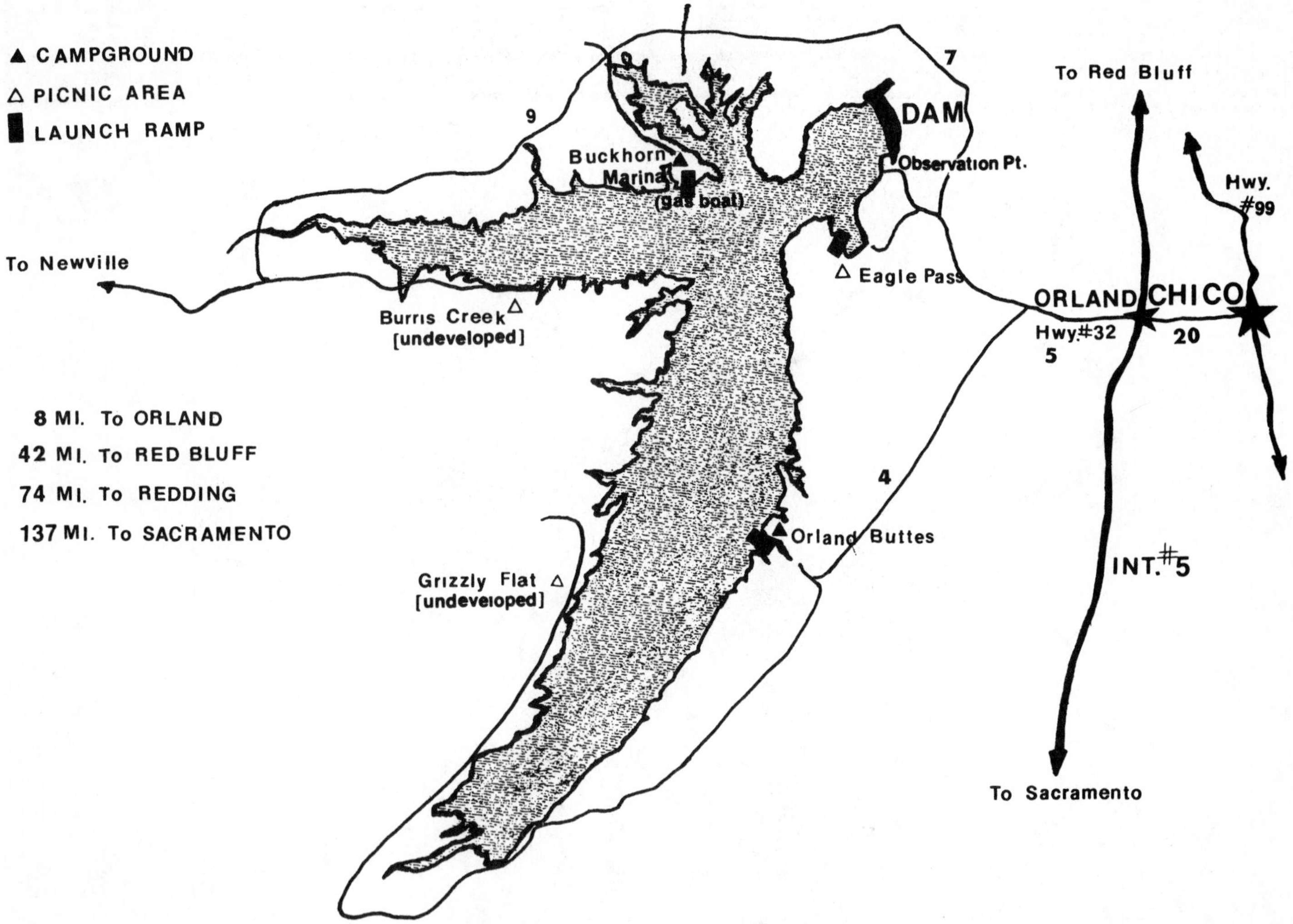
▲ CAMPGROUND
△ PICNIC AREA
LAUNCH RAMP
8 MI. To ORLAND
42 MI. To RED BLUFF
74 MI. To REDDING
137 MI. To SACRAMENTO
To Newville
Buckhorn
Marina
(gas boat)
DAM
Observation Pt.
Eagle Pass
Burris Creek
[undeveloped]
Grizzly Flat
[undeveloped]
Orland Buttes
9
7
4
To Red Bluff
Hwy.
#99
ORLAND
CHICO
Hwy.#32
5
20
INT.#5
To Sacramento

INFORMATION: U. S. Army Corps of Engineers, Orland, Ph. Park Manager 916-865-4781

CAMPING	BOATING	RECREATION	RESORTS
Buckhorn Campground 65 Developed Sites for Tents, R.V.s, Trailers plus Overflow Orland Buttes 35 Developed Sites No Charge Group Use Area	All Boating Allowed 3 Launching Ramps Marina	Fishing Swimming Picnicking Hiking Campfire Programs Nature Trails 100-Acre Motorcycle Park (Open from Memorial Day through February)	Showers 8 Miles to Full Facilities in Orland

STONY GORGE RESERVOIR

The Bureau of Reclamation operates Stony Gorge Reservoir. 40 sites at 2 campgrounds are located on the Northeast side of the Lake at The Figs. There is a 14-day limit or 30 days per year for the use of a campsite. The Pines on the Northwest corner of the Lake can accommodate group picnics of 200 people maximum providing benches, tables and barbecues. There is a boat launching ramp and for 1980, no fees will be charged as there is no drinking water available at the present time.

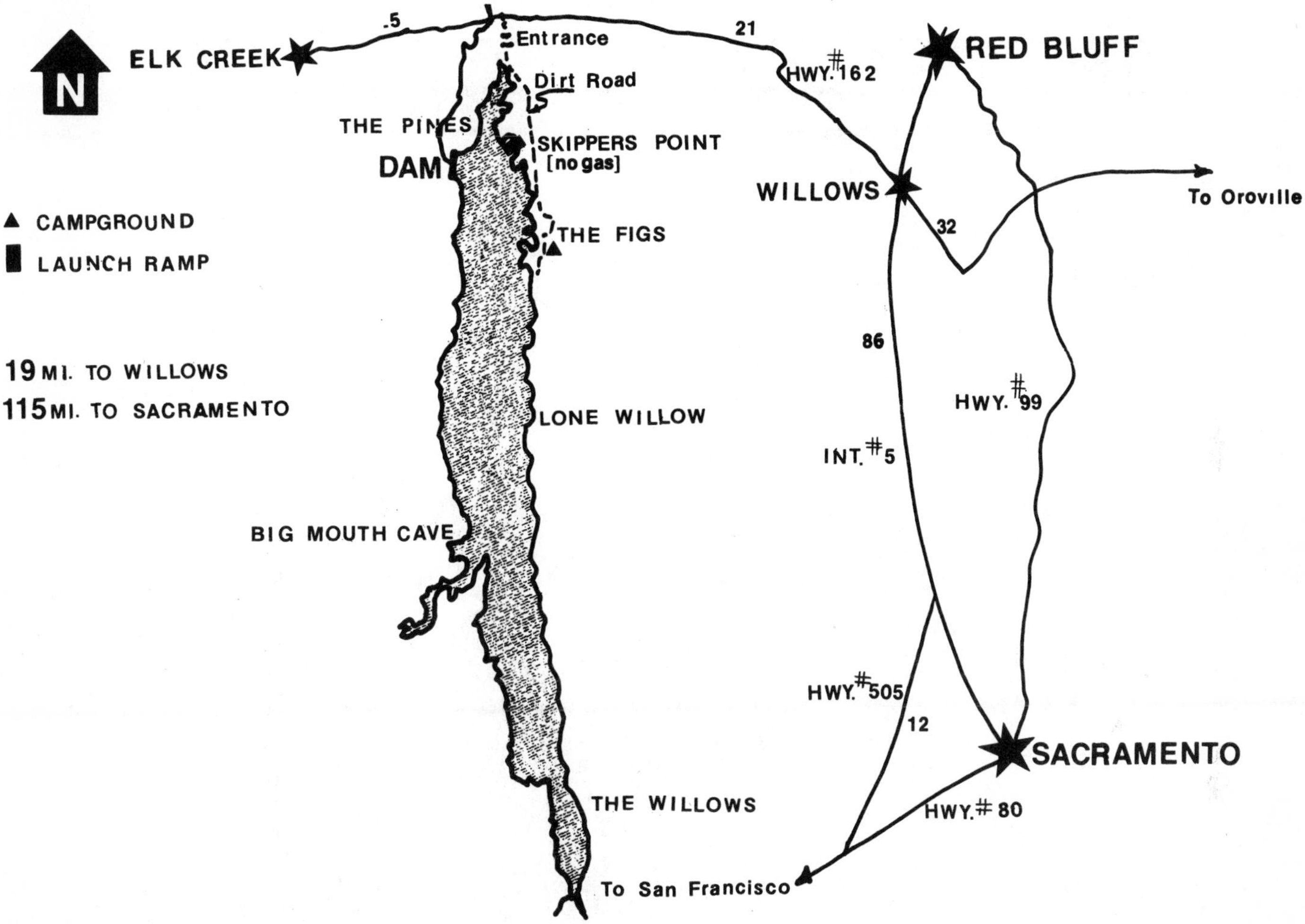
N
ELK CREEK
.5
Entrance
21
RED BLUFF
HWY. #162
Dirt Road
THE PINES
SKIPPERS POINT
[no gas]
DAM
WILLOWS
To Oroville
32
CAMPGROUND
LAUNCH RAMP
THE FIGS
86
19 MI. TO WILLOWS
115 MI. TO SACRAMENTO
LONE WILLOW
HWY. #99
INT. #5
BIG MOUTH CAVE
HWY. #505
12
SACRAMENTO
THE WILLOWS
HWY. # 80
To San Francisco

INFORMATION: Bureau of Reclamation, 1140 Westwood, Willows, Ph. 916-934-7066

CAMPING	BOATING	RECREATION	RESORTS
40 Developed Sites, for Tents, R.V.s and Trailers No drinking water	All Boating Allowed Launch Ramp	Fishing Swimming Picnicking 200 People Group Site	

EAST PARK RESERVOIR

The Bureau of Reclamation operates East Park Reservoir and are presently restocking it with fish. Facilities are limited along the West shore with tables and toilets but no running water. The Lake has a slowly sloping shoreline with small trees and sandy soil. The water should be quite warm in the summer due to relatively shallow water. There is no launching ramp and by the end of summer, the water in the Reservoir is extremely low. For 1980, no fees will be charged.

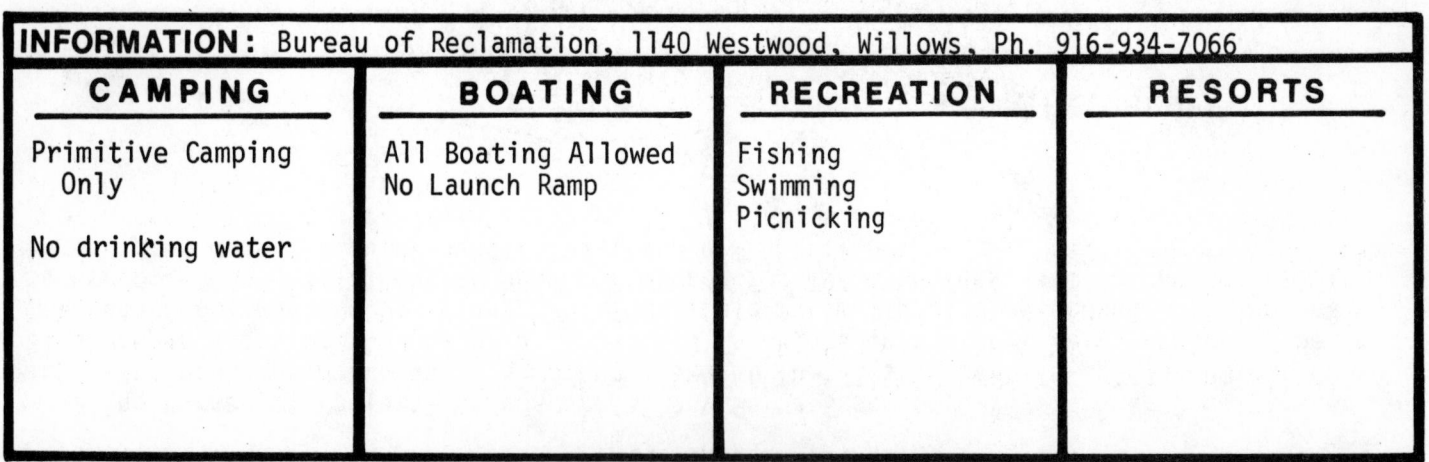

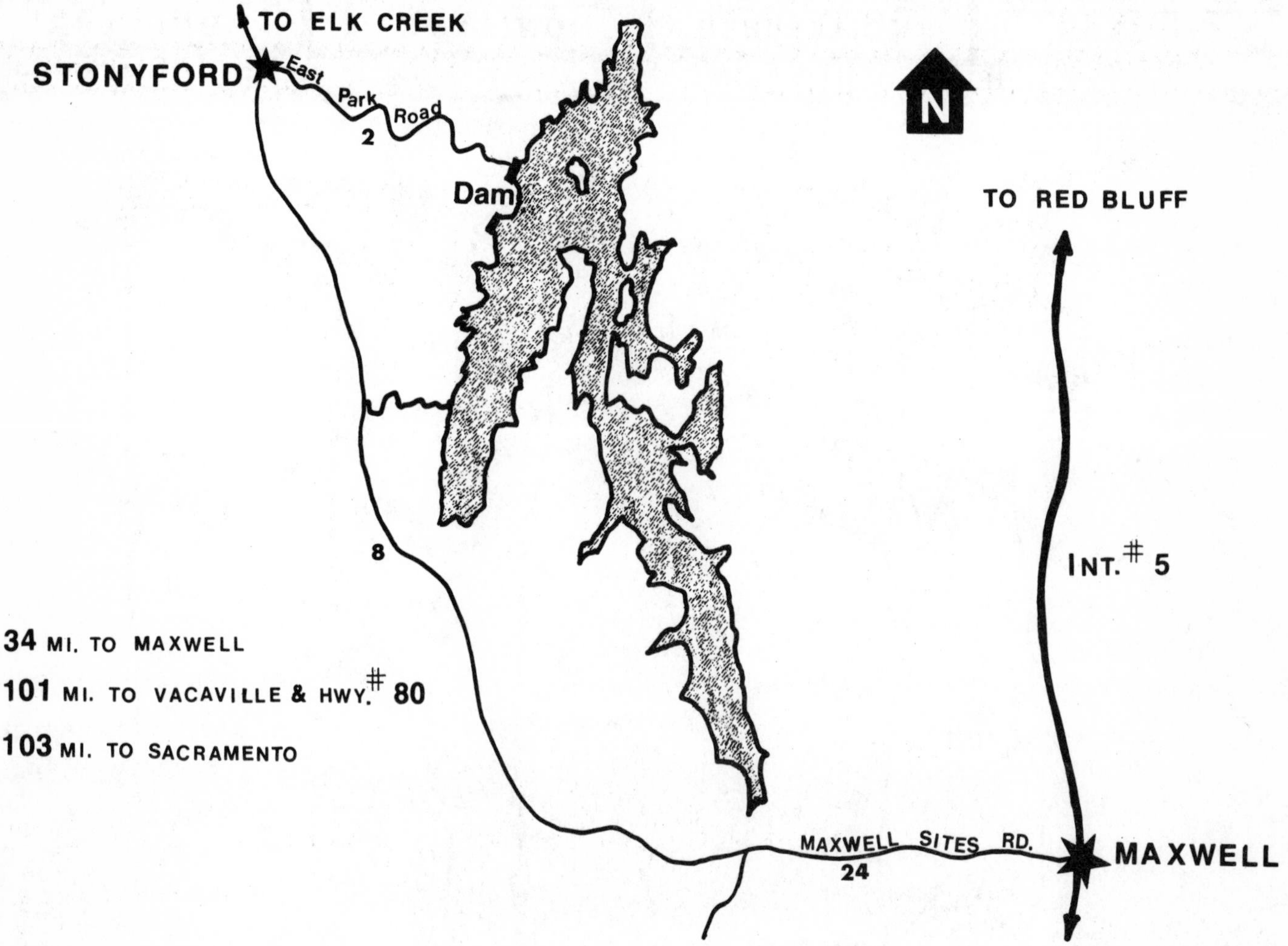
TO ELK CREEK
STONYFORD
East Park Road
2
Dam
N
TO RED BLUFF
8
INT. # 5
34 MI. TO MAXWELL
101 MI. TO VACAVILLE & HWY. # 80
103 MI. TO SACRAMENTO
MAXWELL SITES RD.
24
MAXWELL

INFORMATION: Bureau of Reclamation, 1140 Westwood, Willows, Ph. 916-934-7066

CAMPING	BOATING	RECREATION	RESORTS
Primitive Camping Only No drinking water	All Boating Allowed No Launch Ramp	Fishing Swimming Picnicking	

Lake Oroville, located at 900 feet elevation, has 15,800 surface acres and 167 miles of shoreline. It has the highest Dam in the United States. The Visitor Center is above the Dam on Kelly Ridge Drive and has a souvenir shop, viewing tower and slides and movies. To reach Feather Falls, where the water drops 640 feet into Fall River, take Forbestown Road East 5 miles to Lumpkin Road and turn left to Feather Falls. A 3-1/2 mile hike takes you in and out to the Falls. Lake Oroville is open all year, but the water drops up to 50 feet in the Fall. There are over 250,000 salmon and trout planted each year, and the boating conditions are excellent.

. . . Continued . . .

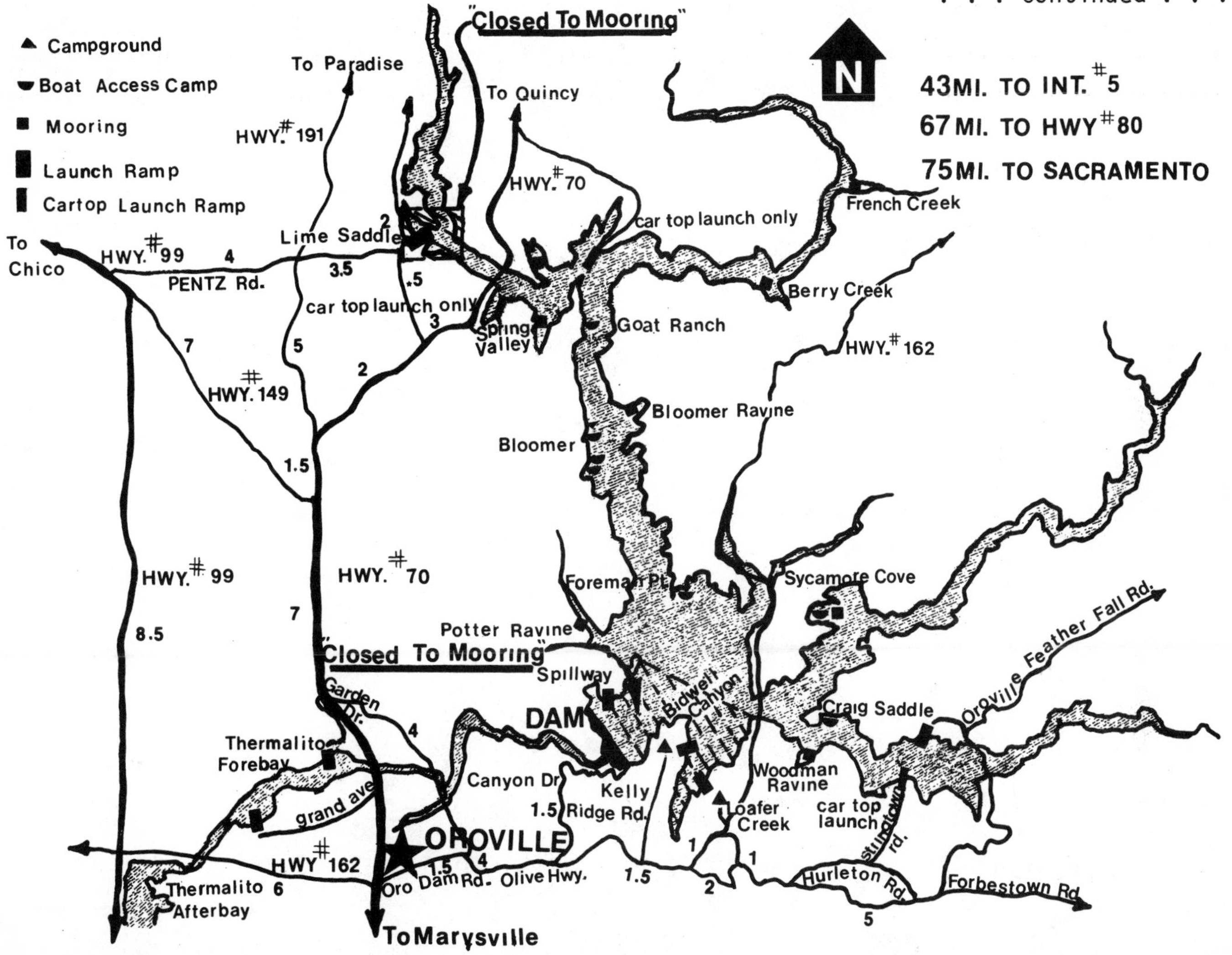
"Closed To Mooring"
Campground
Boat Access Camp
Mooring
Launch Ramp
Cartop Launch Ramp
To Paradise
To Quincy
HWY. #191
HWY. #70
N
43MI. TO INT. #5
67MI. TO HWY #80
75MI. TO SACRAMENTO
French Creek
car top launch only
Lime Saddle
To Chico
HWY. #99
PENTZ Rd.
car top launch only
Spring Valley
Berry Creek
Goat Ranch
HWY. #162
HWY. #149
Bloomer Ravine
Bloomer
HWY. #99
HWY. #70
Foreman Pt.
Sycamore Cove
Potter Ravine
"Closed To Mooring"
Spillway
Oroville Feather Fall Rd.
Garden Dr.
DAM
Bidwell Canyon
Craig Saddle
Thermalito Forebay
Canyon Dr
Kelly
Ridge Rd.
Woodman Ravine
Loafer Creek
car top launch
Stringtown rd.
grand ave
OROVILLE
HWY #162
Thermalito Afterbay
Oro Dam Rd.
Olive Hwy.
Hurleton Rd.
Forbestown Rd.
ToMarysville

INFORMATION: Dept. Parks & Recreation, Sacramento 95811 or Ticketron for Groups

CAMPING	BOATING	RECREATION	RESORTS
137 Developed Sites for Tents, R.V.s, and Trailers 80 Developed Sites with full hook-ups 6 Group Camps Fee: $5-$8 a Day in Season	All Boating Allowed Launching Ramps-$1.50 Full Service Marina Rentals Available: Houseboats, Canoes, Fishing and Pontoon Boats 109 Boat-In Campsites Fee: $3 a Day	Fishing Swimming Picnicking Hiking Horseback Riding Bicycle Paths Visitor's Center Fish Hatchery $2 Fee - Day Use Only	Motels & Restaurants in Oroville Grocery Store Laundromat

LAKE OROVILLE

. . . Continued . . .

Camping Facilities

Loafer Creek - 137 Campsites (tents/trailers), water, toilets, showers, R.V. dump station, 100 picnic sites, swimming beach, launching ramp.

Group Camps - 6 well-developed camps each accommodating 25 people.

Bidwell Canyon - 80 Campsites with full hookups, launching ramp, full facility Marina, boat rentals, store, laundromat.

Reservations for all Sites: Your local Ticketron Outlet or write: Ticketron, P. O. Box 26430, San Francisco 94120

Boat-In Camps

109 Campsites at - Craig Saddle (has drinking water)
Sycamore Cove
Foreman Point
Goat Ranch
Bloomer - Also a Group Camp for 75 people, tables, toilets, but no drinking water. Reservations accepted.

Launch Ramps - Paved

Lime Saddle   Spillway   Bidwell Canyon   Loafer Creek

Mooring: The Lake is open to mooring everywhere except the main body of the Lake (See Map). Lime Saddle Marina Area is also not open to mooring.

THERMALITO FOREBAY

The North end of the Forebay has a 2-lane launch ramp, sandy swim beach, picnic facilities and many lovely trees. This area is for sailboats and other non-power boats only.

The South end of the Forebay has a 4-lane launch ramp and is for power boats and fishing boats only.

Snyder

BUCKS LAKE

Bucks Dam, completed in 1929 as part of the Bucks Creek project, is now under the management of both the U. S. Forest Service and P. G. & E. The Lake is located at 5,155 feet elevation and has 14 miles of shoreline. The Forest Service operates Whitehorse Campground with 20 sites (tents/trailers) with water and toilets. Grizzly Creek has 8 sites (tents/trailers) with toilets. Sundew has 19 campsites with facilities for the handicapped, water, toilets, launch ramp and swim beach. Bucks Lake Lodge, Lakeshore Resort and Haskins Valley Resort have cabins, trailer camping and full boating, restaurant and shopping facilities.

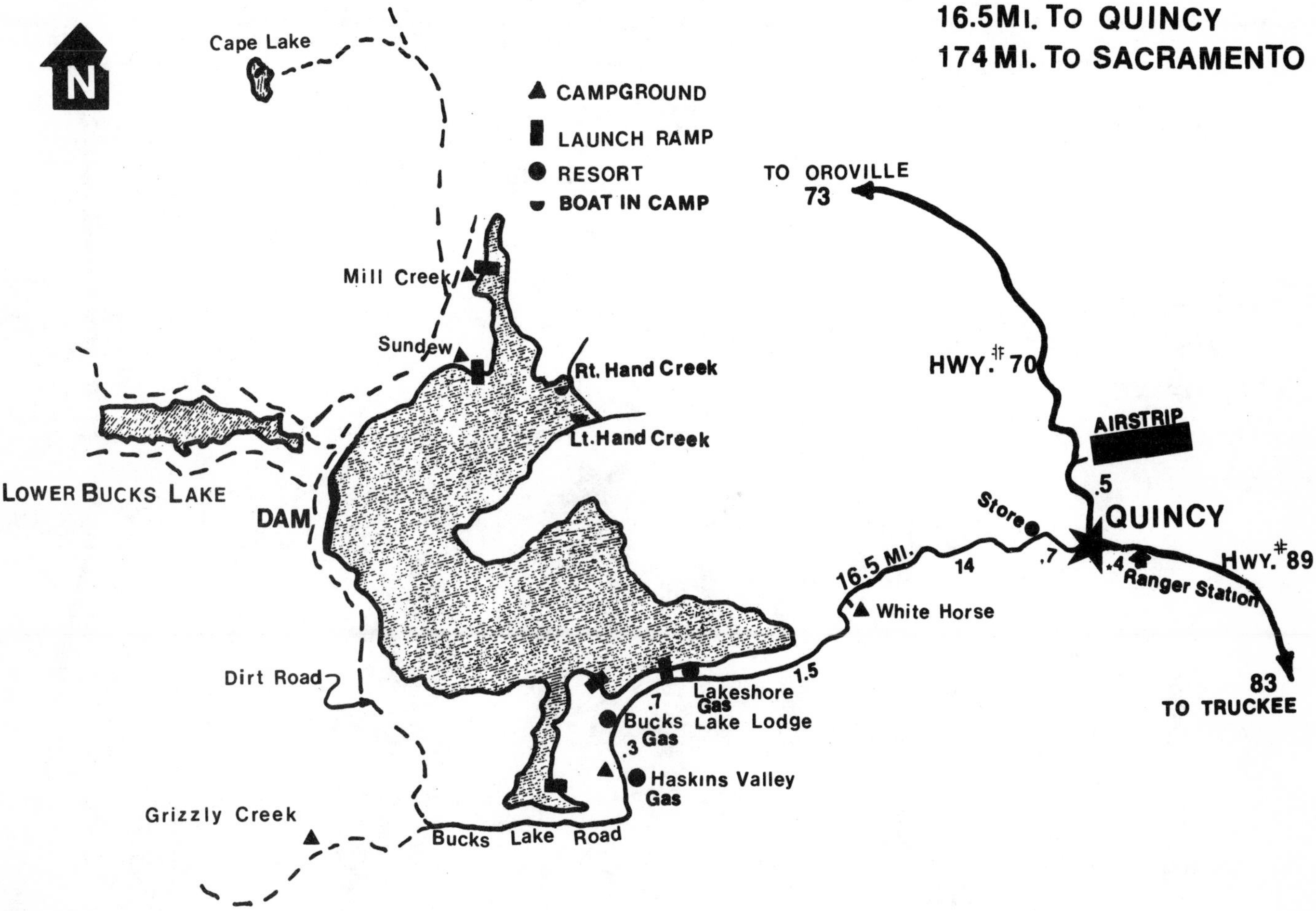

N
Cape Lake
16.5 Mi. To QUINCY
174 Mi. To SACRAMENTO
CAMPGROUND
LAUNCH RAMP
RESORT
BOAT IN CAMP
TO OROVILLE
73
Mill Creek
Sundew
Rt. Hand Creek
Lt. Hand Creek
HWY. #70
AIRSTRIP
.5
Store
QUINCY
LOWER BUCKS LAKE
DAM
16.5 MI.
14
.7
.4
HWY. #89
Ranger Station
White Horse
1.5
Dirt Road
Lakeshore
Gas
.7
Bucks Lake Lodge
Gas
.3
Haskins Valley
Gas
83
TO TRUCKEE
Grizzly Creek
Bucks Lake Road

INFORMATION: District Ranger, U. S. F. S., Oroville 95965 or Resorts

CAMPING	BOATING	RECREATION	RESORTS
47 Developed Sites for Tents, R.V.s, and Trailers - USFS Fee: $3 a Day 65 Developed Sites for Tents, R.V.s, and Trailers - P. G. & E.	All Boating Allowed Rentals Available Launching Ramps Full Service Marinas	Fishing Swimming Hiking Picnicking Horseback Riding	Cabins Snack Bars Restaurant Grocery Stores Laundromat

LITTLE GRASS VALLEY RESERVOIR

Little Grass Valley Reservoir is located in the Plumas National Forest at 5,046 feet elevation with 16 miles of shoreline. Originally the home and hunting grounds of the Maidu Indians, in 1961, the Irrigation District of Oroville constructed the rockfilled Dam. Today the U. S. Forest Service operates 251 campsites. At Wyandotte are 30 campsites (15 tents only, 15 tents/trailers). At Little Beaver are 121 campsites (61 tents only, 60 tents/trailers) and a dump station. At Red Feather are 60 campsites (30 tents only, 30 tents/trailers). At Running Deer are 40 campsites (20 tents only, 20 tents/trailers). All campgrounds have tables, stoves, water and toilets. 26 single family and 2 multiple families picnic sites are at Peninsula and 10 picnic sites are at Black Rock. These have water, toilets, stoves and tables.

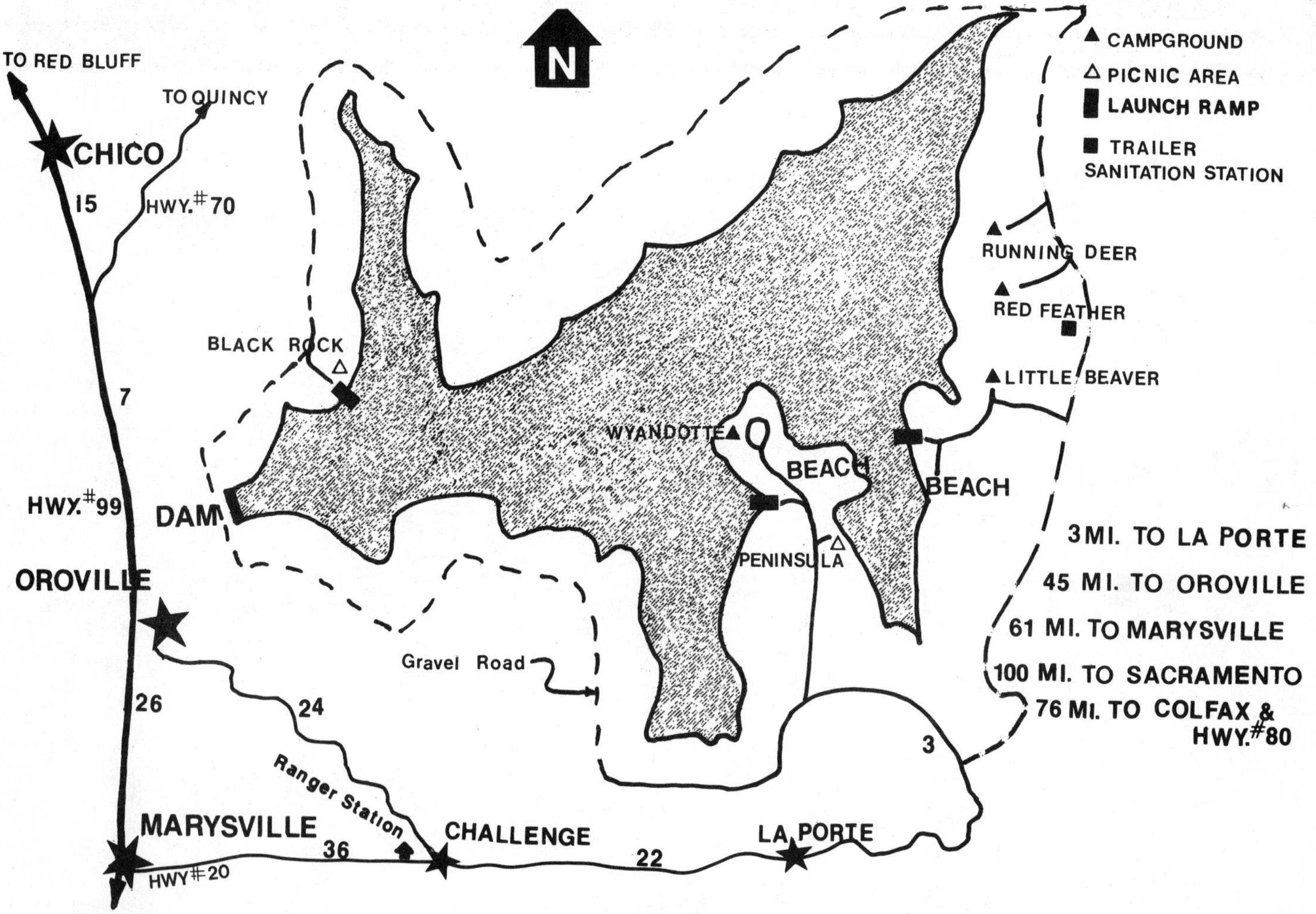
N
TO RED BLUFF
TO QUINCY
CHICO
15
HWY.#70
CAMPGROUND
PICNIC AREA
LAUNCH RAMP
TRAILER
SANITATION STATION
RUNNING DEER
RED FEATHER
LITTLE BEAVER
BLACK ROCK
7
WYANDOTTE
BEACH
BEACH
HWY.#99
DAM
OROVILLE
PENINSULA
3MI. TO LA PORTE
45 MI. TO OROVILLE
61 MI. TO MARYSVILLE
100 MI. TO SACRAMENTO
76 MI. TO COLFAX & HWY.#80
Gravel Road
26
24
3
Ranger Station
MARYSVILLE
36
CHALLENGE
22
LA PORTE
HWY#20

INFORMATION: Challenge Ranger Station, P. O. Box F, Challenge 95925

CAMPING	BOATING	RECREATION	RESORTS
250 Developed Sites for Tents, R.V.s and Trailers (to 22 feet) Fee: $3 a Day	All Boating Allowed 3 Launching Ramps Speed limits in Bays and near swim beach	Fishing Swimming - Change Rooms Picnicking Hiking Ghost Towns	Supplies - 3 miles in La Porte

SLY CREEK RESERVOIR AND LOST CREEK RESERVOIR

One of the best kept secrets around is Sly Creek Reservoir and Lost Creek Reservoir. Many spectacular trees and foliage make these two very pretty Lakes. They are undeveloped with regard to boating and camping facilities so cartop boats only are recommended. You may picnic around the Lakes, but there are no conveniences. Swimming is allowed, but the water in Sly Creek fluctuates greatly in summer. Lost Creek, which is exceptionally pretty, has a constant water level, and the roads around this Reservoir are suitable for pickups only.

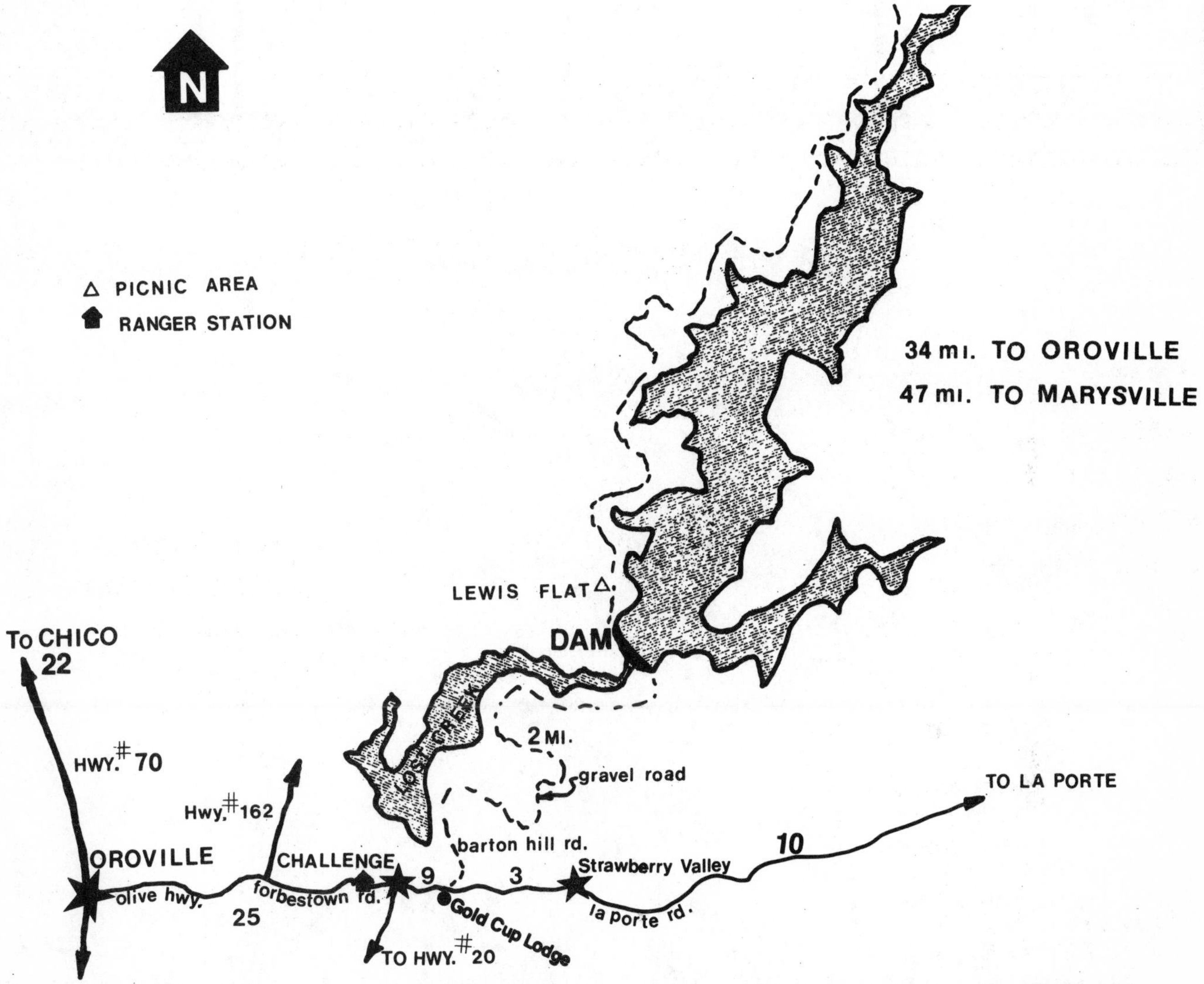

N
△ PICNIC AREA
RANGER STATION
34 mi. TO OROVILLE
47 mi. TO MARYSVILLE
LEWIS FLAT
DAM
To CHICO
22
HWY. #70
Hwy. #162
LOST CREEK
2 MI.
gravel road
TO LA PORTE
barton hill rd.
10
OROVILLE
CHALLENGE
9
3
Strawberry Valley
olive hwy.
forbestown rd.
25
Gold Cup Lodge
la porte rd.
TO HWY. #20

INFORMATION: District Ranger, U. S. Forest Service, P. O. Box F, Challenge 95925

CAMPING	BOATING	RECREATION	RESORTS
No Facilities	Cartop Boats Only Recommended	Fishing Picnicking Swimming	

BULLARDS BAR RESERVOIR

Bullards Bar Reservoir at almost 2,000 feet elevation is surrounded by rugged countryside. The Reservoir lies in a valley with tall hills on three sides and the Dam on the South end. Overnight camping and campfires are restricted to posted, developed recreation sites. The U. S. Forest Service operates Schoolhouse Campground with 67 sites (tents/trailers), and Burnt Bridge with 30 sites (15 tents only, 15 tents/trailers). Water, tables, stoves and toilets are available. The 3 Boat Access camps are Madrone Cove which has 11 units, Frenchy Point with 9 units and Garden Point with 20 units. Each has tables, stoves and floating toilets. Hornwoggle Campground has 5 Group Camps, 4 Camps for 25 people each and 1 Camp for 50 people. Contact the U. S. Forest Service, Bullards Bar Station, Camptonville 95922, Phone: 916-288-3242. 30 picnic units are located at Dark Day, and there is a Youth Camp at Cottage Creek. Launch Ramps are at both these locations.

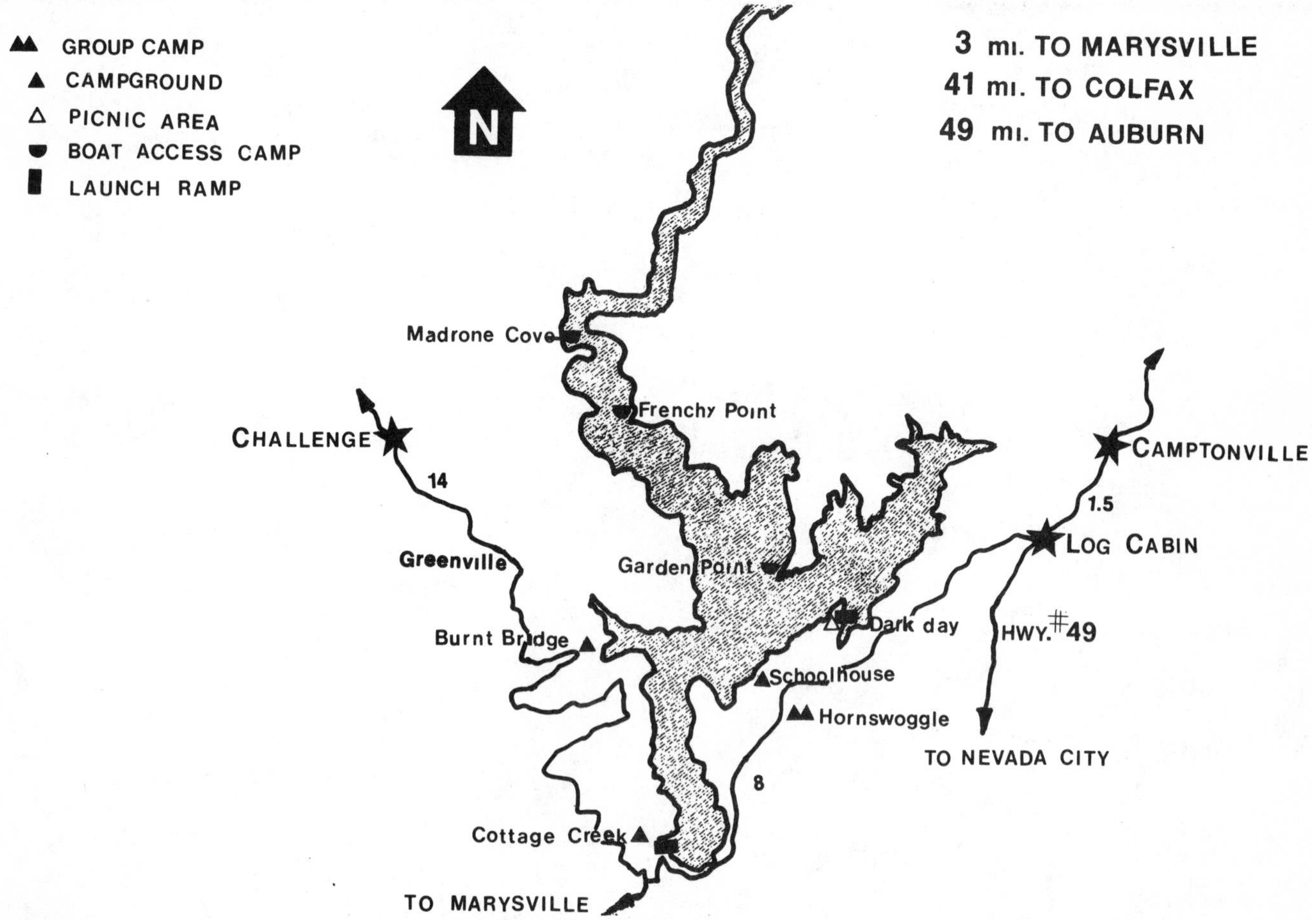
GROUP CAMP
CAMPGROUND
PICNIC AREA
BOAT ACCESS CAMP
LAUNCH RAMP
N
3 mi. TO MARYSVILLE
41 mi. TO COLFAX
49 mi. TO AUBURN
Madrone Cove
Frenchy Point
CHALLENGE
14
CAMPTONVILLE
1.5
LOG CABIN
Greenville
Garden Point
Dark day
HWY. #49
Burnt Bridge
Schoolhouse
Hornswoggle
TO NEVADA CITY
8
Cottage Creek
TO MARYSVILLE

INFORMATION: U. S. Forest Service, Bullards Bar Station, Camptonville 95922

CAMPING	BOATING	RECREATION	RESORTS
97 Developed Sites for Tents, R.V.s and Trailers Fee: $2 a Day Group Camps - 150 People Maximum Phone: 916-288-3242 for Reservations 40 Developed Sites - Boat Access	All Boating Allowed 2 Launch Ramps Waterskiing is Not Advised - Submerged logs	Fishing Hiking Picnicking	Supplies at Camptonville, Challenge, North San Juan and Dobbins - About 5 Miles

GOLD LAKE

Gold Lake is located in the Lakes Basin Recreation area which offers some of the best trout fishing in California and includes 23 smaller Lakes and many streams. The area lies at an elevation of 4,500 feet. The U. S. Forest Service operates 25 developed sites for tents only at Lakes Basin Campground, and a Group Campground for 25 people. Gold Lake Lodge and Elwell Lodge are located near Long Lake, north of Gold Lake, and both have fully equipped housekeeping cabins. There are various other lodges and resorts in this vicinity.

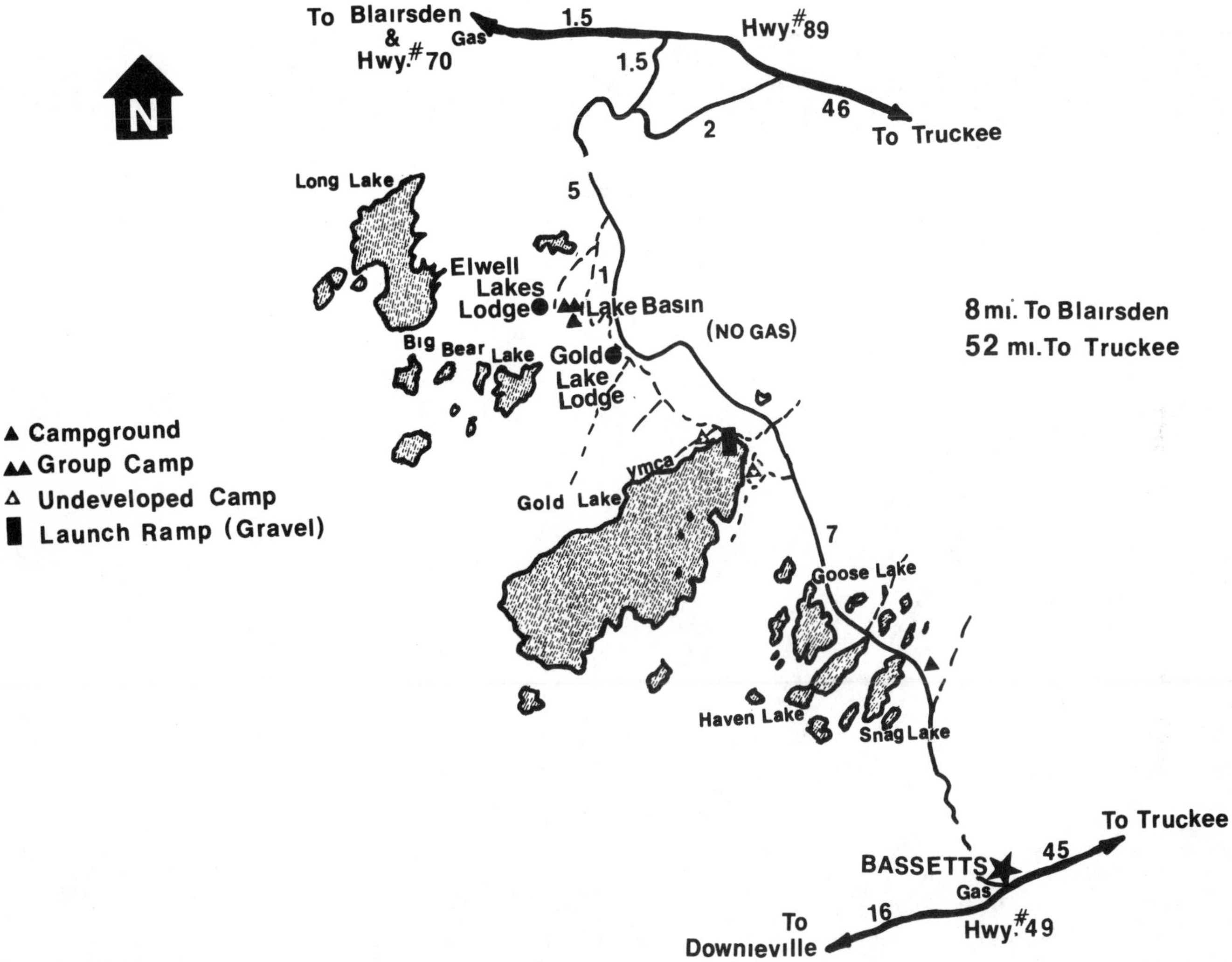

To Blairsden & Hwy.#70
Gas
1.5
Hwy.#89
1.5
2
46
To Truckee
N
Long Lake
5
Elwell Lakes Lodge
1
Lake Basin
(NO GAS)
8 mi. To Blairsden
52 mi. To Truckee
Big Bear Lake
Gold Lake Lodge
▲ Campground
▲▲ Group Camp
△ Undeveloped Camp
▮ Launch Ramp (Gravel)
ymca
Gold Lake
7
Goose Lake
Haven Lake
Snag Lake
To Truckee
BASSETTS
45
Gas
16
To Downieville
Hwy.#49

INFORMATION: Beckwourth Ranger District, Plumas National Forest, Blairsden 96103

CAMPING	BOATING	RECREATION	RESORTS
25 Developed Sites for Tents Only Group Camp - 25 People Reservations: U. S. Forest Service	All Boating Allowed Boat Rentals	Fishing Swimming Hiking Horseback Riding	Housekeeping Cabins: Gold Lake Lodge Gold Lake Road Blairsden 96103 Ph: 916-836-2350 or Elwell Lodge P.O. Box 68 Blairsden 96103 Ph: 916-836-2347

LAKE DAVIS

Lake Davis, at 5,775 feet elevation with 32 miles of shoreline, has trees down to the water's edge and an island in the center. Winds are steady making this an ideal sailing Lake. The U. S. Forest Service operates 125 campsites and a two-lane paved launching ramp at this time. There are 70 sites at Grasshopper Flat and 55 sites at Grizzly for both tents and trailers. Tables, grills, water and toilets are available as well as a dump station. 55 sites at Lightning Tree are for self-contained vehicles only. There are launch ramps at Honker Cove and Lightning Tree as well as the Mallard Cove Cartop Launch Area. All other areas around the Lake are for Day Use only and most supplies can be purchased at stores near Portola. There are many points of interest nearby including an old sheep camp with corral and adobe beehive oven used by the Basque Sheepherders on the West side of the Lake. Smith Peak lookout provides a nice view of the Lake and visitors are welcome to learn about the job of a fire lookout.

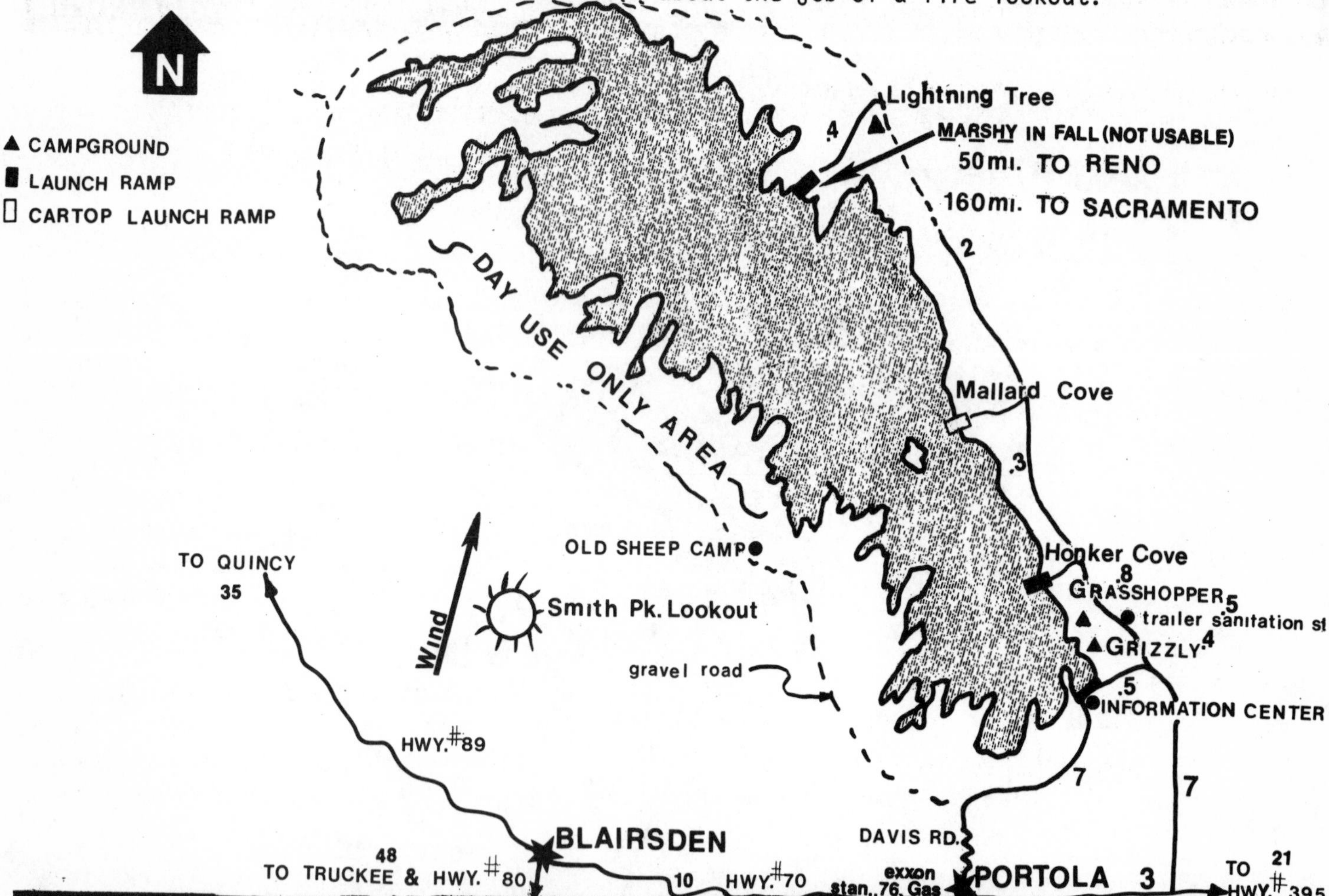
N
▲ CAMPGROUND
▮ LAUNCH RAMP
▯ CARTOP LAUNCH RAMP
Lightning Tree
4
MARSHY IN FALL (NOT USABLE)
50mi. TO RENO
160mi. TO SACRAMENTO
2
DAY USE ONLY AREA
Mallard Cove
.3
OLD SHEEP CAMP
Honker Cove
.8
GRASSHOPPER
5
trailer sanitation st
GRIZZLY
4
.5
INFORMATION CENTER
TO QUINCY
35
Wind
Smith Pk. Lookout
gravel road
HWY. #89
7
7
DAVIS RD.
BLAIRSDEN
48
TO TRUCKEE & HWY. #80
10
HWY. #70
exxon
stan. 76 Gas
PORTOLA
3
TO HWY. #395
21

INFORMATION: Mohawk Ranger Station, P. O. Box 7, Blairsden 96103, Ph. 916-836-2575

CAMPING	BOATING	RECREATION	RESORTS
125 Developed Sites for Tents, R.V.s and Trailers Fee: $3 a Day 55 Sites for Self-Contained R.V.s and Trailers Only - No Fee	Boating Allowed Launch Ramps (Lightning Tree is not usuable when low water) Cartop boat launch area.	Fishing Hiking Picnicking Swimming	Stores Motels and Full Facilities 7 miles in Portola.

FRENCHMAN LAKE

Frenchman Lake is at 5,588 feet elevation with 21 miles of shoreline. Excavation has revealed many Indian artifacts as well as a Sequoia log determined to be 10 million years old. Chilcoot Campground has 40 sites (5 tents only for walk-ins, 35 tents/trailers). Frenchman has 62 sites (25 tents only, 37 tents/trailers) and a 4-lane launch ramp. Spring Creek has 39 sites (tents/trailers), and Big Cove has 38 sites (tents/trailers). 19 are single family and 19 are multiple families. All sites have water, toilets, fireplaces and tables. Cottonwood has 12 multiple family units and 8 single family units as well as a Group Camp. Groups may make reservations by contacting the District Ranger, U.S.F.S., Milford 96121, Phone: 916-253-2223.

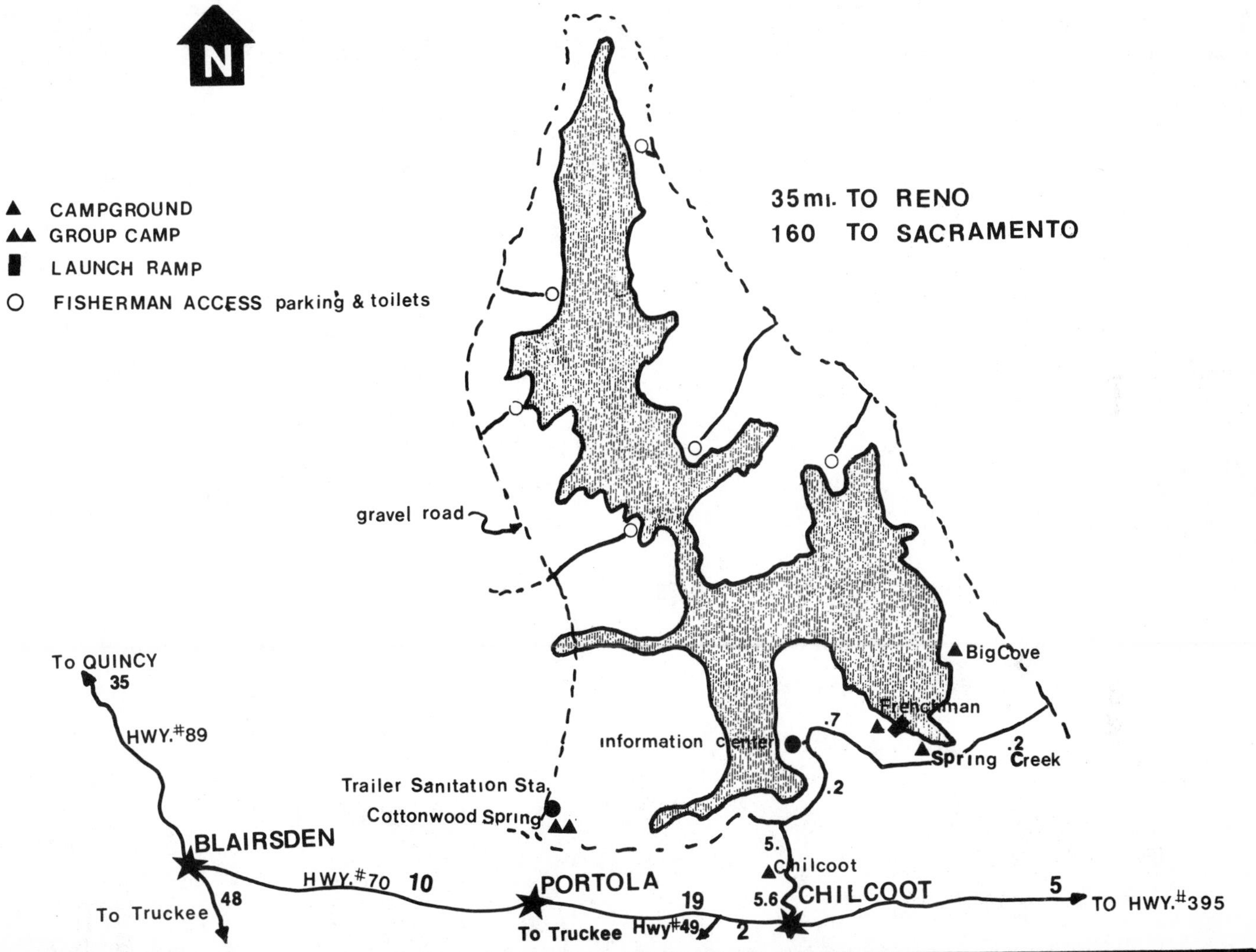
N
CAMPGROUND
GROUP CAMP
LAUNCH RAMP
FISHERMAN ACCESS parking & toilets
35mi. TO RENO
160 TO SACRAMENTO
gravel road
Big Cove
Frenchman
information center
.7
.2
Spring Creek
.2
Trailer Sanitation Sta.
Cottonwood Spring
To QUINCY
35
HWY.#89
BLAIRSDEN
HWY.#70
10
PORTOLA
19
5.
Chilcoot
5.6
CHILCOOT
5
TO HWY.#395
To Truckee
48
To Truckee
Hwy#49
2

INFORMATION: District Ranger, U.S.F.S. Milford 96121, Phone: 916-253-2223

CAMPING	BOATING	RECREATION	RESORTS
179 Developed Sites for Tents, R.V.s, Trailers up to 22 feet. 30 Group Camping - Reservations Fee: $3 a Day Single $5 a Day Multiple Group Camp - $10 to $40 a Day	All Boating Allowed 5 MPH Speed Limits in some areas. Launch Ramp	Fishing Picnicking Swimming Hiking	Supplies at Chilcoot - 8 Miles.

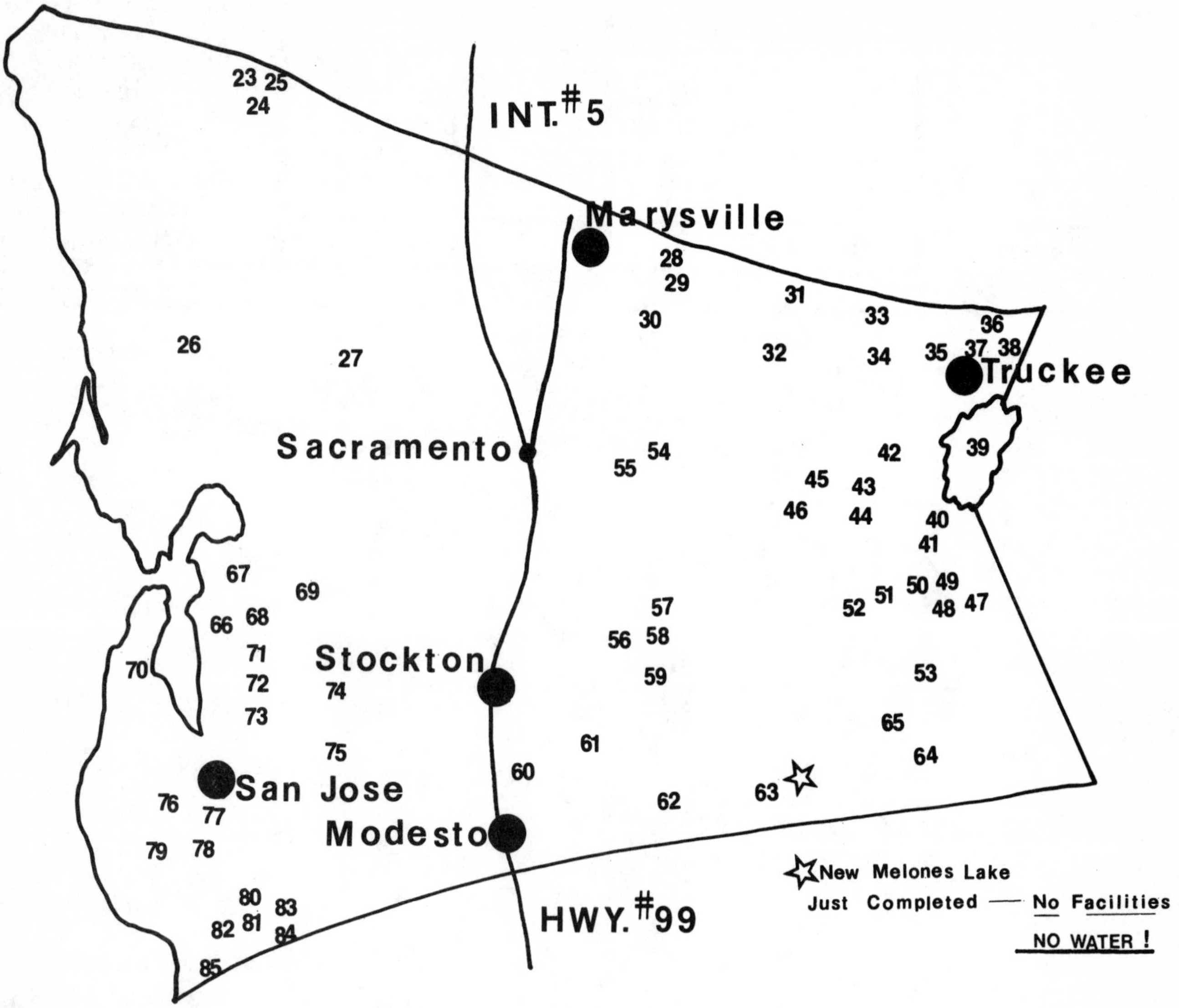
INT. #5
Marysville
Truckee
Sacramento
Stockton
San Jose
Modesto
HWY. #99
New Melones Lake
Just Completed — No Facilities
NO WATER !
23 25
24
26
27
28
29
30
31
32
33
34
35
36
37 38
39
40
41
42
43
44
45
46
47
48
49
50
51
52
53
54
55
56
57
58
59
60
61
62
63
64
65
66
67
68
69
70
71
72
73
74
75
76
77
78
79
80
81
82
83
84
85

* Numbers As Shown Represent Lakes In Numerical Order In Book.

SECTION II

SECTION II

23. BLUE LAKES - LAKE COUNTY
24. CLEAR LAKE
25. INDIAN VALLEY
26. SPRING LAKE
27. LAKE BERRYESSA
28. COLLINS LAKE
29. ENGLEBRIGHT RESERVOIR
30. CAMP FAR WEST RESERVOIR
31. SCOTTS FLAT LAKE
32. ROLLINS LAKE
33. LAKE SPAULDING
34. LAKE VALLEY RESERVOIR AND KELLY LAKE
35. DONNER LAKE
36. STAMPEDE RESERVOIR
37. PROSSER CREEK RESERVOIR
38. BOCA RESERVOIR
39. LAKE TAHOE
40. FALLEN LEAF LAKE
41. ECHO LAKE
42. LOON LAKE
43. UNION VALLEY RESERVOIR
44. ICE HOUSE RESERVOIR
45. STUMPY MEADOWS RESERVOIR
46. SLY PARK - JENKINSON LAKE
47. INDIAN CREEK RESERVOIR
48. BLUE LAKES - ALPINE COUNTY
49. WOODS & RED LAKES
50. CAPLES LAKE
51. SILVER LAKE
52. LOWER BEAR RIVER RESERVOIR
53. LAKE ALPINE
54. FOLSOM LAKE
55. LAKE NATOMA
56. LAKE CAMANCHE
57. LAKE AMADOR
58. PARDEE LAKE
59. NEW HOGAN RESERVOIR
60. OAKWOOD LAKE
61. WOODWARD RESERVOIR
62. LAKE TULLOCH
63. LYONS LAKE
64. PINECREST LAKE
65. BEARDSLEY RESERVOIR
66. LAKE MERRITT
67. LAFAYETTE RESERVOIR
68. SAN PABLO RESERVOIR
69. CONTRA LOMA RESERVOIR
70. LAKE MERCED
71. CULL CANYON RESERVOIR
72. DON CASTRO RESERVOIR
73. SHADOW CLIFFS
74. DEL VALLE RESERVOIR
75. LAKE ELIZABETH
76. STEVENS CREEK
77. LAKE VASONA
78. LEXINGTON RESERVOIR
79. LOCH LOMOND RESERVOIR
80. CALERO RESERVOIR
81. CHESBRO RESERVOIR
82. UVAS RESERVOIR
83. ANDERSON LAKE
84. COYOTE RESERVOIR
85. PINTO LAKE

The Blue Lakes in Lake County are at about 1,400 feet elevation. This is a delightful area for fishing and quiet relaxation. There are 6 private Resorts around the Lake offering complete vacation facilities. Trout, Black Bass, Blue Gill and Catfish are often plentiful in this clear, spring-fed Lake.

. . . Continued . . .

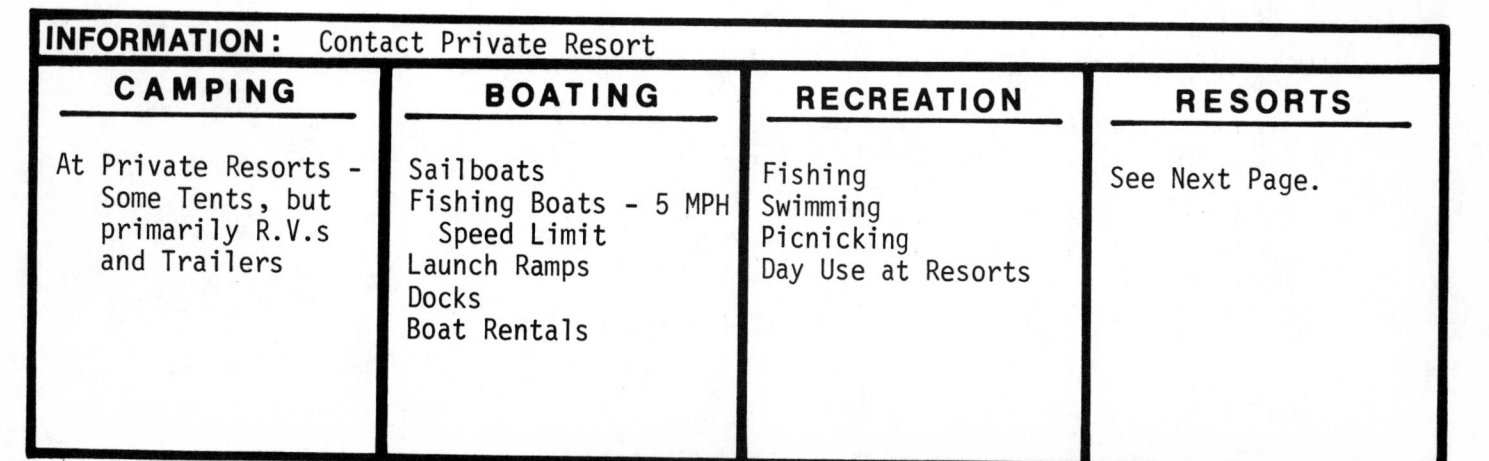

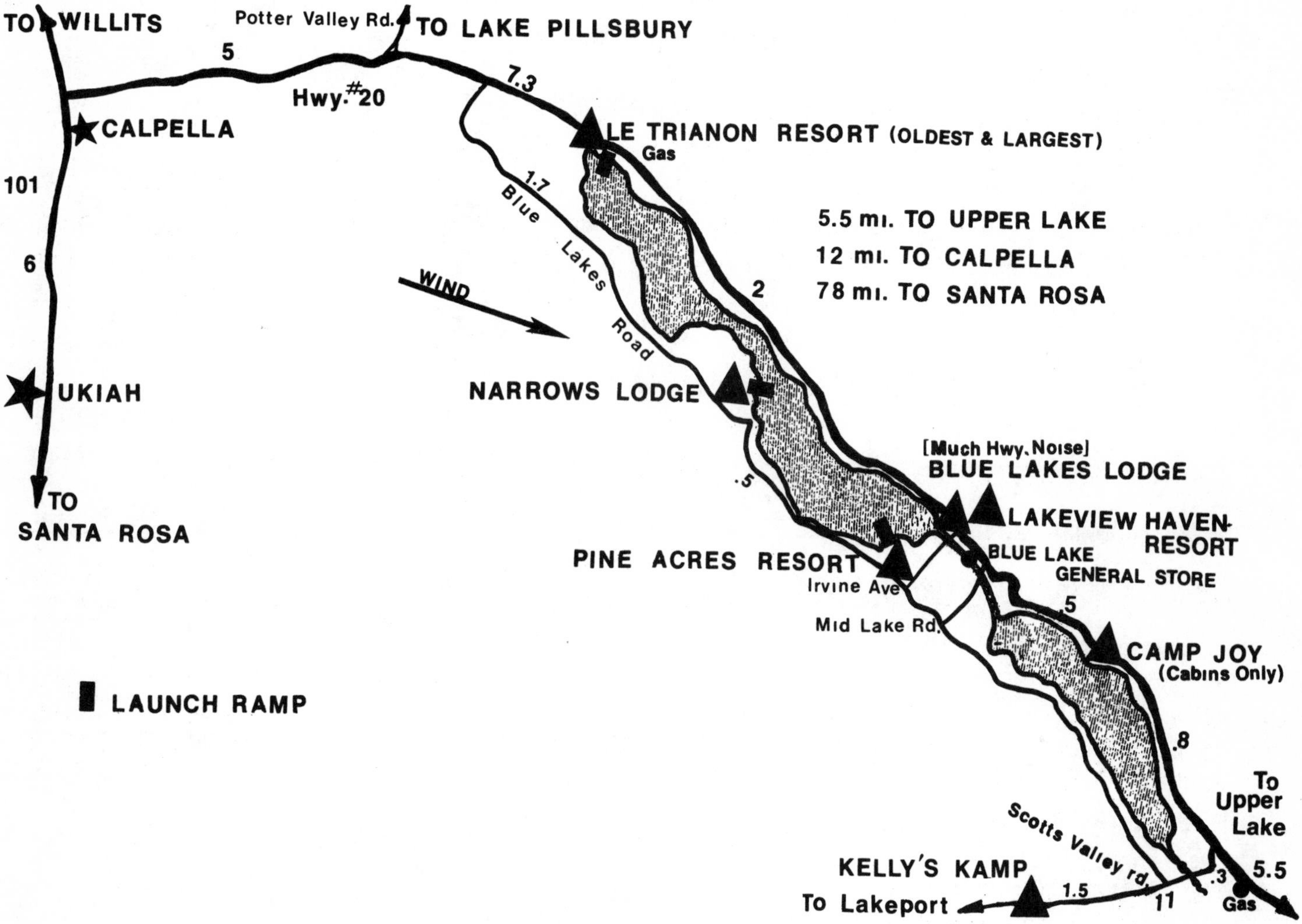
TO WILLITS
Potter Valley Rd.
TO LAKE PILLSBURY
5
Hwy. #20
7.3
CALPELLA
LE TRIANON RESORT (OLDEST & LARGEST)
Gas
101
1.7
Blue Lakes Road
5.5 mi. TO UPPER LAKE
12 mi. TO CALPELLA
78 mi. TO SANTA ROSA
6
WIND
2
UKIAH
NARROWS LODGE
.5
[Much Hwy. Noise]
BLUE LAKES LODGE
LAKEVIEW HAVEN RESORT
TO SANTA ROSA
PINE ACRES RESORT
BLUE LAKE GENERAL STORE
Irvine Ave
.5
Mid Lake Rd.
CAMP JOY
(Cabins Only)
LAUNCH RAMP
.8
To Upper Lake
Scotts Valley rd.
KELLY'S KAMP
.3
5.5
1.5
11
To Lakeport
Gas

INFORMATION: Contact Private Resort

CAMPING	BOATING	RECREATION	RESORTS
At Private Resorts - Some Tents, but primarily R.V.s and Trailers	Sailboats Fishing Boats - 5 MPH Speed Limit Launch Ramps Docks Boat Rentals	Fishing Swimming Picnicking Day Use at Resorts	See Next Page.

Privately Owned

Le Trianon Resort
Star Route 2, Box 757
Ukiah 95482
Phone: 707-275-2262

Le Trianon, the oldest Resort on the Blue Lakes, offers 3 sizes of housekeeping cabins as well as nice areas for tent camping, R.V.s or trailers with 400 picnic tables, electricity, water, toilets and showers. There is a launch ramp, dock, swim area and boat rentals along with R.V. storage. A cocktail lounge, store, snack bar and recreation room complete this full facility Resort.

Narrows Lodge
Star Route 2, Box 827
Ukiah 95482
Phone: 707-275-2718

The Narrows Lodge Resort provides all the comforts of modern conveniences in a lovely tree-studded setting. There are fully equipped housekeeping cabins and a motel unit offered at reasonable prices. The R.V. Trailer Park has complete hookups, and the Resort has a launching ramp, fishing dock and swim area. Excellent meals and cocktails can be enjoyed at the Dinner House. By the way, gnats and mosquitos stay away from this lovely area.

Pine Acres Blue Lake Resort
5328 Blue Lakes Road
Upper Lake 95485
Phone: 707-275-9920

This Resort has a motel as well as fully equipped housekeeping cabins and hookups for R.V.s and trailers. There is a fishing dock, launch ramp, boat rentals and store.

Blue Lakes Lodge
Star Route 2, Box 815
Ukiah 95482
Phone: 707-275-2178

Motel, Restaurant, launch ramp, fishing dock, boat rentals and swim area are available but there is considerable highway noise.

Lakeview Haven Resort and Camp Joy are also along the Lake and have a motel and cabins along with a R.V./Trailer Park.

Kelly's Kamp
8220 Scotts Valley Road
Upper Lake 95485
Phone: 707-263-5754

Kelly's Kamp is located at the South end of Blue Lakes, 1-1/2 miles from Highway 20 and 10 miles North of Lakeport at Clear Lake.

Sites are available for tents and R.V.s (full hookups), water, barbecues, toilets and hot showers.

CLEAR LAKE

Clear Lake is 18 miles long, 8 miles wide, with 100 miles of shoreline. It is the largest natural Lake in California, and studies indicate it is at least 100,000 years old and could be 1 to 4 million years old. By 1940, gnats had become a serious problem and the water was clouded with dirt and algae. Lake smelt were introduced to eat the gnats, and today the ecological balance has largely been restored. The California Department of Parks and Recreation operates an outstanding campground at the State Park 4 miles from Kelseyville. There are many sheltered coves and extensive boating facilities. A complete list of private Resorts can be obtained from the Lake County Chamber of Commerce, P. O. Box 517, Lakeport 95453. Reservations are a must on weekends in season.

. . . Continued . . .

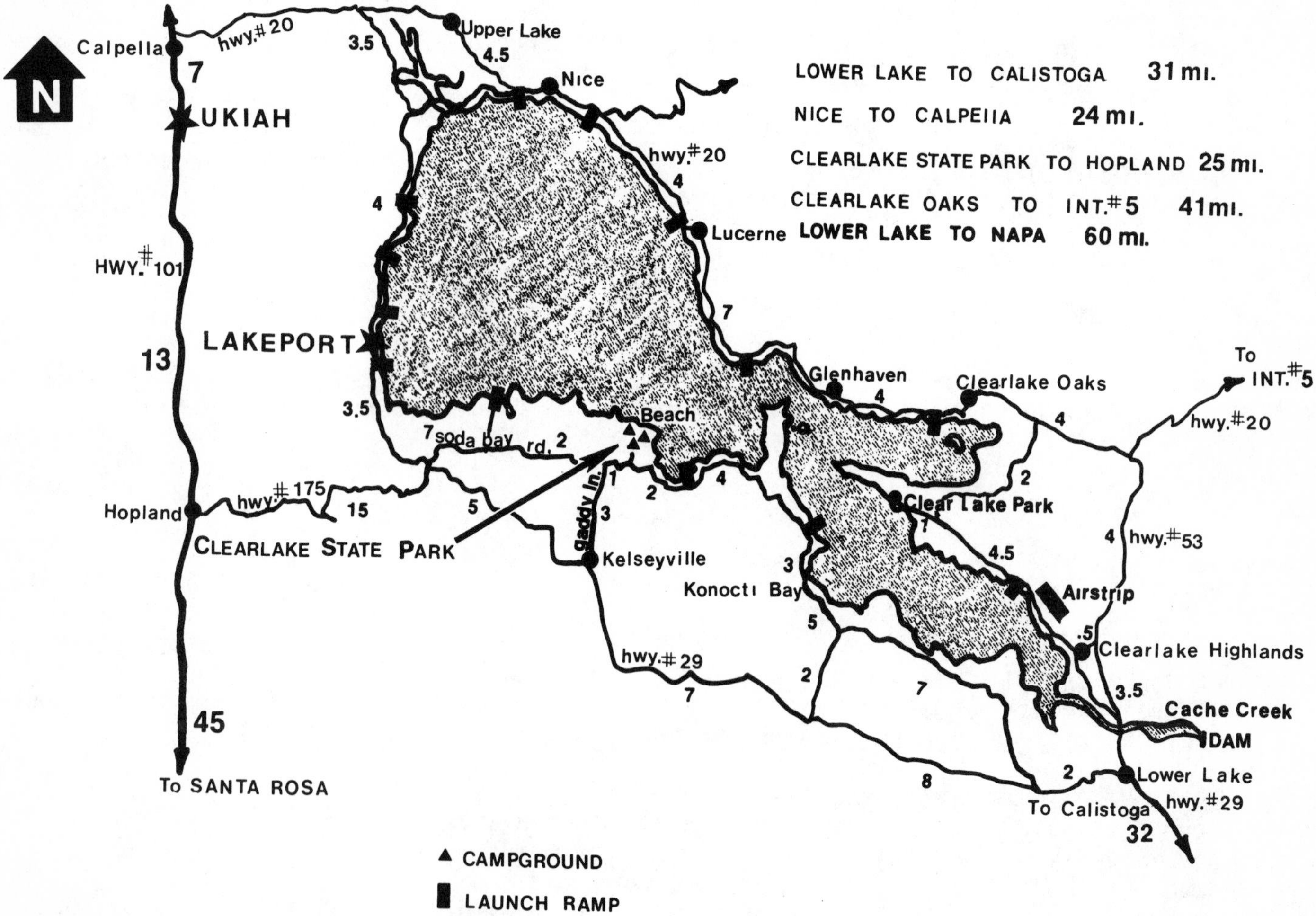

N
Calpella
hwy.#20
7
UKIAH
HWY.#101
13
LAKEPORT
45
To SANTA ROSA
Hopland
hwy.#175
15
CLEARLAKE STATE PARK
Upper Lake
4.5
3.5
Nice
hwy.#20
4
Lucerne
7
Glenhaven
Clearlake Oaks
Beach
soda bay rd.
Gaddy ln.
Kelseyville
Konocti Bay
hwy.#29
Clear Lake Park
Airstrip
Clearlake Highlands
Cache Creek
DAM
Lower Lake
To Calistoga
hwy.#29
32
To INT.#5
hwy.#20
hwy.#53
LOWER LAKE TO CALISTOGA 31 mi.
NICE TO CALPEIIA 24 mi.
CLEARLAKE STATE PARK TO HOPLAND 25 mi.
CLEARLAKE OAKS TO INT.#5 41 mi.
LOWER LAKE TO NAPA 60 mi.
▲ CAMPGROUND
▮ LAUNCH RAMP

INFORMATION: State Park - Ticketron, P.O. Box 26430, San Francisco 94120

CAMPING	BOATING	RECREATION	RESORTS
82 Developed Sites for Tents, R.V.s, and Trailers - State Park System Fee: $4 a Day Numerous Privately Owned Facilities - See 24 a and 24 b.	All Boating Allowed Launch Ramps Boat Rentals	Fishing Swimming Hiking Picnicking Complete Vacation Facilities	See Lists on 24 a and 24 b for tent, R.V. and trailer facilities Numerous Cabins, Motels, Lodges and Restaurants. Contact Chamber of Commerce for complete list.

Clear Lake State Park - Camping Facilities

82 Campsites (tents/trailers), water, toilets, dump station, showers, barbecues, launch ramp, swim beach, campfire programs, nature hikes. Fee: $4.00 a Day. Reservations are through your local Ticketron outlet or write: Ticketron, P. O. Box 26430, San Francisco 94130. $1.50 Day Use Only for picnicking, swimming and fishing. Boat launching facilities for Day Use are $3.00.

Private Resorts are much too numerous to include all of them but the following is a list of several Resorts that have Boat Launching and Marina Facilities. All Phone Numbers are Area Code 707.

Town	Housekeeping Cabins		Trailers, R.V.s or Camping
Lakeport	Anchorage Inn 950 N. Main St. 263-5417	Sandy Cove Cottages 1950 Lakeshore Blvd. 263-5387	Aqua Village Trailer Park 1350 S. Main St. 263-4411
	Chalet Apt. Motel 2802 Lakeshore Blvd. 263-5040	Santa Rita Resort 2569 Lakeshore Blvd. 263-4309	Marv's Trailer Park 2502 Lakeshore Blvd. 263-5392
	El Dorado Motel 3945 Lakeshore Blvd. 253-4071	Skylark Motel 1120 N. Main St. 263-6151	Northport Trailer Resort 5020 Lakeshore Blvd. 263-3232
	4 Seasons 3575 Lakeshore Blvd. 263-5762	Stillwood Resort 2812 Lakeshore Blvd. 263-5411	Robin Hill 5830 Robin Hill Dr. 263-0450
	H & H Rocky Point 3750 Lakeshore Blvd. 263-4513	Sunrise Resort 3325 Lakeshore Blvd. 263-4380	Vail's Camp 37 Lafferty Road 263-6478
	Lakeport Harbor Motel 910 N. Main St. 263-4241 (Good)	Western Hills Resort 3555 Lakeshore Blvd. 263-6674	
	Rocky Point Resort 3894 Lakeshore Blvd. 263-4673	Will-O-Point Resort 1 First St. 263-5407 (Good Full Service Resort - Free Ramp)	
Soda Bay	Edgewater Resort 6420 Soda Bay Road 279-1295 (Good Full Service Resort)	Jim's Soda Bay Resort 6380 Soda Bay Road 279-4837	Edgewater Resort 6420 Soda Bay Road 279-1295
	Ferndale Resort 6190 Soda Bay Road 279-4866		

. . . Continued . . .

. . . Continued . . .

Town	Housekeeping Cabins		Trailers, R.V.s or Camping
Konocti Bay	Konocti Harbor Inn 8727 Soda Bay Road 279-4281	Ski Haven Resort 8946 Soda Bay Road 277-7181	Bayshore 9130 Soda Bay Road 277-7138 (Also sales, repairs and storage)
Clearlake Highlands	Austin's Resort 14067 Lakeshore Dr. 994-6451	Lamplighter Resort 14165 Lakeshore Dr. 994-2129 (Nice facility)	Kingfisher Resort 5845 Old Highway 53 994-3500
	B & B Lighthouse 5895 Old Highway 53 994-3030	Ross's Log Cabins 14335 Lakeshore Dr. 994-2125	Lakeland Resort 5575 Old Highway 53 994-2273
	Garner's Resort 6236 Old Highway 53 994-6267	Ship-N-Shore Resort 13885 Lakeshore Dr. 994-6672 (Good Full Service Facility)	
	Jules Resort 14195 Lakeshore Dr. 994-6491	Tamarack Lodge Lakeshore Dr. 994-6660	
	Konocti Kourt 14365 Lakeshore Dr. 994-2110	Trombetta's Beach Resort 5865 Old Highway 53 994-2417	
Clearlake Park	Honeymoon Cove 8 Miles from Lakeshore Dr. at tip of Peninsula 994-3415		Holiday Island 12145 Lakeshore Dr. 994-6723
			Pine Dell Resort 4 Miles Northwest of Post Office on Lake 994-4161
Clearlake Oaks	Bob's Resort 12555 Highway 20 998-3328	Lake Marina Motel 10215 E. Highway 20 998-3787	Knollwood Park 9850 E. Highway 20 998-3636
	Harbor Motel 130 Short St. 998-3587	Sully's Resort 10165 E. Highway 20 998-3888	M & M Campgrounds 13050 Island Dr. 998-9943

. . . Continued . . .

. . . Continued . . .

Town	Housekeeping Cabins		Trailers, R.V.s or Camping
Glenhaven	Indian Beach Resort 9945 E. Highway 29 998-3760	Ripley's Marina Resort On Highway 20 998-3203	Glenhaven Beach Resort 9625 Highway 20 998-3406
	Plaag's Resort 9595 Harbor Dr. 998-3757	Shamrock Resort 114 Harbor Dr. 998-3331	Harbor Vista Park 9510 Highway 20 998-3331
	Glenhaven Inn 9435 Highway 20 998-3260	Starlite Resort 9495 E. Highway 20 998-3232	
Lucerne	Beachcomber Resort 6345 Highway 20 274-6639	Circle View Resort 6520 E. Highway 20 274-1319	Arrow Recreational Park 6720 E. Highway 20 274-7715
	Cal-Ohio Resort 6339 E. Highway 20 274-6611	Lake Sands Resort 6335 E. Highway 20 274-7732	Bamboo Hollow Mobile Park 5877 Lake St. 274-7751
Nice	Aurora Resort 2980 Lakeshore Blvd. 274-9947	Redbud Lodge Resort 3997 E. Highway 20 274-1994	Holiday Harbor 3746 E. Highway 20 274-1136
	Baywood Beach Resort 3806 Lakeshore Blvd. 274-1289	Talley's Resort 3826 Lakeshore Blvd. 274-1177	North Shore Resort 2345 Lakeshore Blvd. 274-7771
	Clear Lake Lodge E. Highway 20 274-1544	Treehaven Resort 3987 E. Highway 20 274-6642	Tony's Campground 2570 Lakeshore Blvd. 274-3315
Lower Lake and Cache Creek	Cache Creek Auto Court 16021 Dam Road 994-6127		Oak Grove Trailer Park 16150 Tish-A-Tang Road 994-4377
	Lotowana Village 14825 Clement Dr. 994-5344		Oaks Waterfront Park 7664 Highway 53 994-6255
			Shaw's Shady Acres on Cache Creek 994-2236

Marina - 3 Miles North of Konocti Bay at Buckingham Point is located "C" Braito's Buckingham Marina with launch ramp, berths, fuel and supplies.

INDIAN VALLEY RESERVOIR

Construction of Indian Valley Reservoir started in 1973 and has just opened to the public for recreation. Since there is a 10 MPH speed limit on the Lake, it is a delightfully quiet place for fishing boats, sailboats and canoes. Caution is advised, however, as there are many submerged trees. Bass and trout fishing along the inlets can be good, especially night and morning. Swimming is permitted and the water is crystal clear and unusually warm. There are 2 Launch Ramps at the South and North end of the Lake. You can camp around the Lake at many quiet areas, but the only developed site is at the Dam. At Blue Oak Campground towards Highway 20, there are tables and firepits at 10 sites, but no water is available and no fee is charged.

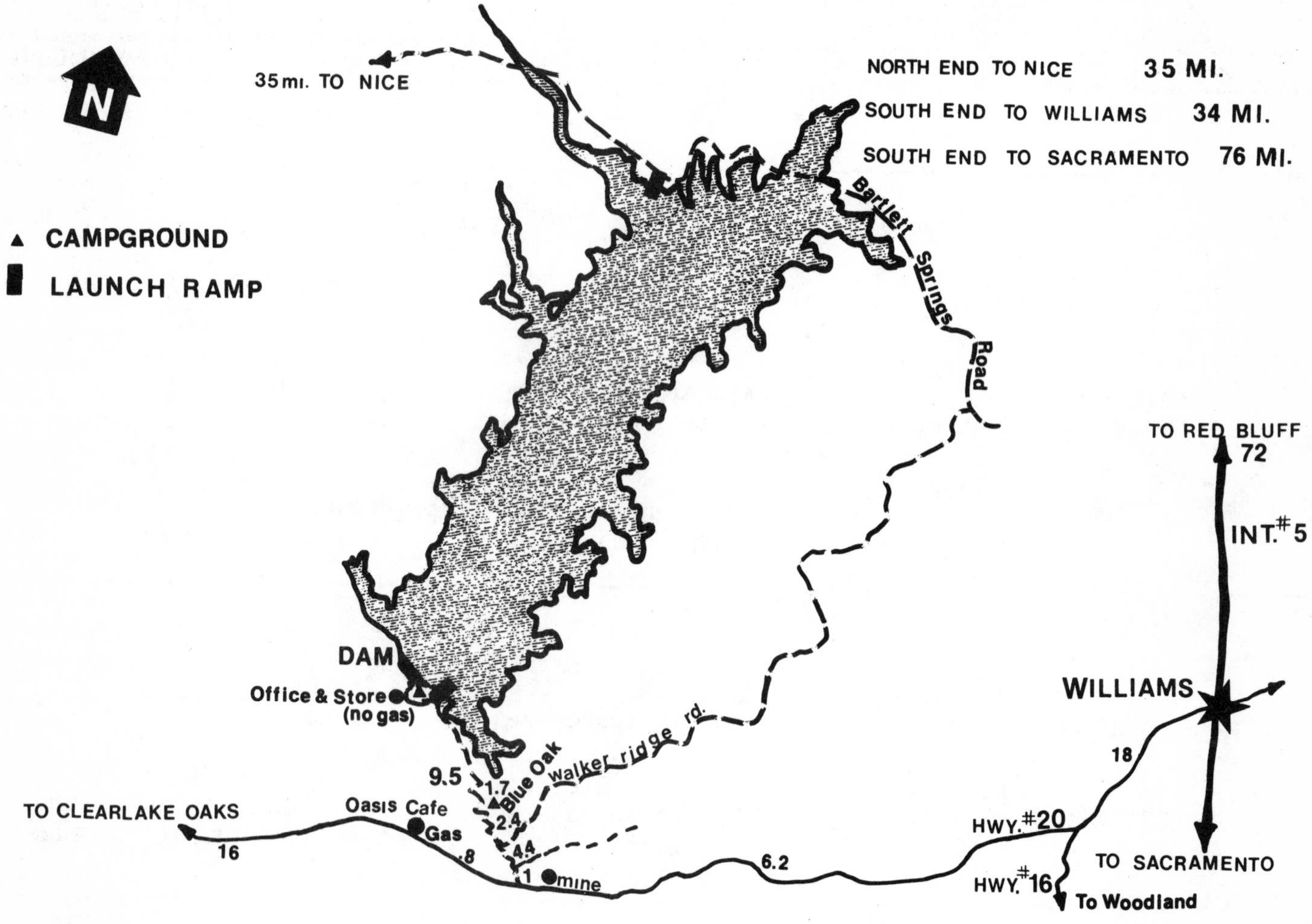
N
35mi. TO NICE
NORTH END TO NICE 35 MI.
SOUTH END TO WILLIAMS 34 MI.
SOUTH END TO SACRAMENTO 76 MI.
▲ CAMPGROUND
LAUNCH RAMP
Bartlett Springs Road
TO RED BLUFF
72
INT.#5
DAM
Office & Store
(no gas)
WILLIAMS
walker ridge rd.
18
9.5
1.7
Blue Oak
2.4
TO CLEARLAKE OAKS
Oasis Cafe
Gas
16
.8
44
1
mine
6.2
HWY.#20
TO SACRAMENTO
HWY.#16
To Woodland

INFORMATION: Yolo County Flood Control, 427 Cleveland St., Woodland 95695

CAMPING	BOATING	RECREATION	RESORTS
Camping is Allowed Developed Sites Under Construction Near the Dam 10 Sites at Blue Oak No Fee, No Water	10 MPH Speed Limit on Lake. 5 MPH Speed Limit within 200 yards of shore. 2 Paved Launch Ramps	Fishing Swimming Picnicking Hiking (No Shooting)	Oasis Cafe for Meals

SPRING LAKE

Spring Lake was opened in 1974 by the Sonoma County Parks Department. It is a small Lake about 1/2 mile long, 1/4 mile wide, and has 2 miles of shoreline. The Park has 320 acres of wooded areas with grass down to the water's edge. It is open to all boating except power boats. There are two small islands in the Lake which was originally built for flood control, and many of the buildings are built to be submerged during the winter. For this reason, there are three Dams back from the edge of the Lake. There is a 3-acre swimming lagoon open from Memorial Day to Labor Day which is spring fed and the water temperature is 85 degrees. The Park is open all year and includes 34 campsites, hot showers, toilets and 150 people maximum Group Picnic Area with barbecues. A paved bike trail is available as well as hiking trails, horseback riding trails, horse trailer parking, food and drink concession stand. The facilities are very well maintained so this is a pretty Reservoir and Park to visit.

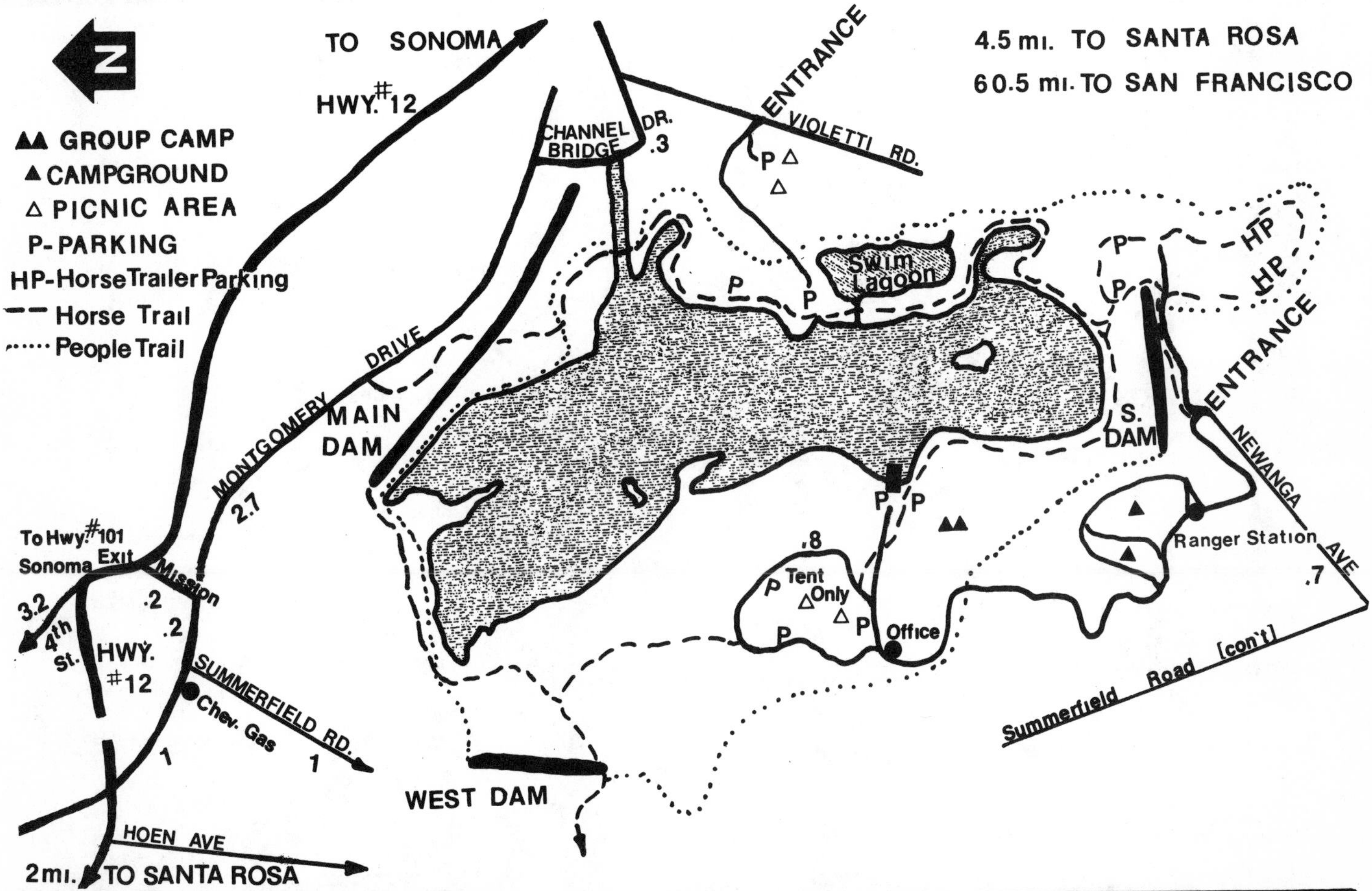
N
TO SONOMA
HWY.#12
4.5 mi. TO SANTA ROSA
60.5 mi. TO SAN FRANCISCO
ENTRANCE
VIOLETTI RD.
CHANNEL BRIDGE
DR. .3
▲▲ GROUP CAMP
▲ CAMPGROUND
△ PICNIC AREA
P- PARKING
HP-Horse Trailer Parking
Horse Trail
People Trail
Swim Lagoon
HP
HP
ENTRANCE
DRIVE
MONTGOMERY
MAIN DAM
2.7
S. DAM
NEWANGA AVE
Ranger Station
.7
.8
Tent Only
Office
To Hwy.#101 Sonoma Exit
Mission
3.2
4th St.
.2
.2
HWY. #12
SUMMERFIELD RD.
Chev. Gas
1
1
Summerfield Road [con't]
WEST DAM
HOEN AVE
2mi. TO SANTA ROSA

INFORMATION: Sonoma Co. Regional Parks, 2403 Professional Dr. #100, Santa Rosa 95401

CAMPING	BOATING	RECREATION	RESORTS
34 Developed Sites - 29 Family, and 5 Walk-ins. 50 Unit Group Campground Fee: $5 a Day $1 a Day for Walk-ins $1 a Day for Your Dog	No Power Boats Launch Ramp Rentals: Canoes, Kayaks, Sailboats, Rowboats, Paddle-boats, Tubes. (Children under 5 yrs. not allowed in boats)	150 Picnic Units Group Picnicking Call Park Dept. - 707-527-2041 Ranger - 707-538-8092 Swimming in Lagoon Fishing, Hiking, Horseback Riding Bicycling Trails Day Use Fee - $1.50	Snack Bar Showers adjacent to Swim Lagoon Restrooms Lockers - 10¢ Day Use Hours - 10 a.m. to 7 p.m.

Lake Berryessa is at 440 feet elevation, about 25 miles long and has 165 miles of shoreline. Complete vacation facilities are available at 7 different Resorts.

. . . Continued . . .

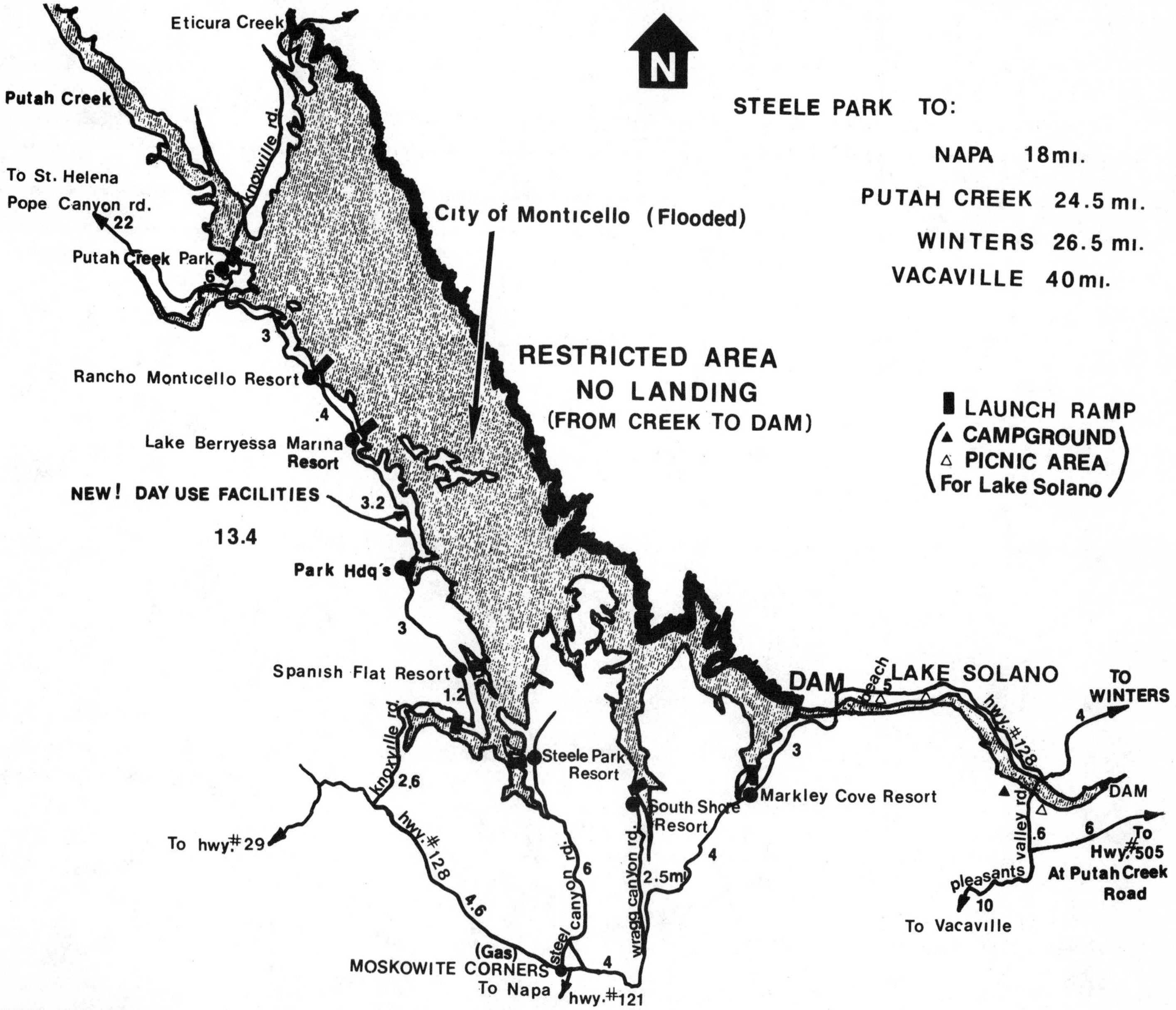
Eticura Creek
N
Putah Creek
STEELE PARK TO:
NAPA 18mi.
PUTAH CREEK 24.5 mi.
WINTERS 26.5 mi.
VACAVILLE 40mi.
To St. Helena
Pope Canyon rd.
22
City of Monticello (Flooded)
knoxville rd.
Putah Creek Park
6
3
RESTRICTED AREA
NO LANDING
(FROM CREEK TO DAM)
Rancho Monticello Resort
.4
LAUNCH RAMP
CAMPGROUND
PICNIC AREA
For Lake Solano
Lake Berryessa Marina Resort
NEW! DAY USE FACILITIES
3.2
13.4
Park Hdq's
3
Spanish Flat Resort
1.2
DAM
beach
5
LAKE SOLANO
TO WINTERS
hwy. #128
4
knoxville rd.
2.6
Steele Park Resort
3
South Shore Resort
Markley Cove Resort
DAM
To hwy.#29
hwy.# 128
6
steel canyon rd.
wragg canyon rd.
2.5mi
4
valley rd.
.6
6
To Hwy.#505 At Putah Creek Road
pleasants
10
To Vacaville
4.6
(Gas)
MOSKOWITE CORNERS
To Napa
4
hwy.#121

INFORMATION: Individual Resort - See Next Page

CAMPING	BOATING	RECREATION	RESORTS
570 Developed Sites at 7 Resorts for Tents, R.V.s and Trailers. Full Hookups	All Boating Allowed	Swimming	Motels & Cabins
Fee: $4.50 a Day - Tent Camping	RESTRICTED AREA - See Map	Fishing	Trailer Parks
$6.50 a Day - R.V.s and Trailers	Launch Ramps	Picnicking	Snack Bars
	Boat Rentals	Hiking	Restaurants
	Full Service Marina		Stores
	No Power Boats on Lake Solano		Swimming Pools

LAKE BERRYESSA

. . . Continued . . .

It is illegal to camp, picnic, launch or land a boat on any portion of the East Shore of the Lake from Eticuera Creek to Monticello Dam. There are 570 campsites at the 7 Resorts and a variety of other facilities. Low hills surround much of the shoreline and some areas can be very steep. The water averages 70 to 75 degrees during the summer and swimming and waterskiing are good although water can drop 30 feet by late summer. You can check with the Bureau of Reclamation for the projected drop each year. Winds are usually light and variable for sailing. Fishing can be excellent for trout, bass, steelhead, catfish and crappie. Check at Resorts for best time, equipment and bait.

RESORTS

Putah Creek Park - Phone: 707-966-2116 - Motel, R.V. and Trailer Park with 20 new units - full hookups - Launch Ramp, Berths, Boat Rentals, Full Service Marina, Restaurant and Bar, Swim Beach, Snack Bar and Marine Repair (Phone: 707-966-2408).

Rancho Monticello Resort - Phone: 707-966-2188 - Camping, R.V.s, Trailers, Launch Ramp, Boat Rentals, Store, Swim Beach, Snack Bar, Storage, Marine Repair (Phone: 707-966-2216).

Lake Berryessa Marina - Phone: 707-966-2161 - Camping, R.V.s, Trailers, Hookups, Launch Ramp, Berths, Boat Rentals, Marina, Store, Restaurant, Swim Beach.

Spanish Flat Resort - Phone: 707-966-2101 - Camping, R.V.s, Trailers, Housekeeping Mobile Homes, Launch Ramps (one for low water), Berths, Boat Rentals (ski boats, fishing boats, jet skis), Full Service Marina, Store, Restaurant, Bar, Swim Beach, Snack Bar.

Steele Park Resort - Phone: 707-966-2123 - The largest Resort at Berryessa - Camping, R.V.s and Trailer Park, Motel, Housekeeping Cottages, Launch Ramp, Berths, Boat Rentals, Full Service Marina, Store, Good Restaurant, Bar, Swim Beach, Pool, Miniature Golf, Snack Bar.

South Shore Resort - Phone: 707-966-2172 - Camping, R.V.s and Trailers, Launch Ramp, Boat Rentals and Storage, Full Service Marina, Store, Restaurant, Bar, Swim Beach.

Markley Cove - Phone: 707-966-2134 - Limited Facilities.

LAKE SOLANO

The water here is very cold but there are many lovely trees and a County Park with campsites at $4 per Day and $1 for your dog. Power boats are not allowed. Parking fee on weekends is $1.

COLLINS LAKE

Collins Lake, in the delightful Motherlode Country, is at 1,200 feet elevation with 12-1/2 miles of shoreline. 75 campsites offer some hookups, toilets, water, tables, barbecues, and an unusual service for $8.00 which will move in and set up your stored trailer in a reserved site before your arrival and return it to storage when you leave. Reservations are accepted by phone or mail. Fees are subject to slight increase from time to time. This is one of the finest fishing Lakes in California and is stocked with Trophy Trout. Fishing is legal 24 hours a day, except no trout or salmon fishing at night, so catfishermen can enjoy the nights, too. Collins Lake is open exclusively to fishermen from September 15 to May 15. Waterskiing is permitted from May 15 to September 15 in designated areas.

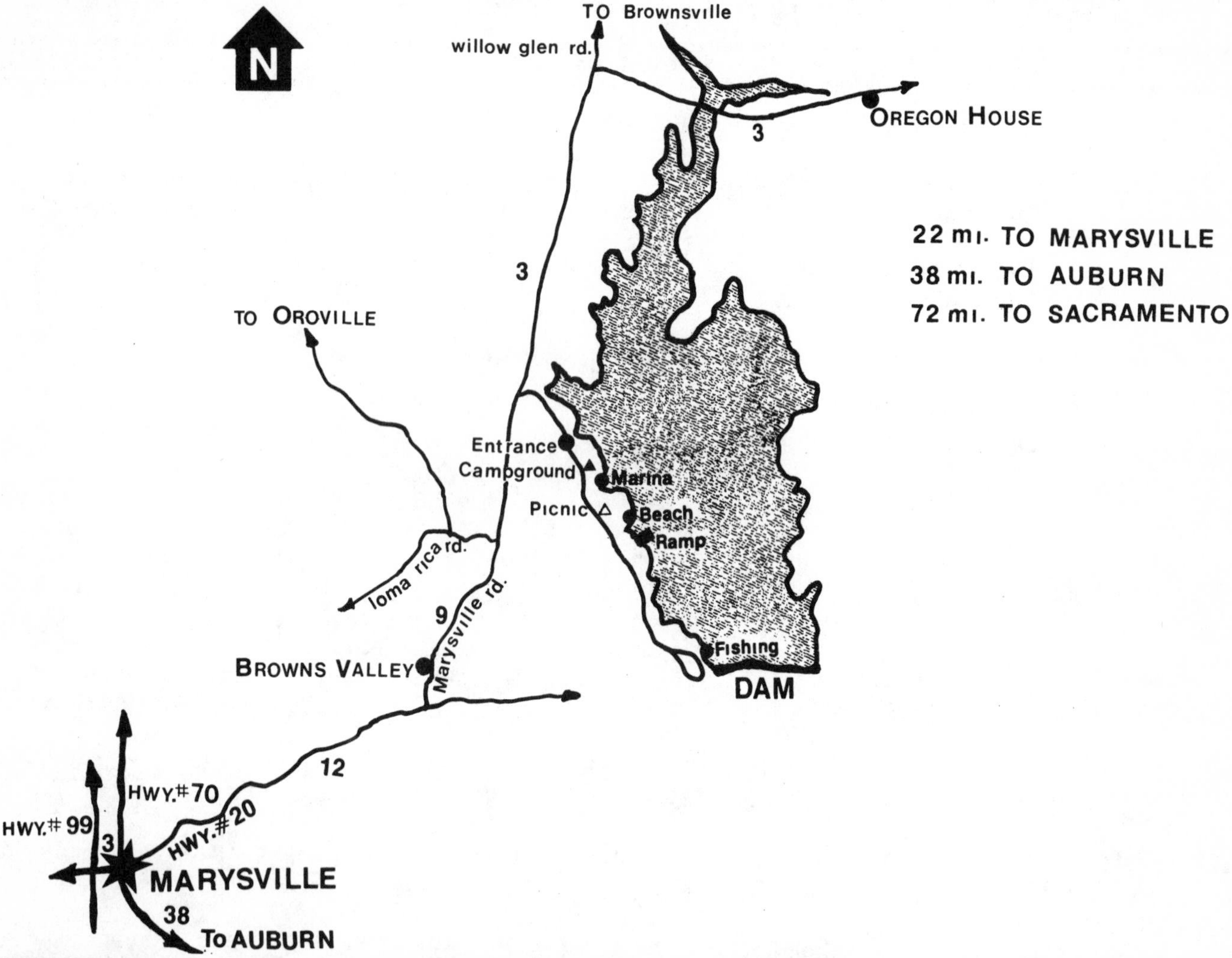
N
TO Brownsville
willow glen rd.
OREGON HOUSE
3
TO OROVILLE
Entrance
Campground
Marina
Picnic
Beach
Ramp
loma rica rd.
9
Marysville rd.
BROWNS VALLEY
Fishing
DAM
12
HWY.#70
HWY.#99
3
HWY.#20
MARYSVILLE
38
To AUBURN
22 mi. TO MARYSVILLE
38 mi. TO AUBURN
72 mi. TO SACRAMENTO

INFORMATION: Collins Lake, Oregon House 95962, Ph. 916-692-1600

CAMPING	BOATING	RECREATION	RESORTS
75 Developed Sites for Tents, R.V.s and Trailers Also Camp Areas with no Facilities. Fee: $5 a Day - Site $6 - Electric and Water Hook-up $7 - Sewer also.	Fishermen Only - Sept. 15 - May 15 Waterskiing Also - May 15 - Sept. 15 Launch Ramp Boat Rentals and Moorage Boat & Trailer Storage	Fishing Swimming Picnicking - Group Picnic Area Hiking Day Use Only - $2 per Vehicle to 4 people	Group or Club Discounts Store Hot Showers - 25¢

ENGLEBRIGHT RESERVOIR

Englebright Reservoir is a boat camper's bonanza! Launching is at Skippers Cove Marina and then you can proceed up the Lake to a campsite. There are over 300 available at campgrounds along the Lake shore with tables, barbecue pits and toilets. No reservations are taken. The surface area of the Lake covers 815 acres, and there are 24 miles of shoreline at 527 feet elevation. The Lake winds around like a snake and most of the shoreline is steep and rocky except at the campgrounds. There are some sandy beaches and pine and small oak trees above the high water line. Drive-in Campgrounds are under construction, but if you enjoy boat camping, this is well worth a trip.

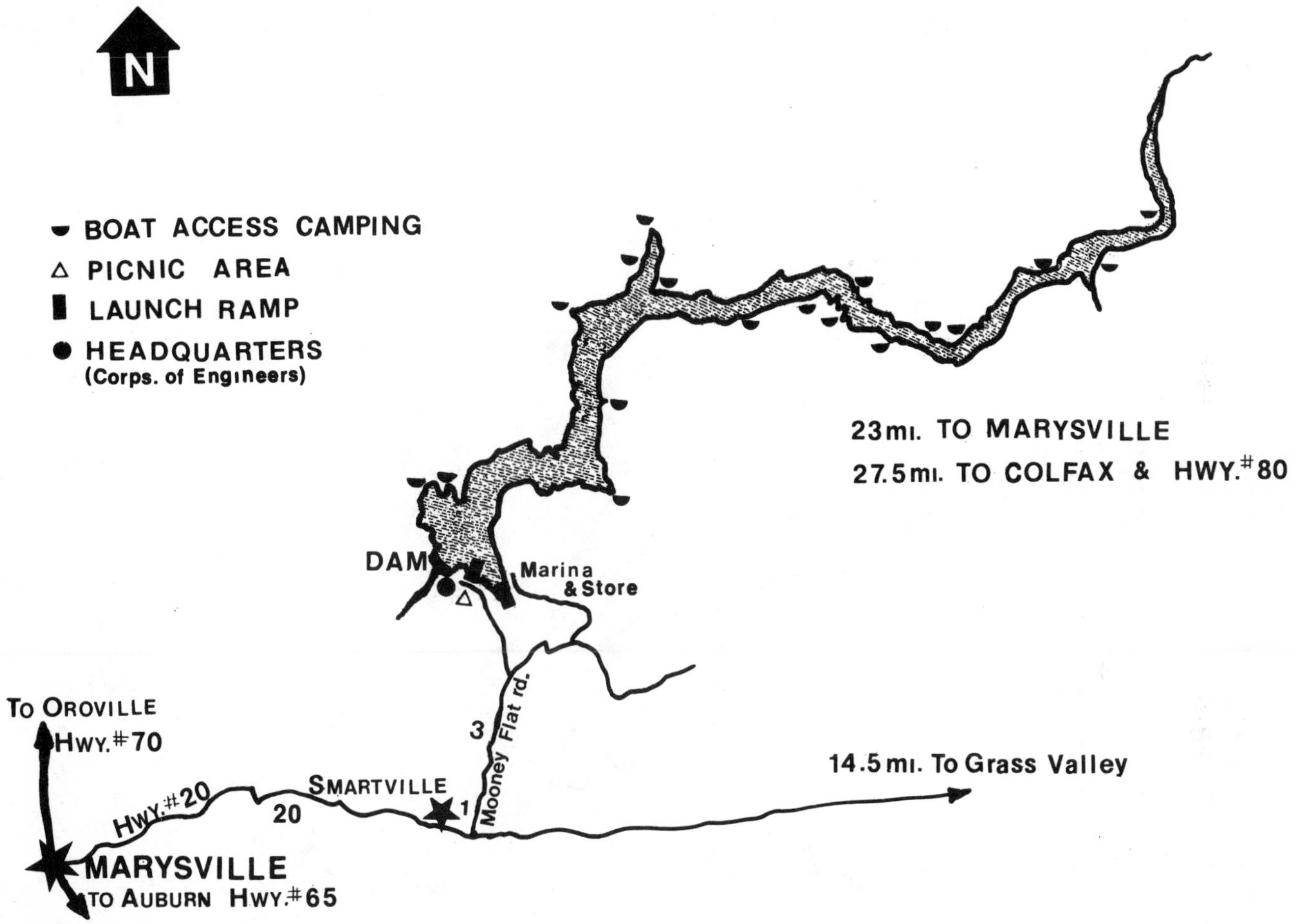
N
BOAT ACCESS CAMPING
PICNIC AREA
LAUNCH RAMP
HEADQUARTERS
(Corps. of Engineers)
23mi. TO MARYSVILLE
27.5mi. TO COLFAX & HWY.#80
DAM
Marina
& Store
Mooney Flat rd.
3
1
To OROVILLE
HWY.#70
HWY.#20
20
SMARTVILLE
14.5mi. To Grass Valley
MARYSVILLE
TO AUBURN HWY.#65

INFORMATION: Skippers Cove, P. O. Box 5, Smartville 95977 - Ph. 916-639-2272

CAMPING	BOATING	RECREATION	RESORTS
300 Developed Boat-Access Sites Drive-In Sites Under Construction	All Boating Allowed Rental Boats Houseboat Moorings Boat Slips - Covered and Open	Fishing Swimming Picnicking Hiking Waterskiing	Store Gas - Propane Hot Sandwiches Beer and Wine

CAMP FAR WEST RESERVOIR

Camp Far West Reservoir water is used for irrigation. The Lake is at 300 feet elevation and the water temperature rises up to 85 degrees in the summer when the climate can be quite hot. The Reservoir is open all year although the water is extremely low at the end of summer. The North Entrance closes at the end of summer also. The Lake has boat camping, 2 launch ramps, boat rentals and 106 campsites located in two different areas with water and toilets. There are picnic tables and group reservations can be made. Bass fishing can be very good.

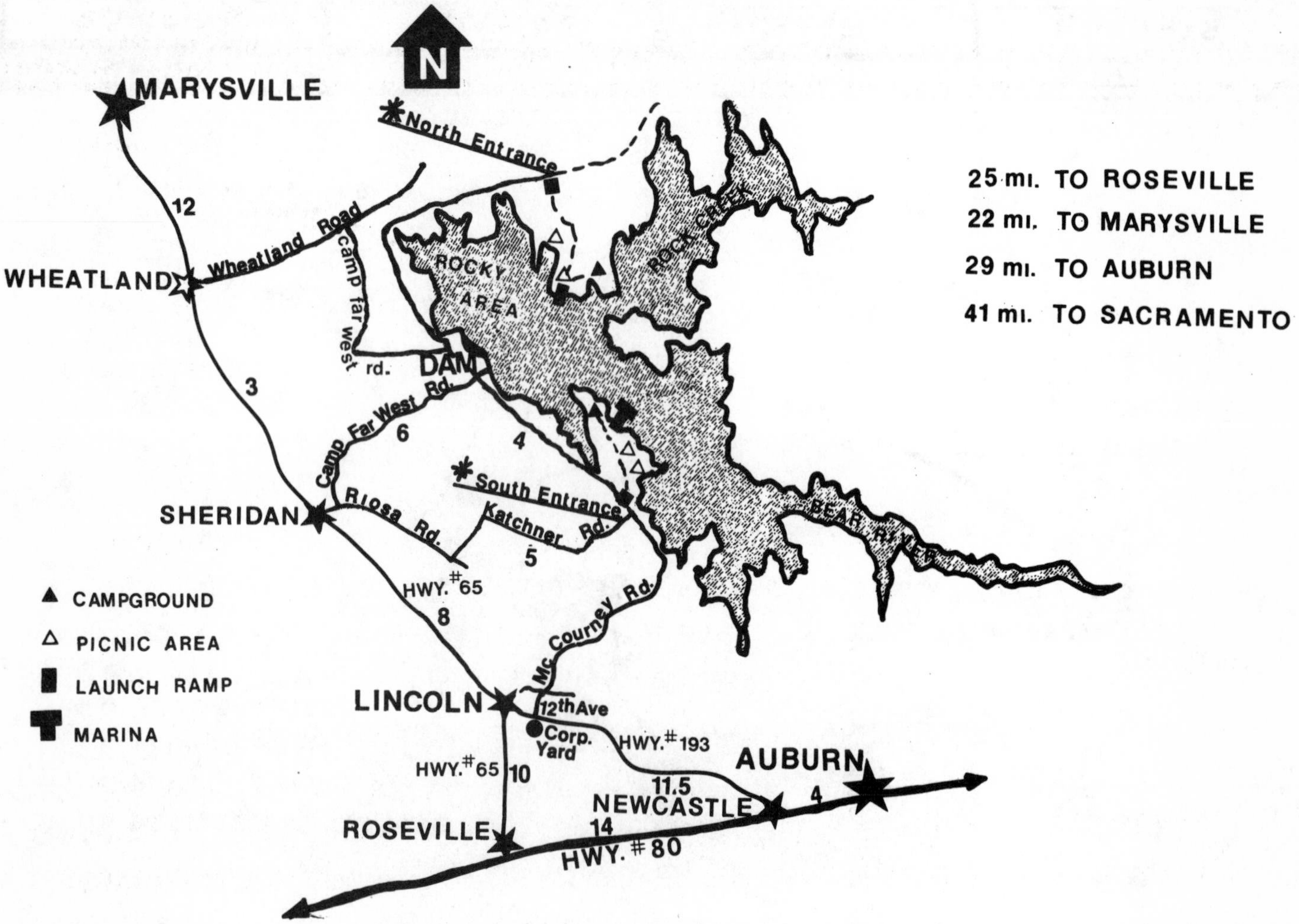
N
MARYSVILLE
North Entrance
12
WHEATLAND
Wheatland Road
camp far west rd.
ROCKY AREA
ROCK CREEK
DAM
3
Camp Far West Rd.
6
4
South Entrance
SHERIDAN
Riosa Rd.
Katchner Rd.
5
BEAR RIVER
HWY. #65
8
Mc Courney Rd.
LINCOLN
12th Ave
Corp. Yard
HWY. #193
HWY. #65
10
AUBURN
11.5
NEWCASTLE
4
14
ROSEVILLE
HWY. #80
CAMPGROUND
PICNIC AREA
LAUNCH RAMP
MARINA
25 mi. TO ROSEVILLE
22 mi. TO MARYSVILLE
29 mi. TO AUBURN
41 mi. TO SACRAMENTO

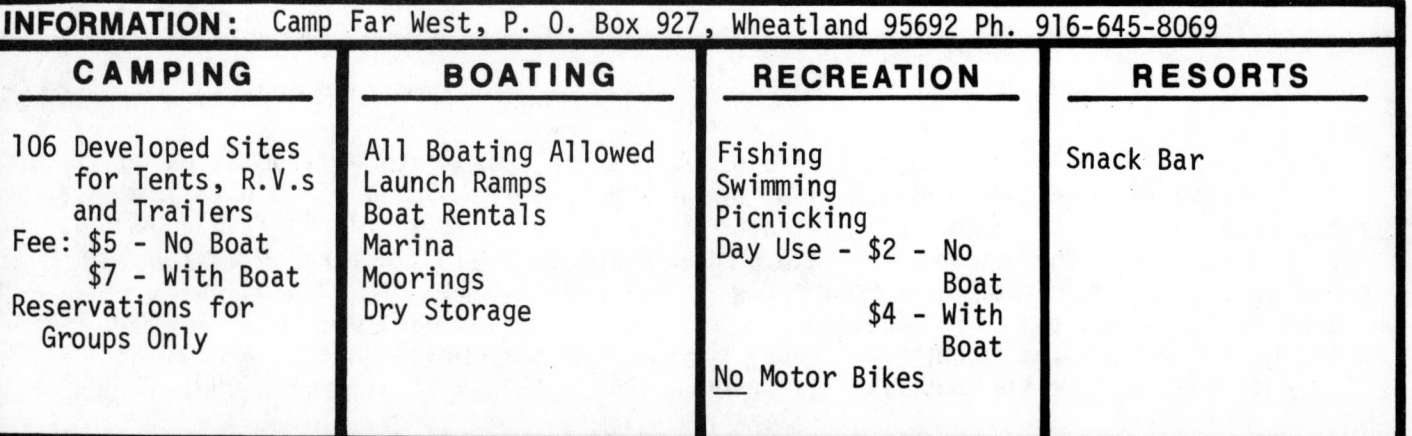

INFORMATION: Camp Far West, P. O. Box 927, Wheatland 95692 Ph. 916-645-8069

CAMPING	BOATING	RECREATION	RESORTS
106 Developed Sites for Tents, R.V.s and Trailers Fee: $5 - No Boat $7 - With Boat Reservations for Groups Only	All Boating Allowed Launch Ramps Boat Rentals Marina Moorings Dry Storage	Fishing Swimming Picnicking Day Use - $2 - No Boat $4 - With Boat No Motor Bikes	Snack Bar

SCOTTS FLAT LAKE

Scotts Flat Lake is a private facility, at about 3,100 feet elevation, with 172 campsites that have water and toilets. The full facility Marina has launch ramps, boat rentals, moorings and dry storage. No motorbikes or motorcycles are allowed in the Park. This can be a good mountain Lake for trout fishing and the scenery is lovely.

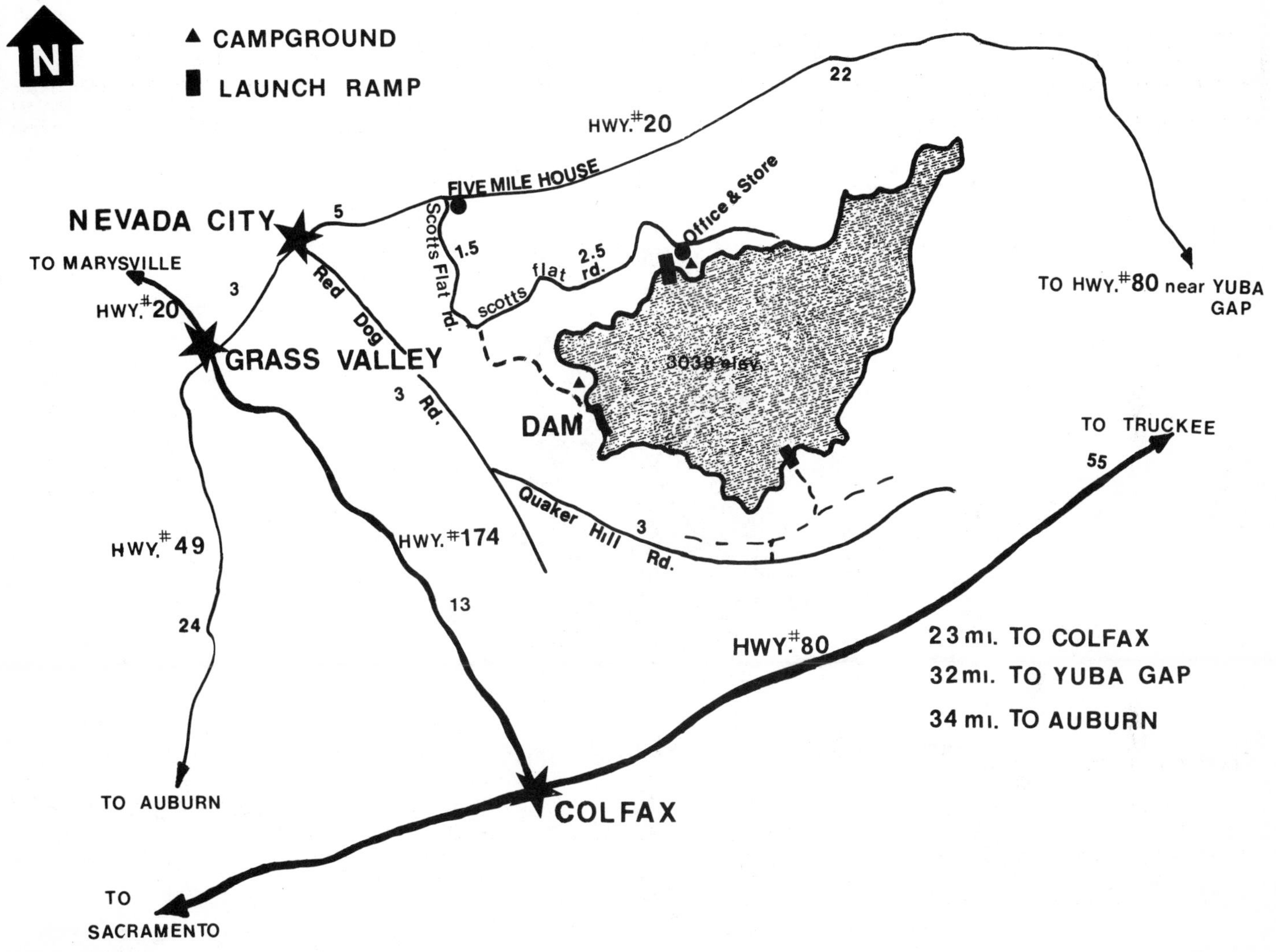
N
▲ CAMPGROUND
▮ LAUNCH RAMP
HWY.#20
22
FIVE MILE HOUSE
Office & Store
NEVADA CITY
5
TO MARYSVILLE
HWY.#20
3
Red Dog
Scotts Flat rd.
1.5
scotts flat rd.
2.5
TO HWY.#80 near YUBA GAP
GRASS VALLEY
3038 elev.
3 Rd.
DAM
TO TRUCKEE
55
Quaker Hill Rd.
3
HWY.#49
HWY.#174
13
24
HWY.#80
23 mi. TO COLFAX
32 mi. TO YUBA GAP
34 mi. TO AUBURN
TO AUBURN
COLFAX
TO SACRAMENTO

INFORMATION: Scotts Flat Lake, Washington Star Route, Box 126, Nevada City 95959

CAMPING	BOATING	RECREATION	RESORTS
172 Developed Sites for Tents, R.V.s and Trailers Reservations Accepted Phone: 916-265-5302	Boating Allowed - Waterskiing Launch Ramps Boat Rentals Mooring and Dry Storage	Fishing Swimming Hiking Goldpanning Picnicking No Motorbikes or Motorcycles	Store Coffee Shop Bait & Tackle Shop Hot Showers

ROLLINS LAKE

Rollins Lake is at 2,100 feet elevation with 800 surface acres and 26 miles of shoreline. It has four facilities with 250 campsites including water, toilets, showers, tables and barbecue pits. Orchard Springs is the best for Group camping with easy access and a ramp and swim beach. Greenhorn is the major Day Use area although it has an area for camping and camper caravans along with a ramp and swim beach. The Peninsula area has a launch ramp and is very pretty but has the hardest access so it is more secluded and private. All campsites are by water access. Long Ravine is the major weekend camping area with a ramp and swim beach. The water is clean with good swimming and the facilities are nicely kept. Much of the shoreline is steep and rocky with the hills covered with dense pine and oak trees.

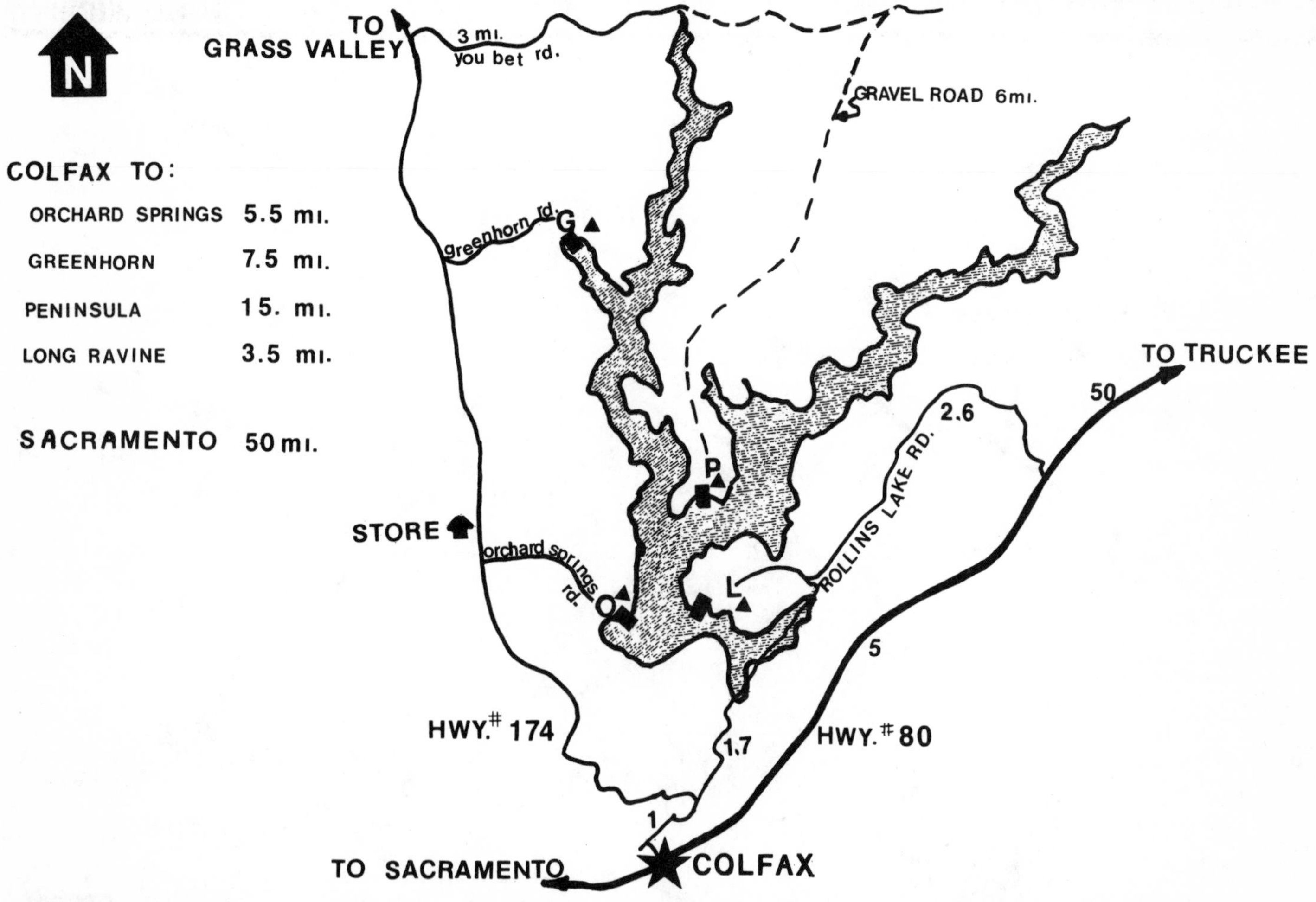
N
TO GRASS VALLEY
3 mi.
you bet rd.
GRAVEL ROAD 6mi.
COLFAX TO:
ORCHARD SPRINGS 5.5 mi.
GREENHORN 7.5 mi.
PENINSULA 15. mi.
LONG RAVINE 3.5 mi.
SACRAMENTO 50 mi.
greenhorn rd.
G
TO TRUCKEE
50
2.6
P
ROLLINS LAKE RD.
STORE
orchard springs rd.
O
L
5
HWY.# 174
1.7
HWY.# 80
1
TO SACRAMENTO
COLFAX

INFORMATION: Rollins Lake, P.O. Box 77, Chicago Park 95712, Ph. 916-346-2212

CAMPING	BOATING	RECREATION	RESORTS
250 Developed Sites for Tents, R.V.s and Trailers Fee: $6 a Day plus $2 per dog Reservations Accepted at $1 per site 30 Boat-In Sites - Must be reserved	All Boating Allowed Some Areas - 5 MPH Speed Limit Launch Ramp Boat Rentals: Canoes, Paddleboats Marina	Fishing Swimming Picnicking Day Use Only - $2.50	Store Snack Bar Restaurant Dancing Mini-Marts

LAKE SPAULDING

Lake Spaulding is at 5,009 feet elevation, high in the Sierra Nevadas. Its Dam was built in 1912 for water supply to the goldminers for hydraulic mining. It is now a P.G.&E. facility. The Lake freezes over and is at a very low level during the winter months so the open season is from June to October. The campground is at the South end of the Lake with 25 sites as well as overflow camping, water, tables, firepits and a launch ramp. At the North end are undeveloped Boat-in campsites. The water is crystal clear and huge granite boulders dot the shoreline between tall pine trees, all making for quite a spectacular setting.

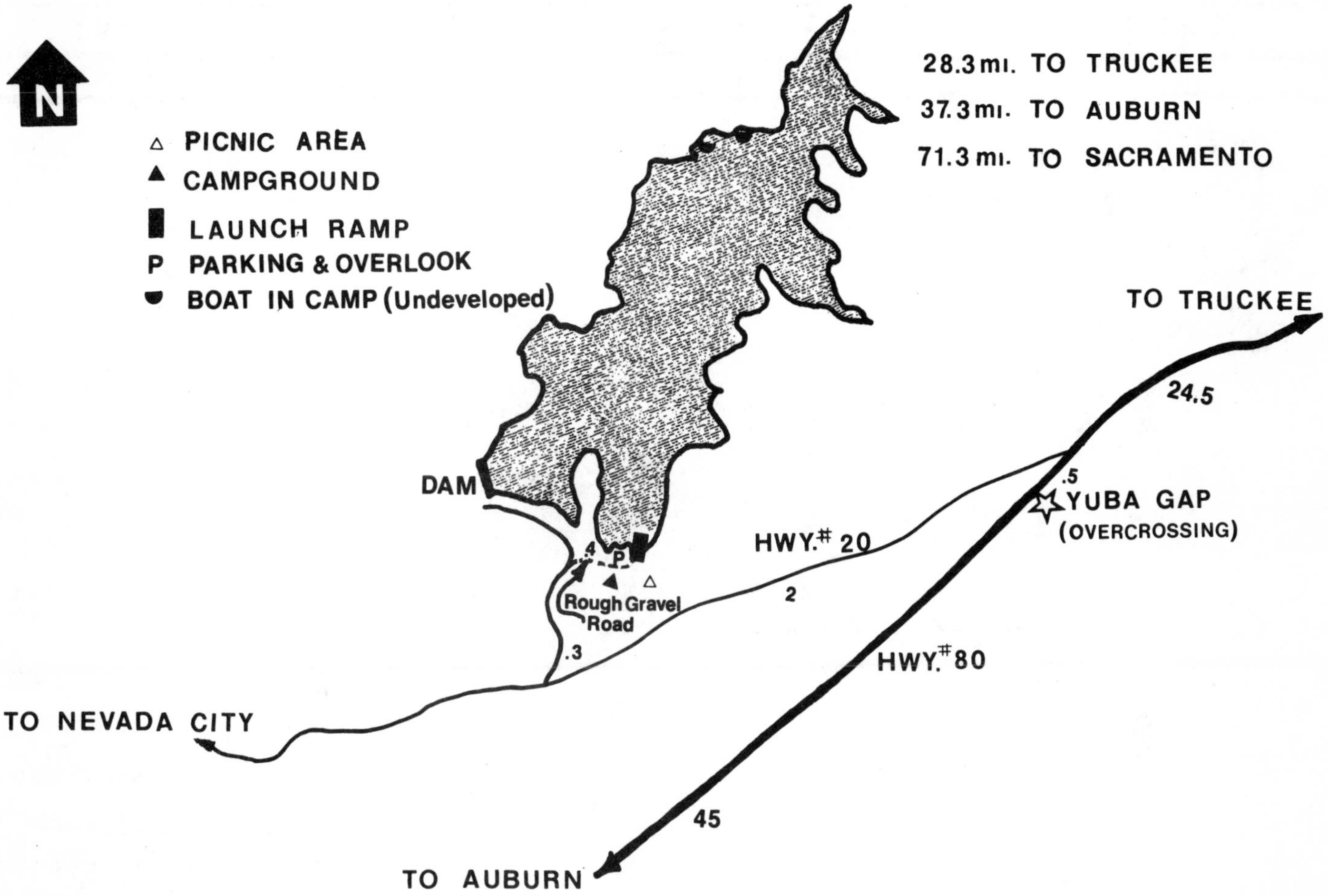
N
28.3 mi. TO TRUCKEE
37.3 mi. TO AUBURN
71.3 mi. TO SACRAMENTO
PICNIC AREA
CAMPGROUND
LAUNCH RAMP
P PARKING & OVERLOOK
BOAT IN CAMP (Undeveloped)
TO TRUCKEE
24.5
DAM
.5
YUBA GAP
(OVERCROSSING)
.4
P
HWY.# 20
2
Rough Gravel Road
.3
HWY.# 80
TO NEVADA CITY
45
TO AUBURN

INFORMATION: P. G. & E., 327 Church Street, Colfax 95713

CAMPING	BOATING	RECREATION	RESORTS
25 Developed Sites for Tents, R.V.s and Trailers Plus Overflow Fee: $3 a Day Some Sites - Undeveloped Boat-Ins	All Boating Allowed Launch Ramp (usuable at low water)	Fishing Swimming Picnicking Hiking	

LAKE VALLEY RESERVOIR

Lake Valley Reservoir is at 5,800 feet elevation. The shoreline is surrounded by tall trees and granite boulders with clear, cold water. The launch ramp is at the Silvertip Picnic Area. Lodgepole Campground has 18 campsites with trailer spaces to 20 feet, tables, firepits, water and toilets. The sites are very pretty, situated under the trees near the Lake. Silvertip picnic area has 10 units. No waterskiing is allowed, and the steep shoreline and steady west wind allows for good sailing.

KELLY LAKE

Coming out from Lake Valley Reservoir to Highway 80, you take the second right turn to Kelly Lake. This is a small, lovely Lake well worth a day's outing, with 5 picnic sites, tables, firepits and toilets.

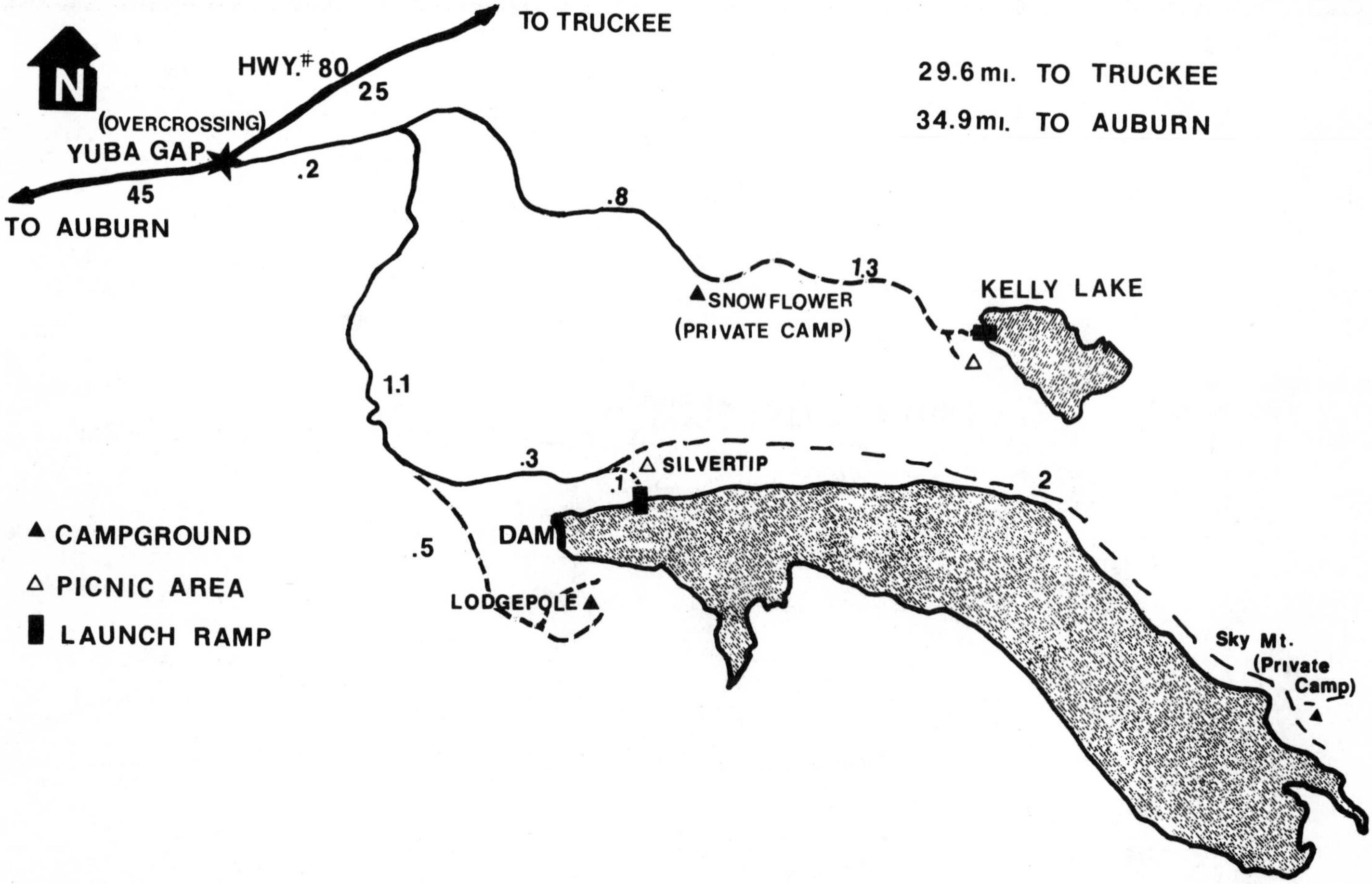
TO TRUCKEE
N
HWY.# 80
25
(OVERCROSSING)
YUBA GAP
.2
45
TO AUBURN
29.6 mi. TO TRUCKEE
34.9 mi. TO AUBURN
.8
1.3
SNOWFLOWER
(PRIVATE CAMP)
KELLY LAKE
1.1
.3
SILVERTIP
.1
2
DAM
.5
LODGEPOLE
CAMPGROUND
PICNIC AREA
LAUNCH RAMP
Sky Mt.
(Private
Camp)

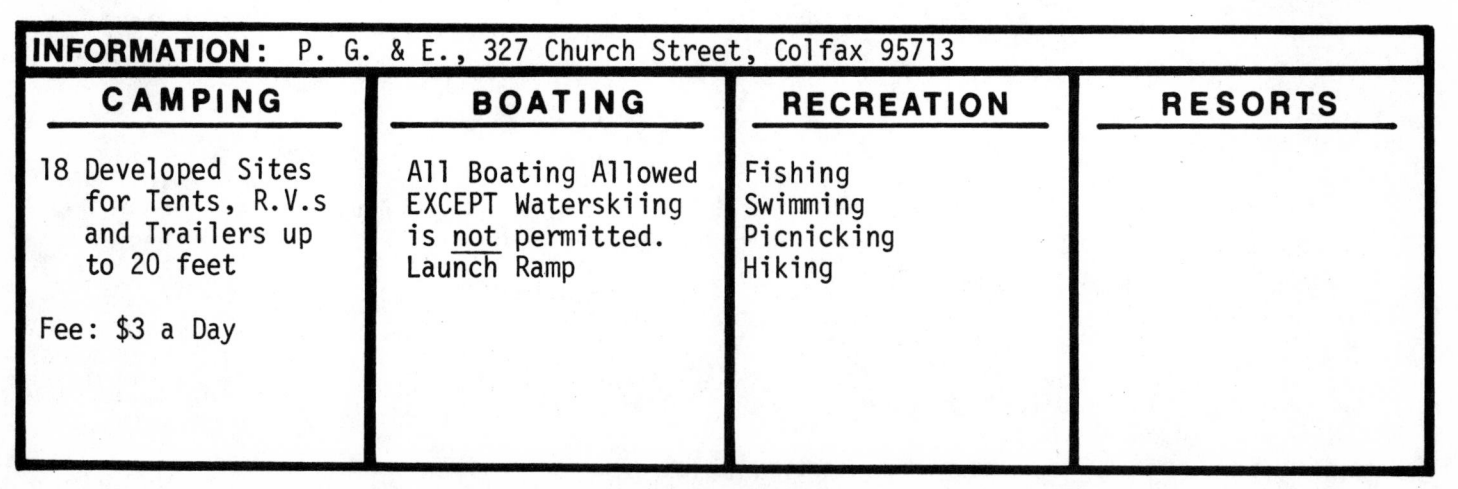

INFORMATION: P. G. & E., 327 Church Street, Colfax 95713

CAMPING	BOATING	RECREATION	RESORTS
18 Developed Sites for Tents, R.V.s and Trailers up to 20 feet Fee: $3 a Day	All Boating Allowed EXCEPT Waterskiing is not permitted. Launch Ramp	Fishing Swimming Picnicking Hiking	

DONNER LAKE

The Donner Lake Memorial State Park is on the East end of the Lake and has 154 campsites with water, toilets and showers, as well as 50 picnic sites along one mile of shoreline. The Park has many tall pine trees, good hiking trails and a museum that is open from 10:00 a.m. to 4:00 p.m. in season. The water is clear and cold, and winds can be very strong in the afternoon with whitecaps on the Lake. The Public Launch Ramp is at the West end of the Lake and there is no charge for its use. Local residents have a sailing club which is very active.

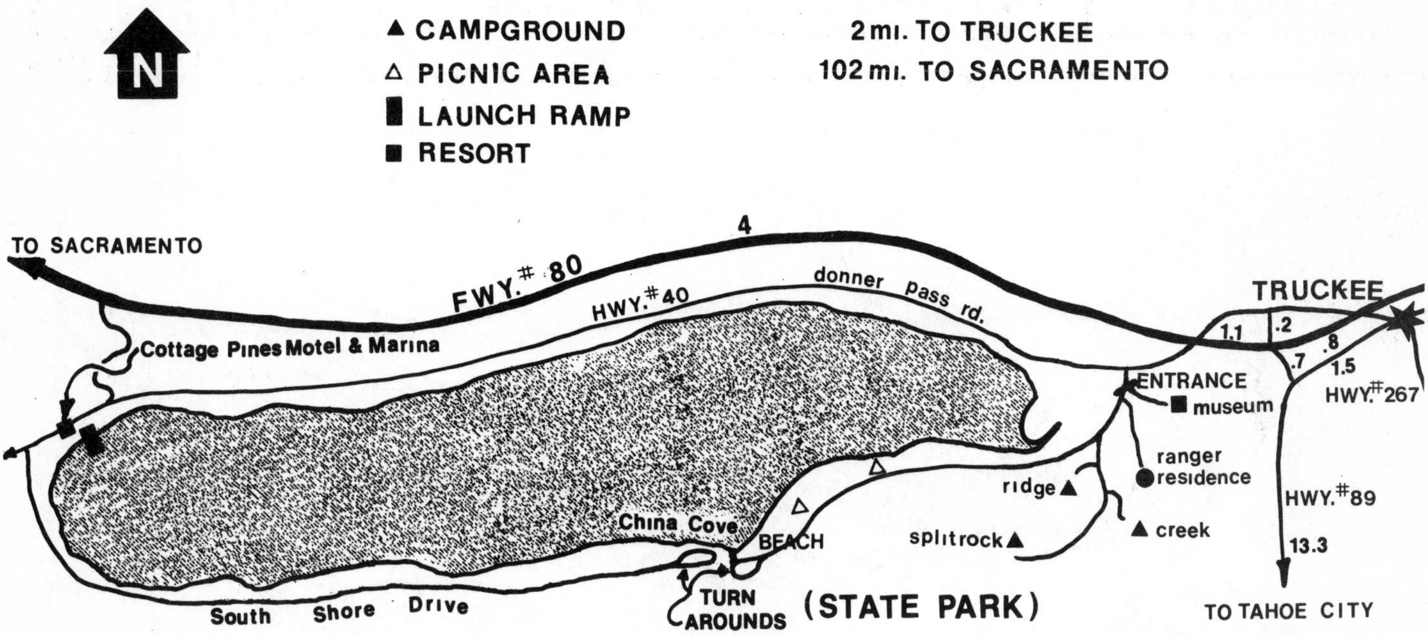
N
▲ CAMPGROUND
△ PICNIC AREA
LAUNCH RAMP
RESORT
2 mi. TO TRUCKEE
102 mi. TO SACRAMENTO
TO SACRAMENTO
4
FWY.# 80
HWY.#40
donner pass rd.
TRUCKEE
1.1
.2
.7
.8
1.5
HWY.#267
Cottage Pines Motel & Marina
ENTRANCE
museum
ranger residence
ridge
splitrock
creek
HWY.#89
13.3
TO TAHOE CITY
China Cove
BEACH
TURN AROUNDS
(STATE PARK)
South Shore Drive

INFORMATION: Ticketron, P. O. Box 26430, San Francisco 94126			
CAMPING	**BOATING**	**RECREATION**	**RESORTS**
154 Developed Sites for Tents, R.V.s and Trailers Reservations through your local Ticketron or above address Fee: $5 a Day	All Boating Allowed No Launching from State Park Public Launch Ramp at West End	Fishing Swimming Picnicking Hiking Day Use Only: $2	Motels, Cabins, Stores on North Shore

Stampede Reservoir is run by the U. S. Forest Service and has 25 miles of shoreline at 6,000 feet elevation. It is a low, open Lake with westerly winds and the boating is good. 252 Campsites are located within the Complex for tents, R.V.s and trailers, with tables, firepits and toilets. Emigrant Group Camp has 5 areas for a maximum of 150 people. For the Group Camp, reservations can be made through the Truckee Ranger District, Ph. 916-587-3558. Sagehen Creek has 9 campsites and Davies Creek has 10 sites for tents, R.V.s and trailers.

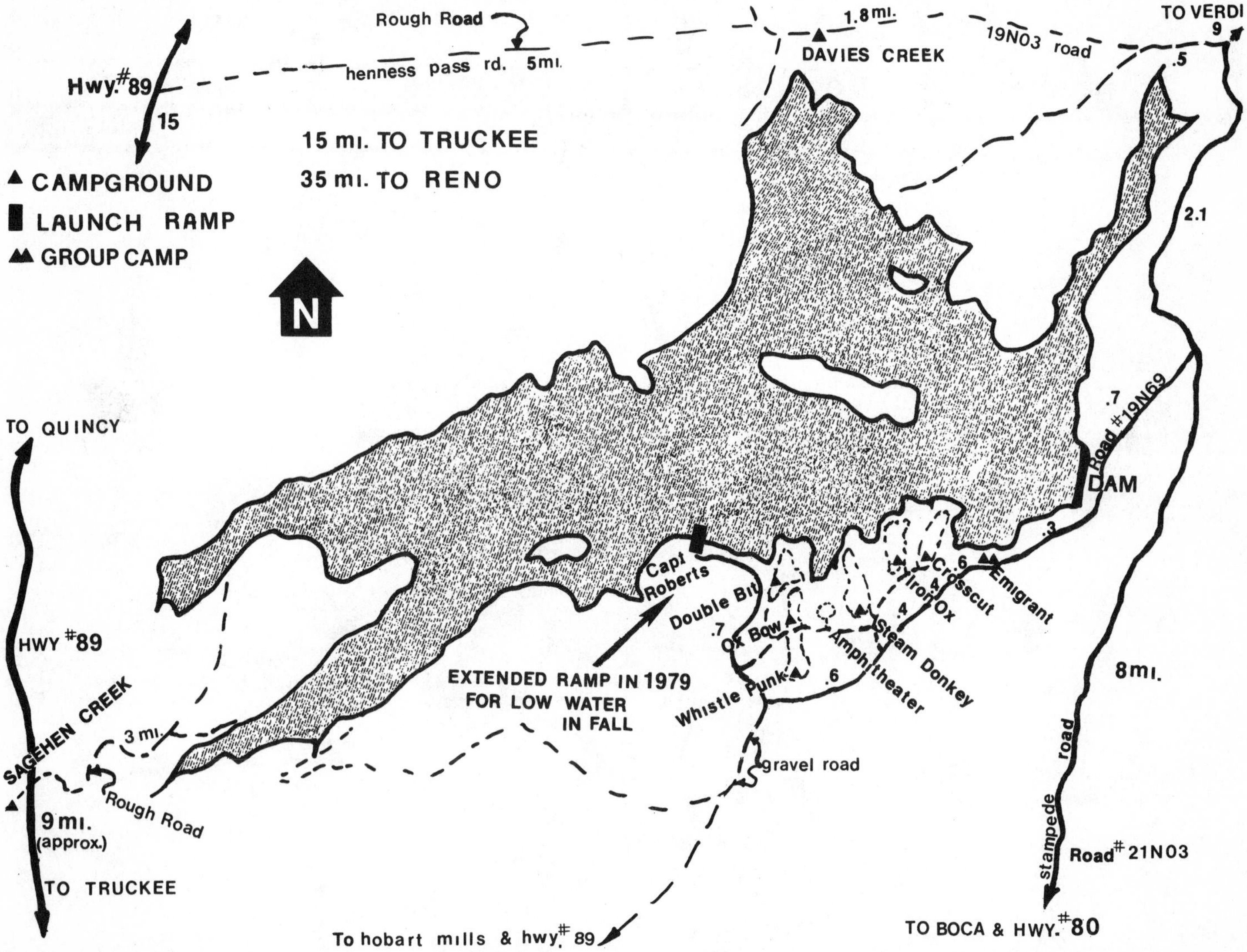
Rough Road
Hwy.#89
15
henness pass rd. 5mi.
1.8mi.
DAVIES CREEK
19N03 road
TO VERDI
9
.5
15 mi. TO TRUCKEE
35 mi. TO RENO
▲ CAMPGROUND
▮ LAUNCH RAMP
▲▲ GROUP CAMP
N
2.1
.7
Road #19N69
DAM
TO QUINCY
.3
Capt Roberts
Double Bit
.7
Ox Bow
Crosscut
Iron Ox
4
6
Emigrant
Steam Donkey
Amphitheater
.6
Whistle Punk
HWY #89
EXTENDED RAMP IN 1979
FOR LOW WATER
IN FALL
8mi.
SAGEHEN CREEK
3 mi.
gravel road
Rough Road
9 mi.
(approx.)
TO TRUCKEE
stampede road
Road# 21N03
To hobart mills & hwy.# 89
TO BOCA & HWY.#80

INFORMATION: U. S. F. S., P. O. Box 399, Truckee 95734 - Phone 916-587-3558

CAMPING	BOATING	RECREATION	RESORTS
252 Developed Sites for Tents, R.V.s and Trailers Fee: $3 a Day Plus 19 Developed Sites on Sagehen and Davies Creeks - No Fee Group Camp to 150.	All Boating Allowed Launch Ramp (No Fee) Water very low in Fall	Fishing Swimming Picnicking Hiking	Full Facilities are available in Truckee, 14 miles Southwest.

PROSSER CREEK RESERVOIR

Prosser Creek Reservoir is in an open canyon surrounded by low hills with 8 miles of shoreline at 5,800 feet elevation. Lakeside has 30 free sites for tents, R.V.s and trailers with toilets only. Prosser has 29 sites (17 tents/12 trailers) with water, toilets and firepits. No camping outside sites is allowed. Prosser Group has one 50 person group site on a reservation basis only. Donner Camp has 4 single family picnic sites.

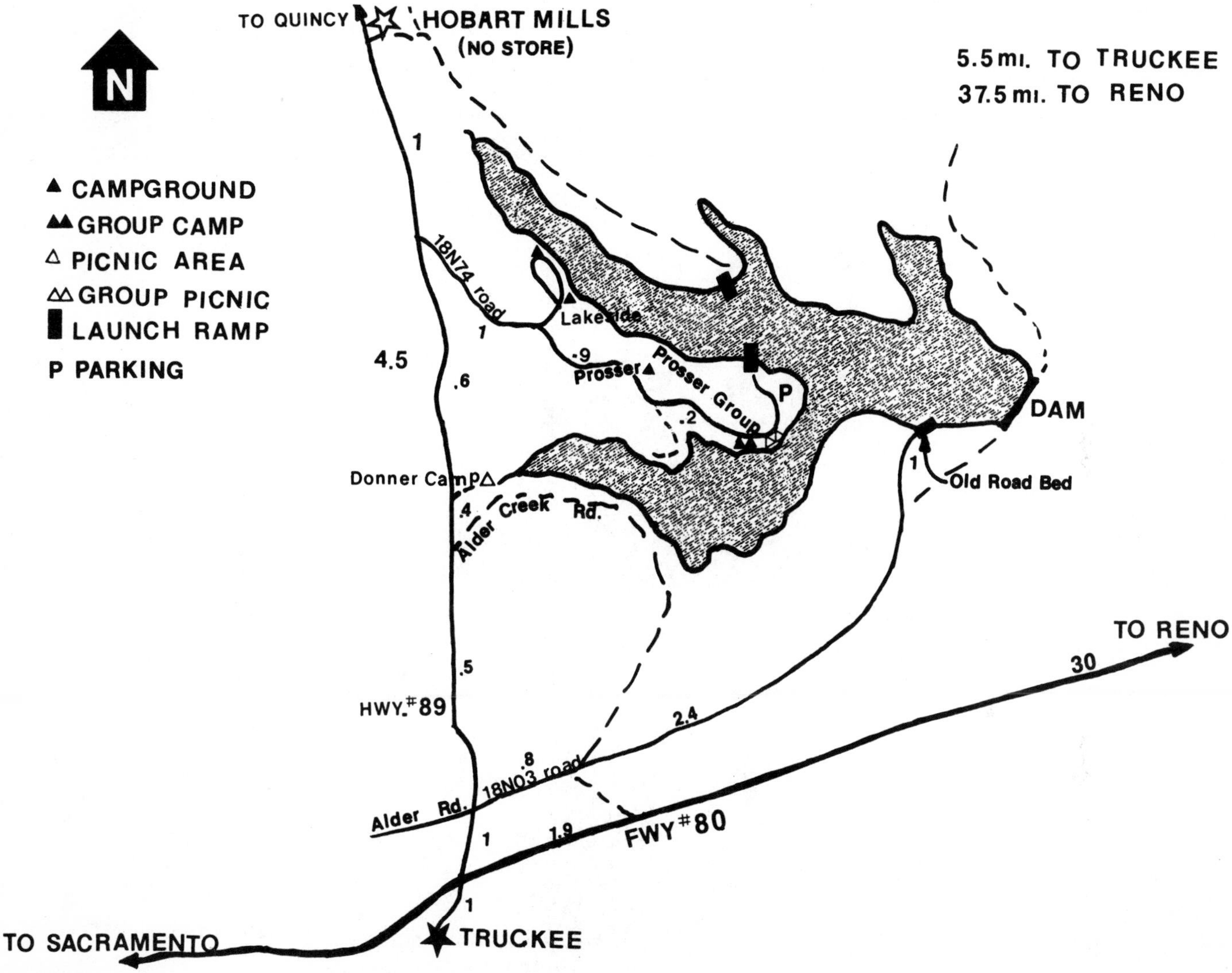

TO QUINCY
HOBART MILLS
(NO STORE)
5.5 mi. TO TRUCKEE
37.5 mi. TO RENO
N
CAMPGROUND
GROUP CAMP
PICNIC AREA
GROUP PICNIC
LAUNCH RAMP
P PARKING
1
18N74 road
Lakeside
1
4.5
.6
.9
Prosser
Prosser Group
P
.2
DAM
1
Old Road Bed
Donner Camp
.4
Alder Creek Rd.
.5
HWY. #89
TO RENO
30
2.4
.8
18NO3 road
Alder Rd.
1
1.9
FWY #80
1
TO SACRAMENTO
TRUCKEE

INFORMATION: U.S.F.S., P. O. Box 399, Truckee 95734, Ph. 916-587-3558			
CAMPING	**BOATING**	**RECREATION**	**RESORTS**
30 Undeveloped Free Sites for Tents, R.V.s and Trailers 29 Developed Sites for Tents, R.V.s and Trailers Fee: $2 a Day	Boating Allowed to 10 MPH Speed Limit Launch Ramps	Fishing Hiking Swimming Picnicking	Full Facilities 5 Miles in Truckee

BOCA RESERVOIR

Boca Reservoir is at 5,700 feet elevation. The Lake has many inlets and is surrounded by tall pine trees with the shoreline a lovely combination of steep bluffs and low grassy areas. It is a good boating Lake with all boating, swimming and water sports allowed although recreation facilities are still in the development stages. Water is at a constant level as it comes from Stampede Reservoir located five miles above Boca. No camping is permitted outside designated sites. Boca has 10 sites and Boyington Mill has 10 sites for tents, R.V.s and trailers. These are in an open flat area. Boca Rest has 25 sites in a very pretty hill area. There are some tables and pit toilets, but water is not available. No fees are charged at this time.

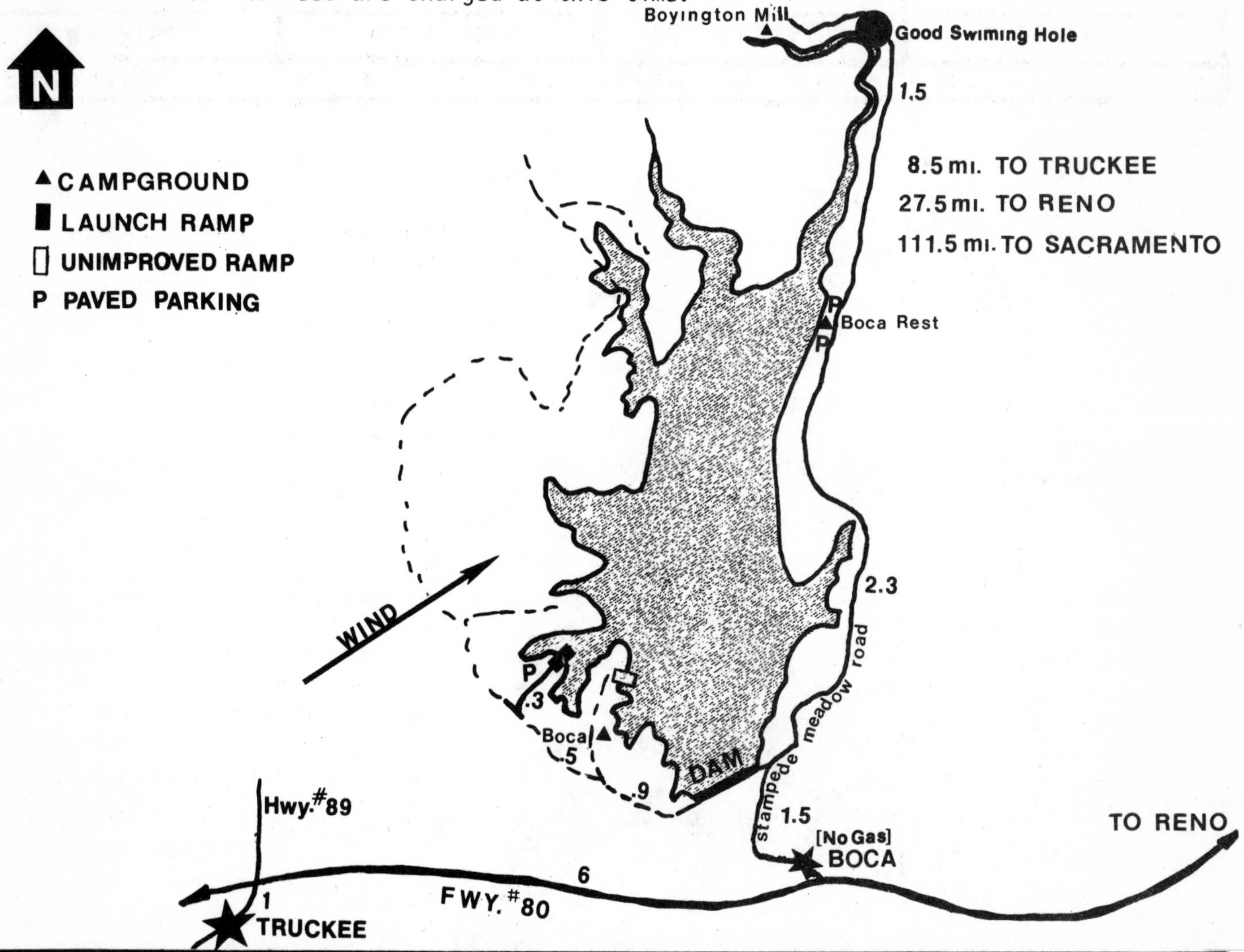
Boyington Mill
Good Swiming Hole
N
1.5
▲CAMPGROUND
LAUNCH RAMP
UNIMPROVED RAMP
P PAVED PARKING
8.5 mi. TO TRUCKEE
27.5 mi. TO RENO
111.5 mi. TO SACRAMENTO
P
Boca Rest
P
2.3
WIND
stampede meadow road
P
.3
Boca
.5
.9
DAM
1.5
Hwy. #89
[No Gas]
BOCA
TO RENO
6
1
TRUCKEE
FWY. #80

INFORMATION: U.S.F.S., P. O. Box 399, Truckee 95734, Ph. 916-587-3558

CAMPING	BOATING	RECREATION	RESORTS
45 Undeveloped Sites for Tents, R.V.s and Trailers - Limited tables and toilets No Water No Fee	All Boating Allowed Launch Ramp	Fishing Picnicking Swimming Hiking	Full Facilities 7-1/2 Miles in Truckee

LAKE TAHOE

As Mark Twain called it, "The Lake in the Sky", is at 6,229 feet elevation and is the largest Lake in California, extending on into Nevada. It is 23 miles long, 13 miles wide and 1,645 feet deep in places. The name comes from the Washoe Indians and means "Big Water". The shoreline remains fairly constant year round and in summer, the water temperature is about 60 degrees.

. . . Continued . . .

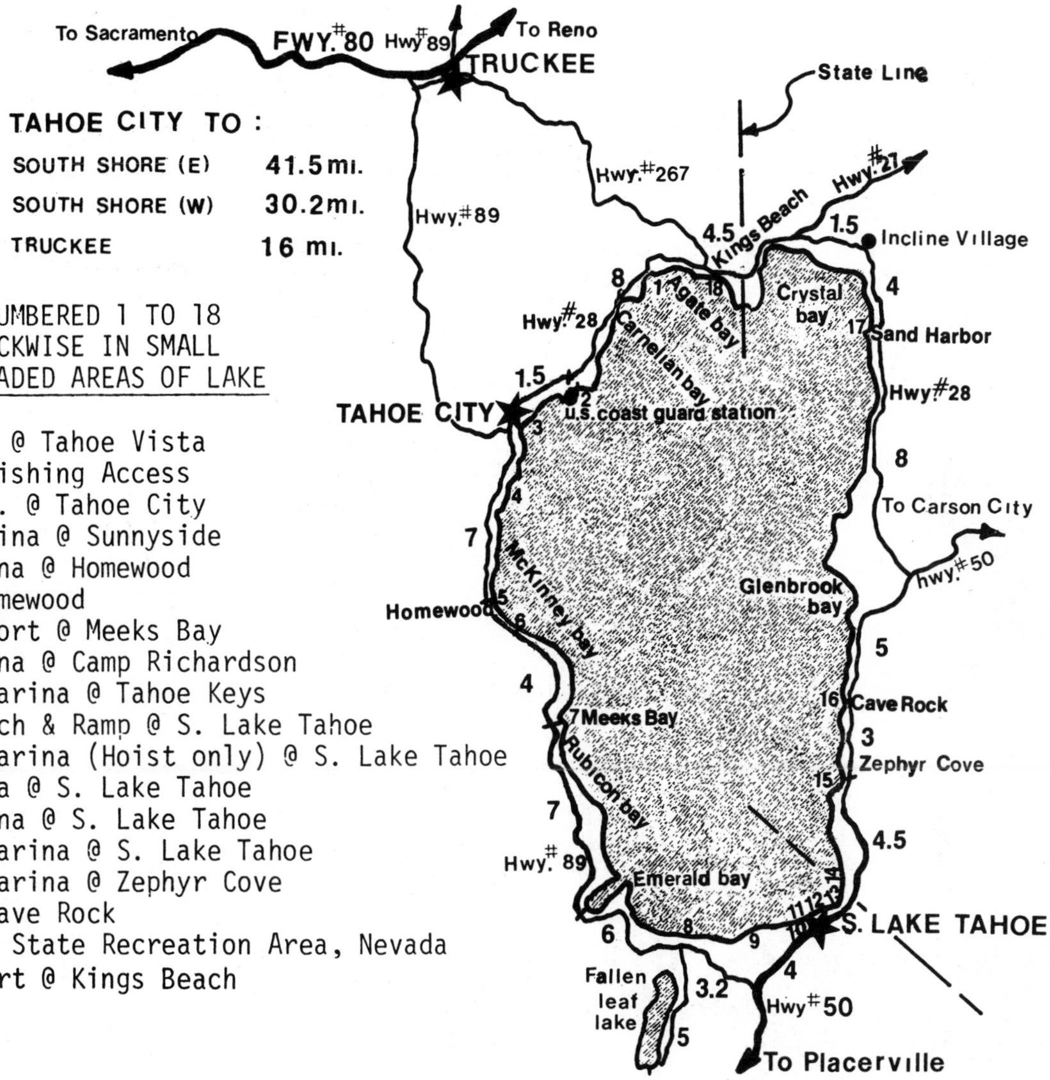

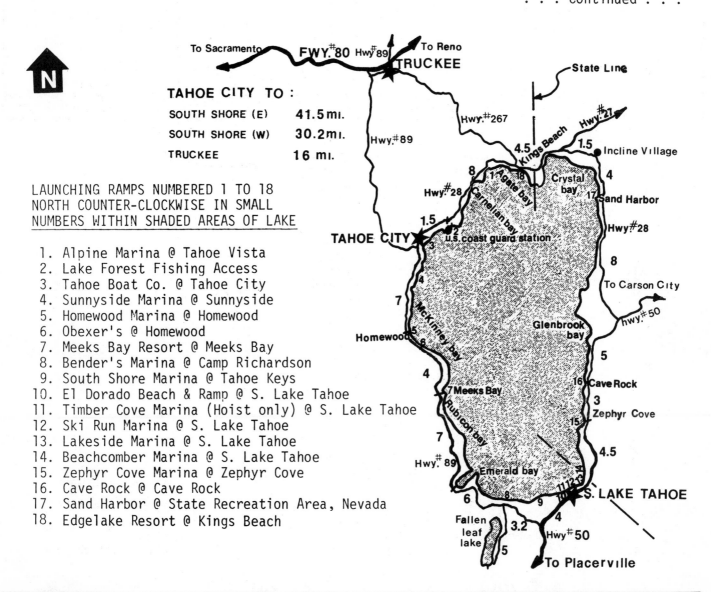

N
To Sacramento
FWY.#80
Hwy#89
To Reno
TRUCKEE
State Line
TAHOE CITY TO :
SOUTH SHORE (E) 41.5 mi.
SOUTH SHORE (W) 30.2 mi.
TRUCKEE 16 mi.
Hwy.#267
Hwy.#27
Hwy.#89
Kings Beach
Incline Village
Crystal bay
Agate bay
Carnelian bay
Sand Harbor
Hwy.#28
TAHOE CITY
U.S. coast guard station
To Carson City
hwy.#50
Glenbrook bay
Homewood
McKinney bay
Cave Rock
Meeks Bay
Zephyr Cove
Rubicon bay
Emerald bay
S. LAKE TAHOE
Fallen leaf lake
Hwy#50
To Placerville

LAUNCHING RAMPS NUMBERED 1 TO 18 NORTH COUNTER-CLOCKWISE IN SMALL NUMBERS WITHIN SHADED AREAS OF LAKE

1. Alpine Marina @ Tahoe Vista
2. Lake Forest Fishing Access
3. Tahoe Boat Co. @ Tahoe City
4. Sunnyside Marina @ Sunnyside
5. Homewood Marina @ Homewood
6. Obexer's @ Homewood
7. Meeks Bay Resort @ Meeks Bay
8. Bender's Marina @ Camp Richardson
9. South Shore Marina @ Tahoe Keys
10. El Dorado Beach & Ramp @ S. Lake Tahoe
11. Timber Cove Marina (Hoist only) @ S. Lake Tahoe
12. Ski Run Marina @ S. Lake Tahoe
13. Lakeside Marina @ S. Lake Tahoe
14. Beachcomber Marina @ S. Lake Tahoe
15. Zephyr Cove Marina @ Zephyr Cove
16. Cave Rock @ Cave Rock
17. Sand Harbor @ State Recreation Area, Nevada
18. Edgelake Resort @ Kings Beach

INFORMATION: Ticketron, P. O. Box 26430, San Francisco 94120 - or See List.

CAMPING	BOATING	RECREATION	RESORTS
Developed Sites for Tents, R.V.s and Trailers around the Lake Boat Access Camps at Emerald Bay	All Boating Allowed Boat Rentals Launch Ramps Full Service Marinas	Fishing Swimming Picnicking Hiking Horseback Riding Backpacking	Hotels-Casinos Motels & Cabins Restaurants Full Facilities

LAKE TAHOE

. . . Continued . . .

Description of Facilities at Launching Ramps Numbered 1 to 18 on Page 39.

1. Alpine Marina 7360 N. Lake Blvd. Tahoe Vista Phone: 916-546-7252	Power Boat Sales, Boat Rentals, Exxon Gas, Full Service Marina.
2. Lake Forest Fishing Access Lake Forest - 2 Miles North of Tahoe City	Access to Launch Ramp Only, Limited Facilities.
3. Tahoe Boat Company 700 N. Lake Blvd. Tahoe City Phone: 916-583-5567	Power Boats and Service, Repairs, Store, Slips, Boat Rentals, Restaurant, Chevron Gas.
4. Sunnyside Marina & Resort P. O. Box 252 1850 West Lake Blvd. Tahoe City Phone: 916-583-4226	Sailboats and Powerboats Sales, Storage, Hoist, Slips or Buoys, Chevron Gas.
5. Homewood Marina High & Dri 5180 Highway 89 Homewood Phone: 916-525-7258	Complete Sailboat Line and Hardware, Powerboats, Marina, Hoist, Gas, Lodge across the street.
6. Obexer's 5290 West Lake Blvd. Homewood Phone: 916-525-7962	Sailboats and Powerboats, Sales and Service, Storage, Chevron Gas, Store, Ramp and Travel Lift, Boat Rentals.
7. Meeks Bay Resort Box "C" Tahoma Phone: 916-525-7242	50-Acre Resort, 120 Berths - Reserve for 7-day Minimum, Ramp, Campsites, 21 Cabins, Trailer Park, Beach, Gift Shop, Snack Bar, Grocery Store, Boat Rentals, Fuel Dock, New R.V. Park.
8. Bender's Marina Camp Richardson P. O. Box 7586 S. Lake Tahoe Phone: 916-541-1777	Powerboats and Canoes, Sales, Service, Repair, Storage, Moorings, Hoist, Supplies, Ramp, Chevron Gas.
9. South Shore Marina Tahoe Keys Blvd. & Venice Dr. S. Lake Tahoe Phone: 916-541-2155	All Boats, Sales and Service, Repairs, Dry Storage, Largest Marina on the Lake, Ramp, Gas, Boat Supplies, Store, Restaurant, Large Travel Lift.

. . . Continued . . .

. . . Continued . . .

10. El Dorado Beach & Ramp S. Lake Tahoe	Park, Picnic Area, Beach, Ramp (Shallow), Public Use Facility near Casinos. Free.
11. Timber Cove Marina & Lodge 3411 Highway 50 S. Lake Tahoe Phone: 916-544-2942	Powerboats, New and Used, Parts, Service, Mooring, Hoist, Rental Boats, Chevron Gas, Restaurant, Bar, Condominiums.
12. Ski Run Marina P. O. Box 14272 S. Lake Tahoe Phone: 916-544-0200	Boat Rentals, Repair, Dry Storage, Full Service Marina, Parts, Boat Sales, Ramp, Jet Skis, Rafts, Chevron Gas, Snack Bar, Miss Tahoe Cruises - Phone: 916-541-3364.
13. Lakeside Marina 828 Park Avenue S. Lake Tahoe Phone: 916-541-6626	Powerboats and Sailboats Sales, Rentals, Launching Storage, Store, Mobil Gas, Lakeside Yacht & Harbor Club.
14. Beachcomber Marina 999 Lakeview Ave. S. Lake Tahoe Phone: 916-544-2426	Ramp, Beach, Dock, Pool, Bar and Grill, Motel with Kitchen Units.
15. Zephyr Cove Marina Zephyr Cove Phone: 916-588-6477	Marina, Ramp, Resort, Restaurant.
16. Cave Rock	Public Launching Facilities, No Fee, Restrooms, Parking, Fishing.
17. Sand Harbor	Excellent Beach, Launch Ramp, Picnic Areas with Many Trees, Restrooms.
18. Edgelake Resort P. O. Box 366 7680 N. Lake Blvd. Kings Beach Phone: 916-546-5974	Ramp, Beach, Pool, Playground, Motel.

This is a partial list of Launching Ramps around Lake Tahoe. All facilities are impossible to list but this gives some idea of the variety available.

. . . Continued . . .

LAKE TAHOE

. . . Continued . . .

Lake Tahoe has a boat camp at Emerald Bay and there are numerous campgrounds around the shore of the Lake run by the Forest Service, The State Park System, the County, and some privately operated. The following is a partial list of facilities.

Operated By the U. S. Forest Service - Reservations Advised in the Summer - See your local Ticketron outlet or write: Ticketron, P. O. Box 26430, San Francisco 94120.

William Kent - 4 Miles South of Tahoe City - 55 campsites for tents, 40 for trailers 24 feet maximum, water, toilets.

Nevada Beach - 1 Mile North of Stateline near Zephyr Cove - 63 campsites for tents, R.V.s and trailers, water, toilets.

Operated by The California State Park System

Emerald Bay State Park - 100 campsites for tents, R.V.s, trailers to 15 feet maximum, showers, toilets, water - 20 Boat Access Only Sites.

Tahoe Recreation Area - 1 Mile North of Tahoe City - 45 campsites for tents, R.V.s, trailers to 20 feet maximum, showers, toilets, water.

Reservations for the above two areas through your local Ticketron outlet or write: Ticketron, P. O. Box 26430, San Francisco 94120.

D. L. Bliss - 3 Miles North of Emerald Bay - 168 campsites for tents, R.V.s, trailers to 18 feet maximum, showers, toilets.

General Creek - 1 Mile South of Tahoma - 175 campsites for tents, R.V.s, trailers to 25 feet maximum, showers, toilets, water.

Pine Flat - 5 Miles South of Tahoma - 25 campsites for tents, showers, toilets, water.

City Campground

South Tahoe El Dorado - On Highway 50, 1 Mile South of Stateline - 144 campsites for tents, R.V.s, Trailers to 18 feet maximum, hookups, showers, toilets.

County Campground

Lake Forest - 3 Miles North of Tahoe City off Highway 89 - 20 campsites, tents, R.V.s, trailers to 18 feet maximum, water, toilets.

Privately-Operated Campgrounds

Tahoe Valley Recreation Area - 1/4 Mile West of "Y" at S. Lake Tahoe - 272 campsites for tents, R.V.s, trailers, hookups, showers, toilets, water.

Camp Richardson - 3 Miles West of "Y" - 180 campsites for tents, R.V.s, trailers and 93 trailers only, water, toilets, showers.

Meek's Bay Resort - 2 Miles South of Tahoma - 90 campsites for tents, R.V.s, trailers, hookups, showers, toilets, water, boat launch, rentals, sandy beach.

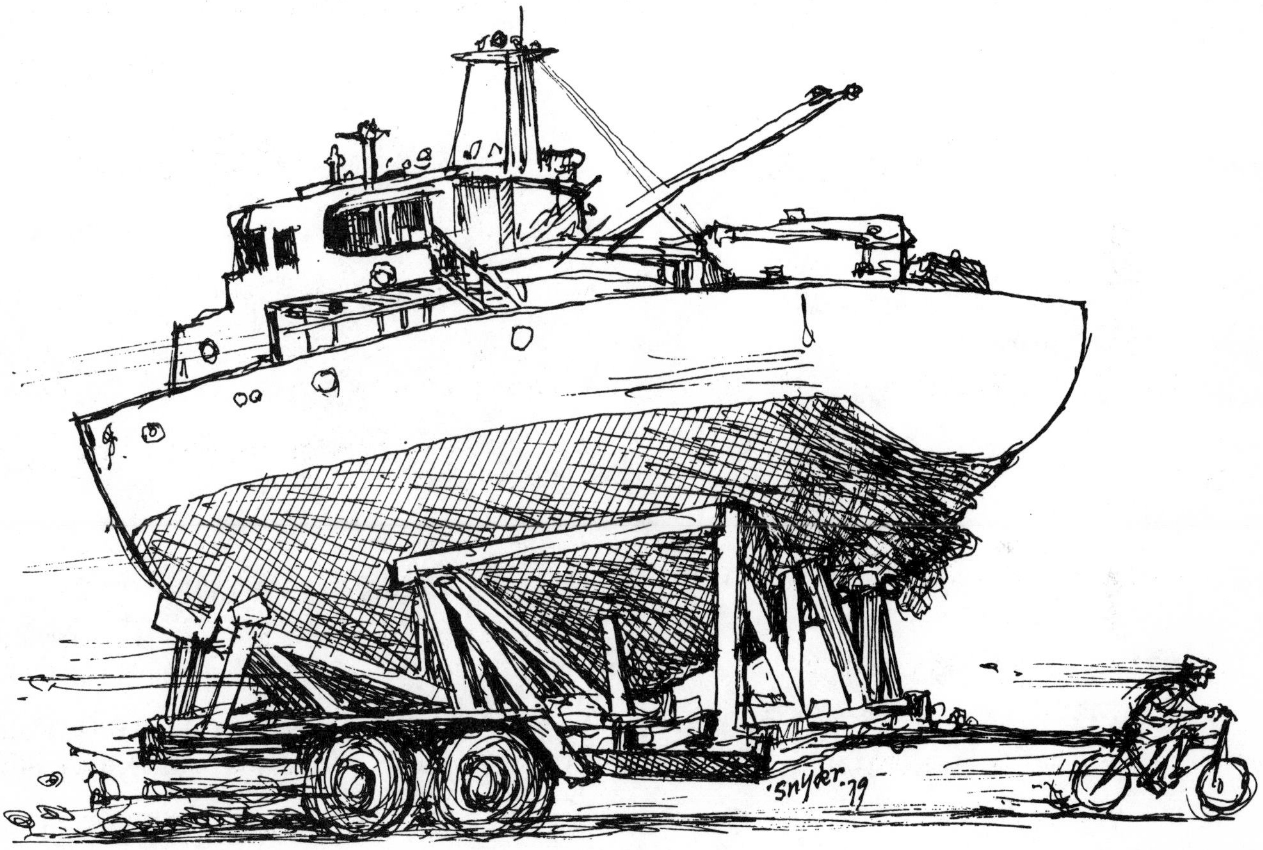
Snyder '79

FALLEN LEAF LAKE

The property around Fallen Leaf Lake is primarily privately owned. Fallen Leaf Lodge is at the South shore and has nice facilities ranging from tent units to lodges that sleep 8 with fireplaces. There are also 25 campsites for tents, R.V.s and trailers with water, toilets and showers. Also the Lodge has a launch ramp, rental boats and good swimming with a sandy beach near the ramp. The water is cold but refreshing. The U. S. Forest Service operates a campground near the Lake with 206 sites (75 tents only/131 tents, R.V.s, trailers) with water, toilets and fire grills. Reservations for this campground can be made through your local Ticketron outlet or write: Ticketron, P. O. Box 26430, San Francisco 94120. This is a nice family recreation area with lovely scenery.

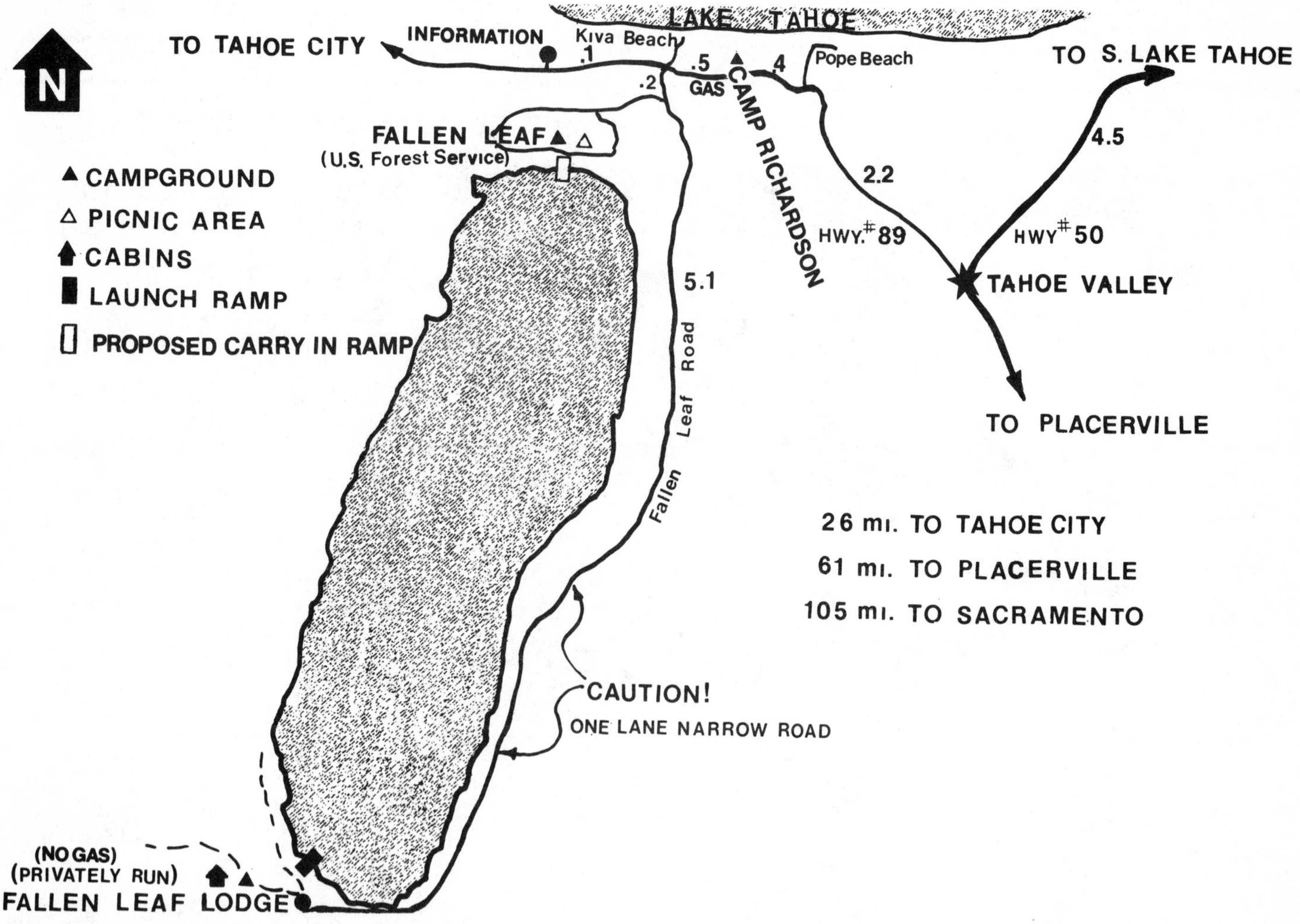
LAKE TAHOE
TO TAHOE CITY
INFORMATION
Kiva Beach
.1
.5
.2
GAS
4
Pope Beach
TO S. LAKE TAHOE
N
FALLEN LEAF
(U.S. Forest Service)
CAMP RICHARDSON
2.2
4.5
HWY. #89
HWY #50
TAHOE VALLEY
TO PLACERVILLE
CAMPGROUND
PICNIC AREA
CABINS
LAUNCH RAMP
PROPOSED CARRY IN RAMP
5.1
Fallen Leaf Road
26 mi. TO TAHOE CITY
61 mi. TO PLACERVILLE
105 mi. TO SACRAMENTO
CAUTION!
ONE LANE NARROW ROAD
(NO GAS)
(PRIVATELY RUN)
FALLEN LEAF LODGE

INFORMATION: U.S.F.S. - Ticketron or Fallen Leaf Lodge, Fallen Leaf 95716

CAMPING	BOATING	RECREATION	RESORTS
U.S. Forest Service 206 Developed Sites for Tents, R.V.s and Trailers - Ticketron Fallen Leaf Lodge 25 Developed Sites for Tents, R.V.s, Trailers	All Boating Allowed Launch Ramp Rental Boats: Sailboats & Rowboats	Fishing Swimming Picnicking Hiking	Fallen Leaf Lodge Phone: 916-541-3366 Must call for Weekend Reservations in Season Various Units Restaurant Store

ECHO LAKE

Echo Lake is nestled in between high mountains near Echo Summit, two miles off Highway 50. The elevation is about 7,500 feet so the water is cold at 50 degrees. Winds can be strong in the afternoons. There are many trails for hiking, backpacking and horseback riding from Echo Lake, but a Permit from the U. S. Forest Service is required to enter the "Desolation Valley Wilderness Area." The closest Ranger Stations are at the "Y" at South Shore Lake Tahoe which is North and at Pollock Pines to the South. Echo Chalet, the only facility on the Lake, is at the South end. There are ten housekeeping cabins, coffee shop, grocery store, gas, boat rentals and a ramp. This area has over 50 accessible Lakes by foot or horses as well as the Rubicon and American Rivers and many other streams so trout fishing can be excellent.

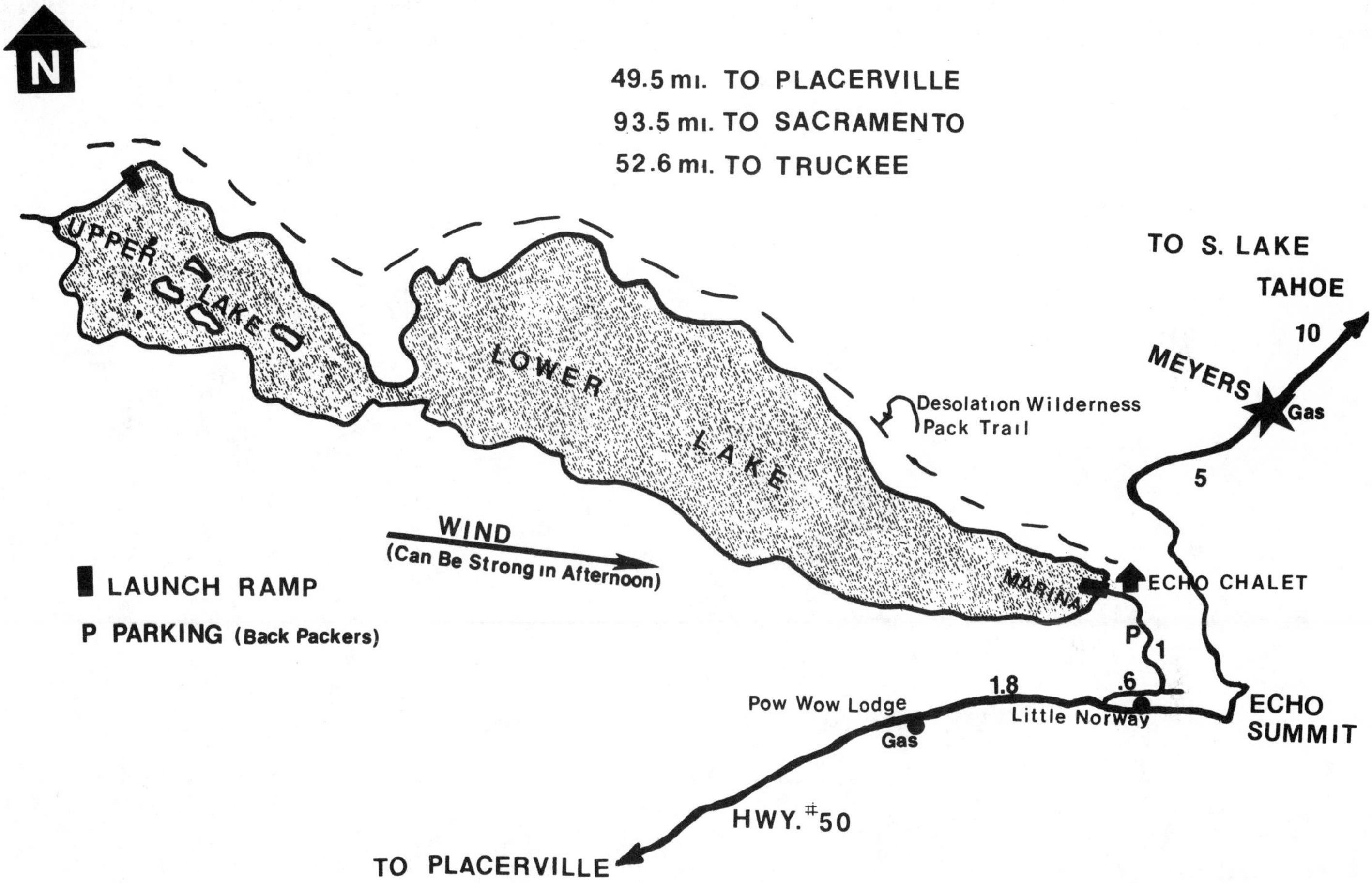
N
49.5 mi. TO PLACERVILLE
93.5 mi. TO SACRAMENTO
52.6 mi. TO TRUCKEE
UPPER LAKE
LOWER LAKE
TO S. LAKE TAHOE
10
MEYERS
Gas
Desolation Wilderness Pack Trail
5
WIND (Can Be Strong in Afternoon)
LAUNCH RAMP
P PARKING (Back Packers)
MARINA
ECHO CHALET
P
1
.6
1.8
Pow Wow Lodge
Gas
Little Norway
ECHO SUMMIT
HWY. #50
TO PLACERVILLE

INFORMATION: Echo Chalet, P. O. Echo Lake 95721, Phone: 916-659-7207

CAMPING	BOATING	RECREATION	RESORTS
Entrance to the Desolation Valley Wilderness Area. No Camping Allowed by U. S. Forest Service Except in Wilderness Area.	All Boating Allowed except No Water-skiing on the Upper Lake Boat Rentals Launching Ramp Full Service Marina	Fishing Hiking Backpacking Swimming Sightseeing Trips by Boat Fishing Trips by Boat Boat Taxi	Echo Chalet - 10 Cottages Store Coffee Shop

LOON LAKE

Loon Lake is part of the Crystal Basin Recreation Area. The U. S. Forest Service operates 10 boat-in camping units at Pleasant and 34 sites (11 tents only/23 tents, R.V.s and trailers) at Loon Lake Campground with tables, barbecues, water and toilets. There are also 18 single family picnic units there. The Lake is at 6,500 feet elevation so the water is very cold and waterskiing is not recommended. There is a two-lane launch ramp and trailhead parking for the Desolation Wilderness is available for backpackers. The trail conditions are good for hikers and horses, and the fishing can be excellent for rainbow and german brown trout. Wentworth Springs has 8 tent sites and at South Fork, there are 17 sites (5 tents only/12 tents, R.V.s, trailers). Gerle Creek Reservoir does not allow motor boats. It has 50 campsites for tents, R.V.s and trailers with water, toilets and barbecues.

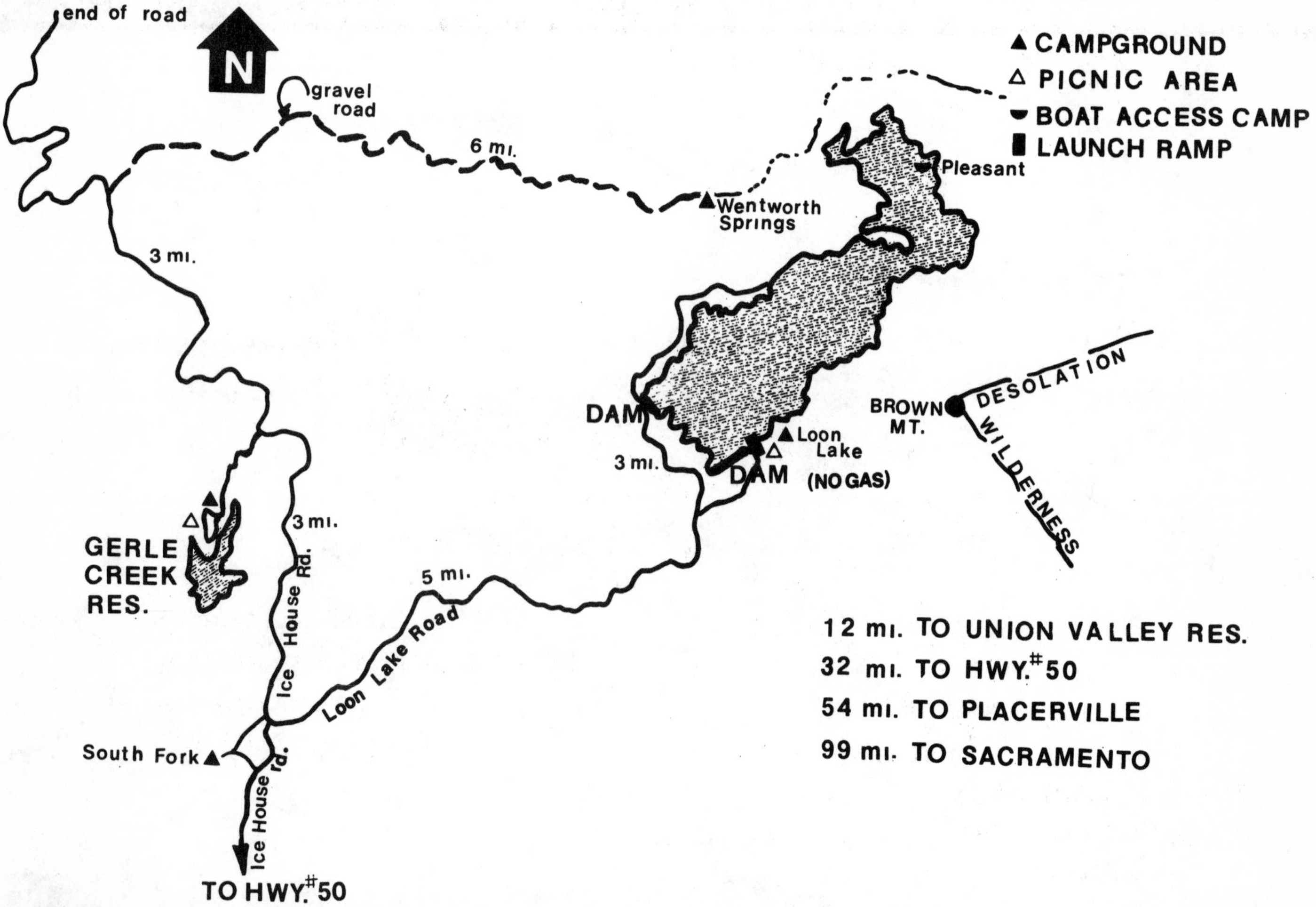
end of road
N
gravel road
6 mi.
Wentworth Springs
Pleasant
CAMPGROUND
PICNIC AREA
BOAT ACCESS CAMP
LAUNCH RAMP
3 mi.
DAM
DAM
Loon Lake
(NO GAS)
3 mi.
BROWN MT.
DESOLATION
WILDERNESS
GERLE CREEK RES.
3 mi.
Ice House Rd.
5 mi.
Loon Lake Road
South Fork
Ice House rd.
TO HWY.#50
12 mi. TO UNION VALLEY RES.
32 mi. TO HWY.#50
54 mi. TO PLACERVILLE
99 mi. TO SACRAMENTO

INFORMATION: U. S. Forest Service, 100 Forni Road, Placerville 95667

CAMPING	BOATING	RECREATION	RESORTS
34 Developed Sites for Tents, R.V.s, Trailers Fee: $3 a Day 25 Sites Near Loon 50 Developed Sites for Tents, R.V.s, Trailers at Gerle Creek Res. Fee: $2 a Day	All Boating Allowed Waterskiing is not recommended. Launch Ramp Gerle Creek Reservoir No Motors	Fishing Picnicking Hiking Entrance to Desolation Wilderness	23 Miles to Ice House Resort and Full Facilities

UNION VALLEY

Union Valley Reservoir is part of the Crystal Basin Recreation Area. It has 2,860 surface acres and is a very good Lake for sailing. Many sailing clubs use the facilities during the summer. The U. S. Forest Service operates 231 camp units by Ticketron reservations only and 40 units on a first-come basis. Wench Creek has 100 camp units (1 tent only/99 tents, R.V.s, trailers) with water, toilets and barbecues, and 2 Group Camps with a capacity for 50 people each by reservation through Ticketron. There are 131 campsites (32 tents only/97 tents, R.V.s, trailers - Single Family, and 2 tents, R.V.s, trailers - Multiple Families) at Sunset Campground. 30 picnic units are at Fashoda as well as a concrete launch ramp, paved parking lot and a trailer sanitary station. Yellow-jacket Campground has 40 campsites (5 tents only/35 tents, R.V.s, trailers) with water, toilets and barbecues and a paved launch ramp. These sites cannot be reserved. This is a lovely Lake with many tall trees and a sand or rock shoreline.

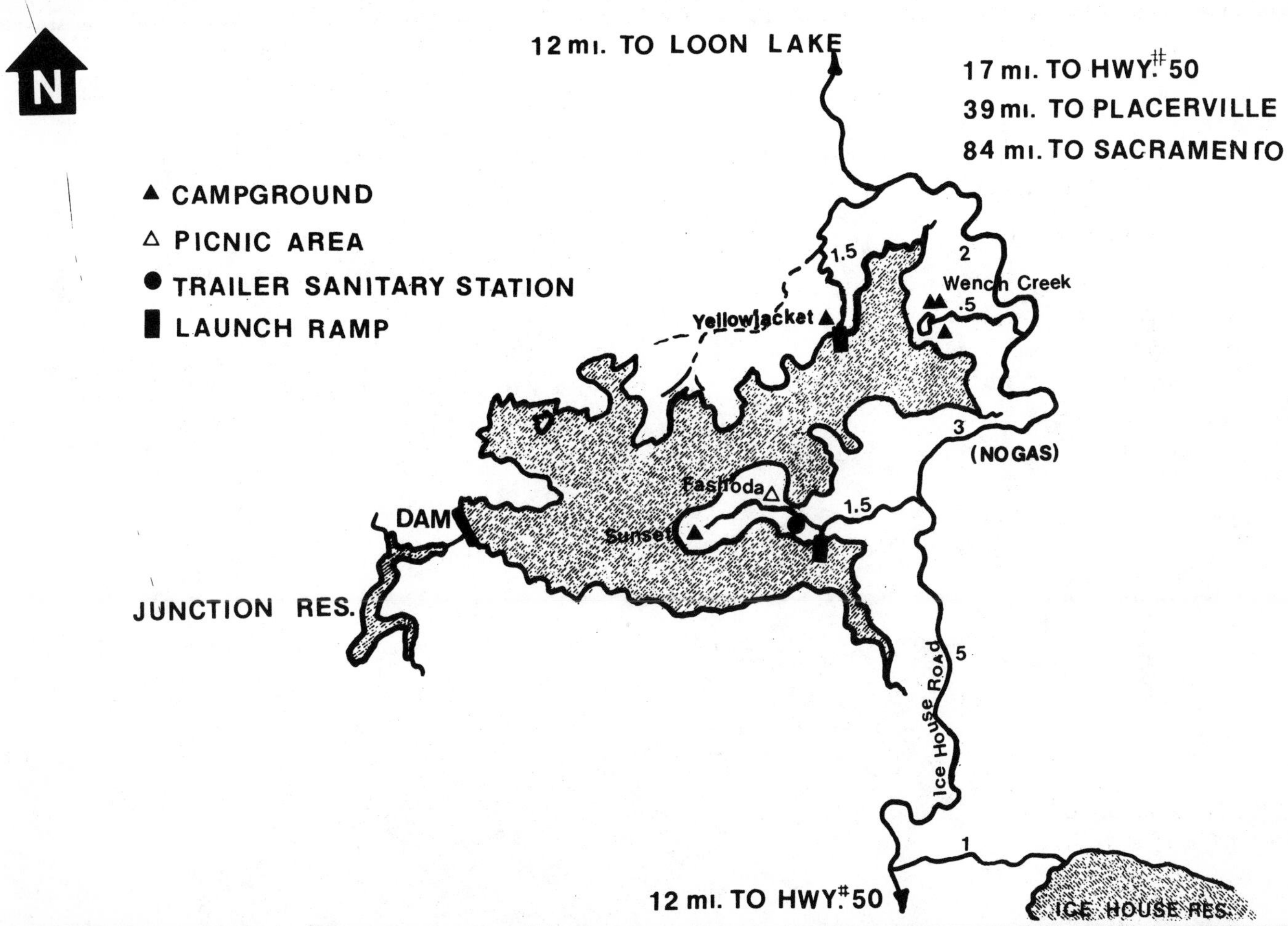
N
12 mi. TO LOON LAKE
17 mi. TO HWY.# 50
39 mi. TO PLACERVILLE
84 mi. TO SACRAMENTO
CAMPGROUND
PICNIC AREA
TRAILER SANITARY STATION
LAUNCH RAMP
1.5
2
Wench Creek
.5
Yellowjacket
3
(NO GAS)
Fashoda
1.5
DAM
Sunset
JUNCTION RES.
5
Ice House Road
1
12 mi. TO HWY.# 50
ICE HOUSE RES.

INFORMATION: Ticketron, P. O. Box 26340, San Francisco 94126

CAMPING	BOATING	RECREATION	RESORTS
271 Developed Sites for Tents, R.V.s and Trailers Fee: $3 a Day	All Boating Allowed Launch Ramps	Fishing Swimming Picnicking Hiking	7-1/2 Miles to Full Facilities

ICE HOUSE RESERVOIR

Ice House Reservoir, a part of the Crystal Basin Recreation Area, has U. S. Forest Service Campgrounds. There are 49 sites (9 tents only/40 tents, R.V.s, trailers) with water, toilets and barbecues as well as 10 picnic units, a launch ramp and dump station, next to the Lake. At Silver Creek there are 11 sites for tents only with toilets and barbecues. The 678 acre Lake is lined with trees and the water is clear and cold. There are nice swimming areas and the roads are paved and well kept. Ice House Resort is privately owned and has motel units, a grocery store, service station and restaurant. Do beware of logging trucks. All types of boating are permitted, and you can fish for Kokanee Salmon and Trout.

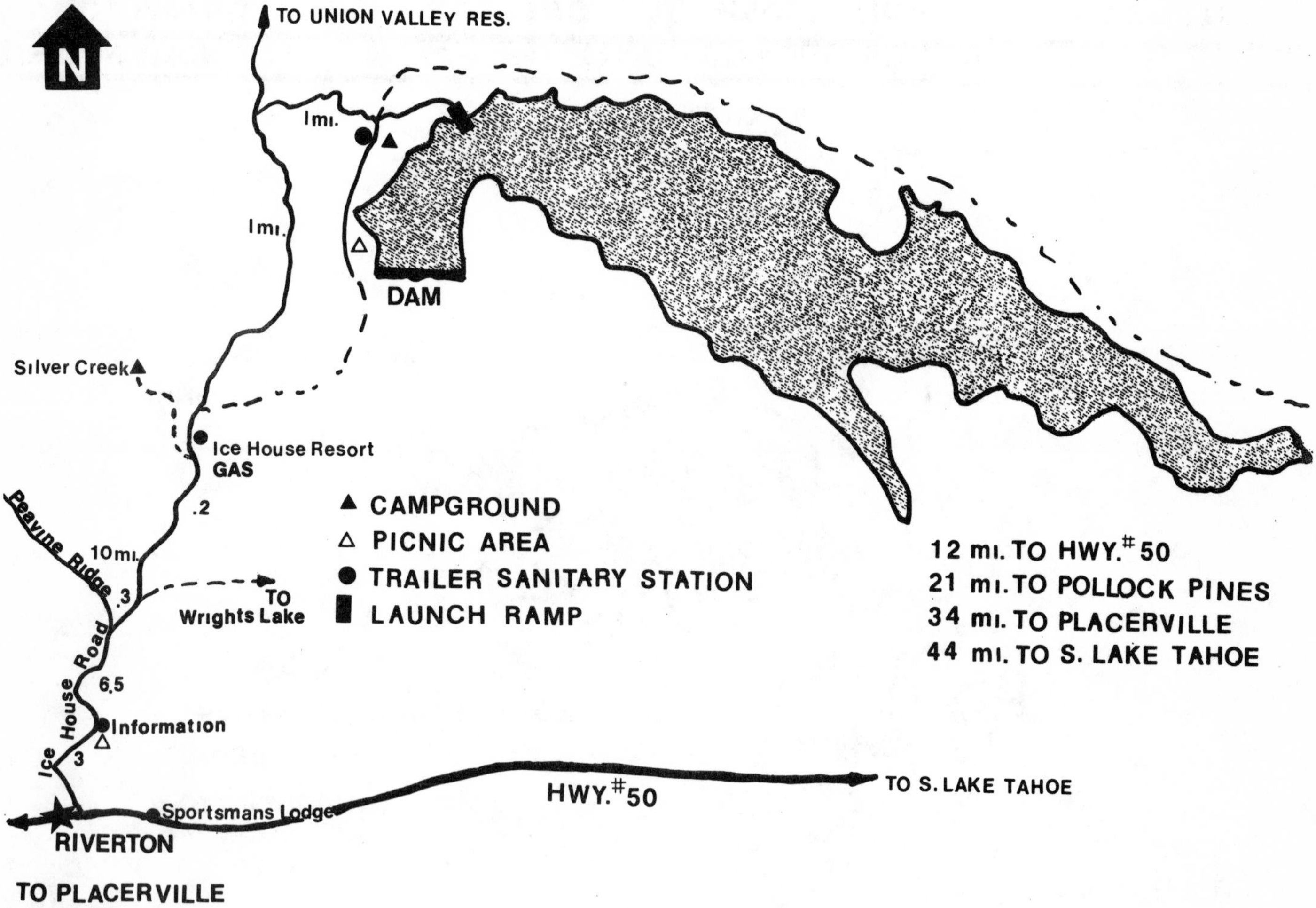

N
TO UNION VALLEY RES.
1mi.
1mi.
DAM
Silver Creek
Ice House Resort
GAS
.2
Peavine Ridge
10mi.
.3
TO
Wrights Lake
Ice House Road
6.5
Information
3
Sportsmans Lodge
RIVERTON
TO PLACERVILLE
HWY.#50
TO S. LAKE TAHOE
▲ CAMPGROUND
△ PICNIC AREA
● TRAILER SANITARY STATION
▮ LAUNCH RAMP
12 mi. TO HWY.#50
21 mi. TO POLLOCK PINES
34 mi. TO PLACERVILLE
44 mi. TO S. LAKE TAHOE

INFORMATION: U. S. Forest Service, 100 Forni Rd., Placerville 95667

CAMPING	BOATING	RECREATION	RESORTS
49 Developed Sites for tents, R.V.s, trailers Fee: $3 a Day 11 Minimum Dev. Sites for tents only No Fee	All Boating Allowed Launch Ramp	Fishing Picnicking Swimming Hiking	Full Facilities at Ice House Resort - Motel Restaurant Grocery Store

STUMPY MEADOWS RESERVOIR

Stumpy Meadows is a delightful Lake surrounded by tall trees and the water is very clean and clear. Swimming is not allowed, and there is a 5 MPH speed limit for boaters which makes the Lake very quiet and peaceful. There are 40 campsites (7 tents only/32 tents, R.V.s, trailers/1 multiple family) with tables, barbecues and water and toilets located at Stumpy Meadows Campground. At Black Oak Group Camp, there are 4 areas accommodating up to 225 people maximum with water, toilets and barbecues. Reservations are through your local Ticketron Outlet or write: Ticketron, P. O. Box 26430, San Francisco 94120. Access to the Lake is by good road and there is a paved launching ramp near the Dam.

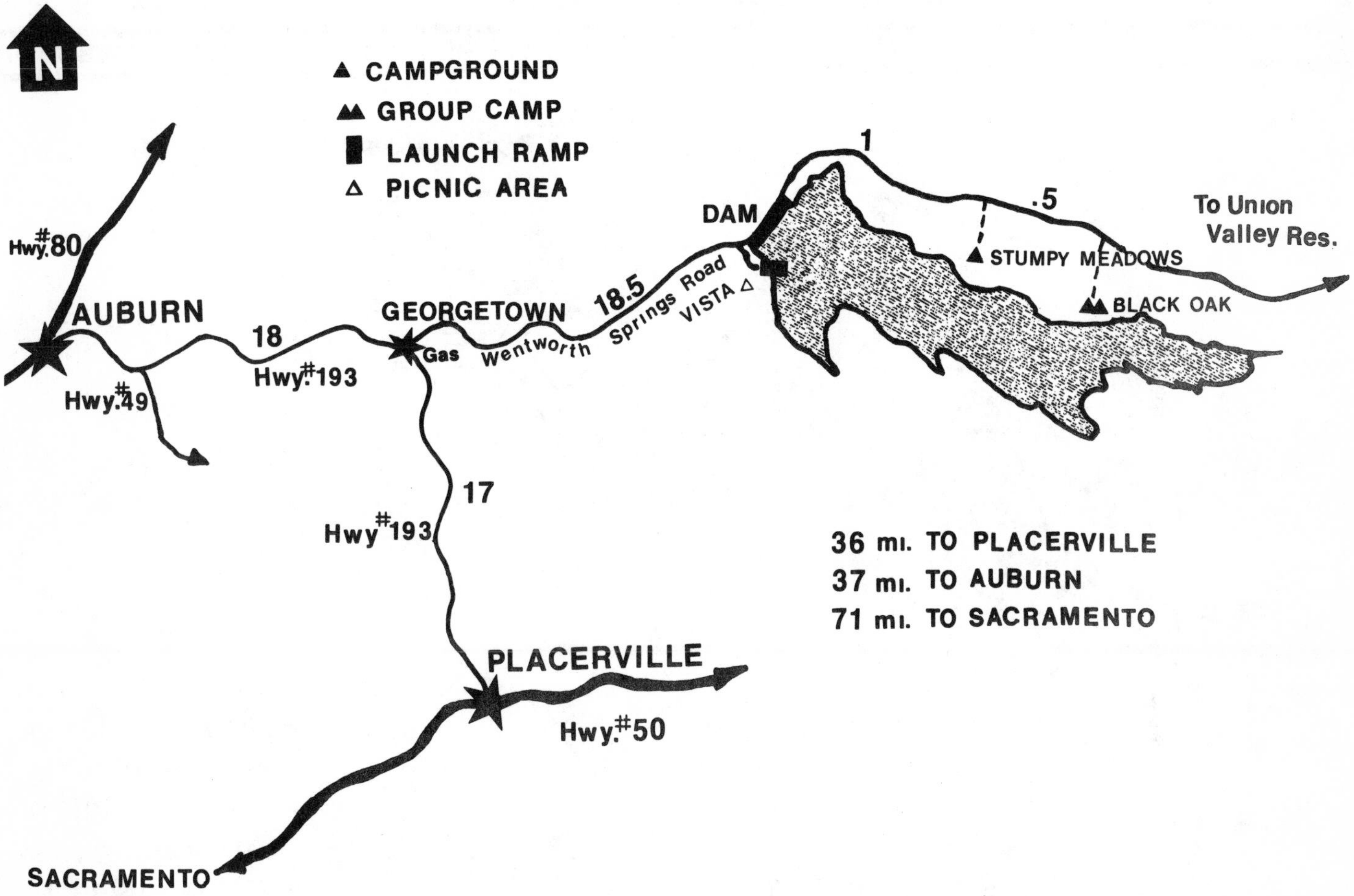
N
▲ CAMPGROUND
▲▲ GROUP CAMP
LAUNCH RAMP
△ PICNIC AREA
Hwy.#80
AUBURN
Hwy.#49
18
Hwy.#193
GEORGETOWN
Gas
Wentworth Springs Road
18.5
VISTA △
DAM
1
.5
STUMPY MEADOWS
BLACK OAK
To Union Valley Res.
17
Hwy#193
PLACERVILLE
Hwy.#50
SACRAMENTO
36 mi. TO PLACERVILLE
37 mi. TO AUBURN
71 mi. TO SACRAMENTO

INFORMATION: U.S.F.S., 100 Forni Rd., Placerville 95667 or Ticketron

CAMPING	BOATING	RECREATION	RESORTS
40 Developed Sites for Tents, R.V.s, Trailers Fee: $2 a Day 4 Group Sites - Maximum - 225 People - Reservations	Boating Allowed to 5 MPH Speed Limit Launching Ramp	Fishing Picnicking Hiking No Swimming	20 Miles to Full Facilities

SLY PARK - JENKINSON LAKE

Jenkinson Lake is located in the Sly Park Recreation Area. It is at about 3,500 feet elevation and has 640 surface acres. The shoreline is sandy in some areas, and the North-east end of the Lake has a 5 MPH speed limit for fishermen. There is a paved launch ramp with floats, a nice small Marina and boat storage area. 9 campgrounds, a group campground and a youth group area are located around the Lake. Swimming, waterskiing, fishing and picnicking are all available. The water is clear, fishing can be good along the coves, and the winds are usually good for sailing.

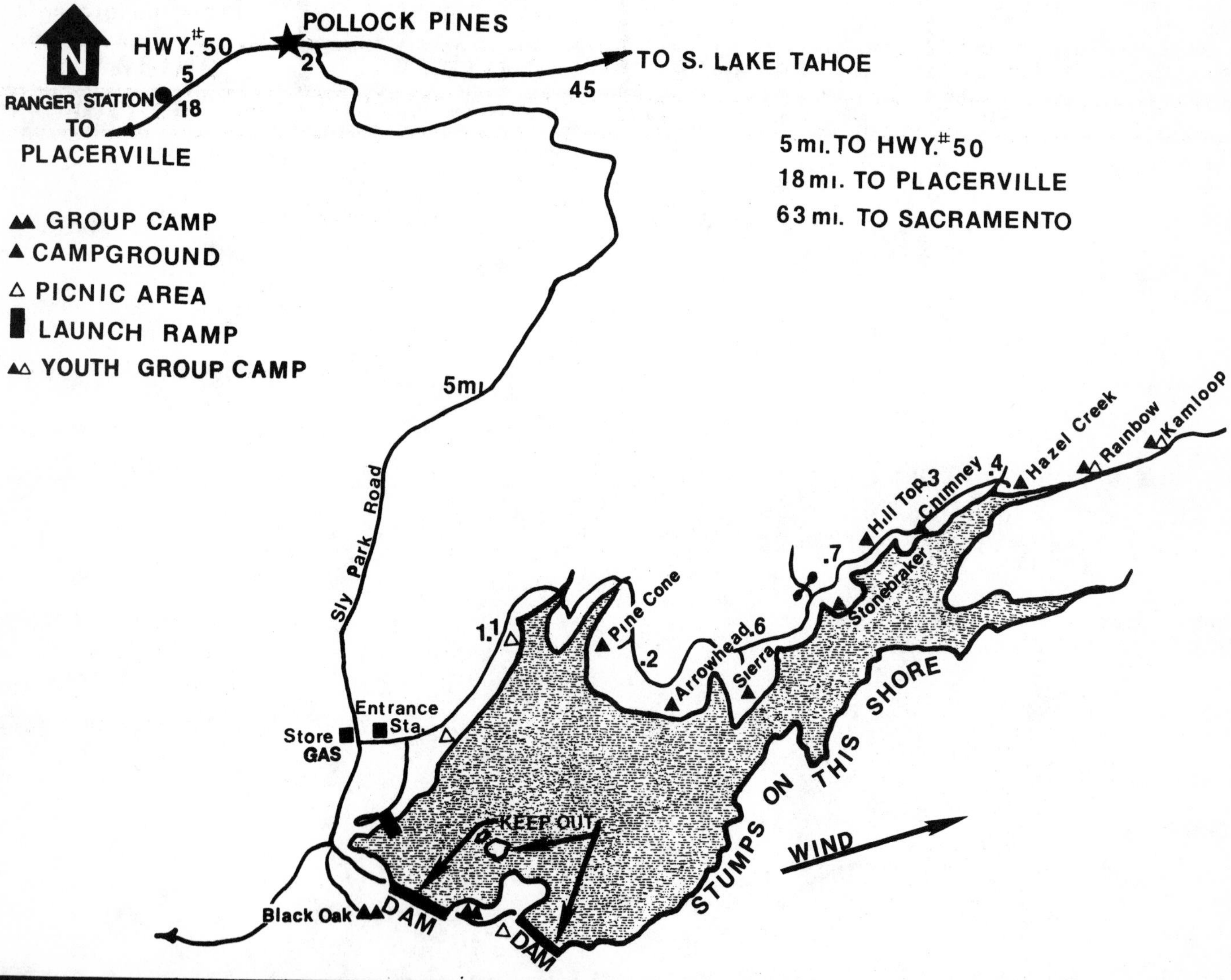
N
HWY.#50
POLLOCK PINES
TO S. LAKE TAHOE
2
5
45
RANGER STATION
18
TO
PLACERVILLE
5mi.TO HWY.#50
18mi. TO PLACERVILLE
63mi. TO SACRAMENTO
GROUP CAMP
CAMPGROUND
PICNIC AREA
LAUNCH RAMP
YOUTH GROUP CAMP
5mi
Sly Park Road
1.1
Pine Cone
.2
Arrowhead.6
Sierra
.7
Hill Top.3
Stonebraker
Chimney .4
Hazel Creek
Rainbow
Kamloop
Entrance Sta.
Store
GAS
KEEP OUT
STUMPS ON THIS SHORE
WIND
Black Oak
DAM
DAM

INFORMATION: El Dorado Irrigation District, P.O. Box 1047, Placerville 95667

CAMPING	BOATING	RECREATION	RESORTS
250 Developed Sites for Tents, R.V.s and Trailers Fee:$3.50 a Day (1st come-1st served) Reservations required for Group and Youth Camp Areas. Write Irrigation District, 916-622-4513	All Boating Allowed Fishing Area - 5 MPH Speed Limit Launch Ramp Fee: $2 Dry Boat Storage	Fishing Swimming Picnicking Hiking Day Use Only: $1.75	Store Sly Park Resort 4782 Sly Park Rd. Pollock Pines 95726 Ph. 916-644-1113 Park Entrance Station Ph. 916-664-2545

INDIAN CREEK RESERVOIR

Indian Creek Reservoir, located at 5,600 feet elevation, is a new facility for Lake recreation. Its 160 surface acres are a result of 27 miles of pipeline from Lake Tahoe's recycled water. There are 19 campsites for tents, R.V.s and trailers with water, toilets and showers. 10 campsites for tents only are located north of the launch ramp. With advance reservations, groups of up to 60 people maximum, tents only, can camp next to the picnic area. This is a lovely Lake situated in the eastern foothills of the Sierra Nevada, and there are wonderful hiking trails with spectacular views.

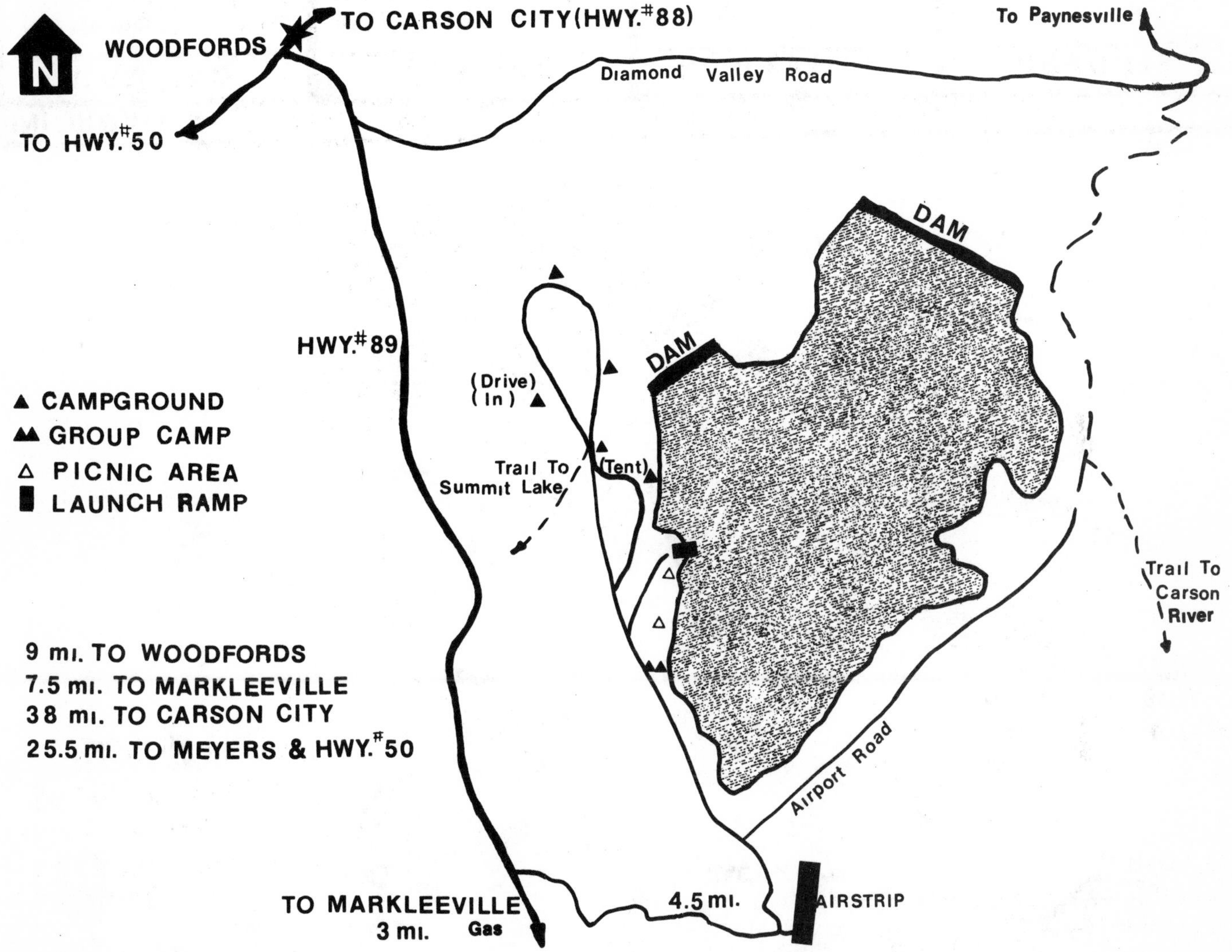

N
WOODFORDS
TO CARSON CITY(HWY.#88)
To Paynesville
Diamond Valley Road
TO HWY.#50
DAM
DAM
HWY.#89
(Drive) (In)
Trail To Summit Lake
(Tent)
Trail To Carson River
▲ CAMPGROUND
▲▲ GROUP CAMP
△ PICNIC AREA
▮ LAUNCH RAMP
9 mi. TO WOODFORDS
7.5 mi. TO MARKLEEVILLE
38 mi. TO CARSON CITY
25.5 mi. TO MEYERS & HWY.#50
Airport Road
TO MARKLEEVILLE 3 mi.
Gas
4.5 mi.
AIRSTRIP

INFORMATION: Bureau of Land Management, Carson City, Nevada 89701, Ph. 702-882-1631

CAMPING	BOATING	RECREATION	RESORTS
19 Developed Sites for Tents, R.V.s, and Trailers Fee: $3 a Day 10 Sites, Tents Only Fee: $2 a Day Group Camp - 60 People Maximum	All Boating Allowed Launch Ramp Waterskiing is <u>not</u> recommended	Fishing Picnicking Hiking	

BLUE LAKES
ALPINE COUNTY

Blue Lakes are located at 8,000 feet elevation. The mornings and nights are cool and the water is cold. Swimming is allowed, and small boats only are permitted on the dirt ramp. The country is rough and remote and fishing can be excellent. Mark Lake, Twin Lake, Meadow Lake and others are in this same area, and you have to hike into those. Campsites operated by P. G. & E. include Lower Blue Lake which has 16 sites with tables, water, toilets and fire pits. 1.5 miles further is Middle Creek with 5 campsites. 1/4 mile further on is Upper Blue Lake Dam with 25 campsites, and 1.3 miles further is Upper Blue Lake with 32 campsites. The first 7 miles of road into Blue Lakes is paved from Highway 88, but the last 5 miles are not paved. On the West Fork of Carson Creek on Blue Lakes Road, about 2 miles in, is Hope Valley Campground which has 26 campsites, 18 trailer spaces, tables and water. This Campground is operated by the U. S. Forest Service.

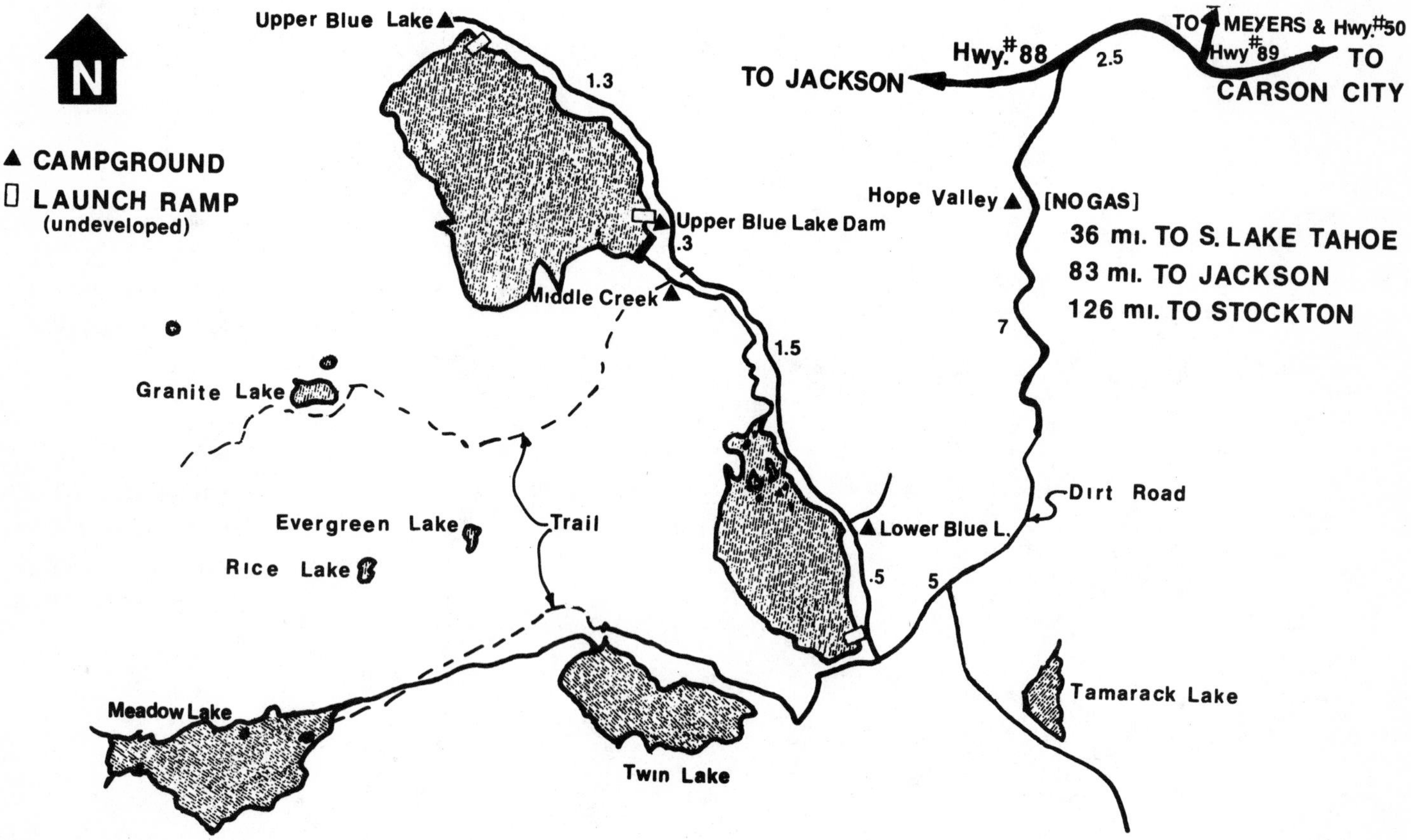
N
▲ CAMPGROUND
▯ LAUNCH RAMP
(undeveloped)
Upper Blue Lake
1.3
Upper Blue Lake Dam
.3
Middle Creek
1.5
Granite Lake
Evergreen Lake
Trail
Rice Lake
Lower Blue L.
.5
5
Meadow Lake
Twin Lake
Tamarack Lake
Dirt Road
7
Hope Valley
[NO GAS]
36 mi. TO S. LAKE TAHOE
83 mi. TO JACKSON
126 mi. TO STOCKTON
TO JACKSON
Hwy.#88
2.5
TO MEYERS & Hwy.#50
Hwy#89
TO CARSON CITY

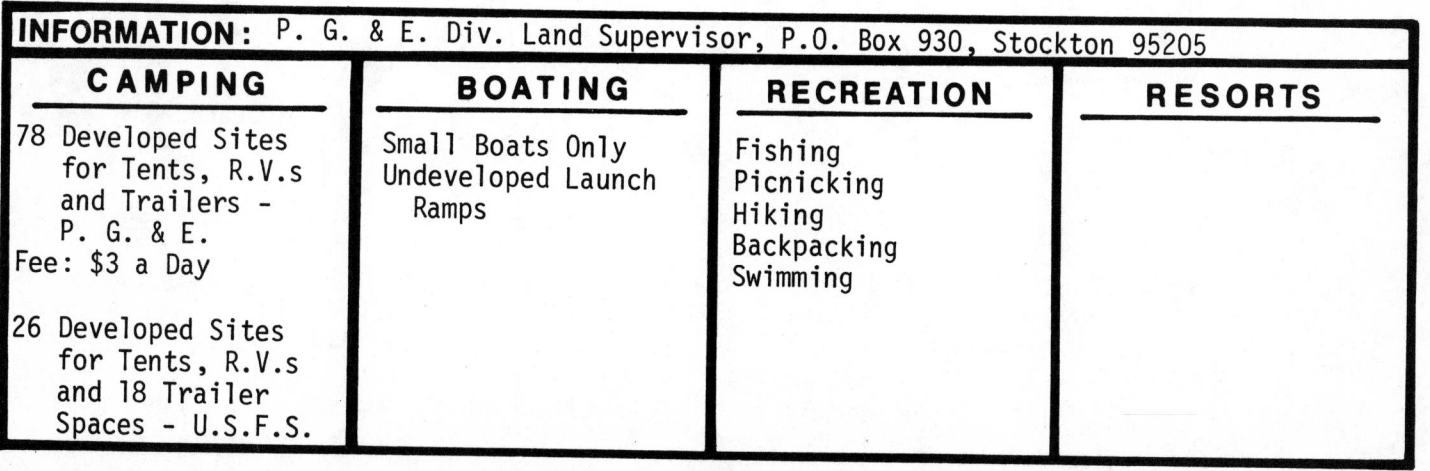

INFORMATION: P. G. & E. Div. Land Supervisor, P.O. Box 930, Stockton 95205

CAMPING	BOATING	RECREATION	RESORTS
78 Developed Sites for Tents, R.V.s and Trailers - P. G. & E. Fee: $3 a Day 26 Developed Sites for Tents, R.V.s and 18 Trailer Spaces - U.S.F.S.	Small Boats Only Undeveloped Launch Ramps	Fishing Picnicking Hiking Backpacking Swimming	

WOODS LAKE

Woods Lake, at 8,200 feet elevation, is a lovely hidden retreat off Highway 88 over Carson Pass. The campground at present has 14 units for tents, R.V.s and trailers with plans for future expansion to 24 units. Tables, water and toilets are available. 8 picnic sites at the water's edge provide excellent paths for the handicapped. Fishing can be good in the Lake as well as streams through this area. (Cover photographs).

RED LAKE

Red Lake has no facilities and is seen from Highway 88 as it winds around the Lake. Winds can be strong in the afternoons and fishing is often quite good.

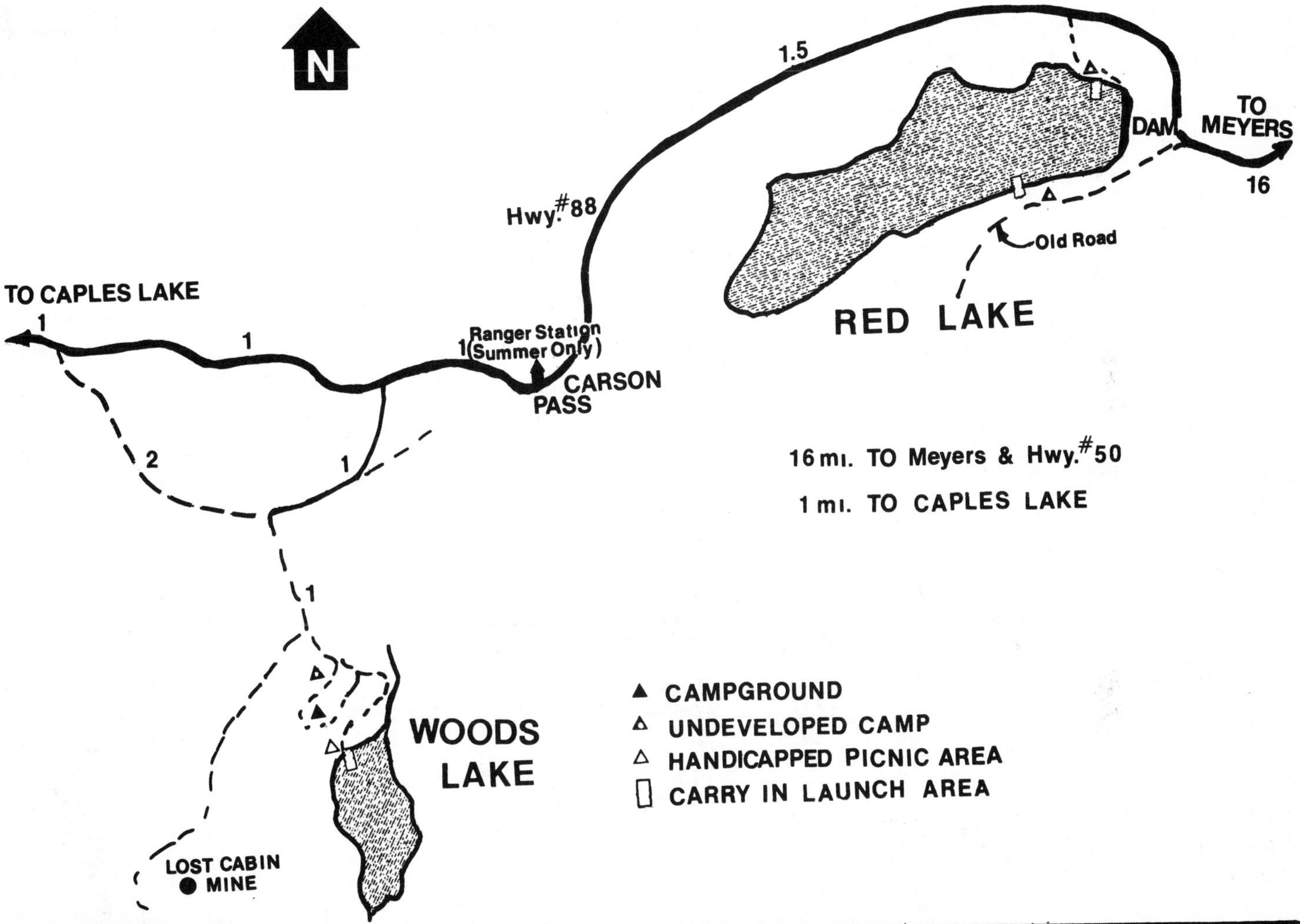
N
1.5
DAM
TO MEYERS
16
Hwy.#88
Old Road
TO CAPLES LAKE
1
1
Ranger Station (Summer Only)
1
CARSON PASS
RED LAKE
2
1
16 mi. TO Meyers & Hwy.#50
1 mi. TO CAPLES LAKE
1
WOODS LAKE
CAMPGROUND
UNDEVELOPED CAMP
HANDICAPPED PICNIC AREA
CARRY IN LAUNCH AREA
LOST CABIN MINE

INFORMATION: Amador Ranger Station, El Dorado National Forest, Ph. 209-223-1623

CAMPING	BOATING	RECREATION	RESORTS
Woods Lake 14 Developed Sites for Tents, R.V.s and Trailers Fee: $1 a Day	Hand Launch Fishing boats, Sailboats, Canoes No motors allowed on Woods Lake	Fishing Picnicking (Good handicapped facilities) Hiking	

CAPLES LAKE

Caples Lake is at 7,950 feet elevation so the nights and mornings are cool and the water is cold. This is a beautiful Lake which lies along the spectacular Highway 88 over Carson Pass. The U. S. Forest Service maintains 35 campsites (20 tents only, 15 tents, R.V.s, trailers) with water, toilets and barbecues. Caples Lake Resort has a large Lodge with rooms right on the Lake and housekeeping cabins also. There is a grocery store, fishing tackle, row and motor boat rentals, 2-lane launching ramp, docking facilities and horseback riding nearby. West on Highway 88 at Kirkwood Lake there are 13 campsites (12 tents only, 1 tents, R.V.s, trailers) with water, toilets and barbecues. The road is not suitable for larger R.V.s or trailers. Motorboats are not allowed. Trout fishing is good from the shore or rowboat. This entire area is a photographer's delight.

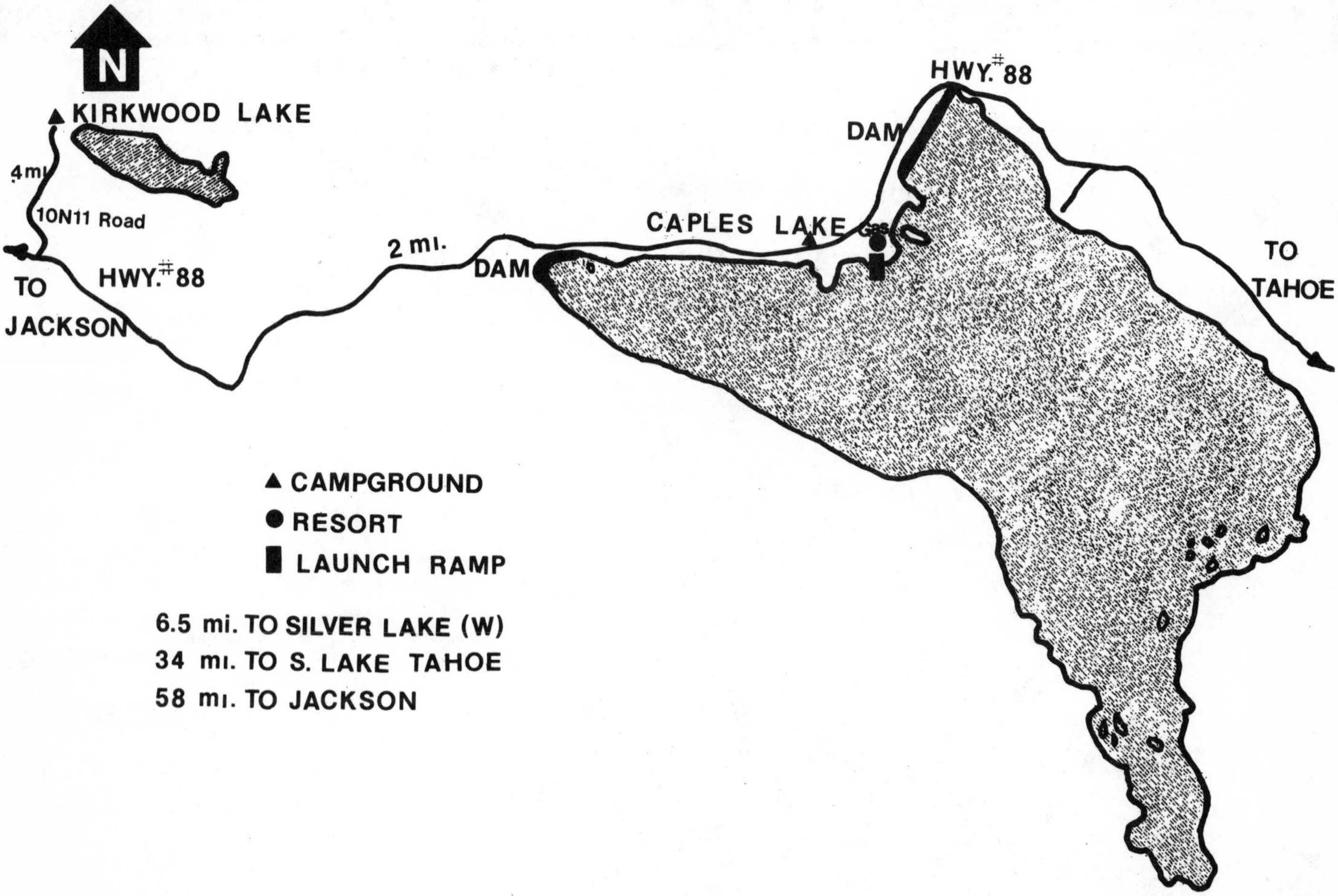
N
KIRKWOOD LAKE
4mi
10N11 Road
TO JACKSON
HWY.# 88
2 mi.
DAM
CAPLES LAKE
Gas
DAM
HWY.# 88
TO TAHOE
▲ CAMPGROUND
● RESORT
■ LAUNCH RAMP
6.5 mi. TO SILVER LAKE (W)
34 mi. TO S. LAKE TAHOE
58 mi. TO JACKSON

INFORMATION: Caples Lake Resort, Box 8, Kirkwood 95646, Ph. 209-258-8888

CAMPING	BOATING	RECREATION	RESORTS
35 Developed Sites for Tents, R.V.s, Trailers - at Caples Lake Fee: $2 a Day 13 Developed Sites for Tents, R.V.s, Trailers - at Kirkwood Lake Fee: $1 a Day	All Boating Allowed Except No Motors on Kirkwood Launch Ramp Boat Rentals Full Facility Marina Water Taxi	Fishing Picnicking Hiking Swimming Horseback Riding	Lodge Housekeeping Cabins Store Restaurant

SILVER LAKE

Silver Lake is on Kit Carson Spur in a granite basin at about 7,300 feet in elevation. It is a natural Lake but in 1877, a Dam was built over the outlet of the Lake and has been rebuilt twice since then. The U. S. Forest Service maintains 97 campsites (47 tents only, 50 tents, R.V.s, trailers) with tables, toilets, barbecues and water. Kay's Silver Lake Resort has housekeeping cabins, launch ramp, coffee shop, gas, store and boat rentals. Kit Carson Lodge has lovely housekeeping accommodations, dining room and full Resort facilities. Plasse's Resort, which was once a trading post, is at the South end of the Lake and has 35 campsites for tents, R.V.s or trailers and 10 spaces with water hookups. There is also a bar, restaurant and store as well as a recreation room, dump station, toilets, hot showers and stables. The Lake water is very clear and cold. Silver Lake is located on the section of Highway 88 which is one of the most scenic roads in the nation, following the Emigrant Trail cut by Kit Carson in 1844.

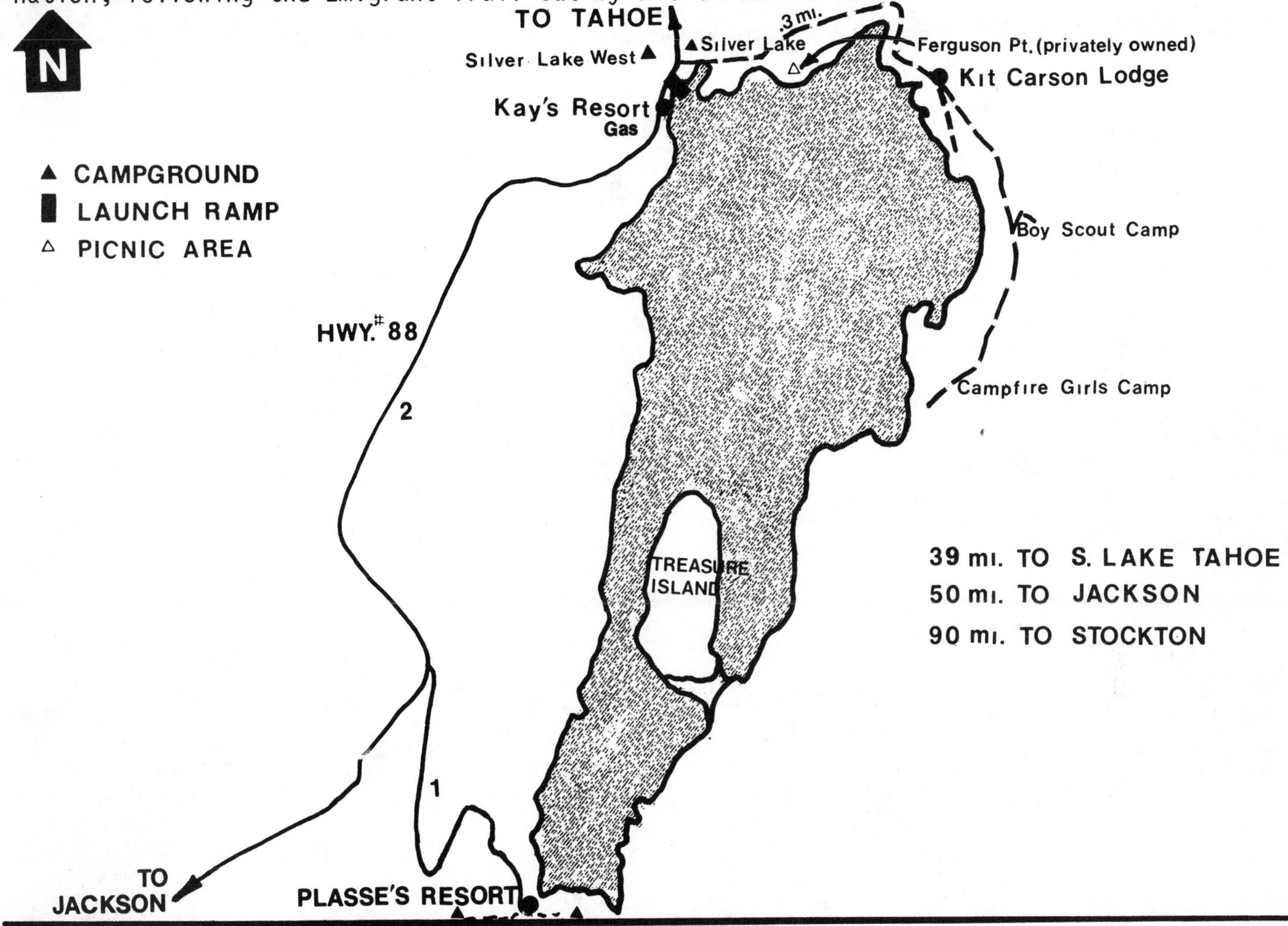

N
TO TAHOE
.3 mi.
Silver Lake
Ferguson Pt. (privately owned)
Silver Lake West
Kit Carson Lodge
Kay's Resort
Gas
CAMPGROUND
LAUNCH RAMP
PICNIC AREA
Boy Scout Camp
HWY.# 88
2
Campfire Girls Camp
TREASURE ISLAND
39 mi. TO S. LAKE TAHOE
50 mi. TO JACKSON
90 mi. TO STOCKTON
1
TO JACKSON
PLASSE'S RESORT

INFORMATION: U. S. Forest Service, 100 Forni Road, Placerville 95667

CAMPING	BOATING	RECREATION	RESORTS
U.S.F.S. 97 Developed Sites for Tents, R.V.s, and Trailers Fee: $2 a Day	All Boating Allowed Launch Ramps Boat Rentals Full Service Marina	Fishing Swimming Hiking Picnicking Horseback Riding	Housekeeping Cabins Stores Restaurants Laundromats

LOWER BEAR RIVER RESERVOIR

Lower Bear River Reservoir is a very pretty Lake at 5,800 feet elevation. The U. S. Forest Service operates 22 sites (13 tents only/9 tents, R.V.s, trailers) at South Shore Campground with water, toilets and barbecues. Bear River Campground is a Group Camp with 3 sites, 2 for 25 people each and 1 for 50 people, with water, toilets and barbecues. For Group Camp Reservations write: District Ranger, P. O. Box 1327, Jackson 95642 (Winter) or Lumberyard Ranger Station, Pioneer 95666 (Summer). The U. S. Forest Service also has a dirt ramp near the Dam. Bear River Resort has 127 campsites for tents, R.V.s and trailers with water, toilets, showers, launch ramp, store and group sites for camping. There are boat rentals as well as trailer rentals and a swim beach. Winds are good for sailing in the afternoon at this Lake, and trout are planted two times a month in season.

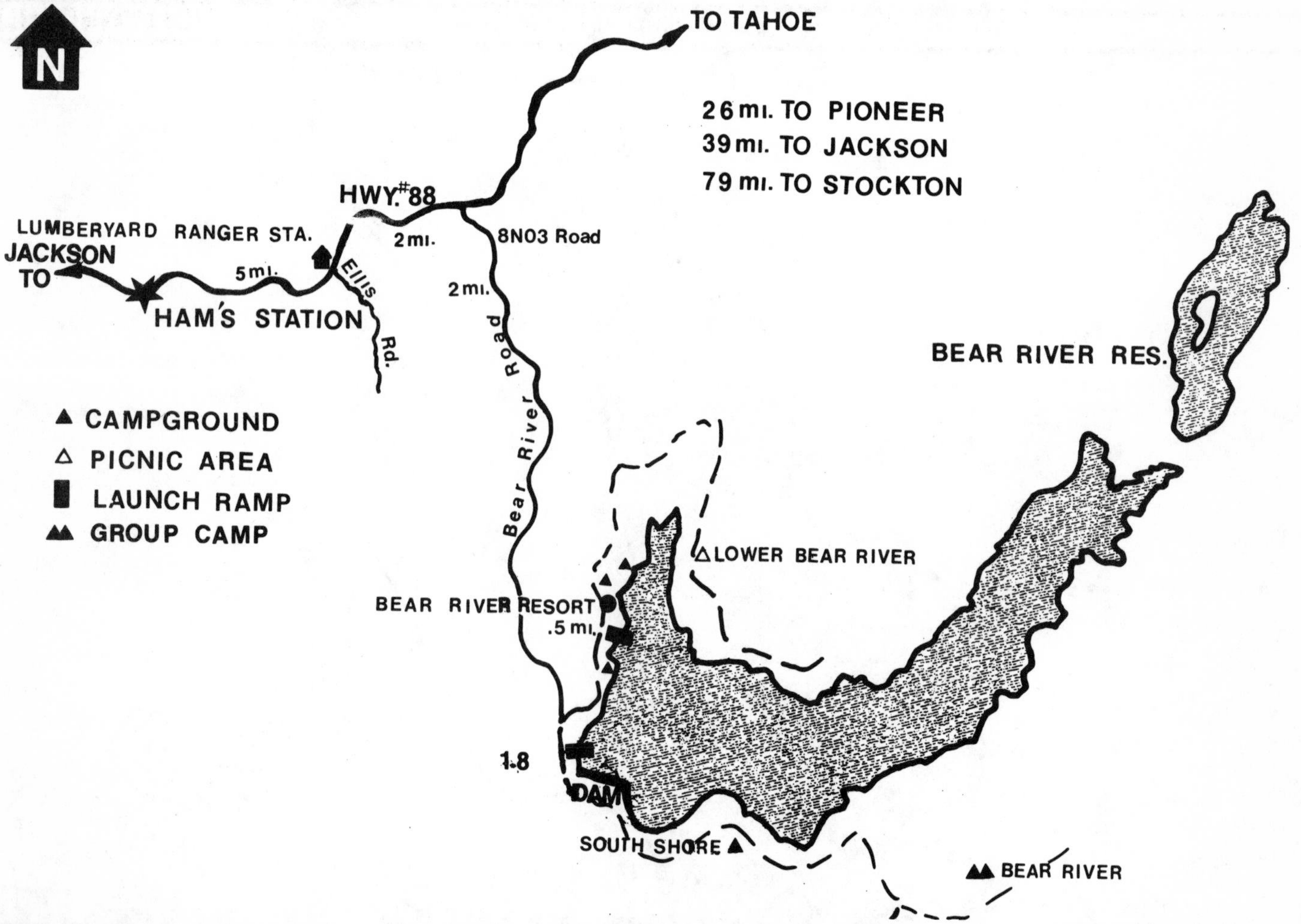
N
TO TAHOE
26 mi. TO PIONEER
39 mi. TO JACKSON
79 mi. TO STOCKTON
HWY. #88
LUMBERYARD RANGER STA.
JACKSON TO
2 mi.
8N03 Road
5 mi.
Ellis Rd.
2 mi.
HAM'S STATION
Bear River Road
BEAR RIVER RES.
CAMPGROUND
PICNIC AREA
LAUNCH RAMP
GROUP CAMP
LOWER BEAR RIVER
BEAR RIVER RESORT
.5 mi.
1.8
DAM
SOUTH SHORE
BEAR RIVER

INFORMATION: U.S.F.S. - see above, Bear River Resort, Kirkwood Star Rte., Pioneer 95666

CAMPING	BOATING	RECREATION	RESORTS
22 Developed Sites for Tents, R.V.s, Trailers - USFS Fee: $2 a Day Group Camp - 100 people maximum USFS - Reservations 127 Developed Sites for Tents, R.V.s Trailers-Resort	All Boating Allowed Launch Ramps Boat Rentals Full Service Marina	Fishing Swimming Picnicking Hiking Day Use at Resort - $3	Store Showers Dump Station Full Vacation Facilities Bear River Resort - Ph. 209-295-4868

LAKE ALPINE

Lake Alpine is located in a picturesque timbered forest at 7,320 feet elevation. It has 180 surface acres and is regularly stocked with rainbow trout. The U. S. Forest Service operates 105 campsites. Silvertip has 23 sites and Lake Alpine Campground has 25 sites for tents, R.V.s and trailers with water, toilets and barbecues. Lake Alpine Picnic Area has 10 units with toilets and a launch ramp. Pine Marten has 32 sites and Silver Valley has 25 sites for tents, R.V.s and trailers with water and toilets. All boating is allowed within a 10 MPH speed limit. This is a good sailing Lake with steady breezes. Historic Lake Alpine Lodge and Resort has cabins, a store and a dining room overlooking the scenic Lake. There are hundreds of more campsites and facilities nearby on Highway 4.

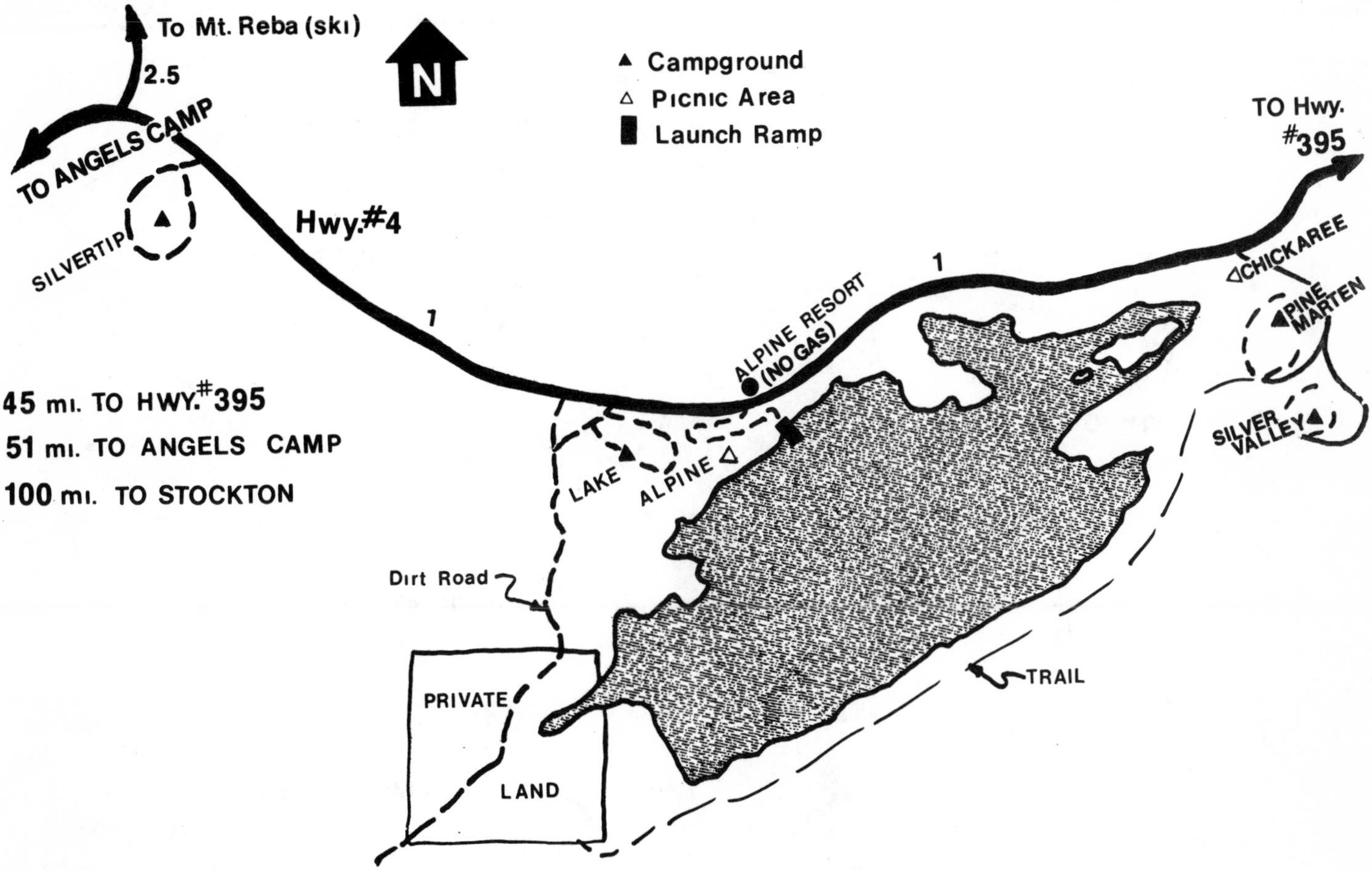
To Mt. Reba (ski)
2.5
N
▲ Campground
△ Picnic Area
▮ Launch Ramp
TO Hwy. #395
TO ANGELS CAMP
SILVERTIP
Hwy. #4
1
1
ALPINE RESORT (NO GAS)
CHICKAREE
PINE MARTEN
SILVER VALLEY
45 mi. TO HWY. #395
51 mi. TO ANGELS CAMP
100 mi. TO STOCKTON
LAKE ALPINE
Dirt Road
TRAIL
PRIVATE LAND

INFORMATION: U.S.F.S. - Calaveras District Headquarters, Arnold 95223

CAMPING	BOATING	RECREATION	RESORTS
105 Developed Sites for Tents, R.V.s and Trailers Fee: $3 a Day	All Boating to 10 MPH Speed Limit Launch Ramp Rental Boats Full Service Marina	Fishing Swimming Picnicking Hiking Horseback Riding	Cabins Restaurant Snack Bar Store

FOLSOM LAKE

Folsom Lake is in the heart of the Gold Country and buried beneath its waters is the site of one of California's oldest gold mining communities, Mormon Island. There are 5 concrete launching ramps around the Lake as well as 2 self-contained boat camping areas. You must register at Granite Bay or Folsom Marina for boat inspections. 150 campsites for tents, R.V.s, and trailers with tables, barbecues and water are located at Beals Point and Peninsula Campgrounds. There is a good full service Marina including boat rentals and about 300 slips at Folsom Marina. Camping reservations can be made through your local Ticketron outlet or write: Ticketron, P. O. Box 26430, San Francisco 94120. There are 50 miles of trails for the hiker or horseback rider, and swimming beaches with lifeguards. Rattlesnake Bar is ideal for the small boater with lovely islands and protected areas.

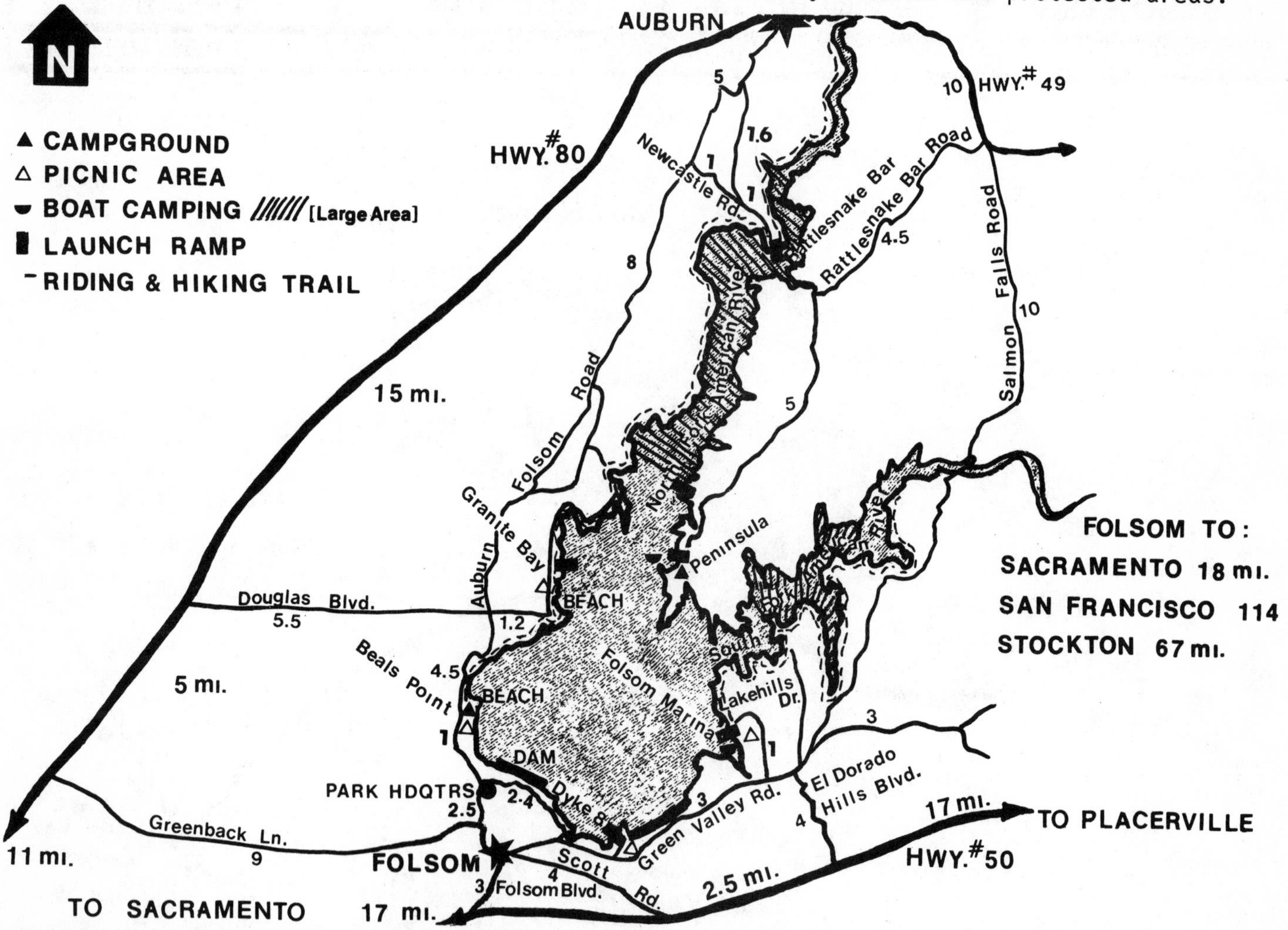
N
▲ CAMPGROUND
△ PICNIC AREA
BOAT CAMPING [Large Area]
LAUNCH RAMP
RIDING & HIKING TRAIL
AUBURN
HWY. # 80
HWY. # 49
Newcastle Rd.
Rattlesnake Bar
Rattlesnake Bar Road
Salmon Falls Road
Folsom Road
Granite Bay
Auburn
Douglas Blvd.
Beals Point
BEACH
Peninsula
Folsom Marina
Lakehills Dr.
DAM
Dyke 8
PARK HDQTRS
Greenback Ln.
FOLSOM
Scott Rd.
Folsom Blvd.
Green Valley Rd.
El Dorado Hills Blvd.
HWY. # 50
TO PLACERVILLE
TO SACRAMENTO
15 mi.
5 mi.
11 mi.
17 mi.
2.5 mi.
FOLSOM TO:
SACRAMENTO 18 mi.
SAN FRANCISCO 114
STOCKTON 67 mi.

INFORMATION: Folsom Lake, 7806 Folsom-Auburn Rd., Folsom 95630, Ph. 916-988-0205

CAMPING	BOATING	RECREATION	RESORTS
150 Developed Sites for Tents, R.V.s and Trailers Fee: $4 a Day Reservations through Ticketron 2 Boat Camping Areas Fee: $2 a Day	All Boating Allowed Boat Rentals Launch Ramps Full Service Marina	Fishing Swimming Hiking Picnicking Horseback Riding Trails Day Use Only - $1.50	1 Mile to Store 6 Miles to Motels

LAKE NATOMA
FOLSOM AFTERBAY

Lake Natoma has 500 surface acres and is the reregulating reservoir for Folsom Dam. The water is very cold as it comes from under the Dam. There is a paved launch ramp at Nimbus Flat and one at Negro Bar as well as a swim beach. 20 campsites are for tents, R.V.s and trailers and can be reserved for Groups. Contact your local Ticketron outlet or write: Ticketron, P. O. Box 26430, San Francisco 94120. Waterskiing is not allowed, and the winds are usually good in the afternoon for sailing. There are shade structures with picnic tables and a car and trailer parking area. Trout and catfish can be caught from shore or boat. Good trails are available for hiking and horseback riding.

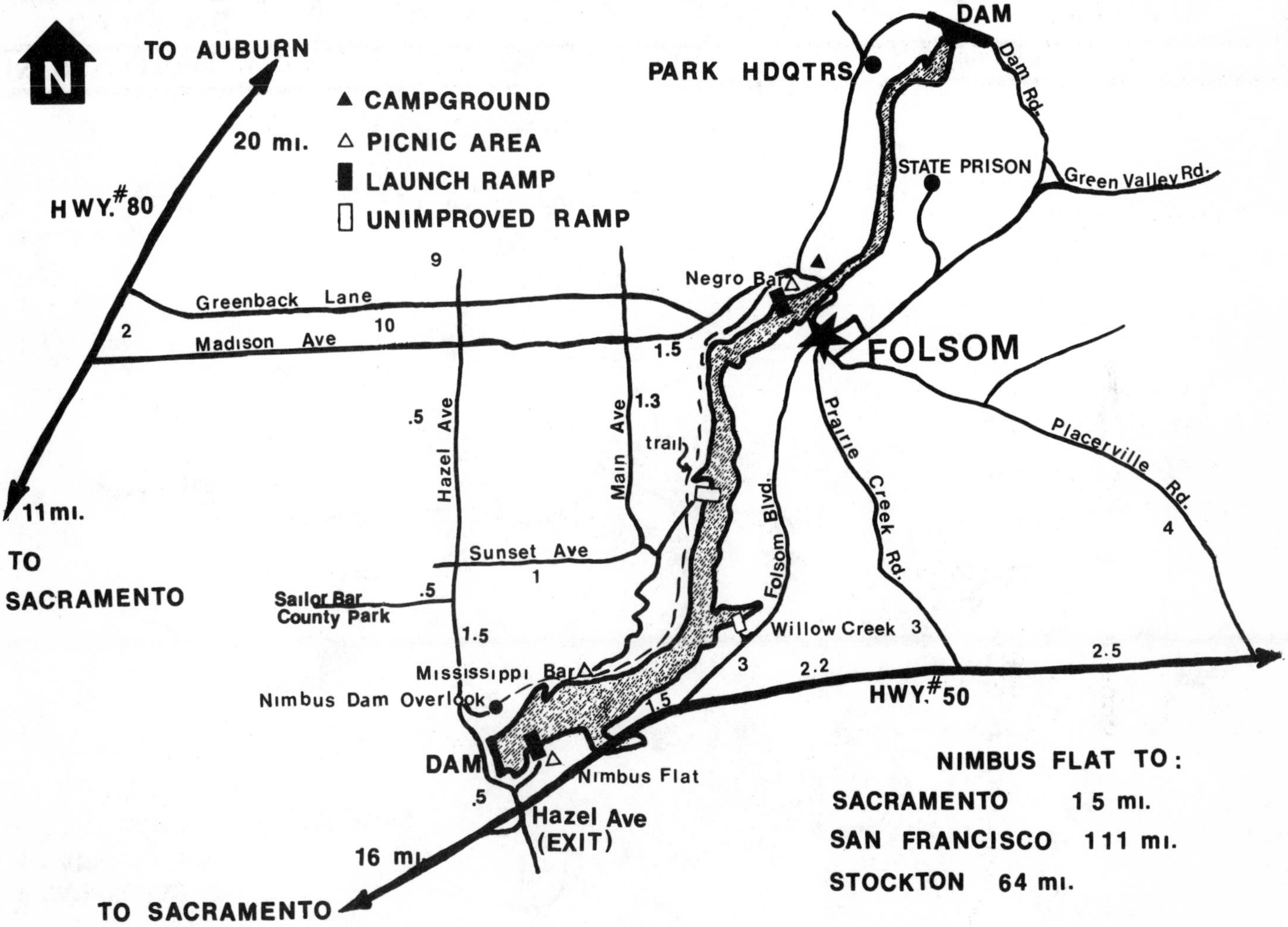

N
TO AUBURN
20 mi.
HWY.#80
11mi.
TO SACRAMENTO
▲ CAMPGROUND
△ PICNIC AREA
LAUNCH RAMP
UNIMPROVED RAMP
DAM
Dam Rd.
PARK HDQTRS
STATE PRISON
Green Valley Rd.
Negro Bar
FOLSOM
Greenback Lane
Madison Ave
2
9
10
1.5
1.3
.5
Hazel Ave
Main Ave
trail
Prairie Creek Rd.
Placerville Rd.
4
Folsom Blvd.
Sunset Ave
1
Sailor Bar County Park
.5
1.5
Willow Creek 3
Mississippi Bar
Nimbus Dam Overlook
3
2.2
2.5
HWY.#50
1.5
DAM
Nimbus Flat
.5
Hazel Ave (EXIT)
16 mi.
TO SACRAMENTO
NIMBUS FLAT TO:
SACRAMENTO 15 mi.
SAN FRANCISCO 111 mi.
STOCKTON 64 mi.

INFORMATION: Folsom Lake, 7806 Folsom-Auburn Rd., Folsom 95630, Ph. 916-988-0205

CAMPING	BOATING	RECREATION	RESORTS
20 Developed Sites for Tents, R.V.s and Trailers Fee: $4 a Day Can be reserved as a Group Camp also - Reservations through Ticketron	All Boating Allowed except No Waterskiing Launch Ramps Fee: $3 a Day	Fishing Swimming Picnicking Hiking Day Use Only: $1.50	1/2 Mile to Full Facilities

LAKE CAMANCHE

Lake Camanche, an East Bay Municipal Utility District Reservoir, has 7,770 surface acres with 54 miles of shoreline. Indian caves are still visible along the Lake shore, and you can pan for gold in the spring when the streams are high. There are two recreational facilities, Camanche North Shore and Camanche Lake Park at the South Shore. Both facilities have swimming lagoons with sandy beaches. This Lake is one of the nicest for water sports as the water is warm and clean, and fishing can be good. There are full Marina facilities at both locations as well as cottages and boat rentals and storage. There are over 15,000 acres of park lands for hiking and horseback riding. Camanche is one of the most complete facility Lakes within easy distance of the San Francisco Bay Area.

. . . Continued . . .

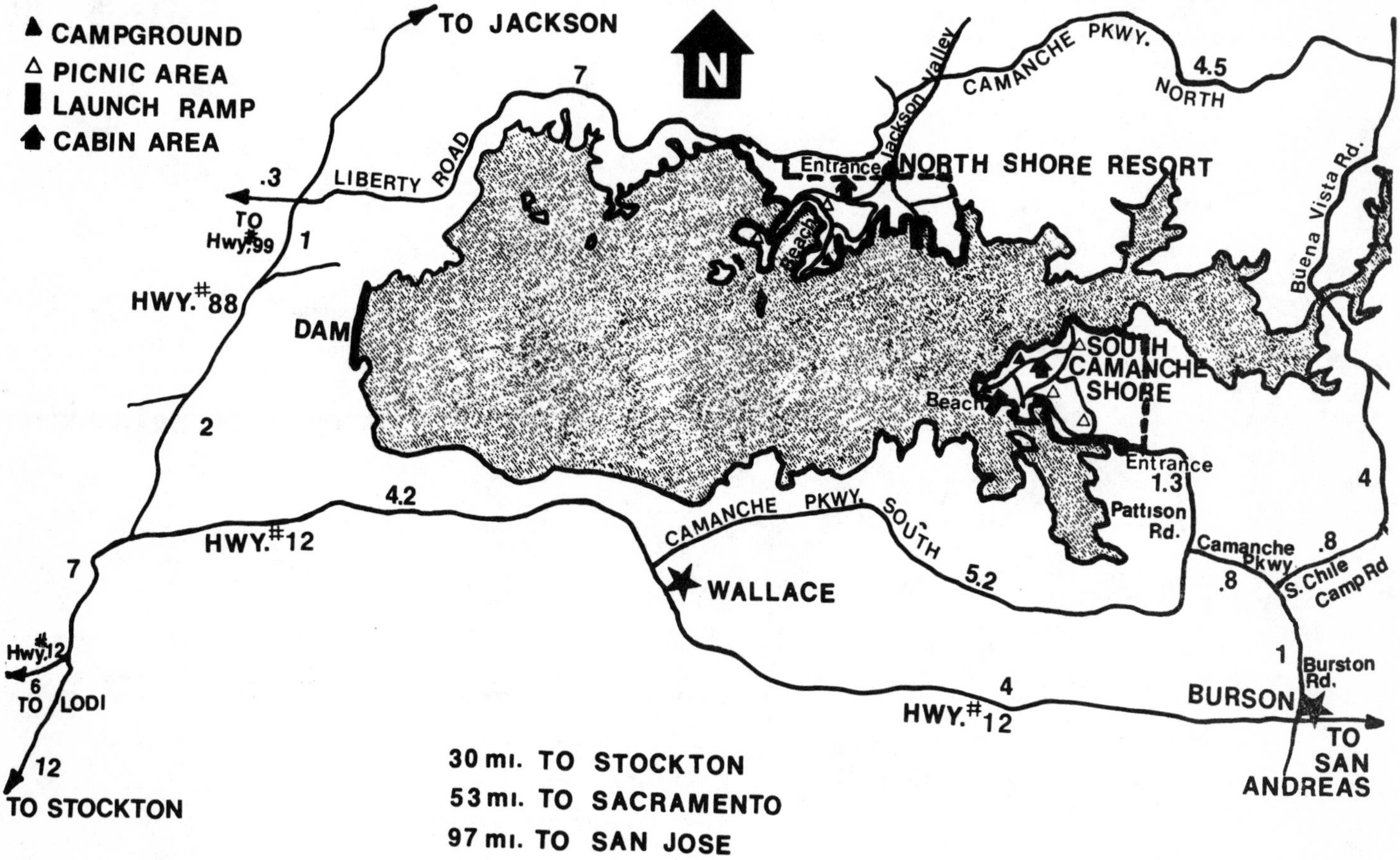

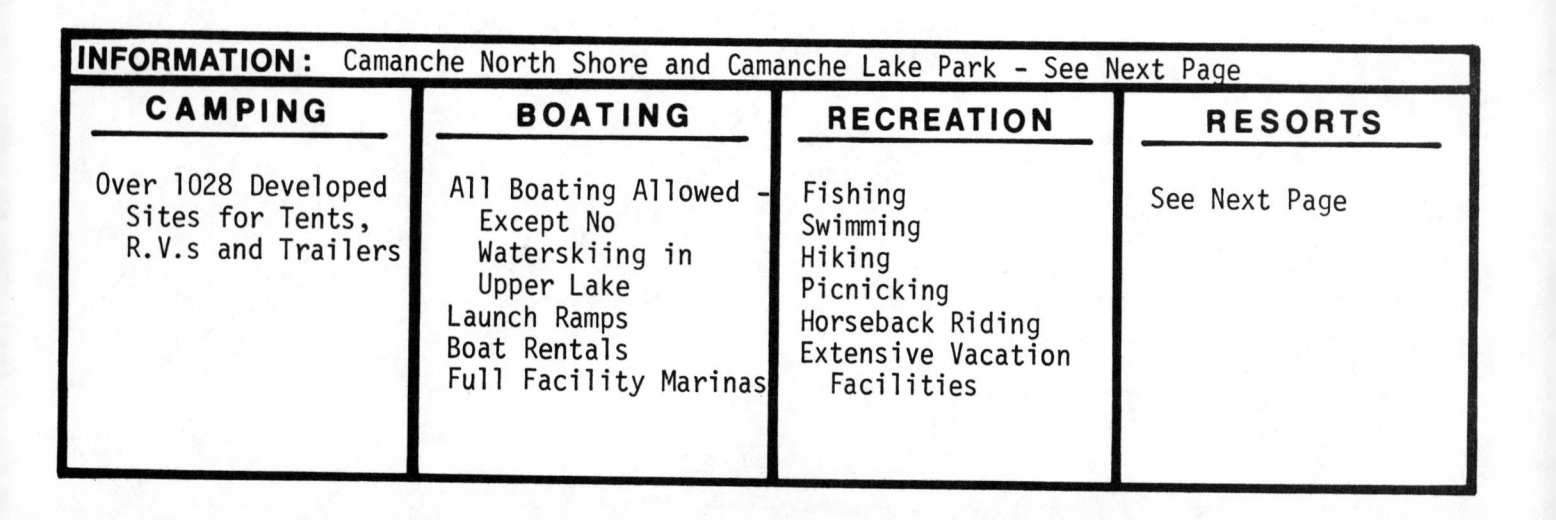

▲ CAMPGROUND
△ PICNIC AREA
▮ LAUNCH RAMP
⬆ CABIN AREA
TO JACKSON
N
7
CAMANCHE PKWY.
4.5
NORTH
Jackson Valley
Buena Vista Rd.
Entrance
NORTH SHORE RESORT
.3
LIBERTY ROAD
TO Hwy.#99
1
HWY.#88
DAM
Beach
SOUTH CAMANCHE SHORE
Beach
2
Entrance
1.3
4
Pattison Rd.
4.2
CAMANCHE PKWY. SOUTH
HWY.#12
7
Camanche Pkwy
.8
S.Chile Camp Rd
5.2
WALLACE
.8
Hwy.#12
6
TO LODI
1
Burston Rd.
4
BURSON
HWY.#12
TO SAN ANDREAS
12
TO STOCKTON
30 mi. TO STOCKTON
53 mi. TO SACRAMENTO
97 mi. TO SAN JOSE

INFORMATION: Camanche North Shore and Camanche Lake Park - See Next Page

CAMPING	BOATING	RECREATION	RESORTS
Over 1028 Developed Sites for Tents, R.V.s and Trailers	All Boating Allowed - Except No Waterskiing in Upper Lake Launch Ramps Boat Rentals Full Facility Marinas	Fishing Swimming Hiking Picnicking Horseback Riding Extensive Vacation Facilities	See Next Page

. . . Continued . . .

Camanche North Shore Resort
Rural Route 1
Ione, California 95640
Phone: 209-763-5121

Over 350 Campsites for Tents, R.V.s and Trailers - Water, toilets, showers, hookups, dump station, trailer storage, laundromat, playgrounds, store, coffee shop
Fee: Starting at $6 a Day.

Marina - 10-lane launch ramp, boat rentals, windsurfer rentals, storage, berths, moorings, fishing and waterskiing equipment rentals, sailing school, bike rentals, store, cafe, canoe river trips, pontoon boat tours, special group rates - phone: 209-763-5166.

Riding Stables - Breakfast rides, cross country, sunset rides, barbecue dinners and campfire, haywagon rides, pony rides, lessons, training, boarding. Phone: 209-763-5295.

Cottages - Rentals - Deluxe Housekeeping Cottages for 2 to 12 people, motel rooms.

Family or Individual Vacation Programs - Hunting, Horse Ranch, Fishing or Golf Weeks or 3-Day Packages.

Camanche Lake Park - South Shore
P. O. Box 92
Wallace, California 95254
Phone: 209-763-5178

Over 678 Campsites for Tents, R.V.s and Trailers - Water, toilets, showers, hookups, dump station, laundromat, store, snack bars.

Marina - 7-lane launch ramp, boat rentals, storage, berths, moorings.

Other Facilities - Housekeeping Cottages, horseback riding, tennis courts, amphitheater with movies and entertainment, group reservations for camping or picnicking, Mobile Home Park and Sales, Recreation Hall.

Please
use Camping
Courtesy
Snyder
Clean
up!

LAKE AMADOR

Lake Amador, formed by an earth and rock-filled Dam and fed by Jackson Creek, is known for about the best bass fishing in Northern California. Waterskiing, speedboating or motorcycling is not allowed. The Lake is open all year and has about 13 miles of shoreline. Most of the facilities are at the Club House which is located at the entrance to the Lake at the Dam on the South end. There are 100 well-developed campsites for tents, R.V.s and trailers and 12 boat-in campsites. Swimming is nice in the 1 acre pond with 75 degree filtered water. Winds are usually good for sailing.

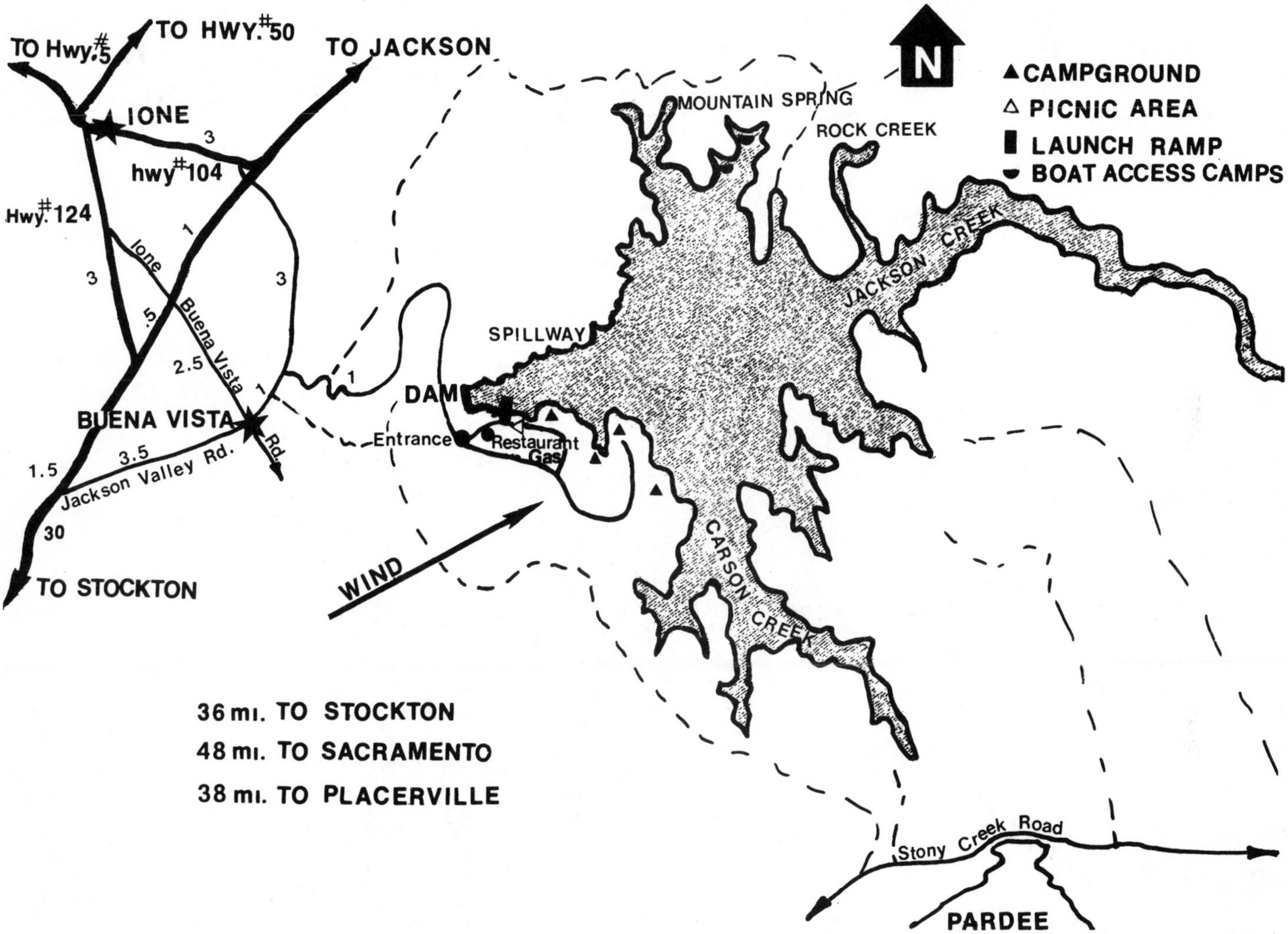

TO Hwy.#5
TO HWY.#50
TO JACKSON
N
▲CAMPGROUND
△ PICNIC AREA
LAUNCH RAMP
BOAT ACCESS CAMPS
IONE
3
hwy#104
Hwy#124
MOUNTAIN SPRING
ROCK CREEK
JACKSON CREEK
Ione
Buena Vista
SPILLWAY
DAM
Entrance
Restaurant
Gas
BUENA VISTA
Rd.
Jackson Valley Rd.
TO STOCKTON
WIND
CARSON CREEK
Stony Creek Road
PARDEE
36 mi. TO STOCKTON
48 mi. TO SACRAMENTO
38 mi. TO PLACERVILLE

INFORMATION: Lake Amador, Route 1, Box 243, Ione 95640, Phone: 209-274-2625

CAMPING	BOATING	RECREATION	RESORTS
100 Developed Sites for Tents, R.V.s and Trailers Fee: $5 a Day Reservations taken - Write Lake Amador 12 Boat-In Camp Sites	Boating Allowed Except No Waterskiing and No Speedboating Boat Rentals Launch Ramp - $1.50 Boat Storage Fishing Floats around Shoreline	Fishing Swimming Picnicking Hiking Bicycle Road No Motorcycles Day Use Only: $2.50	Club House Restaurant Recreation Room Children's Playground with 100 ft. slide

Pardee Lake is the fisherman's dream with trophy-sized rainbow trout planted once a week. The fishing access fee of $1.00 per person per day goes to restocking the Lake. 150 campsites plus 90 R.V. and trailer sites with full hookups are available, and there is a playground for children as well as a restaurant and showers. A good-sized swimming pool adds to the nice vacation facilities. There is a 10-lane concrete launch ramp and all boating is allowed, but no waterskiing or body contact with the water. Law enforcement is very strict so the Lake is quite peaceful. There are 37 miles of shoreline and the waters are fed by the Mokelumme River and then spills water down into Lake Camanche.

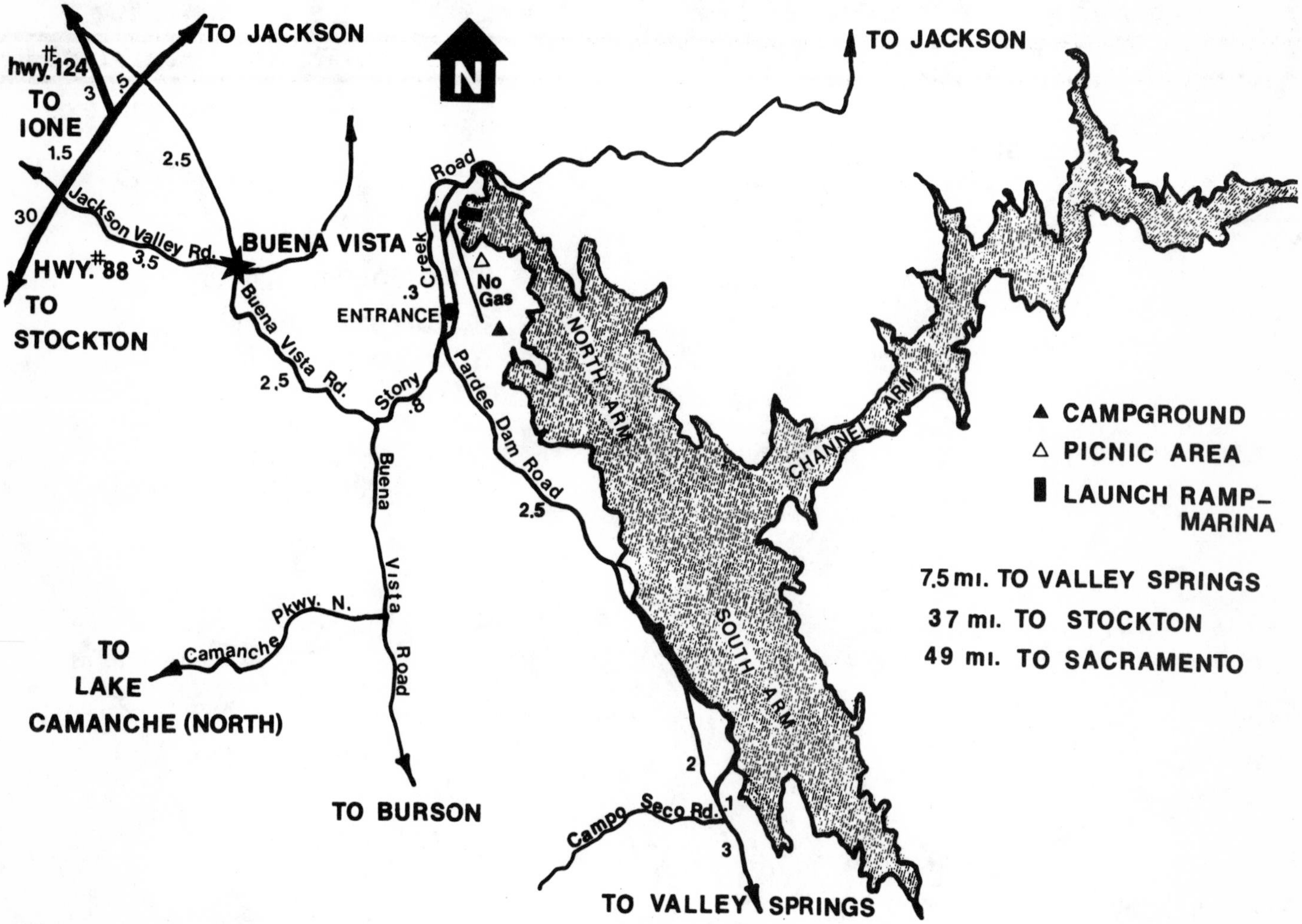
TO JACKSON
hwy. #124
TO IONE
1.5
3
5
2.5
30
Jackson Valley Rd.
3.5
HWY. #88
TO STOCKTON
BUENA VISTA
Buena Vista Rd.
2.5
Stony
.8
Creek
.3
Road
ENTRANCE
No Gas
Pardee Dam Road
2.5
Buena Vista Road
Pkwy. N.
Camanche
TO LAKE CAMANCHE (NORTH)
TO BURSON
TO JACKSON
N
NORTH ARM
CHANNEL ARM
SOUTH ARM
2
1
3
Campo Seco Rd.
TO VALLEY SPRINGS
▲ CAMPGROUND
△ PICNIC AREA
▮ LAUNCH RAMP–MARINA
7.5 mi. TO VALLEY SPRINGS
37 mi. TO STOCKTON
49 mi. TO SACRAMENTO

INFORMATION: Pardee Lake, Route 1, Box 224B, Ione 95640, Phone: 209-772-1472

CAMPING	BOATING	RECREATION	RESORTS
150 Developed Tent Sites 90 Trailer - R.V. Sites No Boat Camping	Boating Allowed Except No Waterskiing Launch Ramp Boat Rentals Full Service Marina	Fishing Fee: $1 Swimming in Pool Picnicking Hiking Tom Sawyer Fishing Island for Children Day Use Only: $2.00	Showers Laundromat Store Restaurant Playground

NEW HOGAN RESERVOIR

New Hogan was named after the old Hogan Dam, now underwater 950 feet upstream. The Reservoir provides about 90,000 acre feet of new water each year for irrigation and domestic water use. 50 miles of shoreline have numerous coves shaded by oak trees along the banks. There are 121 campsites for tents, R.V.s and trailers with toilets and showers at Acorn Campground next to the Entrance, 75 primitive campsites at Oak Knoll Campground, and 30 Boat-In campsites at Deer Flat. Three paved boat ramps with a total of 13 lanes are at the Marina. Nice picnic facilities and a swim area make this Lake ideal for all water sports. Waterskiing is allowed in the central Lake, but many of the coves have 5 MPH speed limits so fishing can also be enjoyed. Fishing is particularly good for trout near the Dam and bass in the two brushy tree coves in the southeast arm and upper arm of the Reservoir.

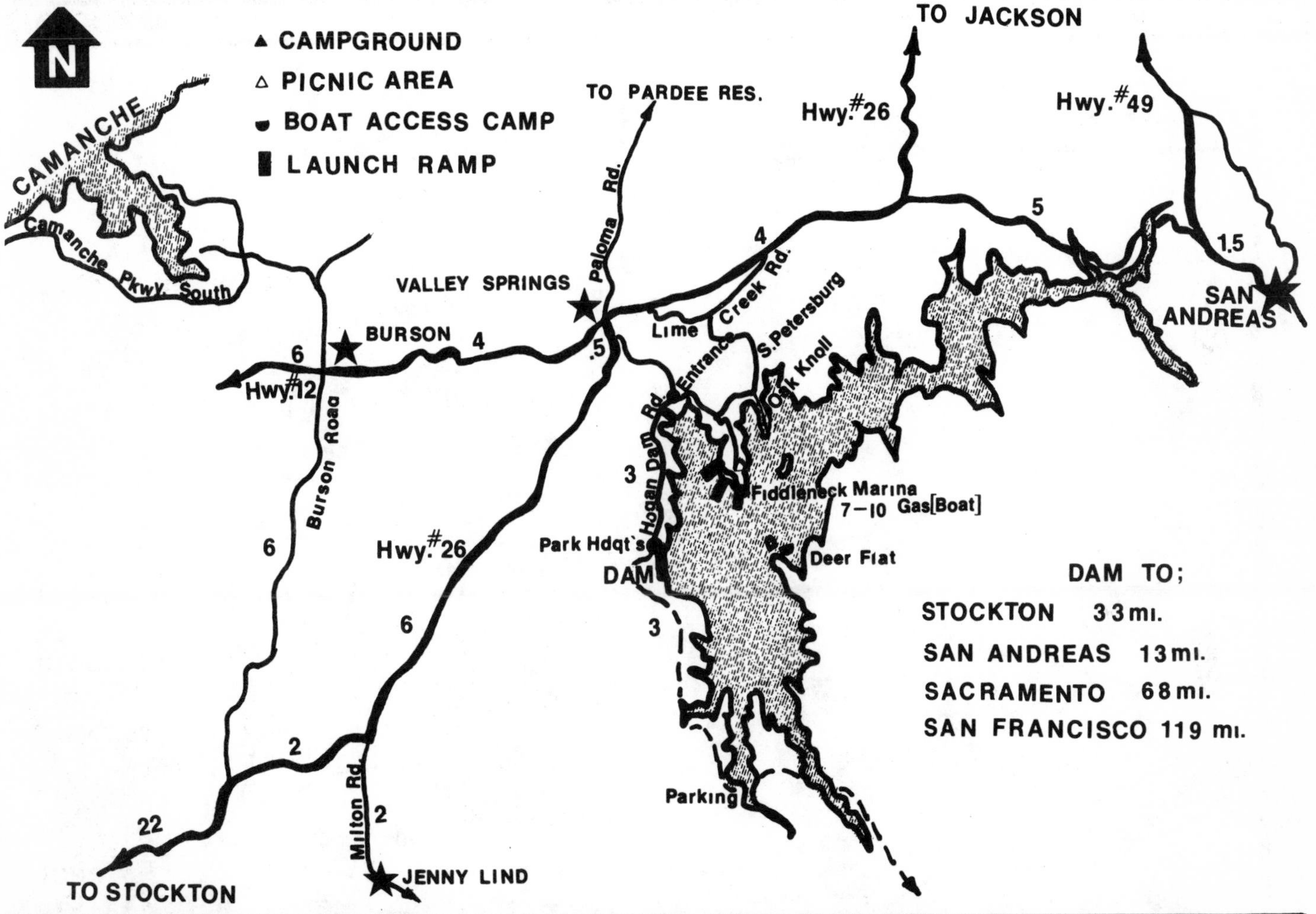

N
▲ CAMPGROUND
△ PICNIC AREA
BOAT ACCESS CAMP
LAUNCH RAMP
TO JACKSON
TO PARDEE RES.
Hwy.#26
Hwy.#49
CAMANCHE
Camanche Pkwy. South
Paloma Rd.
VALLEY SPRINGS
BURSON
Hwy.#12
Burson Road
Lime Creek Rd.
S.Petersburg
Entrance
Oak Knoll
Hogan Dam Rd.
Fiddleneck Marina
7-10
Gas[Boat]
Park Hdqt's
DAM
Deer Flat
SAN ANDREAS
Hwy.#26
Milton Rd.
Parking
JENNY LIND
TO STOCKTON
22
DAM TO;
STOCKTON 33mi.
SAN ANDREAS 13mi.
SACRAMENTO 68mi.
SAN FRANCISCO 119 mi.

INFORMATION: New Hogan Reservoir, Box 128, Valley Springs 95252, Ph. 209-772-1343

CAMPING	BOATING	RECREATION	RESORTS
121 Developed Sites for Tents, R.V.s and Trailers	All Boating Allowed	Fishing	Store
Fee: $3 a Day - April to September 30 Only	Launch Ramps	Swimming	Showers
Free Oct. 1 to March 31	Rental Baots	Picnicking	Gas
75 Undeveloped Sites are Free	Dry Storage	Hiking	Golf Course nearby
30 Boat Access Camps No Water - No Fee	Moorings	Nature Trails	
	Full Service Marina		

OAKWOOD LAKE

Oakwood Lake is an excavation quarry that has been made into a nice Family Resort with sandy beaches and the "world's longest waterslides", 7 in all. There are picnic areas, playground, groceries and tackle, showers, propane, gas, dump station, laundromats, movies and boat rentals. 360 spaces for R.V.s and Trailers are located on lawns going down to the beach with shade trees. Tent camping is also available. The facility is next to the San Joaquin River where all boating is allowed. Children and young people really enjoy the vacation atmosphere of this full facility Resort.

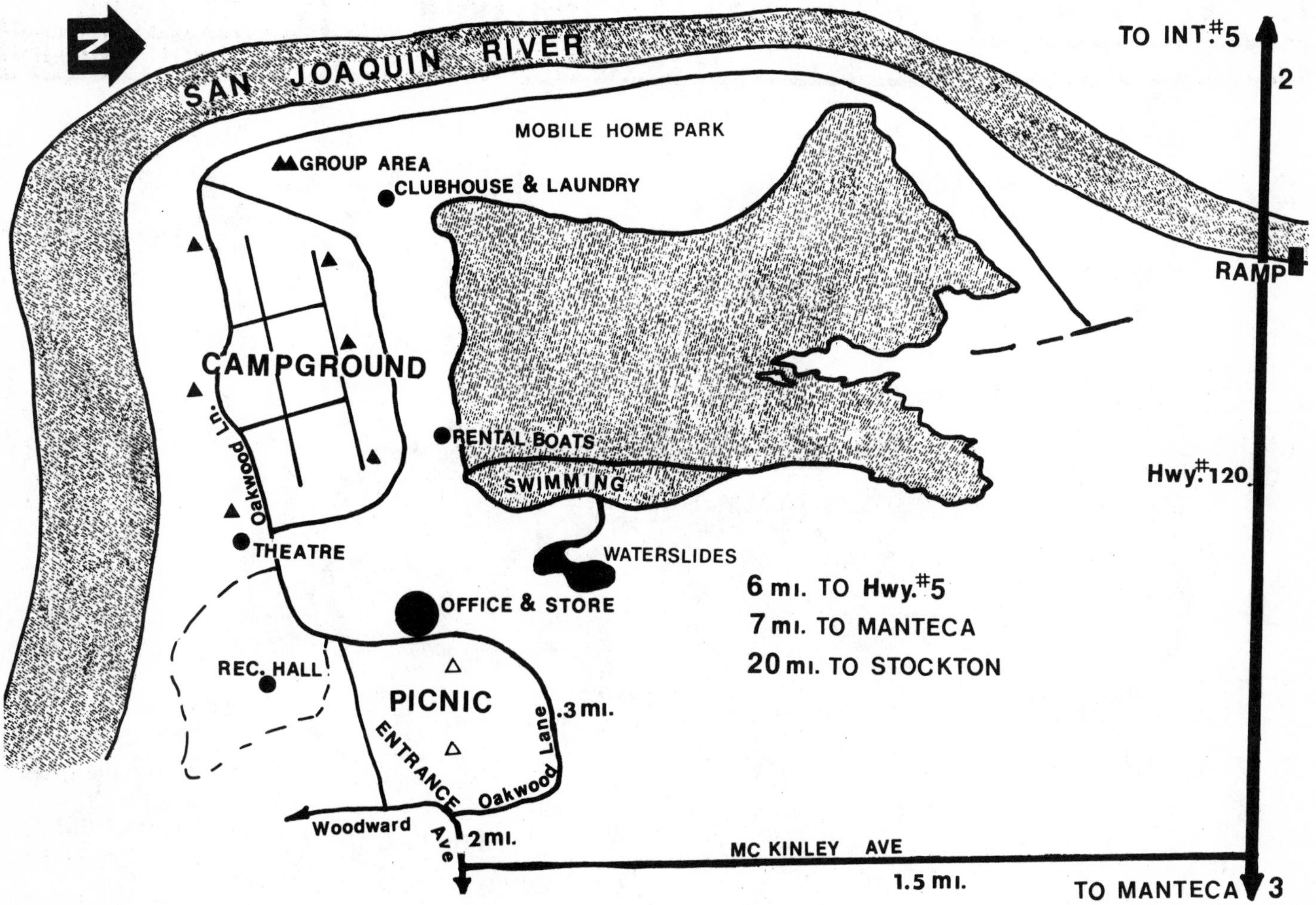
N
SAN JOAQUIN RIVER
TO INT.#5
2
MOBILE HOME PARK
GROUP AREA
CLUBHOUSE & LAUNDRY
RAMP
CAMPGROUND
Oakwood Ln.
RENTAL BOATS
SWIMMING
Hwy.#120
THEATRE
WATERSLIDES
OFFICE & STORE
6 mi. TO Hwy.#5
7 mi. TO MANTECA
20 mi. TO STOCKTON
REC. HALL
PICNIC
.3 mi.
ENTRANCE
Oakwood Lane
Woodward
Ave
2 mi.
MC KINLEY AVE
1.5 mi.
TO MANTECA
3

INFORMATION: Oakwood Lake, 874 E. Woodward, Manteca 95336, Phone: 209-239-9566

CAMPING	BOATING	RECREATION	RESORTS
360 Developed Sites for R.V.s and Trailers - Full Hookups Fee: Starting at $6 a Day Tent Camping Group Area	Boat Rentals: Paddleboats, Jet Skis Dry Storage for Boats and Trailers Launch Ramp Nearby All Boating Allowed on the River	Fishing Swimming Picnicking Full Vacation Facilities Scheduled Events - Dances, Parties, Contests 7 Waterslides	Store Showers Laundromat Recreation Halls Movies Planned Activities Mobile Home Park

WOODWARD RESERVOIR

Woodward Reservoir covers about 2,900 acres and the Lake is divided into areas to allow for waterskiing, sailing and fishing by speed limit restrictions which makes it enjoyable for all boaters. The shoreline is shallow with many trees in the water and coves and inlets. There are 78 campsites for tents, R.V.s and trailers and boat camping is allowed. A launch ramp, grocery store and snack bar are part of this facility operated by the Stanislaus County Regional Park Department.

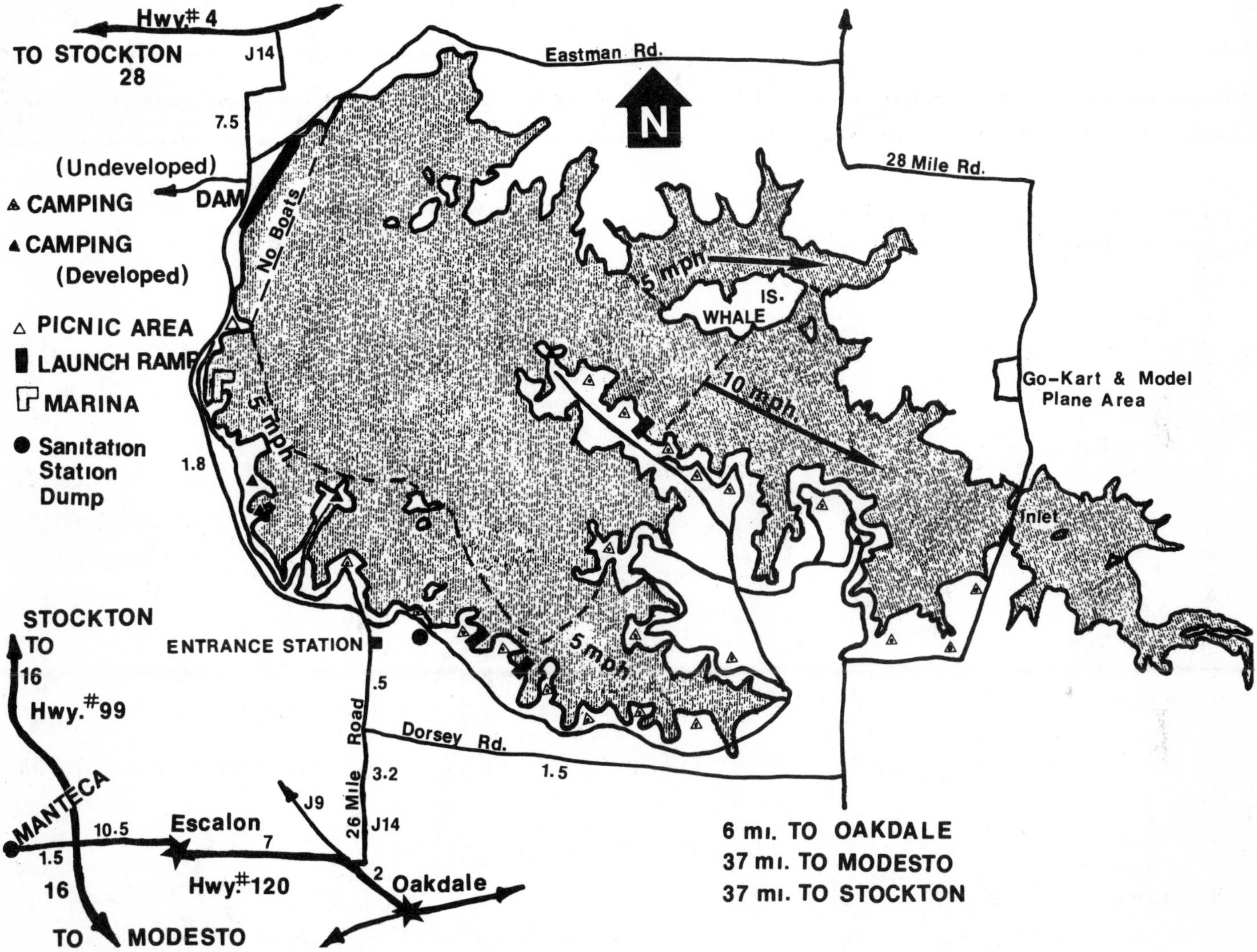
Hwy.# 4
TO STOCKTON
28
J14
7.5
(Undeveloped)
CAMPING
DAM
CAMPING
(Developed)
PICNIC AREA
LAUNCH RAMP
MARINA
Sanitation Station Dump
1.8
No Boats
5 mph.
Eastman Rd.
N
28 Mile Rd.
5 mph
IS.
WHALE
10 mph.
Go-Kart & Model Plane Area
Inlet
STOCKTON
TO
16
Hwy.#99
ENTRANCE STATION
.5
5 mph
Dorsey Rd.
1.5
26 Mile Road
3.2
J14
J9
MANTECA
10.5
Escalon
7
1.5
16
Hwy.#120
2
Oakdale
TO MODESTO
6 mi. TO OAKDALE
37 mi. TO MODESTO
37 mi. TO STOCKTON

INFORMATION: Woodward Reservoir, 14528 - 26 Mile Road, Oakdale 95361

CAMPING	BOATING	RECREATION	RESORTS
78 Developed Sites for Tents, R.V.s, and Trailers Fee: $3 - $5 a Day Boat Camping	All Boating Allowed See Restricted Speed Limit Areas Launch Ramps - $1.50 Rental Boats Full Service Marina	Fishing Swimming Picnicking Hiking Day Use Only: $1.50	Store Snack Bar

Located in the Gold Country, Lake Tulloch occupies two submerged valleys with 55 miles of shoreline. It is nestled between two high plateaus which are open to westerly winds making it a good Lake for sailing. Boating is very popular as the water is warm and clean. Basically there are two shorelines, North and South. Going towards Sonora on Highway 120, South Shore is the first exit. There are 16 developed campsites with covered tables, by reservation, and many other undeveloped sites. In addition, there are 60 level trailer or motorhome sites. At the Lake Tulloch Marina, there is a launch ramp, snack bar and grocery store and gas. North Shore, 5 miles from Highway 120, has two facilities, Poker Flat and Copper Cove. Poker Flat has a luxury motel on the water with boat docks, gas, launch ramp, swimming pool, restaurant and bar with live music in the summer. There is a private sandy beach in front of the motel. Copper Cove has a bar and restaurant on the water, launch ramp, moorings and gas dock.

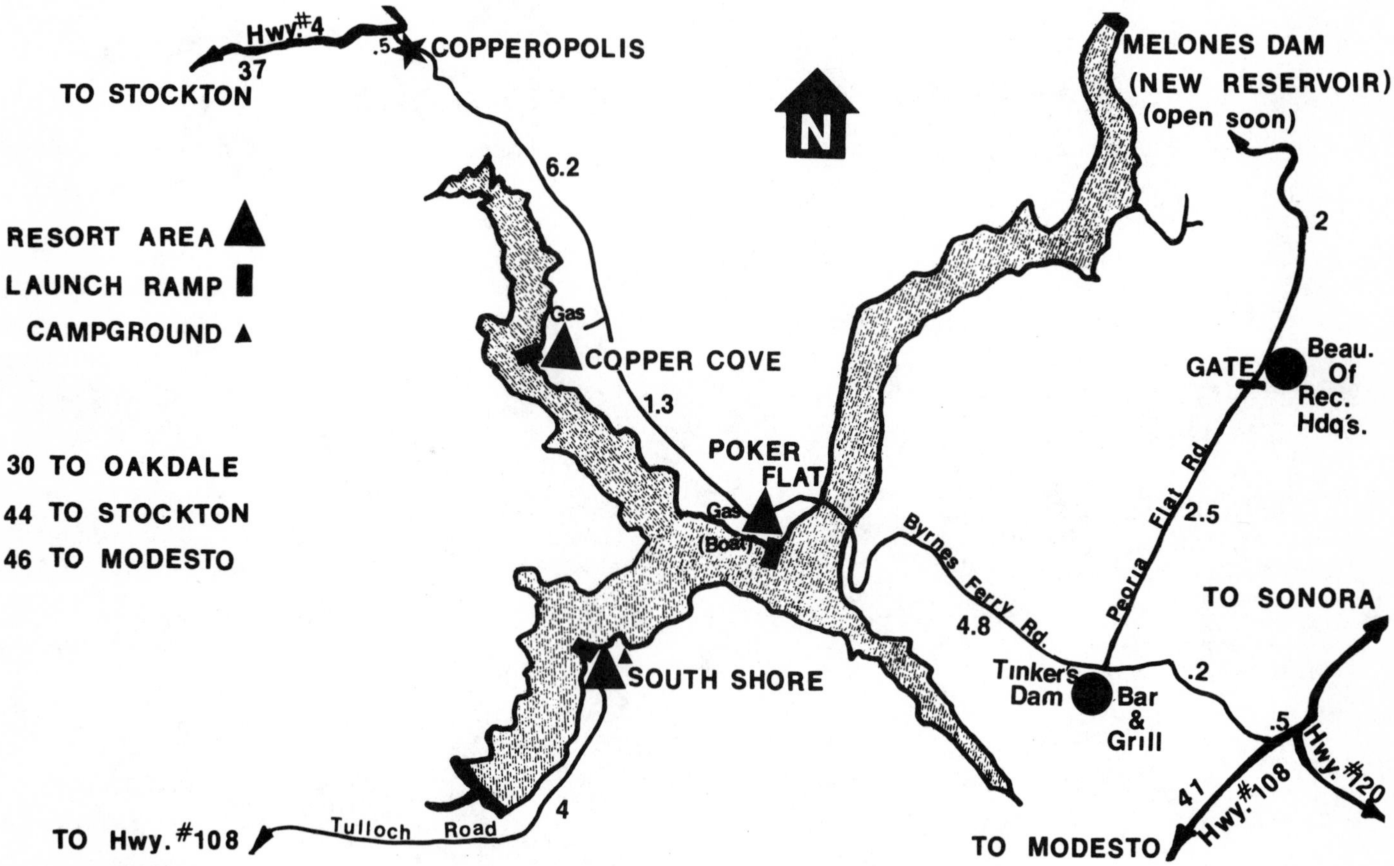
Hwy. #4
.5
COPPEROPOLIS
37
TO STOCKTON
N
MELONES DAM
(NEW RESERVOIR)
(open soon)
6.2
2
RESORT AREA
LAUNCH RAMP
CAMPGROUND
Gas
COPPER COVE
GATE
Beau. Of Rec. Hdq's.
1.3
30 TO OAKDALE
44 TO STOCKTON
46 TO MODESTO
POKER FLAT
Gas
(Boat)
Peoria Flat Rd.
2.5
Byrnes Ferry Rd.
4.8
TO SONORA
SOUTH SHORE
Tinker's Dam
Bar & Grill
.2
.5
Hwy. #120
41
Hwy. #108
TO Hwy. #108
Tulloch Road
4
TO MODESTO

INFORMATION: For Poker Flat, Box 31, Copperopolis 95228, Phone: 209-785-2287			
CAMPING	**BOATING**	**RECREATION**	**RESORTS**
South Shore - 16 Developed Sites for Tents, R.V.s and Trailers Call: 209-881-3335 for Reservations Numerous Undeveloped Sites	All Boating Allowed Launch Ramps	Fishing Swimming Picnicking Resort Facilities at Poker Flat	Motel - Poker Flat Restaurant Bar Store - South Shore Snack Shop

LYONS LAKE

Lyons Lake Resort is a lovely area with spacious, secluded campsites. There are 75 sites for tents, small trailers or R.V.s. Larger ones are not advised due to the road conditions into the Lake. Picnic tables and showers are available and a rocked launch ramp for cartop boats. Only electric motors are permitted on the Lake. Also a coffee shop and supply store are at the Resort. Trolling for trout can be excellent and the photographer will have some beautiful pictures from this area.

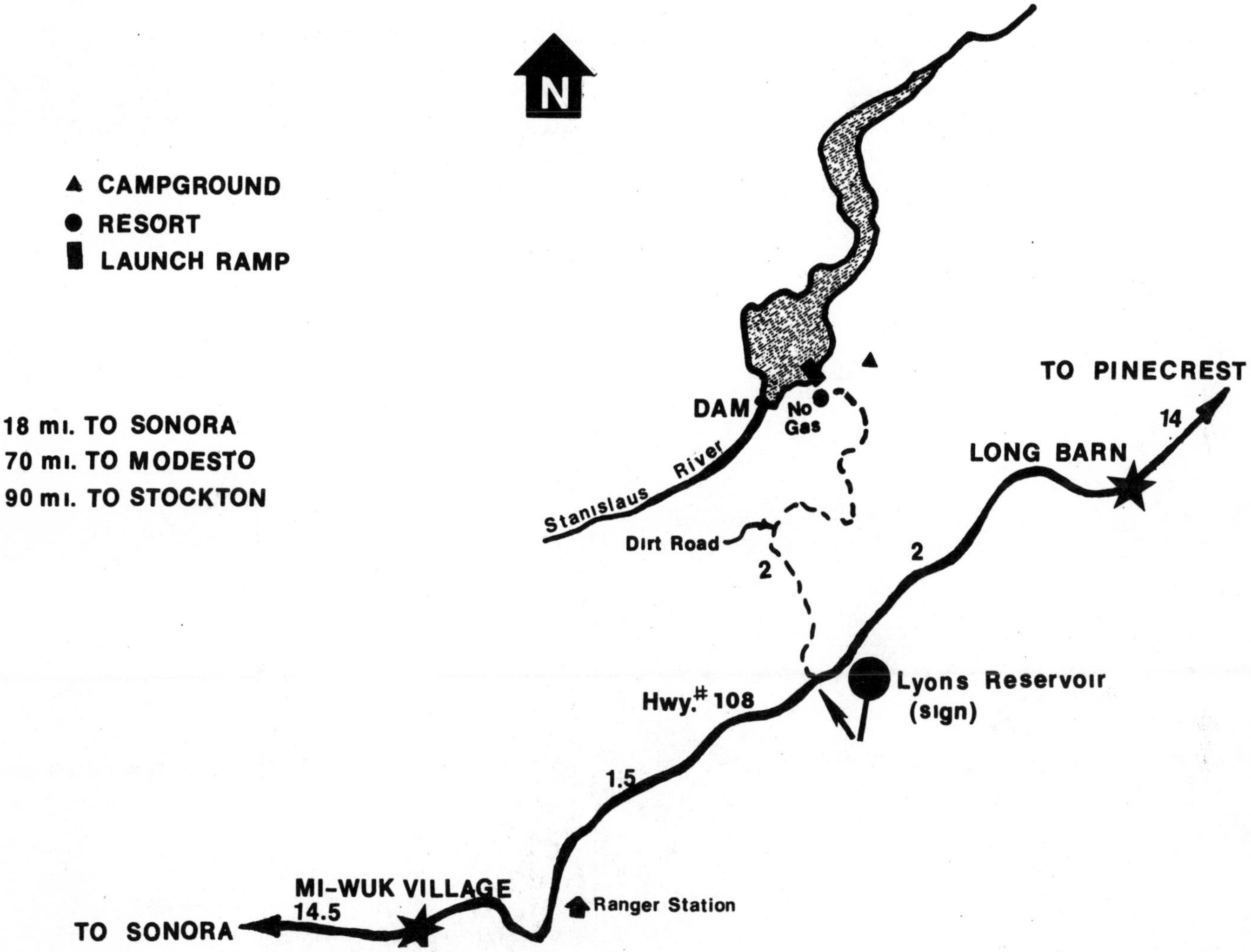
N
▲ CAMPGROUND
● RESORT
▮ LAUNCH RAMP
18 mi. TO SONORA
70 mi. TO MODESTO
90 mi. TO STOCKTON
DAM
No Gas
Stanislaus River
Dirt Road
2
TO PINECREST
14
LONG BARN
2
Lyons Reservoir (sign)
Hwy.# 108
1.5
MI-WUK VILLAGE
14.5
TO SONORA
Ranger Station

INFORMATION: Lyons Lake, Box 1196, Sonora 95370, Phone: 209-586-3724

CAMPING	BOATING	RECREATION	RESORTS
75 Sites for Tents, Small R.V.s and Trailers Fee: $3.75 a Day Reservations Accepted	Cartop Boats Electric Motors Only Launch Ramp Rental Boats	Fishing Picnicking Hiking	Showers Coffee Shop Store Fishing Tackle and Bait

PINECREST LAKE

Pinecrest Lake is at 5,600 feet elevation with 380 surface acres. The U. S. Forest Service operates Pinecrest Campground with 200 developed sites for tents, R.V.s and trailers. Reservations for this campground can be made through your local Ticketron outlet or write: Ticketron, P. O. Box 26430, San Francisco 94120. Meadowview Campground, on a first-come, first-serve basis, has 100 developed sites for tents, R.V.s and trailers, all with water, toilets, tables and barbecues. There are also 40 picnic units next to the beach. Pioneer Trail Group Camp for tents, campers and motorhomes (no trailers), accommodates 200 people maximum. Reservations are through Ticketron. Pinecrest Lake Resort has 2 and 3 bedroom luxury townhouses as well as housekeeping cabins and a well-stocked grocery store, a large sporting goods store, snack bar and restaurant, bar, amphitheater and tennis courts. Rental boats are available and all boating is allowed with a 20 MPH speed limit. There is a new wide launching ramp and a large swimming beach with life guards. Waterskiing is not permitted. Trout are planted weekly so fishing can be good. This is an ideal family area offering complete facilities.

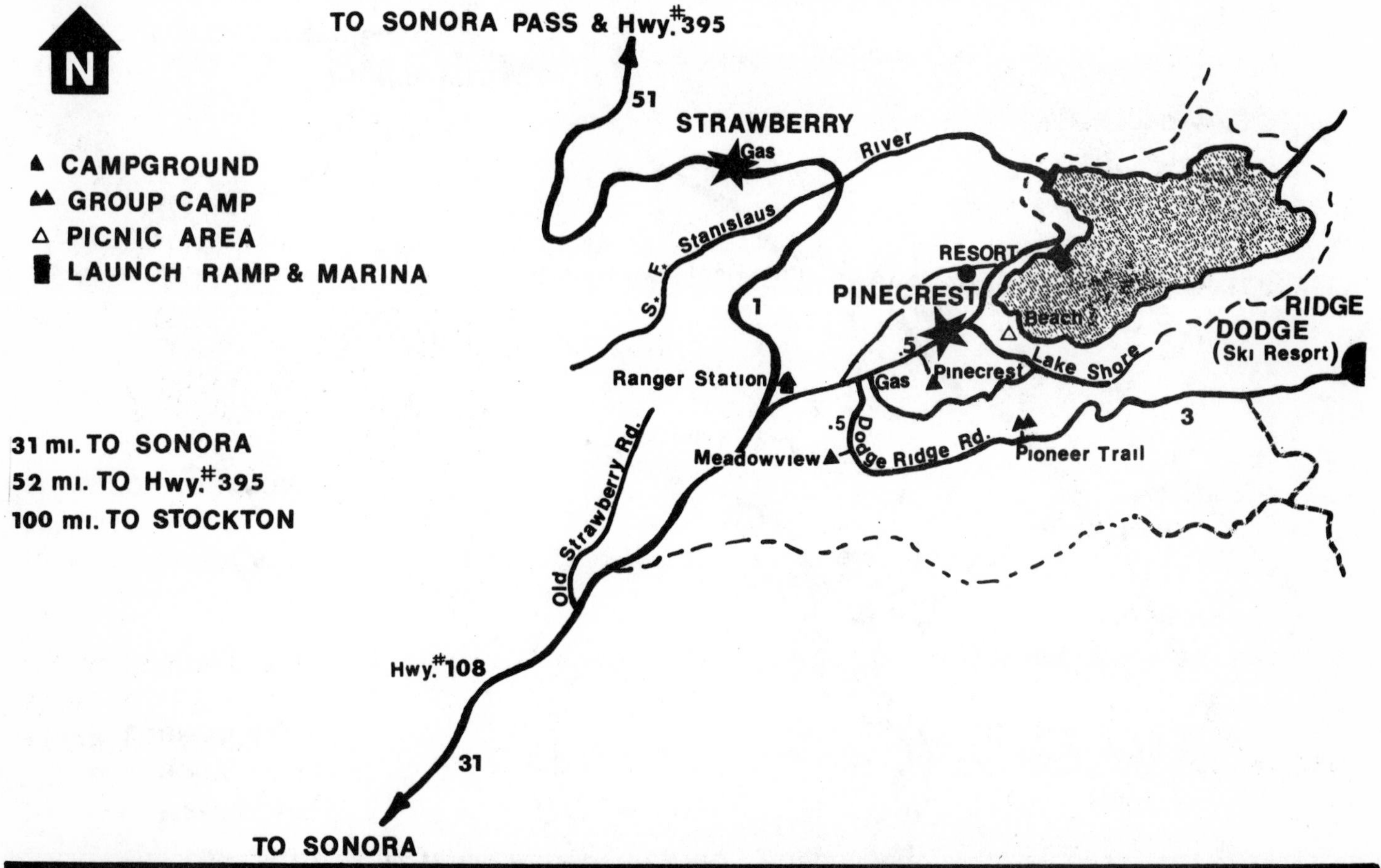
TO SONORA PASS & Hwy.#395
N
51
STRAWBERRY
Gas
River
CAMPGROUND
GROUP CAMP
PICNIC AREA
LAUNCH RAMP & MARINA
S. F. Stanislaus
RESORT
PINECREST
1
Beach
RIDGE
DODGE
(Ski Resort)
.5
Ranger Station
Gas
Pinecrest
Lake Shore
3
.5
Dodge Ridge Rd.
Pioneer Trail
Meadowview
31 mi. TO SONORA
52 mi. TO Hwy.#395
100 mi. TO STOCKTON
Old Strawberry Rd.
Hwy.#108
31
TO SONORA

INFORMATION: Summit Ranger District, Star Route, Box 1295, Sonora 95370

CAMPING	BOATING	RECREATION	RESORTS
300 Developed Sites for Tents, R.V.s and Trailers Fees: $3 - $4 a Day Group Camp - 200 people maximum	All Boating Allowed Up to 20 MPH Speed Limit No Waterskiing Launch Ramp Boat Rentals Full Service Marina	Fishing Swimming Picnicking Hiking Bicycle Roads Tennis Movies	Pinecrest Lake Resort P. O. Box 1216 Pinecrest 95364 Phone: 209-965-3411

BEARDSLEY RESERVOIR

Beardsley Reservoir is located at 3,405 feet elevation. The road is paved all the way in, and there is a 4-lane concrete launch ramp, toilets, drinking water and a 44-space paved parking lot. Primitive camping is on the North side of the Dam in very rugged terrain. Big boulders, rock and sand shoreline and trees just above the high water mark make for a beautiful setting. There are 27 picnic sites near the launch ramp. The winds can be very strong in the afternoon so fishing is best in the morning. This Reservoir is a delightful spot to spend a day if you are in the Pinecrest area with good sailing and waterskiing.

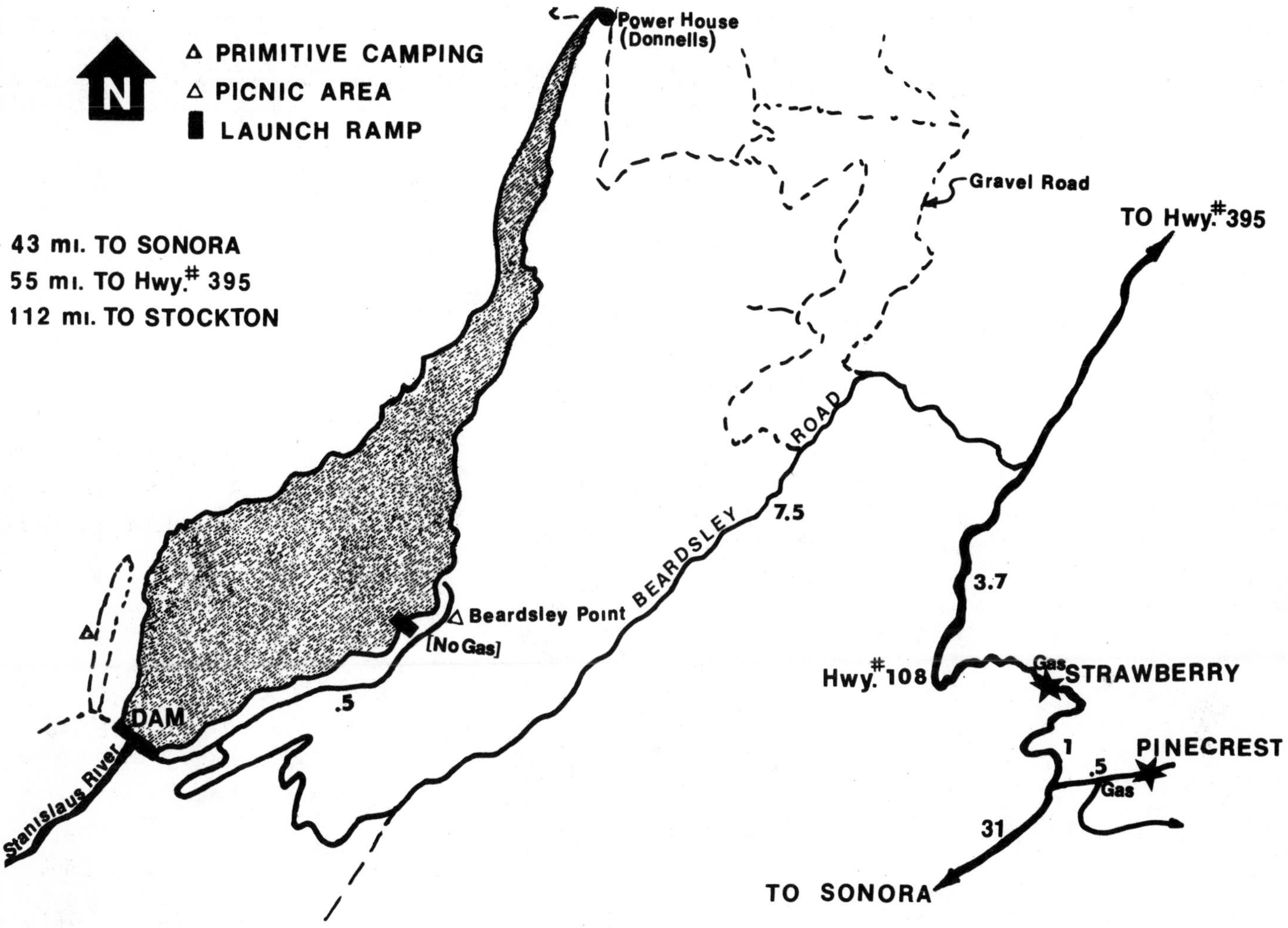
N
PRIMITIVE CAMPING
PICNIC AREA
LAUNCH RAMP
43 mi. TO SONORA
55 mi. TO Hwy.# 395
112 mi. TO STOCKTON
Power House (Donnells)
Gravel Road
TO Hwy.# 395
BEARDSLEY ROAD
7.5
3.7
Beardsley Point
[No Gas]
.5
DAM
Stanislaus River
Hwy.# 108
Gas
STRAWBERRY
1
.5
PINECREST
Gas
31
TO SONORA

INFORMATION: Summit Ranger District, U. S. Forest Service, Box 1295, Sonora			
CAMPING	**BOATING**	**RECREATION**	**RESORTS**
Primitive Camping Only	All Boating Allowed Launch Ramp	Fishing Picnicking Swimming	

LAKE MERRITT

Lake Merritt, a 160-acre saltwater Lake, was actually an arm of San Francisco Bay at the end of San Antonio Creek in Oakland. A Dam was built in 1874 to form Lake Merritt. The Lake is 6 to 10 feet deep with 3.18 miles of shoreline. It is the home of Lake Merritt Sailing Club, Lake Merritt Rowing Club and Oakland Women's Rowing Club. Rentals of rowboats, sailboats, canoes and paddle boats are available, and there is a launch ramp and hoist with several floating docks. For over 25 years, Lake Merritt has provided sailing and canoeing lessons for children and adults. The Merritt Queen, an authentic replica of a Mississippi Riverboat, leaves from the Sailboat House for 30-minute historical tours every day during summer and on weekends throughout the year. It can also be chartered by schools, churches and other organized groups. This is a good sailing Lake with mostly steady light winds. Picnicking areas dot the grassy shoreline around the Lake.

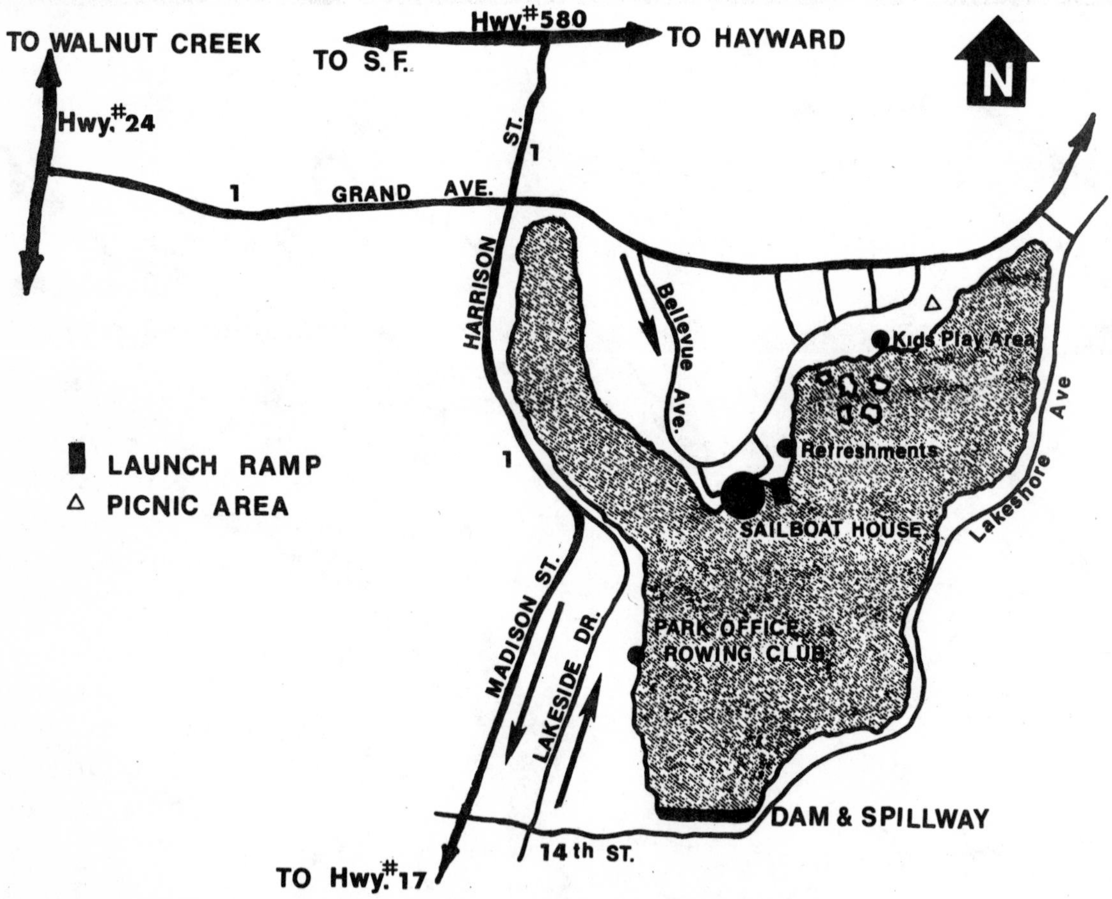
TO WALNUT CREEK
Hwy.#580
TO S.F.
TO HAYWARD
N
Hwy.#24
ST.
1
1
GRAND AVE.
HARRISON
Bellevue Ave.
Kids Play Area
Ave
Lakeshore
1
LAUNCH RAMP
PICNIC AREA
Refreshments
SAILBOAT HOUSE
MADISON ST.
LAKESIDE DR.
PARK OFFICE
ROWING CLUB
DAM & SPILLWAY
14th ST.
TO Hwy.#17

INFORMATION: Lake Merritt Park, 1520 Lakeside Dr., Oakland, Phone: 415-444-3807

CAMPING	BOATING	RECREATION	RESORTS
No Camping Day Use Only	All Boating Allowed to 10 HP - 15 MPH Primarily Sailing, Rowing & Canoeing Launch Ramp Hoist - Dry Storage Boat Rentals Sailing & Canoeing Lessons	Picnicking Bicycle & Walking Paths	Adjoining Full Facilities in Oakland

LAFAYETTE RESERVOIR

Lafayette Reservoir is a pretty Lake nestled in the rolling hills of Lafayette in Contra Costa County. Motorboats and swimming are not permitted, and you can only bring in cartop sailboats, canoes, kayaks, fishing boats and some types of inflatable boats as there is no launch ramp. A bait shop, boat and canoe rentals, fishing docks, bicycle and hiking trails are part of this facility. 135 picnic tables, some with barbecues, surround the Reservoir, and several are accessible only by boat or path. The Department of Fish and Game plant 60,000 trout a year and the Lake also has black bass, catfish and crappie. The Reservoir is owned and maintained by the East Bay Municipal Utility District and is for Day Use only.

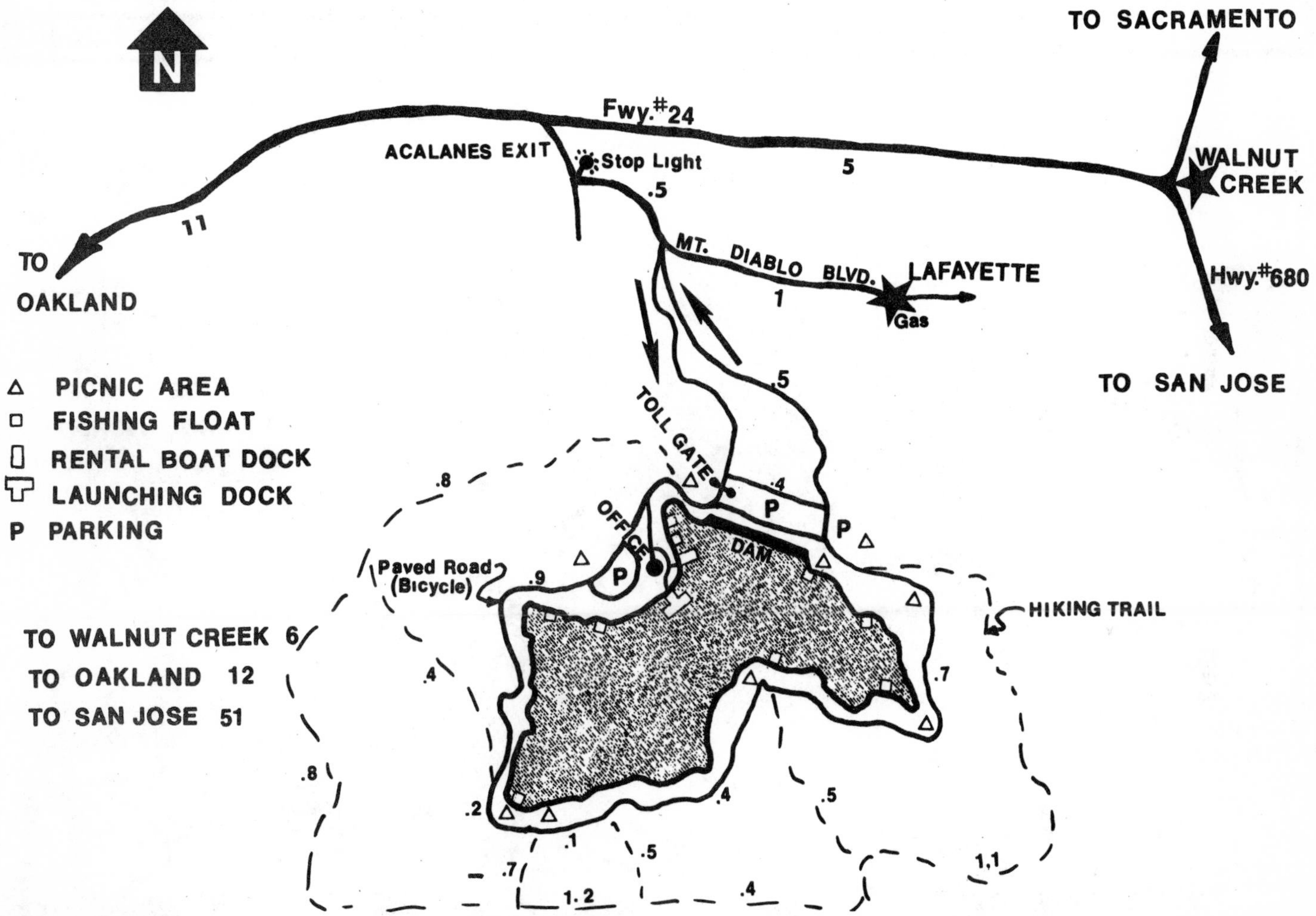

N
TO SACRAMENTO
Fwy.#24
ACALANES EXIT
Stop Light
.5
5
WALNUT CREEK
11
TO OAKLAND
MT. DIABLO BLVD.
LAFAYETTE
1
Gas
Hwy.#680
TO SAN JOSE
.5
TOLL GATE
PICNIC AREA
FISHING FLOAT
RENTAL BOAT DOCK
LAUNCHING DOCK
P PARKING
OFFICE
DAM
Paved Road (Bicycle)
HIKING TRAIL
TO WALNUT CREEK 6
TO OAKLAND 12
TO SAN JOSE 51

INFORMATION: EBMUD, Box 24055, Oakland 94623, Phone: 415-284-9669

CAMPING	BOATING	RECREATION	RESORTS
No Camping Day Use Only	Cartop Boats Fee: $2 a Day, $15 a Year, $7.50 a Season. Boat Rentals - Canoes Rowboats, Paddle Boats, Electric Motorboats	Fishing Picnicking Hiking Bicycling Parking Fee: $1.00 on Weekdays, $2.00 on Weekends $30 - Annual Pass $15 - Season Pass	

SAN PABLO RESERVOIR

CLOSED UNTIL 1981 FOR REPAIRS TO DAM

...o Reservoir is a day-use facility only. The northern end of the Lake is she... grove of eucalyptus trees which makes a very pretty setting. Sailing and rowing ... are allowed but no body contact with the water. You can launch sailboats ... rowboats. There are nice picnic sites overlooking the water with 110 table... Trails around the Reservoir lead to Tilden and Briones Regional Parks and ... the hiker, horseback rider and bicyclist.

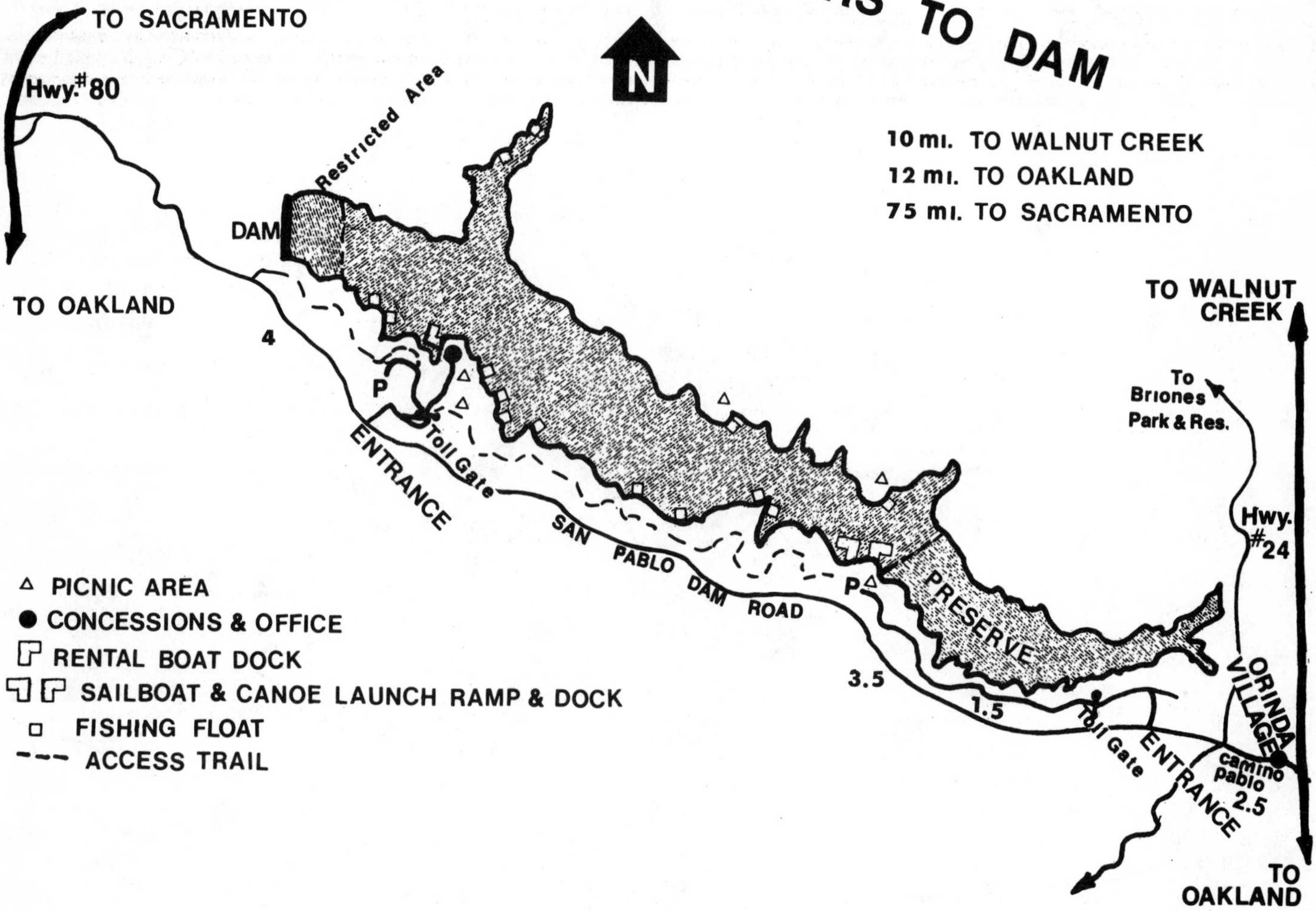
TO SACRAMENTO
Hwy.#80
Restricted Area
N
DAM
TO OAKLAND
4
P
Toll Gate
ENTRANCE
SAN PABLO DAM ROAD
P
PRESERVE
3.5
1.5
Toll Gate
ENTRANCE
camino pablo
2.5
ORINDA VILLAGE
TO OAKLAND
TO WALNUT CREEK
To Briones Park & Res.
Hwy. #24
10 mi. TO WALNUT CREEK
12 mi. TO OAKLAND
75 mi. TO SACRAMENTO
△ PICNIC AREA
● CONCESSIONS & OFFICE
RENTAL BOAT DOCK
SAILBOAT & CANOE LAUNCH RAMP & DOCK
□ FISHING FLOAT
--- ACCESS TRAIL

INFORMATION: EBMUD, P. O. Box 24055, Oakland, Phone: 415-223-1661

CAMPING	BOATING	RECREATION	RESORTS
No Camping Day Use Only	Privately Owned Sailboats & Canoes Only Launch Ramp Dock Fee: $2 a Day Boat Rentals - Rowboats with or without motors	Fishing Picnicking Hiking Bicycling and Horseback Riding Trails Parking: $1 a Day	

CONTRA LOMA RESERVOIR

Contra Loma Regional Park covers an area of 772 acres with 71 surface acres for the Lake. Swimming is allowed from May 5 to October 1 between 11:00 a.m. and 6:00 p.m. with a life guard present. Boating is limited to sail, row or electric motors only, and boats can be no longer than 17 feet. There are hiking, bicycle and horseback riding trails and a boat launch. Rowboats are for rent, and picnic facilities have 60 tables, barbecues, drinking water and toilets. Group reservations are available. This Reservoir is for Day Use Only from 7:00 a.m. to 9:00 p.m.

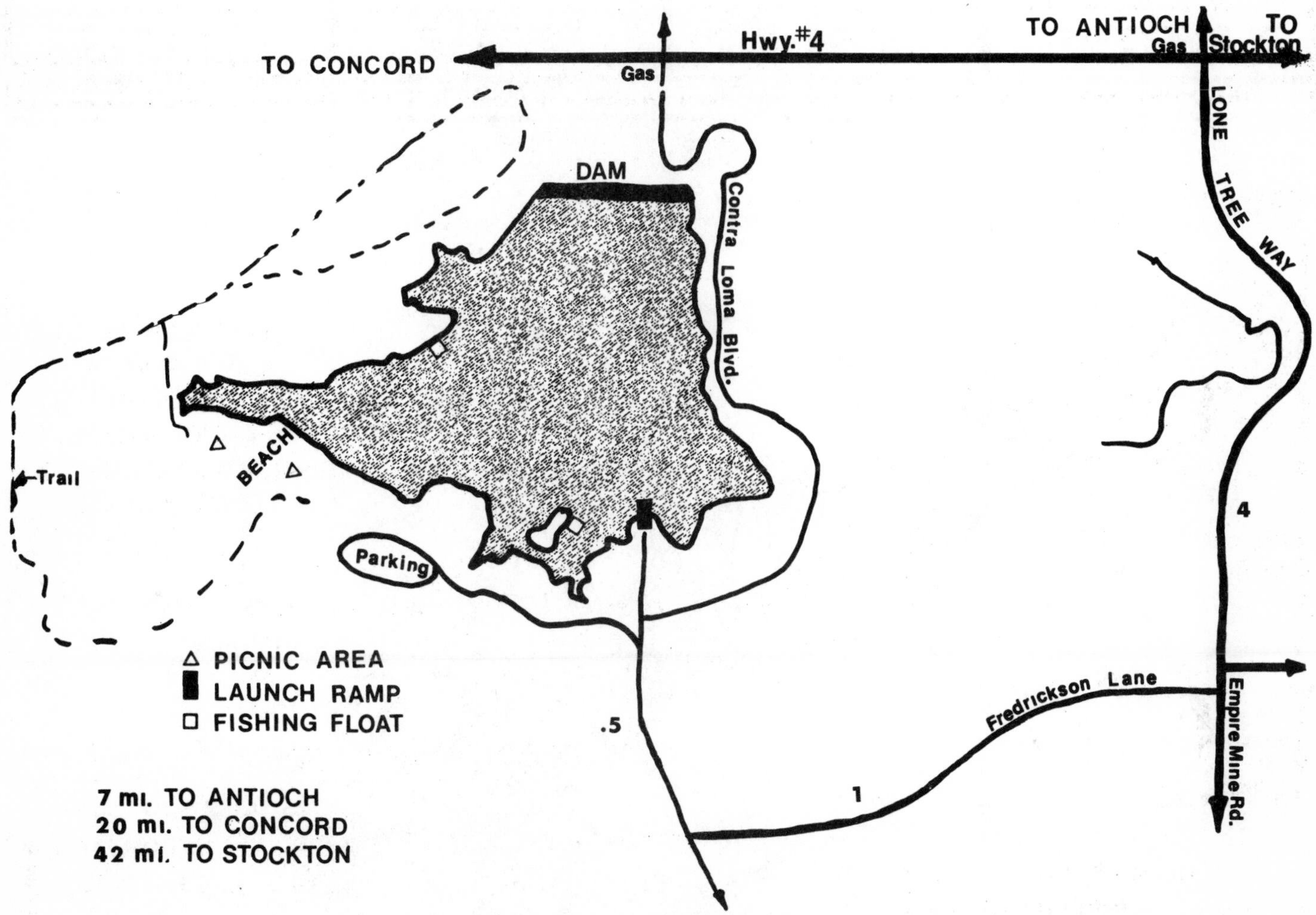
TO CONCORD
Hwy.#4
TO ANTIOCH
TO Stockton
Gas
Gas
LONE TREE WAY
DAM
Contra Loma Blvd.
Trail
BEACH
Parking
4
.5
1
Fredrickson Lane
Empire Mine Rd.
△ PICNIC AREA
LAUNCH RAMP
□ FISHING FLOAT
7 mi. TO ANTIOCH
20 mi. TO CONCORD
42 mi. TO STOCKTON

INFORMATION: East Bay Reg. Parks, 11500 Skyline, Oakland, Phone: 415-531-9300

CAMPING	BOATING	RECREATION	RESORTS
No Camping Day Use Only	Carry-In Sailboats & Rowboats Electric Motors Only Rental Boats Launch Ramp Fee: $10-Year with Inspection - Valid at all East Bay Regional Parks	Fishing - $1 a Day or $7.50 a Year - Valid at all East Bay Regional Parks Swimming - Hiking Bicycle & Horseback Riding Trails Parking: $1-Weekdays $2-Weekends, Holidays	

LAKE MERCED

Lake Merced is a nice small facility for Day Use only. If you bring your own sailboat, it can be from 8 feet to 18 feet in length. There is no ramp, but a hoist and floats. You can rent sailboats or rowboats at the Lake Merced Boathouse, which also offers excellent sailing courses by accredited instructors. There are picnic tables, barbecues, drinking water and toilets available as well as hiking and bicycle trails. Trout are planted once a week in season, but swimming is not permitted.

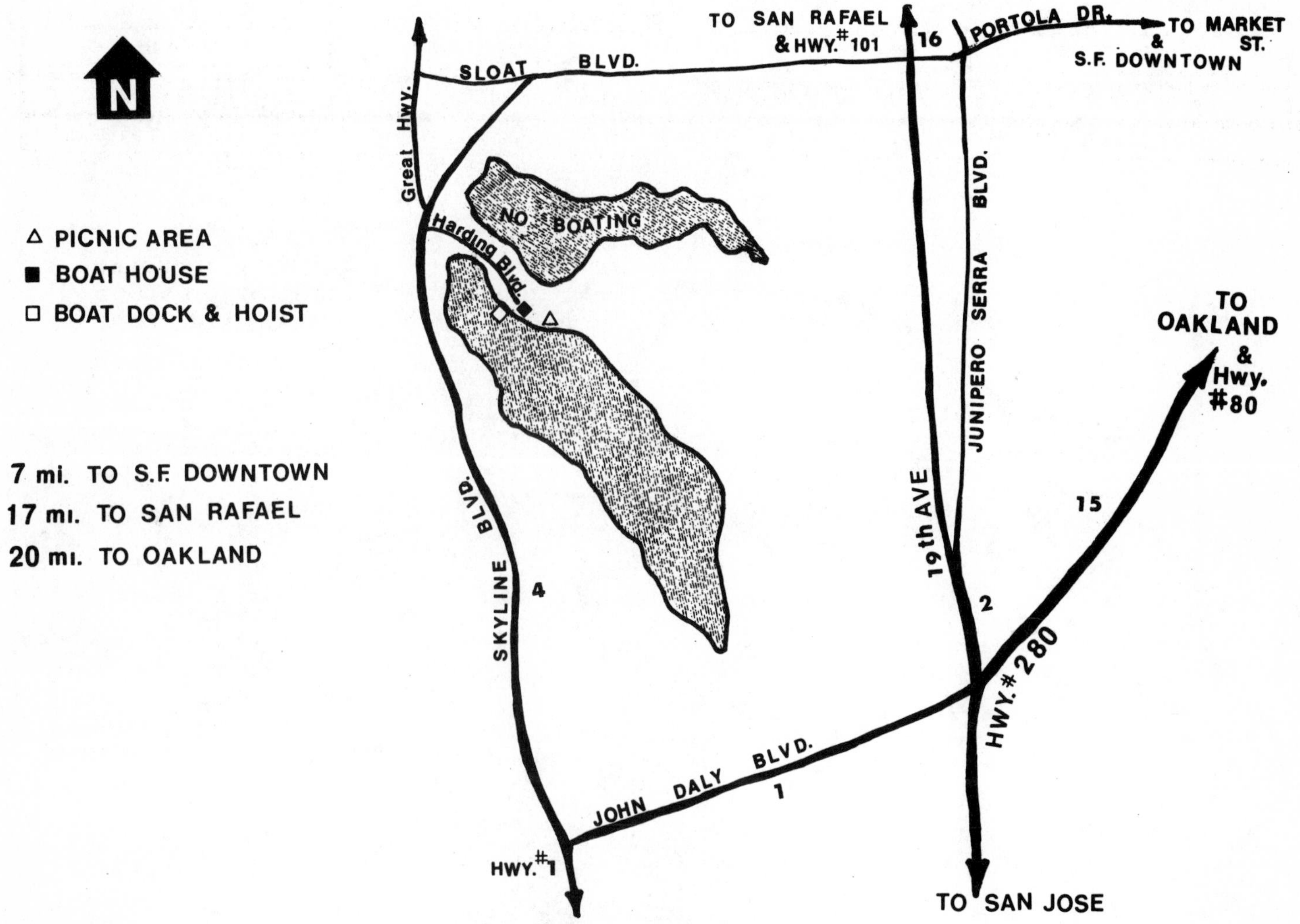
N
△ PICNIC AREA
■ BOAT HOUSE
□ BOAT DOCK & HOIST
7 mi. TO S.F. DOWNTOWN
17 mi. TO SAN RAFAEL
20 mi. TO OAKLAND
TO SAN RAFAEL & HWY.#101
16
PORTOLA DR.
TO MARKET ST. & S.F. DOWNTOWN
SLOAT BLVD.
Great Hwy.
Harding Blvd.
NO BOATING
JUNIPERO SERRA BLVD.
19th AVE
TO OAKLAND & Hwy. #80
15
2
HWY.# 280
SKYLINE BLVD.
4
JOHN DALY BLVD.
1
HWY.#1
TO SAN JOSE

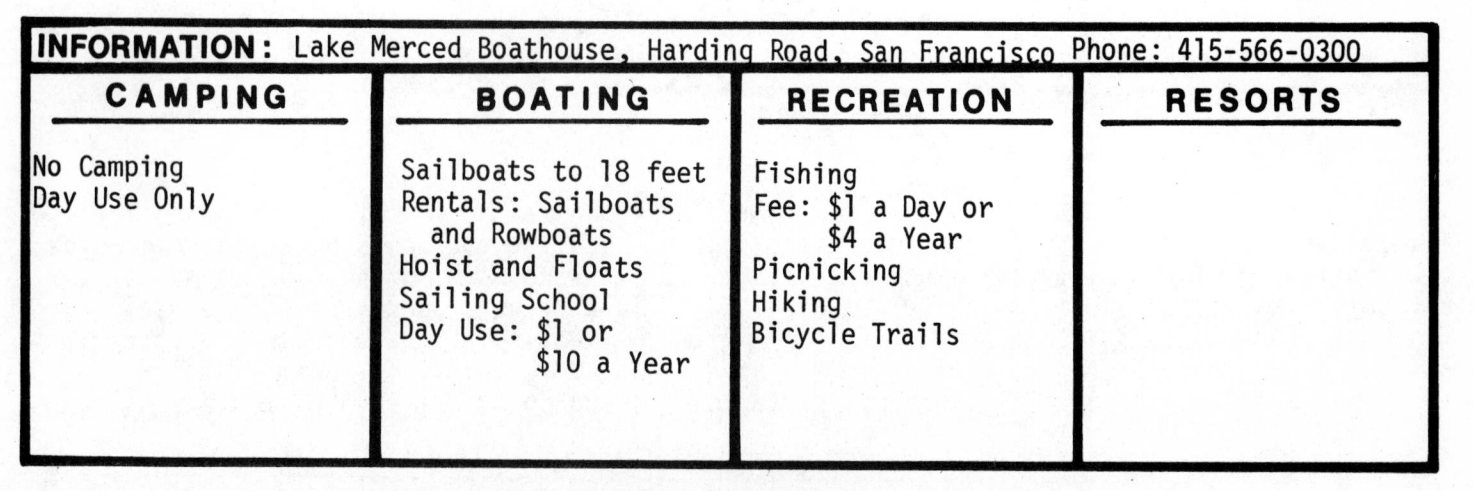

INFORMATION: Lake Merced Boathouse, Harding Road, San Francisco Phone: 415-566-0300

CAMPING	BOATING	RECREATION	RESORTS
No Camping Day Use Only	Sailboats to 18 feet Rentals: Sailboats and Rowboats Hoist and Floats Sailing School Day Use: $1 or $10 a Year	Fishing Fee: $1 a Day or $4 a Year Picnicking Hiking Bicycle Trails	

CULL CANYON RESERVOIR

In 1966, Cull Canyon Reservoir and Park received the Governor's Design Award for Excellence and Beauty for Recreational Development in California. This 100-acre Park has a 19-acre Lake and a special Lagoon for swimming with a sandy beach. There are hiking and horseback riding trails. The picnic area has 28 tables, barbecue pits, water and a volleyball court. You can carry in rowboats and sailboats up to 17 feet and only electric motors are allowed. The Lake is stocked with large-mouth bass, black crappie, sunfish and catfish. Cull Canyon is for Day Use Only.

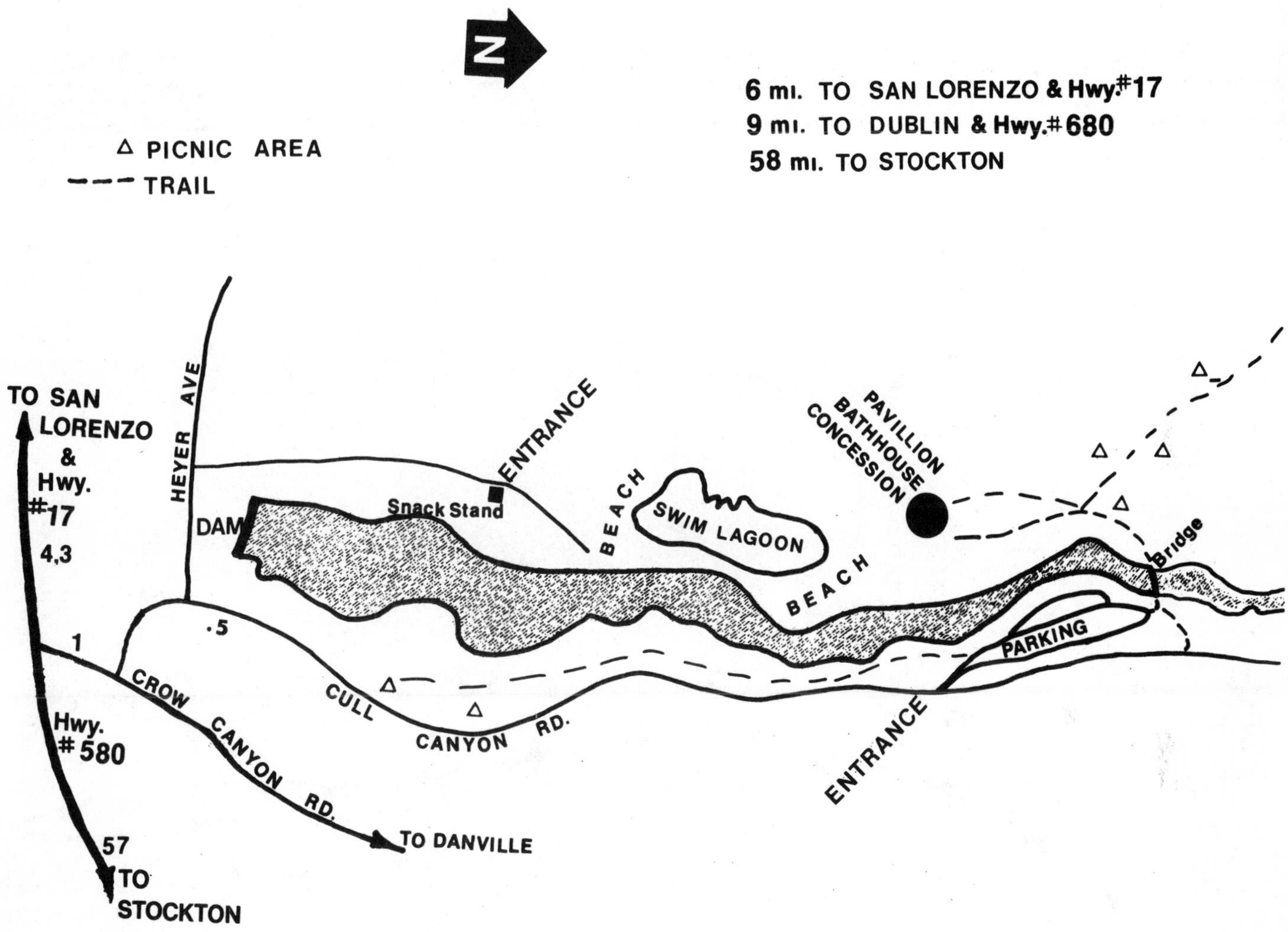
N
6 mi. TO SAN LORENZO & Hwy.#17
9 mi. TO DUBLIN & Hwy.#680
58 mi. TO STOCKTON
△ PICNIC AREA
--- TRAIL
TO SAN LORENZO & Hwy. #17
4,3
1
Hwy. #580
57
TO STOCKTON
HEYER AVE
DAM
.5
CROW CANYON RD.
TO DANVILLE
CULL CANYON RD.
ENTRANCE
Snack Stand
BEACH
SWIM LAGOON
PAVILLION
BATHHOUSE
CONCESSION
BEACH
PARKING
Bridge
ENTRANCE

INFORMATION: East Bay Reg. Parks, 11500 Skyline, Oakland, Phone: 415-531-9300

CAMPING	BOATING	RECREATION	RESORTS
No Camping Day Use Only	Carry-In Sailboats & Rowboats to 17 feet Electric Motors Only Fee: $10 - Year with Inspection - Valid at all East Bay Regional Parks	Fishing - $1 a Day or $7.50 a Year - Valid at all East Bay Regional Parks Swimming in Lagoon - Adults - $1 and Children - 25¢ May 5 to October 1 Hiking Trails	Picnicking Groups of 50 or more can Reserve Call: 415-531-9043

DON CASTRO RESERVOIR

Don Castro Reservoir is another delightful part of the East Bay Regional Park System. It is about 100 acres with a 25 surface acre Lake. There is a sandy lagoon for swimming. Fishing, hiking and picnic tables are available as well as a Snack Bar. Boating is for carry-in sailboats and rowboats up to 17 feet, electric motors only. This Lake is for Day Use Only.

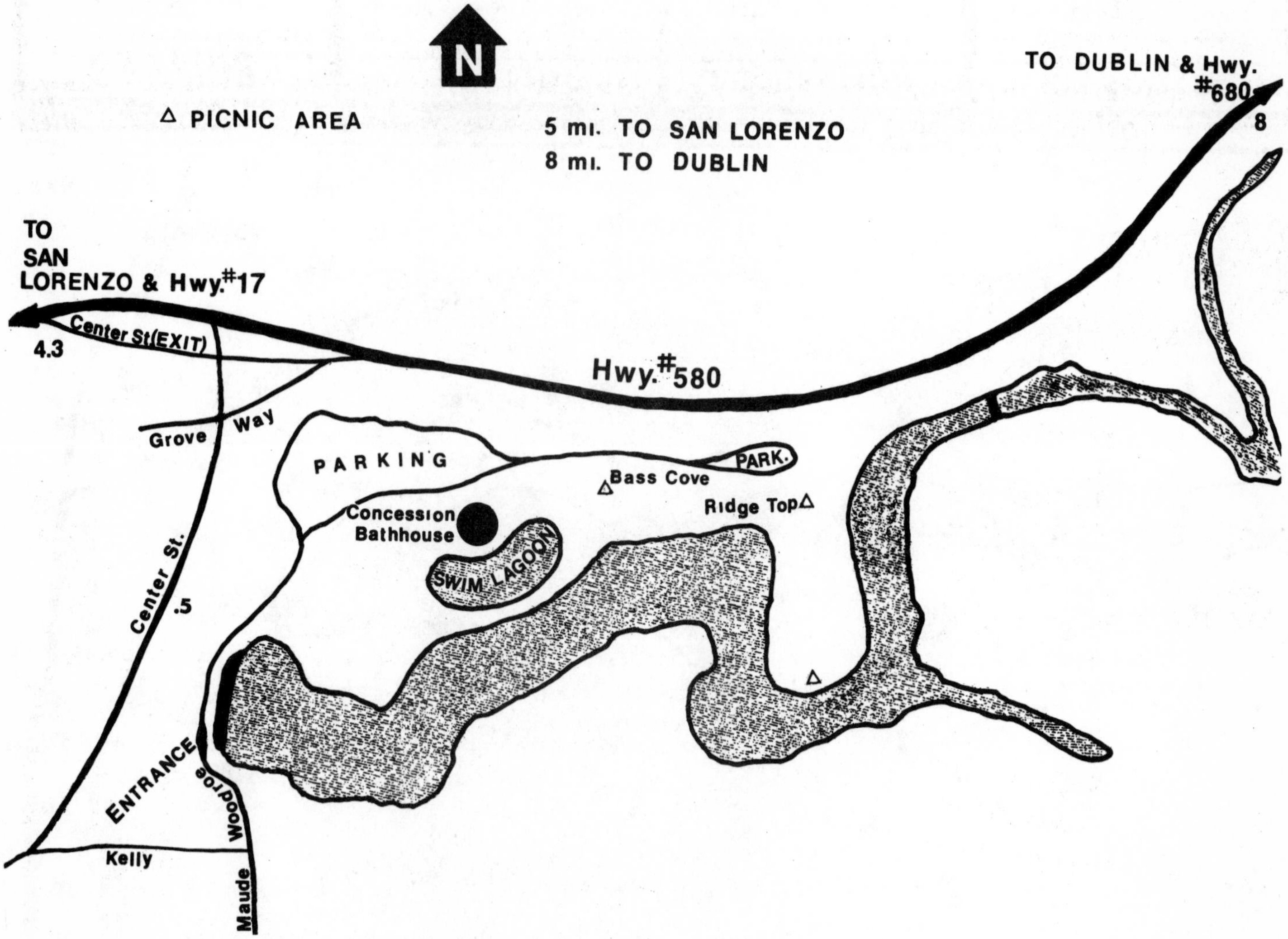
N
△ PICNIC AREA
5 mi. TO SAN LORENZO
8 mi. TO DUBLIN
TO DUBLIN & Hwy. #680
8
TO SAN LORENZO & Hwy.#17
Center St(EXIT)
4.3
Hwy.#580
Grove Way
PARKING
PARK.
Bass Cove
Ridge Top
Concession Bathhouse
SWIM LAGOON
Center St.
.5
ENTRANCE
Woodroe
Kelly
Maude

INFORMATION: East Bay Reg. Parks, 11500 Skyline, Oakland, Phone: 415-531-9300

CAMPING	BOATING	RECREATION	RESORTS
No Camping Day Use Only	Carry-In Sailboats and Rowboats to 17 feet Electric Motors Only Fee: Year's Permit - $5 - Valid at All East Bay Regional Parks	Fishing - Fee: $1 a Day or $7.50 a yr. Valid at All East Bay Regional Parks Swimming in Lagoon - Fee: $1 - Adults & 25¢ - Children Hiking Picnicking	Snack Bar

SHADOW CLIFFS RESERVOIR

Shadow Cliffs Reservoir has been transformed from a bleak sand and gravel quarry into a lovely recreation facility. It is part of the East Bay Regional Park District and is a total of 249 acres with a 90 acre Lake. There is a nice sandy swim beach and a launch ramp for boats up to 17 feet. Lifeguards are present from May 5 through September 30. Picnic tables and barbecues are around the Lake and a 1-1/2 acre grassy area. Rental boats are available and there is a special area for Model Boats. Park hours are from 8:00 a.m. to Dark. This Reservoir is for Day Use Only.

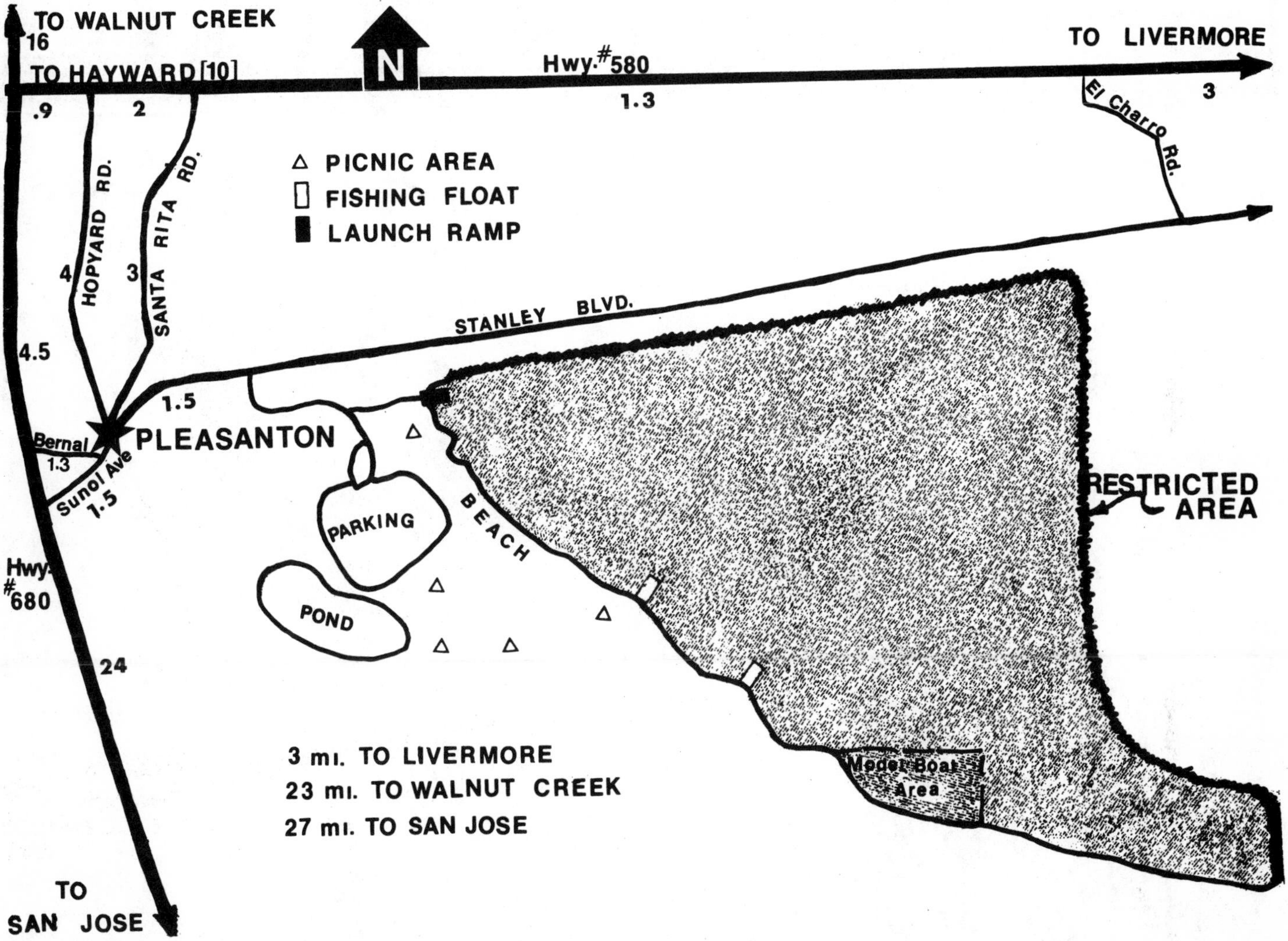

TO WALNUT CREEK
16
TO HAYWARD [10]
N
Hwy.#580
TO LIVERMORE
.9
2
1.3
3
El Charro Rd.
HOPYARD RD.
SANTA RITA RD.
4
3
△ PICNIC AREA
FISHING FLOAT
LAUNCH RAMP
STANLEY BLVD.
4.5
1.5
PLEASANTON
Bernal
1.3
Sunol Ave
1.5
PARKING
BEACH
POND
RESTRICTED AREA
Hwy. #680
24
Model Boat Area
3 mi. TO LIVERMORE
23 mi. TO WALNUT CREEK
27 mi. TO SAN JOSE
TO SAN JOSE

INFORMATION: East Bay Regional Parks, 11500 Skyline, Oakland, Phone: 415-531-9300

CAMPING	BOATING	RECREATION	RESORTS
Day Use Only	Small Boats to 17 ft. Launch Ramp Rental Boats Fee: $10 a Year with Inspection - Valid at all East Bay Regional Parks	Fishing - $1 a Day or $7.50 a Year - Valid at all East Bay Regional Parks Swimming Hiking Picnicking Parking: $1 - Weekday $2 - Weekend	

DEL VALLE RESERVOIR

Del Valle Park, 8 miles South of Livermore, offers 3,445 acres for recreation. It was once a portion of the largest Mexican Land Grant in Alameda County. The Lake has 750 surface acres and 16 miles of shoreline where you can hike or picnic. 110 campsites for tents, R.V.s or trailers, some hookups, have tables, barbecues, drinking water, showers and are located at the Family Campground. .There are also Youth Group Campgrounds available. For reservations by Youth Groups, call: 415-531-9043. All boating is allowed on the Reservoir with a 10 MPH speed limit. There are rental boats and a 4-lane launching ramp.

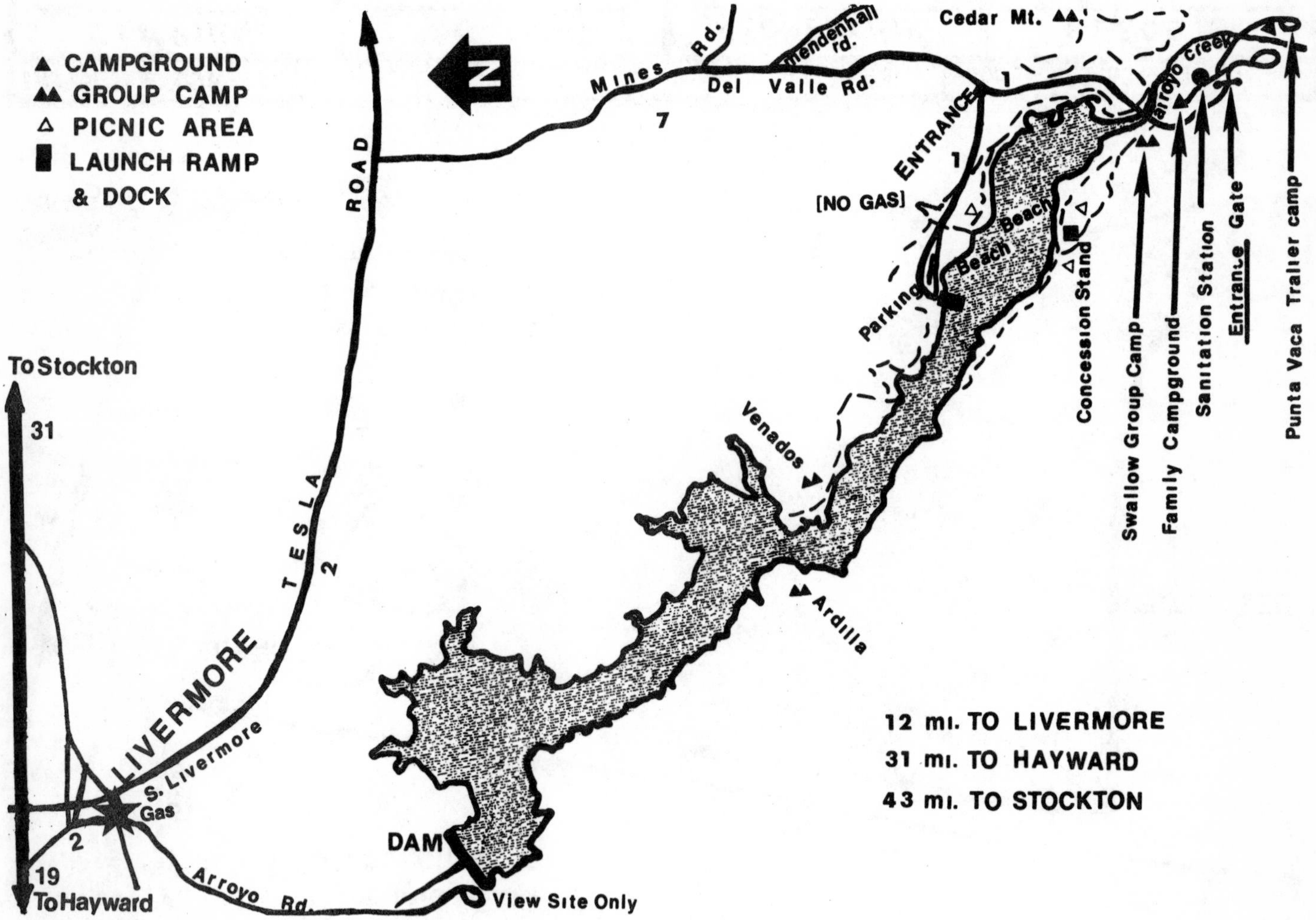
▲ CAMPGROUND
▲▲ GROUP CAMP
△ PICNIC AREA
■ LAUNCH RAMP & DOCK
N
ROAD
Mines Rd.
Del Valle Rd.
Mendenhall rd.
7
Cedar Mt.
Arroyo Creek
ENTRANCE
1
[NO GAS]
Beach
Parking
Concession Stand
Swallow Group Camp
Family Campground
Sanitation Station
Entrance Gate
Punta Vaca Trailer camp
Venados
Ardilla
TESLA
2
LIVERMORE
S. Livermore
Gas
To Stockton
31
19
To Hayward
Arroyo Rd.
DAM
View Site Only
12 mi. TO LIVERMORE
31 mi. TO HAYWARD
43 mi. TO STOCKTON

INFORMATION: East Bay Reg. Parks, 11500 Skyline, Oakland, Phone: 415-531-9300

CAMPING	BOATING	RECREATION	RESORTS
110 Developed Sites for Tents, R.V.s and Trailers Fee: $6 In Season $3 Off Season Youth Group Camps - Hike-In - 40 people each. For Reserv. Phone: 415-531-9043	Boating Allowed to 10 MPH Speed Limit Launch Ramp Fee: $1 - Cartop Boat $2 - Trailered Rental Boats	Fishing Swimming Picnicking - Groups 50 to 75 people Reserv. Phone: 415-531-9043 Hiking Bicycle & Horseback Riding Trails Parking: $2 in Season	Snack Bar

LAKE ELIZABETH

Lake Elizabeth, a 63-surface acre Lake, is open from 8:00 a.m. until sunset all year. There is a Fishing Derby every month for children 15 years old and under. Many courses are available with instructors for Basic Sailing, Canoeing, Racing Sailing, and Senior and Junior Lifesaving. Registration starts in June at The Recreation Office, 3375 County Drive in Fremont. The Park has a nice Swimming Lagoon and beach. Winds are from the West and in the afternoon can become quite strong due to the flatness of the land around the Lake. There is a 2-lane launch ramp and boat house with large floating docks. Motorboats are not allowed. 95 picnic tables and barbecue pits as well as restrooms and extensive parking facilities make this Lake a nice spot for a day's outing.

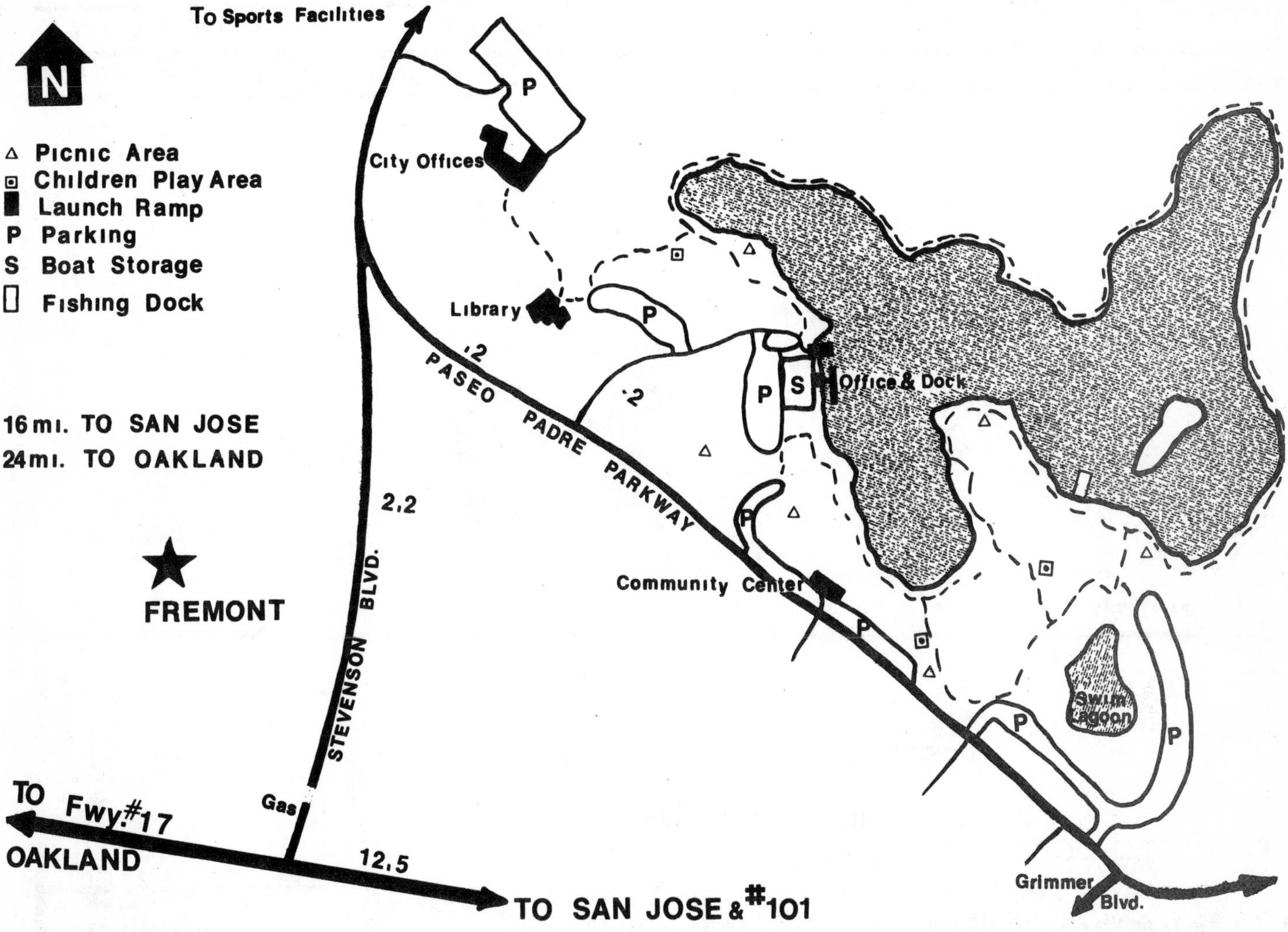

To Sports Facilities
N
Picnic Area
Children Play Area
Launch Ramp
P Parking
S Boat Storage
Fishing Dock
City Offices
Library
Office & Dock
Community Center
PASEO PADRE PARKWAY
STEVENSON BLVD.
.2
2.2
16 mi. TO SAN JOSE
24 mi. TO OAKLAND
FREMONT
Swim Lagoon
TO OAKLAND
Fwy.#17
Gas
12.5
TO SAN JOSE & #101
Grimmer Blvd.

INFORMATION: Boathouse, P.O. Box 5006, Fremont 94538, Phone: 408-791-4340

CAMPING	BOATING	RECREATION	RESORTS
No Camping Day Use Only 40 Car/Trailer Parking Spaces	No Motors Allowed Launch Ramp Boat Rentals Dry Storage Instructions	Fishing Swimming Lagoon Picnicking Hiking Bicycle Paths Tennis Courts - 18 Softball Fields - 2 Soccer Fields - 3 Vita Course	Snack Bar Showers & Dressing Rooms Picnic Groups can be Reserved for Groups

STEVENS CREEK RESERVOIR

Stevens Creek Reservoir is nestled in a canyon with many trees and rolling hills making a very pretty setting. Due to repairs needed on the Dam, the water level has been dropped to at least 12 feet below the launch ramp until work is completed. Small sailboats or rowboats are allowed but no motors, and swimming is not permitted. There are nice hiking and horseback riding trails. Reservations can be made for group picnics of 25 or more people. Call the Park Department at 408-299-2913. The Reservoir is open for Day Use Only from 8:00 a.m. to Sunset all year.

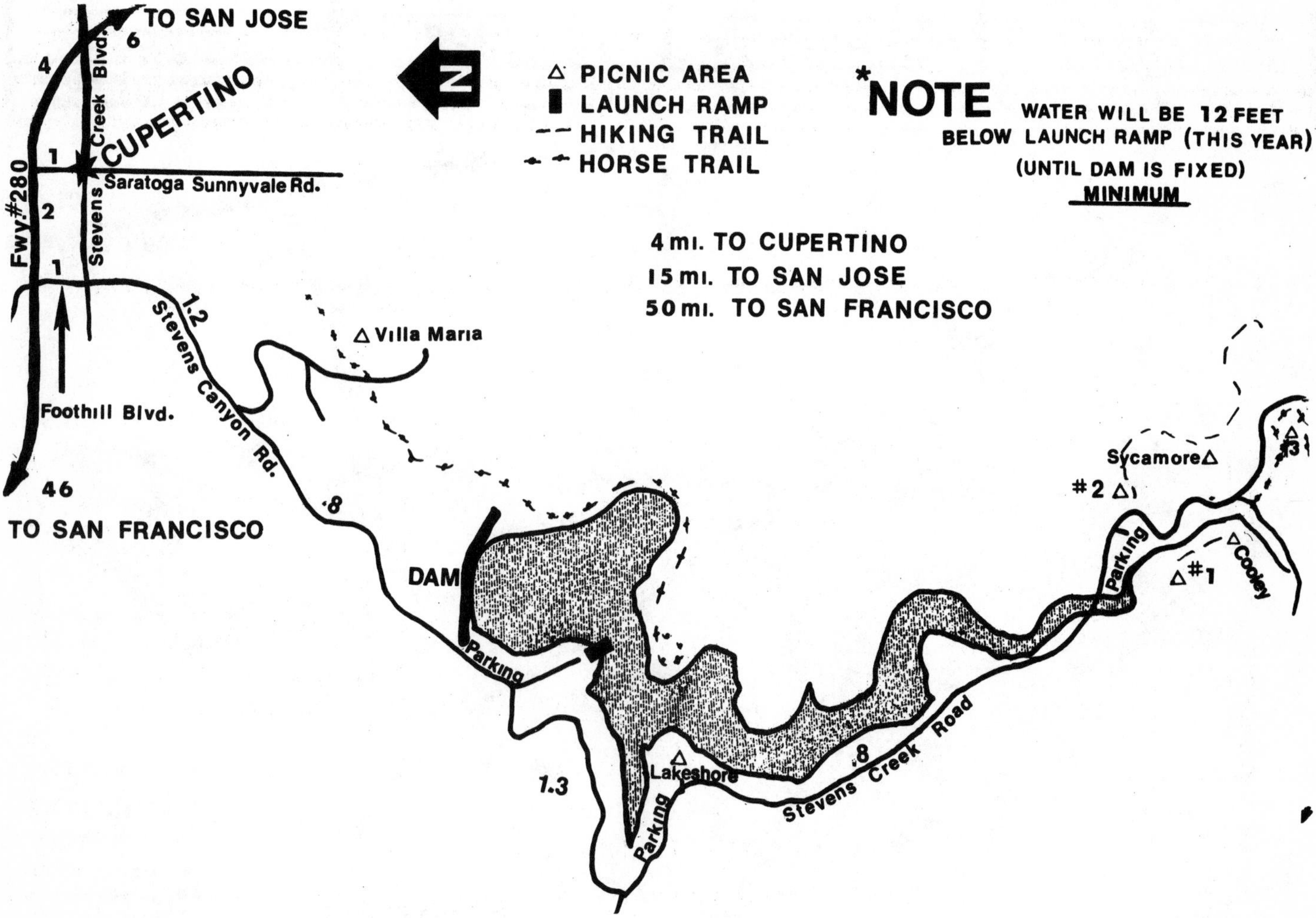
TO SAN JOSE
CUPERTINO
Stevens Creek Blvd.
Saratoga Sunnyvale Rd.
Fwy.#280
Foothill Blvd.
46
TO SAN FRANCISCO
Stevens Canyon Rd.
1.2
.8
Villa Maria
DAM
Parking
1.3
Lakeshore
Parking
Stevens Creek Road
Sycamore
#2
#1
Cooley
#3
N
PICNIC AREA
LAUNCH RAMP
HIKING TRAIL
HORSE TRAIL
*NOTE WATER WILL BE 12 FEET BELOW LAUNCH RAMP (THIS YEAR) (UNTIL DAM IS FIXED) MINIMUM
4 mi. TO CUPERTINO
15 mi. TO SAN JOSE
50 mi. TO SAN FRANCISCO

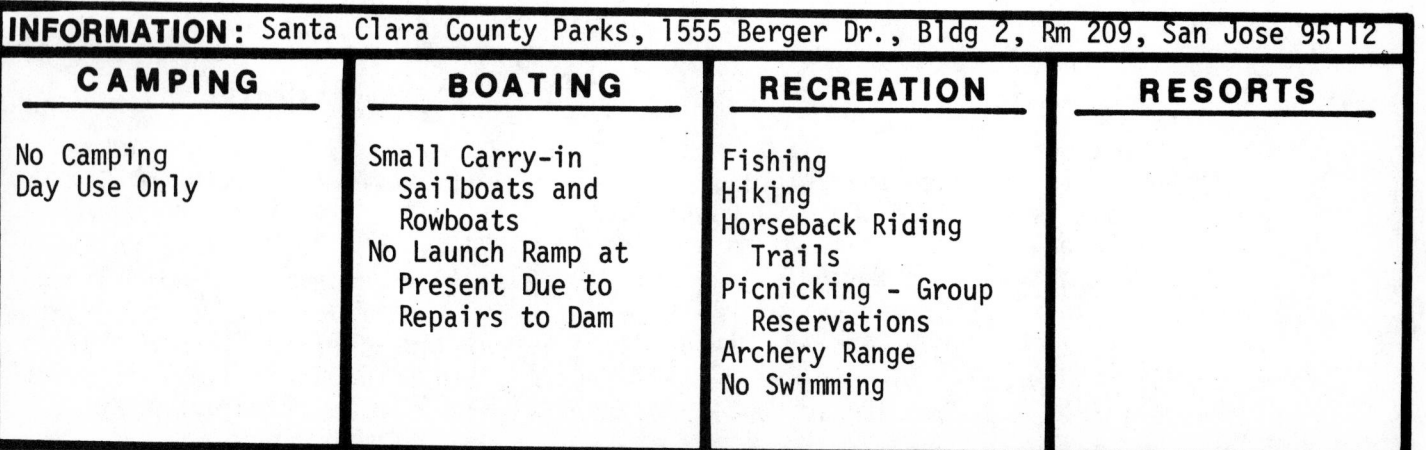

INFORMATION: Santa Clara County Parks, 1555 Berger Dr., Bldg 2, Rm 209, San Jose 95112

CAMPING	BOATING	RECREATION	RESORTS
No Camping Day Use Only	Small Carry-in Sailboats and Rowboats No Launch Ramp at Present Due to Repairs to Dam	Fishing Hiking Horseback Riding Trails Picnicking - Group Reservations Archery Range No Swimming	

LAKE VASONA

Lake Vasona is a delightful family Park open for Day Use Only from 8:00 a.m. to Sunset. There are good picnic facilities, boat rentals and a playground and children's train. Rowing, sailing and fishing are allowed but no swimming is permitted. The winds are usually light, and there are many shade trees and grassy areas. Reservations can be made for Group picnics of 25 or more people. Call the Park Department at: 408-299-2912.

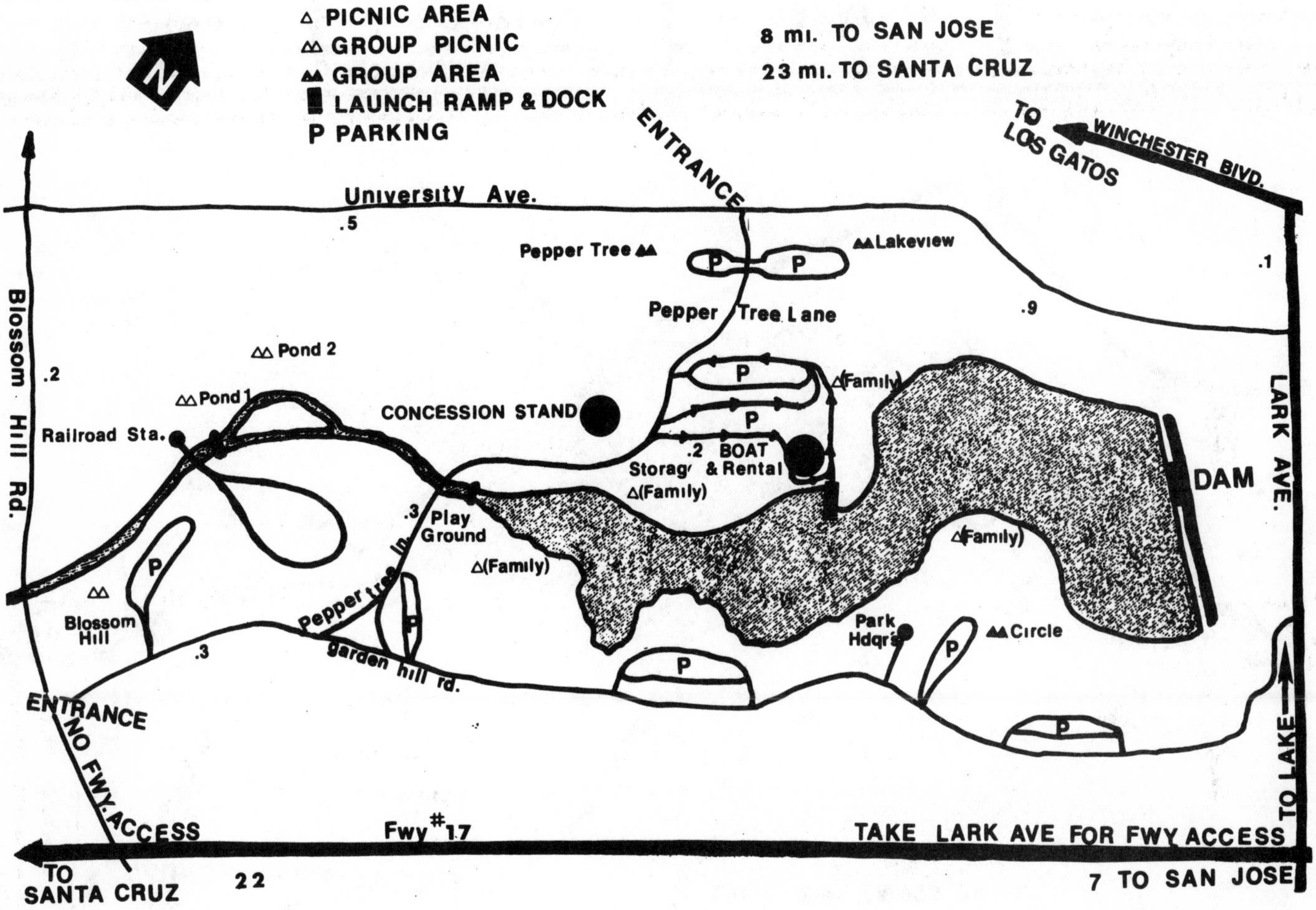

N
PICNIC AREA
GROUP PICNIC
GROUP AREA
LAUNCH RAMP & DOCK
P PARKING
8 mi. TO SAN JOSE
23 mi. TO SANTA CRUZ
ENTRANCE
TO LOS GATOS
WINCHESTER BLVD.
University Ave.
.5
Pepper Tree
Lakeview
.1
Pepper Tree Lane
.9
Blossom Hill Rd.
.2
Pond 2
Pond 1
Railroad Sta.
CONCESSION STAND
(Family)
.2 BOAT
Storage & Rental
(Family)
LARK AVE.
DAM
.3
Play Ground
(Family)
(Family)
Pepper tree ln.
Blossom Hill
Park Hdqrs
Circle
.3
garden hill rd.
ENTRANCE
NO FWY. ACCESS
Fwy #17
TAKE LARK AVE FOR FWY ACCESS
TO LAKE
TO SANTA CRUZ
22
7 TO SAN JOSE

INFORMATION: Santa Clara County Parks, 1555 Berger Dr., Bldg. 2, Rm. 209, San Jose 95112

CAMPING	BOATING	RECREATION	RESORTS
No Camping Day Use Only	Sailboats and Rowboats No Motors Launch Ramp $2 a Day Boat Rentals Dry Storage	Fishing Hiking Picnicking - Group Reservations Playground	Snack Bar Saratoga Springs Picnic & Campgrounds for R.V.s & Tents, 22801 Big Basin Way, Saratoga - minutes away.

LEXINGTON RESERVOIR

Lexington Reservoir, 844 surface acres, permits power boating and waterskiing on even-numbered days only. Sailboats and boats with less than 10 HP motors are allowed on odd-numbered days only. At the end of summer, the water can be very low and in past years, it has been impossible to use the launching ramp at that time. Swimming is not allowed. The Highway side or West side of the Lake is the best shoreline for picnicking as the rest is very steep. The Lake is open to westerly winds which can become quite strong in the afternoons. Part of the Santa Clara County Park system, this Reservoir is for Day Use Only.

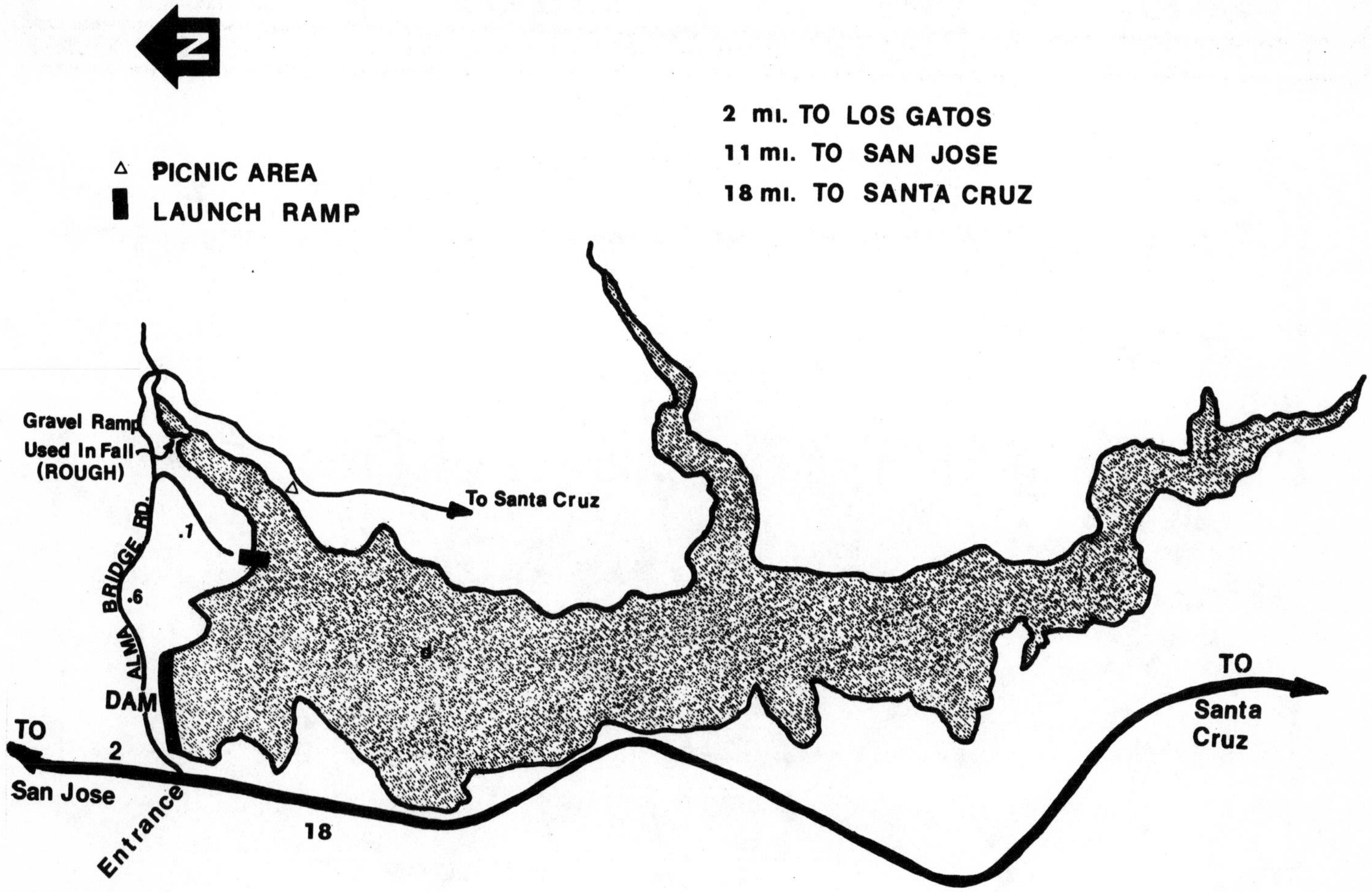
N
2 mi. TO LOS GATOS
11 mi. TO SAN JOSE
18 mi. TO SANTA CRUZ
PICNIC AREA
LAUNCH RAMP
Gravel Ramp
Used In Fall
(ROUGH)
To Santa Cruz
ALMA BRIDGE RD.
.1
.6
DAM
TO
2
San Jose
Entrance
18
TO
Santa
Cruz

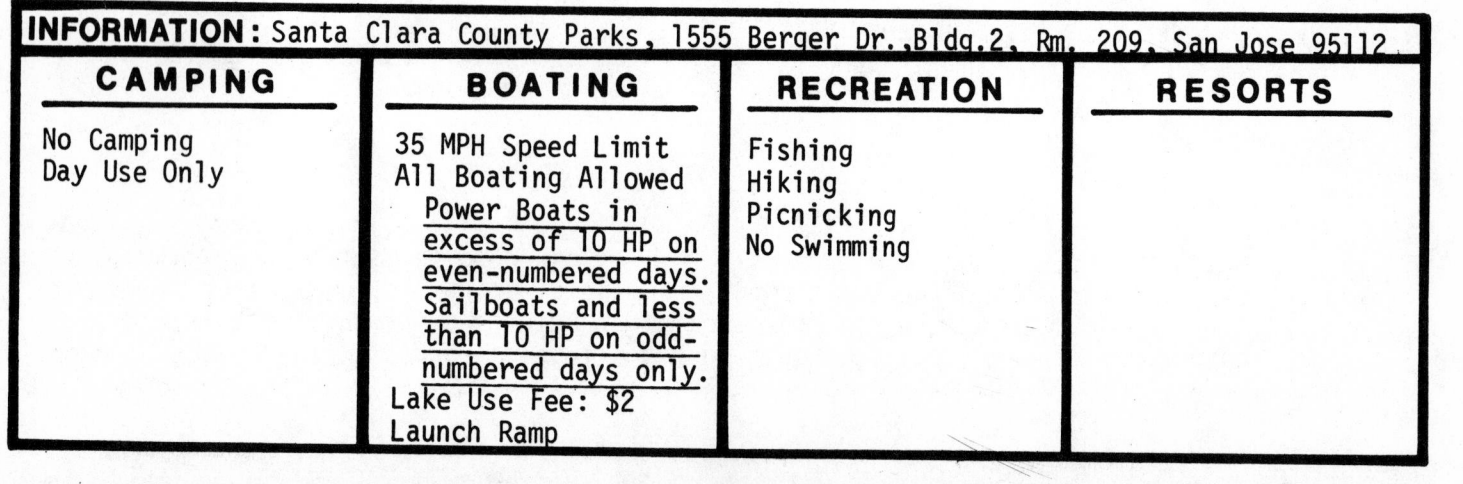

INFORMATION: Santa Clara County Parks, 1555 Berger Dr.,Bldg.2, Rm. 209, San Jose 95112

CAMPING	BOATING	RECREATION	RESORTS
No Camping Day Use Only	35 MPH Speed Limit All Boating Allowed Power Boats in excess of 10 HP on even-numbered days. Sailboats and less than 10 HP on odd-numbered days only. Lake Use Fee: $2 Launch Ramp	Fishing Hiking Picnicking No Swimming	

LOCH LOMOND RESERVOIR

Loch Lomond Reservoir is located in the Santa Cruz Mountains with trees and foliage down to the shoreline in a very lovely setting. Breezes are usually light from the West. The Reservoir is closed Wednesdays and Thursdays in season, and is closed completely from September 16 through February each year. Included in the facility are picnic tables, hiking trails and a Junior Ranger Program. Rental boats, snack shop and a tackle shop are also available. Rowboats up to 18 feet are permitted with hand launching and electric motors for trolling are allowed, but no sailboats and no powerboats. Swimming and camping are not permitted at this Day Use only Reservoir.

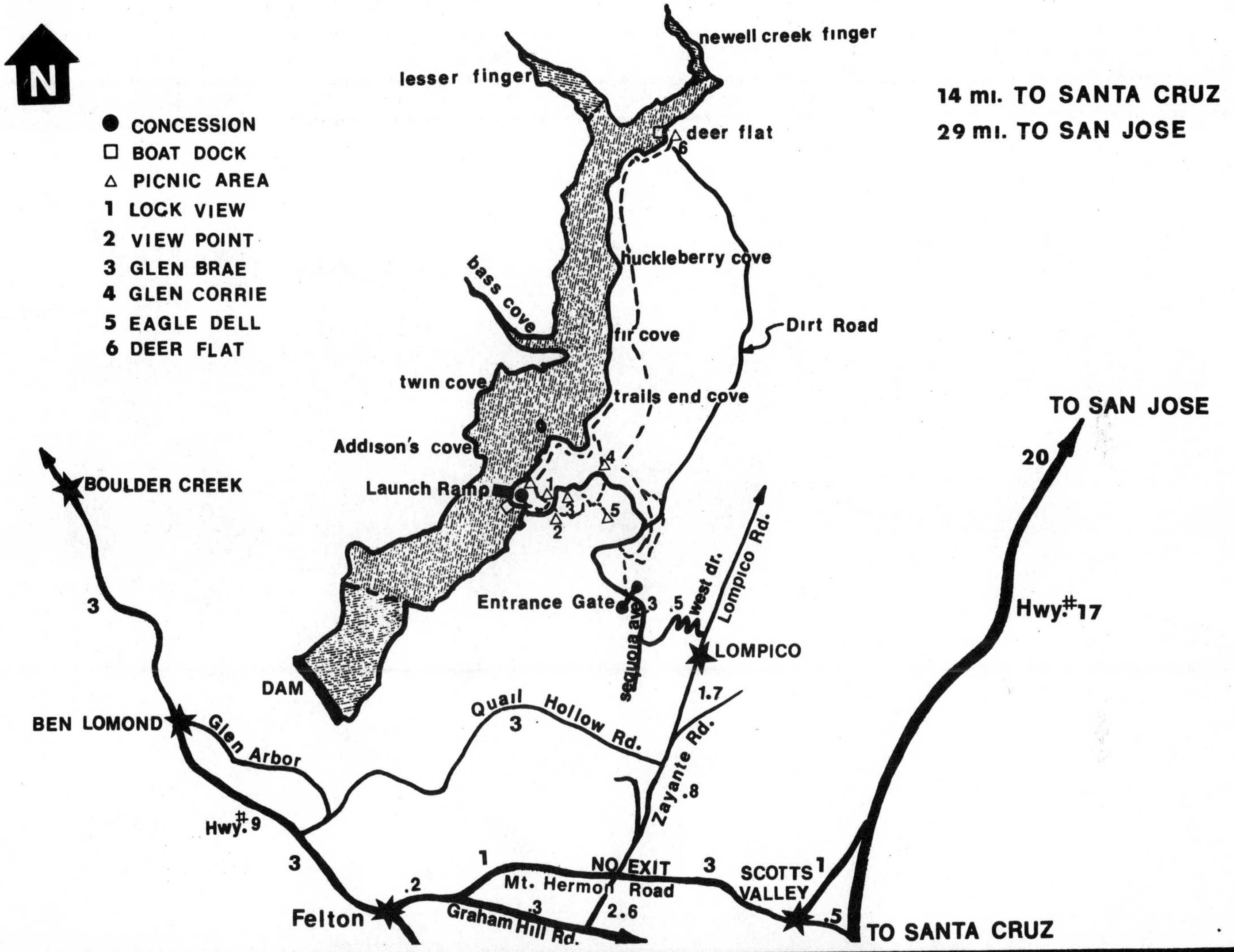
N
CONCESSION
BOAT DOCK
PICNIC AREA
1 LOCK VIEW
2 VIEW POINT
3 GLEN BRAE
4 GLEN CORRIE
5 EAGLE DELL
6 DEER FLAT
14 mi. TO SANTA CRUZ
29 mi. TO SAN JOSE
newell creek finger
lesser finger
deer flat
huckleberry cove
bass cove
fir cove
Dirt Road
twin cove
trails end cove
Addison's cove
Launch Ramp
Entrance Gate
west dr.
Lompico Rd.
sequoia ave
LOMPICO
BOULDER CREEK
DAM
BEN LOMOND
Glen Arbor
Quail Hollow Rd.
Zayante Rd.
Hwy. #9
Felton
Graham Hill Rd.
Mt. Hermon Road
NO EXIT
SCOTTS VALLEY
TO SANTA CRUZ
TO SAN JOSE
Hwy. #17
20

INFORMATION: Loch Lomond Recreation Area, Phone: 408-335-7424

CAMPING	BOATING	RECREATION	RESORTS
No Camping Day Use Only	Canoes - 13' and over, Rafts - 3 Chambers - 6' and over, Rowboats to 18 feet, Electric Motors Only Dock - Fee: $2 a Day Rental Boats: Row Boats - $2 an Hr., $7-5 Hrs., $12 - All Day, With Motors - $4 an Hr $10-5 Hrs. $20-All Day	Fishing Hiking - 2 Guided Hikes a Day Picnicking Day Use Fees: $2 - Car, $3.50 - Car & Boat $4 - Car & Trailer Hike-In - 50¢	Snack Shop - Phone: 408-335-9911 Supplies

CALERO RESERVOIR

Calero Reservoir has 493 surface acres and is for Day Use Only from 8:00 a.m. to Sunset. This is a good facility for powerboats, and waterskiing is very popular. The sandy swim beach has a life guard in season, but no shade trees, and the surrounding area is very flat and open. There are picnic areas with barbecues and ample parking for boaters. The launch ramp is closed during low water period, usually from September or October through January or February.

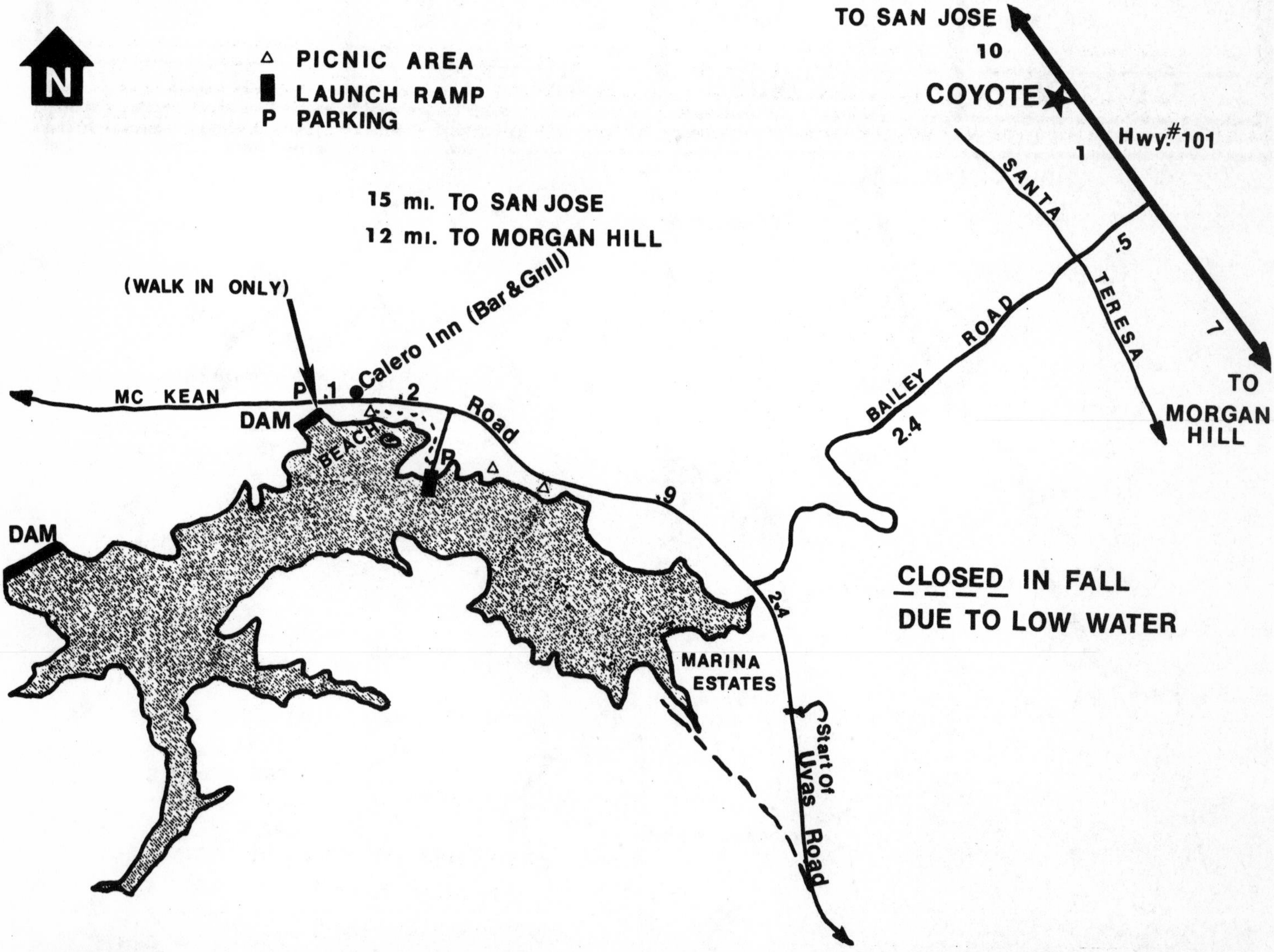
N
△ PICNIC AREA
▮ LAUNCH RAMP
P PARKING
TO SAN JOSE
10
COYOTE
Hwy.#101
1
SANTA
.5
TERESA
7
TO MORGAN HILL
ROAD
BAILEY
2.4
15 mi. TO SAN JOSE
12 mi. TO MORGAN HILL
(WALK IN ONLY)
Calero Inn (Bar&Grill)
MC KEAN
P .1
.2
Road
DAM
BEACH
P
.9
DAM
2.4
CLOSED IN FALL
DUE TO LOW WATER
MARINA ESTATES
Start of Uvas Road

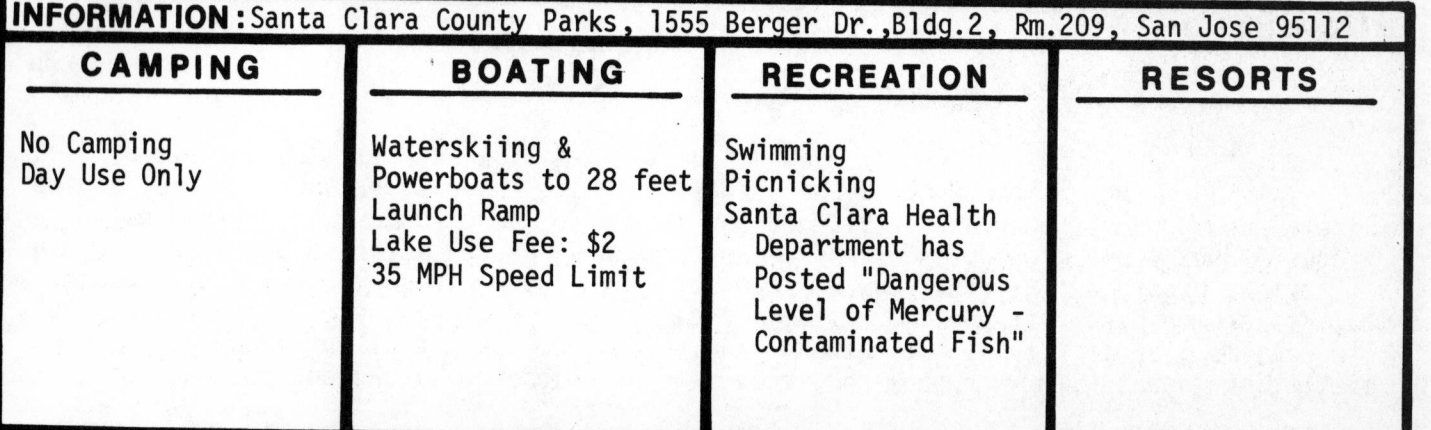

INFORMATION: Santa Clara County Parks, 1555 Berger Dr., Bldg.2, Rm.209, San Jose 95112

CAMPING	BOATING	RECREATION	RESORTS
No Camping Day Use Only	Waterskiing & Powerboats to 28 feet Launch Ramp Lake Use Fee: $2 35 MPH Speed Limit	Swimming Picnicking Santa Clara Health Department has Posted "Dangerous Level of Mercury - Contaminated Fish"	

CHESBRO RESERVOIR

Chesbro Reservoir is a small, pretty Lake with good fishing for black bass, catfish and crappie. It is quite peaceful for sailboats and rowboats only as powerboats are not allowed. It is open for Day Use from 8:00 a.m. to Sunset as part of the Santa Clara County Parks System. There is a launching ramp and picnic tables, but swimming is not permitted.

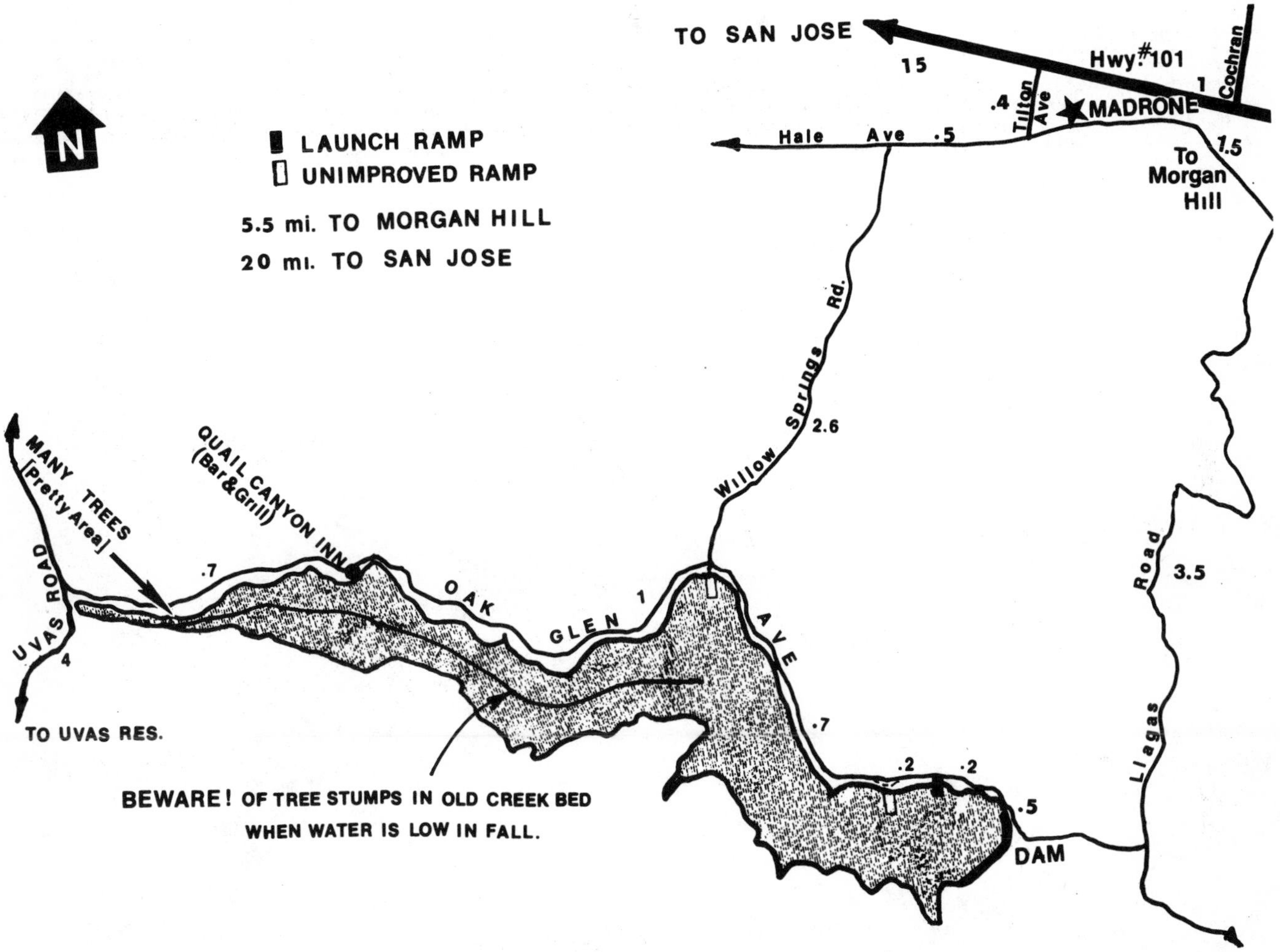
TO SAN JOSE
15
Hwy.#101
1
Cochran
.4
Tilton Ave
MADRONE
Hale Ave .5
1.5
To Morgan Hill
N
LAUNCH RAMP
UNIMPROVED RAMP
5.5 mi. TO MORGAN HILL
20 mi. TO SAN JOSE
Willow Springs Rd.
2.6
MANY TREES [Pretty Area]
QUAIL CANYON INN (Bar&Grill)
.7
OAK GLEN 1
AVE
UVAS ROAD
4
TO UVAS RES.
Road
3.5
Llagas
.7
.2
.2
.5
DAM
BEWARE! OF TREE STUMPS IN OLD CREEK BED WHEN WATER IS LOW IN FALL.

INFORMATION: Santa Clara County Parks, 1555 Berger Dr., Bldg.2, Rm.209, San Jose 95112

CAMPING	BOATING	RECREATION	RESORTS
No Camping Day Use Only	Sailboats & Rowboats Electric Motors Only Launch Ramp with Floating Dock Lake Use Fee: $2	Fishing Picnicking	Quail Canyon Inn Bar & Grill

UVAS RESERVOIR

Uvas Reservoir with 725 acres is in an open valley surrounded by rolling hills and a few trees. The Lake is for sailboats and rowboats with electric motors only. Powerboats are not allowed. Picnic areas are near the launching ramp, and swimming is not permitted. This is for Day Use Only from 8:00 a.m. to Sunset. Uvas Canyon Park, 4 miles West on Croy Road, has family and group camping facilities as well as nice hiking trails. Uvas Meadows, 1.8 miles South of the Dam has camping and R.V. sites, picnicking, heated pool and a snack bar.

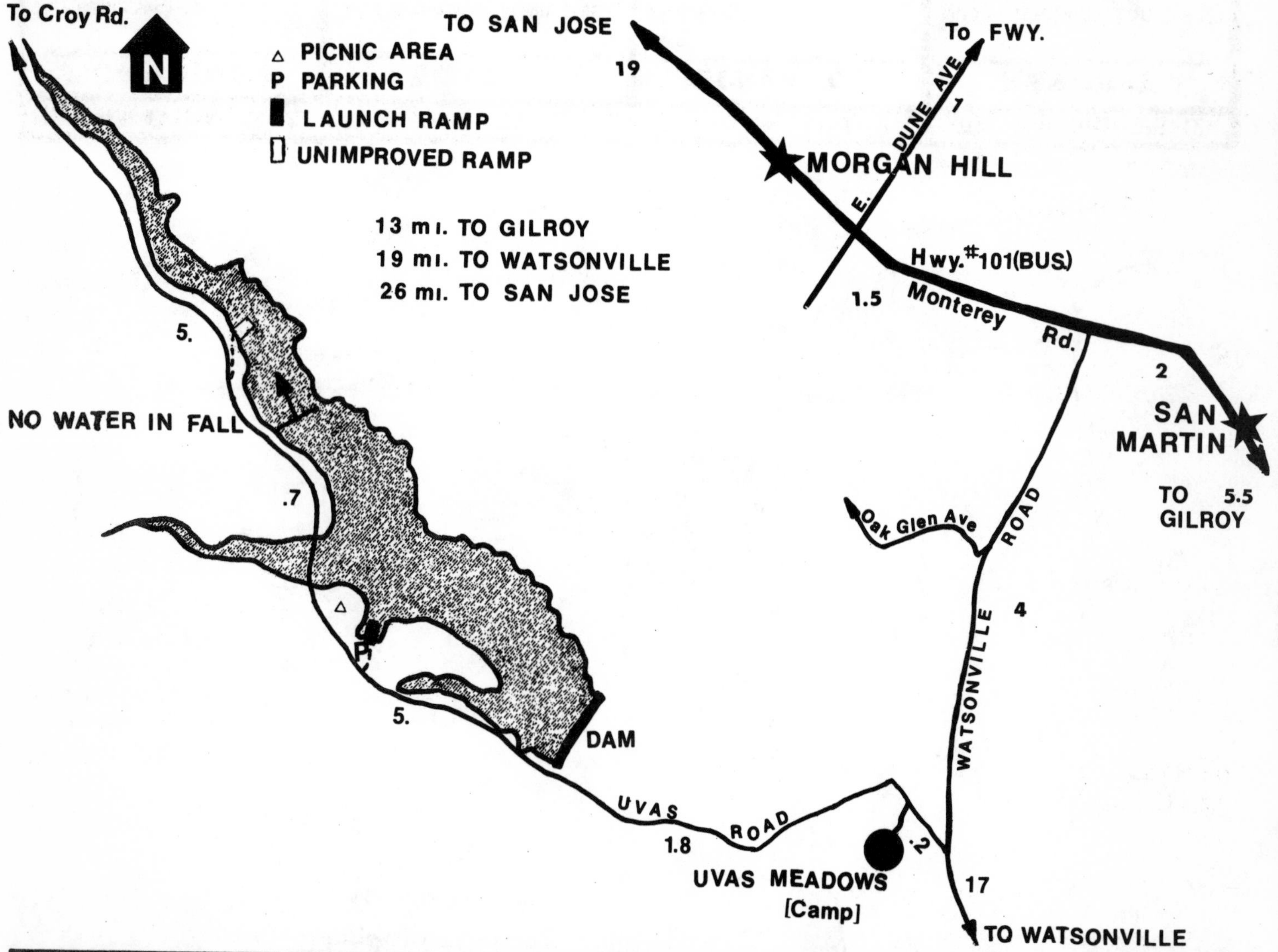
To Croy Rd.
N
△ PICNIC AREA
P PARKING
LAUNCH RAMP
UNIMPROVED RAMP
13 mi. TO GILROY
19 mi. TO WATSONVILLE
26 mi. TO SAN JOSE
TO SAN JOSE
19
To FWY.
E. DUNE AVE
1
MORGAN HILL
Hwy.#101(BUS)
1.5
Monterey Rd.
2
SAN MARTIN
TO 5.5 GILROY
NO WATER IN FALL
5.
.7
Oak Glen Ave
ROAD
4
WATSONVILLE
5.
DAM
UVAS ROAD
1.8
.2
UVAS MEADOWS
[Camp]
17
TO WATSONVILLE

INFORMATION: Santa Clara County Parks, 1555 Berger Dr.,Bldg.2, Rm. 209, San Jose 95112

CAMPING	BOATING	RECREATION	RESORTS
No Camping at Lake Day Use Only Nearby is Uvas Canyon Park with Campsites - 4 miles West on Croy Road and Uvas Meadows - Camping & R.V.s - 1.8 miles south of Dam	Sailboats and Rowboats Electric Motors Only Launch Ramp Lake Use Fee: $2	Fishing Picnicking	

ANDERSON LAKE

Anderson Lake, 7 miles long, is the largest body of fresh water in Santa Clara County. There are two launching ramps and all types of boating are allowed. Waterskiing is very popular and usually there are good afternoon winds for sailing. The water does drop down in the Fall each year. You can launch cartop boats on the Southeast shore and there are picnic areas below the Dam off Cochran Road. A picnic area, boat access only, is about 1/2 mile from the Dam on the Northwest shore. Fishing can be quite good in the morning and evening. Holiday Marina, located on the West side of the Lake in Holiday Estates, a private community, has a market for supplies, gas and boat parts as well as a launching ramp and docks.

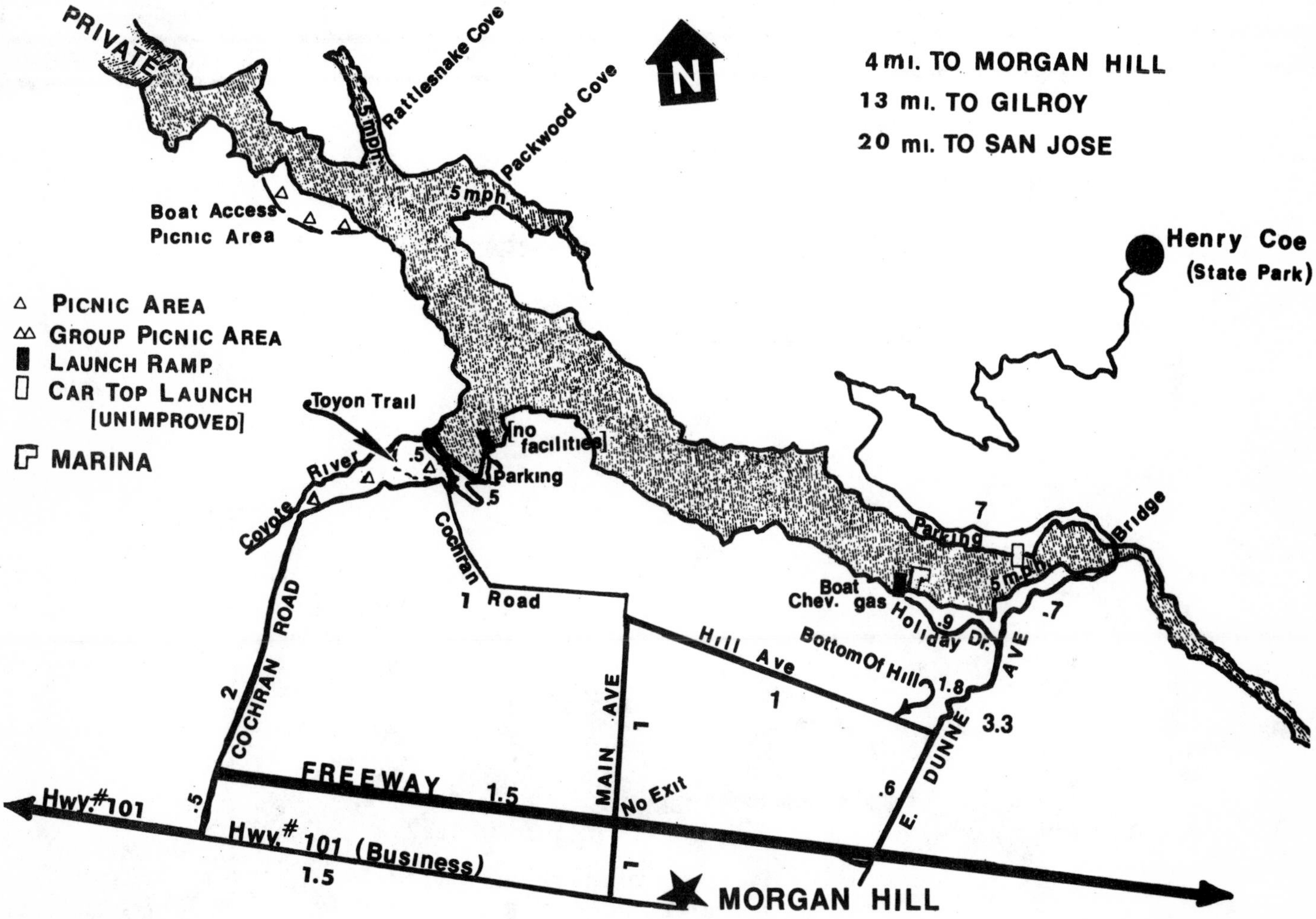
PRIVATE
Rattlesnake Cove
5 mph
Packwood Cove
5mph.
N
4mi. TO MORGAN HILL
13 mi. TO GILROY
20 mi. TO SAN JOSE
Boat Access Picnic Area
Henry Coe (State Park)
PICNIC AREA
GROUP PICNIC AREA
LAUNCH RAMP
CAR TOP LAUNCH [UNIMPROVED]
MARINA
Toyon Trail
[no facilities]
Parking
.5
Coyote River
Cochran Road
1
7
Parking
Bridge
5mph
Boat
Chev. gas
Holiday Dr.
.9
.7
Bottom Of Hill
1.8
Hill Ave
1
DUNNE AVE
3.3
COCHRAN ROAD
2
MAIN AVE
1
FREEWAY 1.5
No Exit
.6
E.
Hwy.#101
.5
Hwy.# 101 (Business)
1.5
1
MORGAN HILL

INFORMATION: Santa Clara County Parks, 1555 Berger Dr., Bldg.2, Rm.209, San Jose 95112

CAMPING	BOATING	RECREATION	RESORTS
No Camping Day Use Only	All Boating Allowed Launch Ramps Docks Full Service Marina Rental Boats Speed Limit - 35 MPH Noise Level Control is strictly enforced Lake Use Fee: $2	Fishing Hiking Horseback Riding Trails Picnicking - Group Reservations for 25 people or more	Store Supplies

COYOTE RESERVOIR

Coyote Reservoir, with 760 acres, has facilities for lakeside camping, picnicking, hiking, fishing and all types of boating. A good swim beach has life guards in season, and the Lake is quite pretty especially in some areas where there are more trees and foliage. This can be a good sailing Lake, open at the Northwest end, so the wind goes down the length. Coyote Reservoir is open year around from 8:00 a.m. to Sunset for Day Use and has a 14-day limit for campers. For reservations, campers may call 408-299-2912.

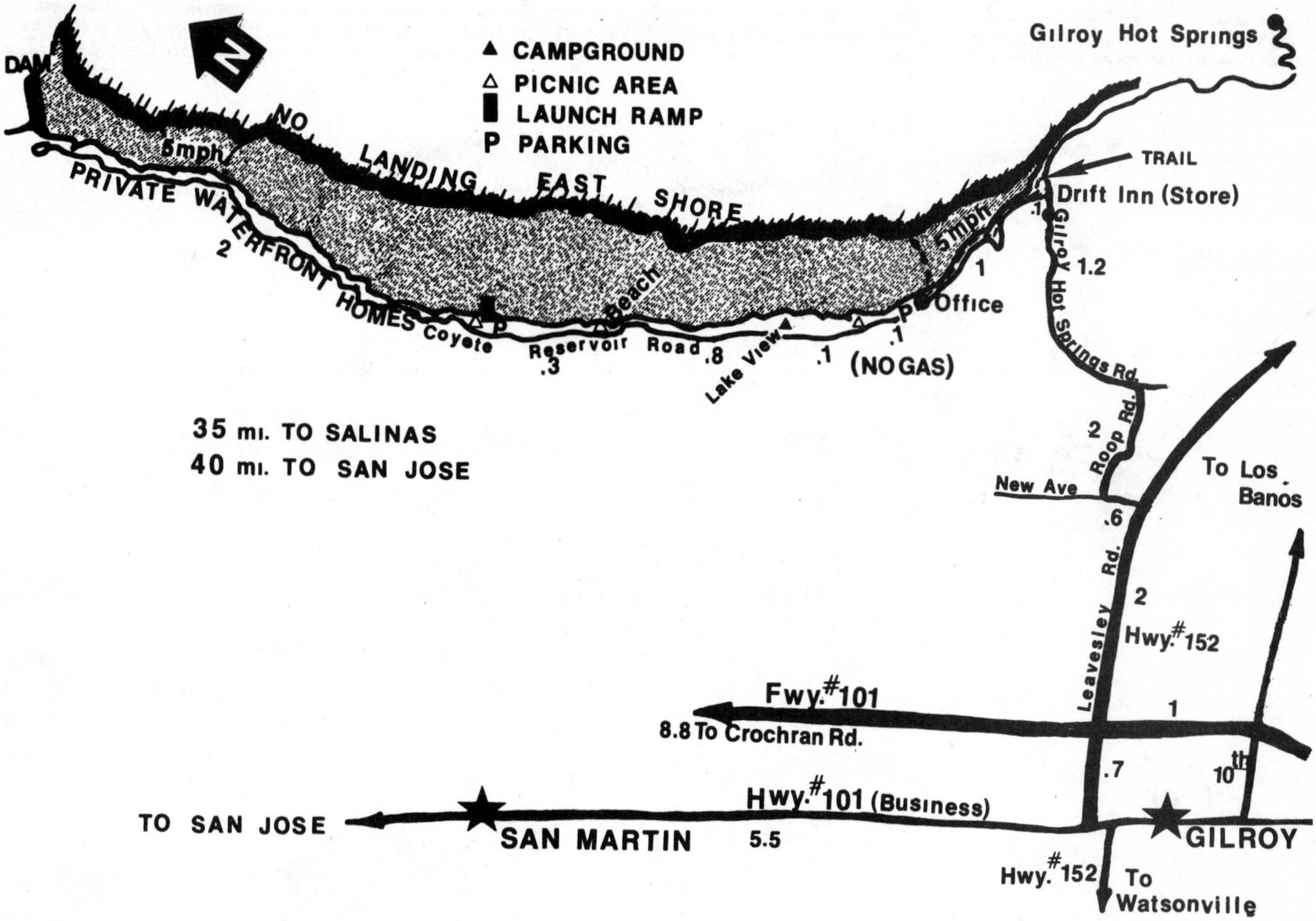

DAM
N
▲ CAMPGROUND
△ PICNIC AREA
▮ LAUNCH RAMP
P PARKING
Gilroy Hot Springs
TRAIL
Drift Inn (Store)
NO LANDING EAST SHORE
5mph
5mph
PRIVATE WATERFRONT HOMES
2
Beach
Coyote Reservoir Road
.3
.8
Lake View
.1
.1
(NO GAS)
Office
1
.1
1.2
Gilroy Hot Springs Rd.
2
Roop Rd.
New Ave
.6
To Los Banos
35 mi. TO SALINAS
40 mi. TO SAN JOSE
Leavesley Rd.
2
Hwy.#152
Fwy.#101
8.8 To Crochran Rd.
1
.7
10th
Hwy.#101 (Business)
TO SAN JOSE
SAN MARTIN
5.5
GILROY
Hwy.#152
To Watsonville

INFORMATION: Santa Clara County Parks, 1555 Berger Dr., Bldg.2, Rm.209, San Jose 95112

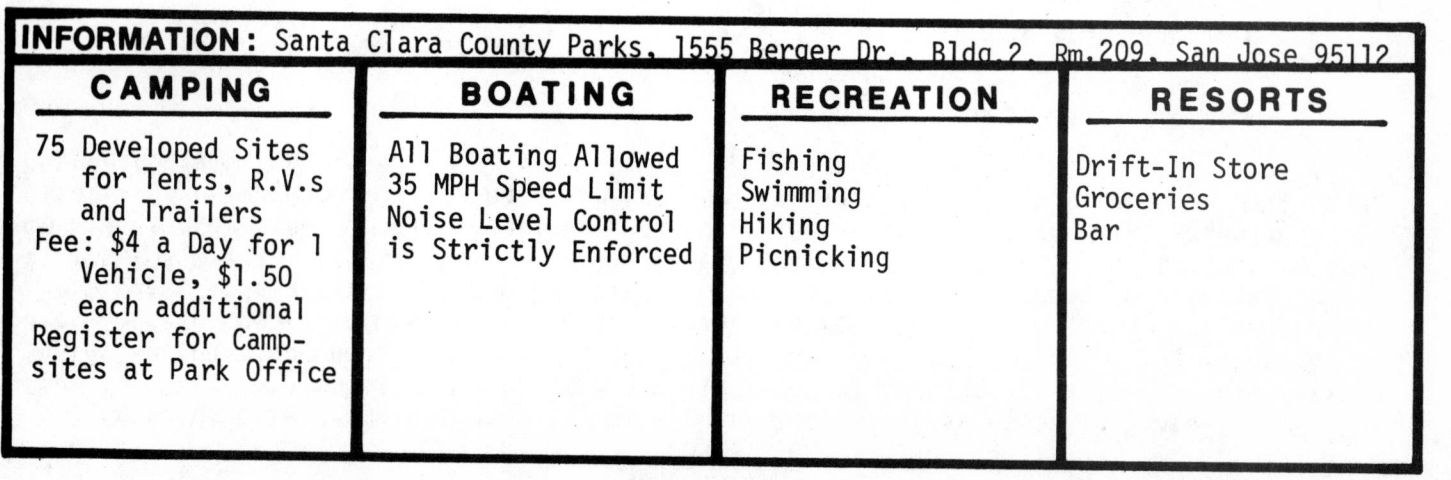

CAMPING	BOATING	RECREATION	RESORTS
75 Developed Sites for Tents, R.V.s and Trailers Fee: $4 a Day for 1 Vehicle, $1.50 each additional Register for Campsites at Park Office	All Boating Allowed 35 MPH Speed Limit Noise Level Control is Strictly Enforced	Fishing Swimming Hiking Picnicking	Drift-In Store Groceries Bar

PINTO LAKE

Pinto Lake is quite a nice facility and there can be excellent fishing. All boating is allowed - Except Note - Every Wednesday and Thursday and the third weekend of each month, sailboats, rowboats and motorboats of not more than 7-1/2 HP have the exclusive use of the Lake. At other times, waterskiing is permitted, and you can launch at the Pinto Lake Park facility. Rowboats can be rented and swimming is permitted only in designated area. There are group picnic areas, tables and barbecues. Camping in tents or sleeping on the ground is not allowed at this Lake. There are 33 hookup sites with electricity and water for travel trailers, campers and R.V.s, and 8 spaces without hookups. This is closed to overnight usage by recreational vehicles on Wednesdays at 2:00 p.m. until Thursday at 2:00 p.m. The Marmo's facility off of Amesti Road, has tent camping, walk-in and trailer sites. There is a launch ramp for up to 7-1/2 HP boats, tables, barbecues and restrooms. The 50 campsites have hot showers nearby.

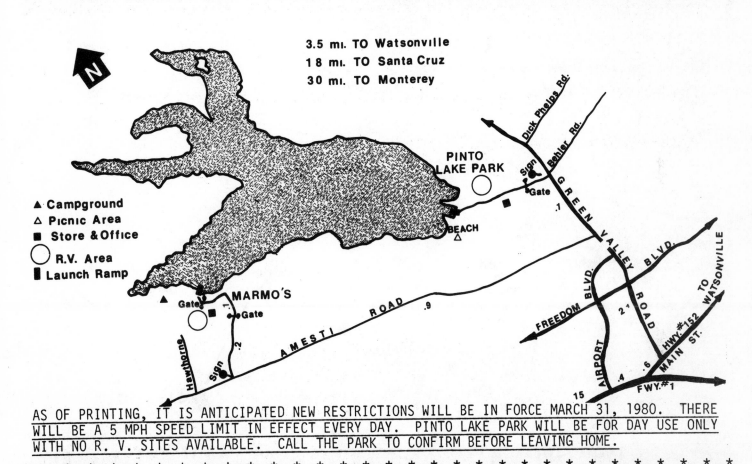

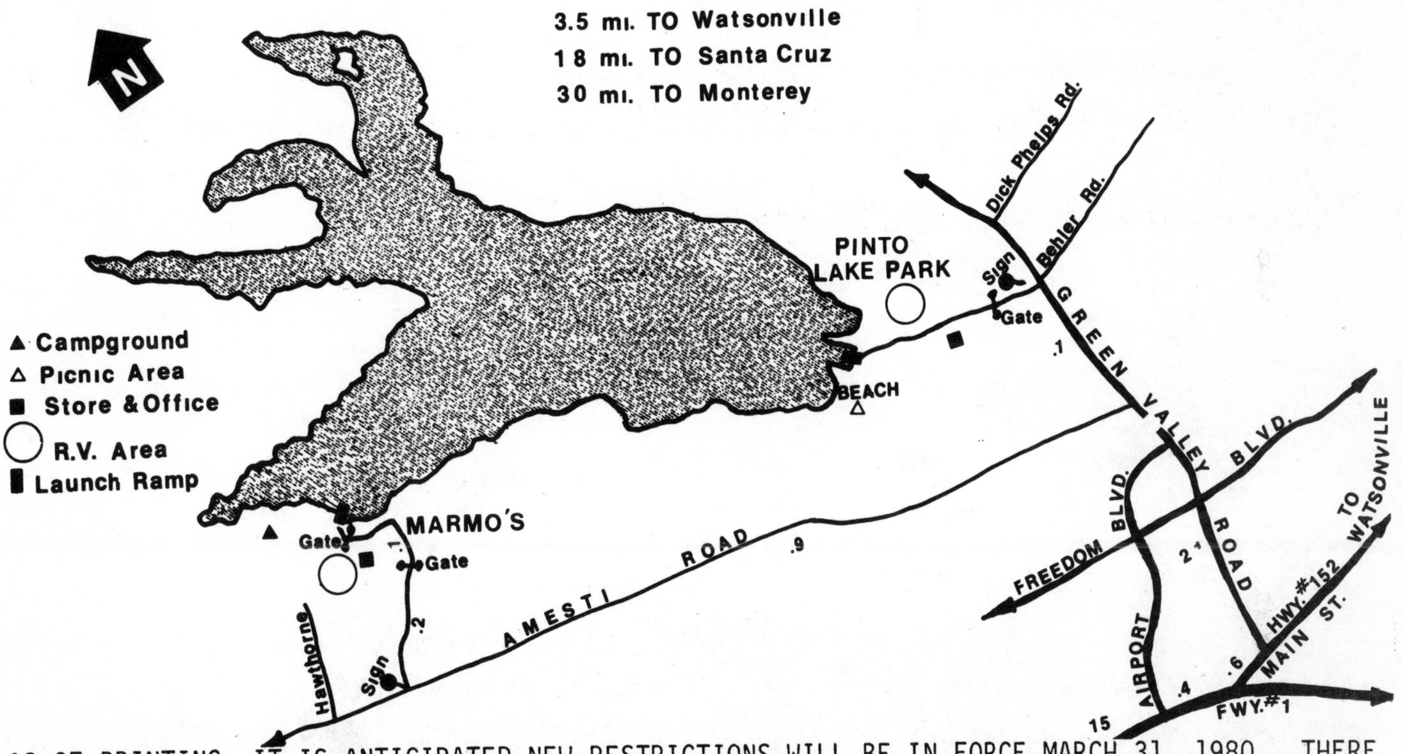
3.5 mi. TO Watsonville
18 mi. TO Santa Cruz
30 mi. TO Monterey
N
Campground
Picnic Area
Store & Office
R.V. Area
Launch Ramp
PINTO LAKE PARK
BEACH
Sign
Gate
Dick Phelps Rd.
Behler Rd.
GREEN VALLEY ROAD
MARMO'S
Gate
Sign
Hawthorne
AMESTI ROAD
FREEDOM BLVD.
AIRPORT BLVD.
TO WATSONVILLE
HWY. #152
MAIN ST.
FWY. #1
.1
.2
.9
2
.6
.4
15

AS OF PRINTING, IT IS ANTICIPATED NEW RESTRICTIONS WILL BE IN FORCE MARCH 31, 1980. THERE WILL BE A 5 MPH SPEED LIMIT IN EFFECT EVERY DAY. PINTO LAKE PARK WILL BE FOR DAY USE ONLY WITH NO R. V. SITES AVAILABLE. CALL THE PARK TO CONFIRM BEFORE LEAVING HOME.

* *

INFORMATION: Pinto Lake Park, Phone: 408-722-5011, Marmo's, Phone: 408-722-4533

CAMPING	BOATING	RECREATION	RESORTS
Pinto Lake Park - 33 Hookup Sites for R.V.s and Trailers - $5 a Day 8 No Hookups - $4 a Day Marmo's - 50 Sites for Tents, R.V.s and Trailers	All Boating Allowed Except 7-1/2 HP Motor Maximum on Wednesdays, Thursdays and 3rd Weekend of each month. Launch Ramps Rental Boats	Fishing Picnicking - Group Reservations - Park Manager, P. O. Box 53 Freedom 95019 Bicycle Paths	Snack Bar

* Numbers As Shown Represent Lakes In Numerical Order In Book.

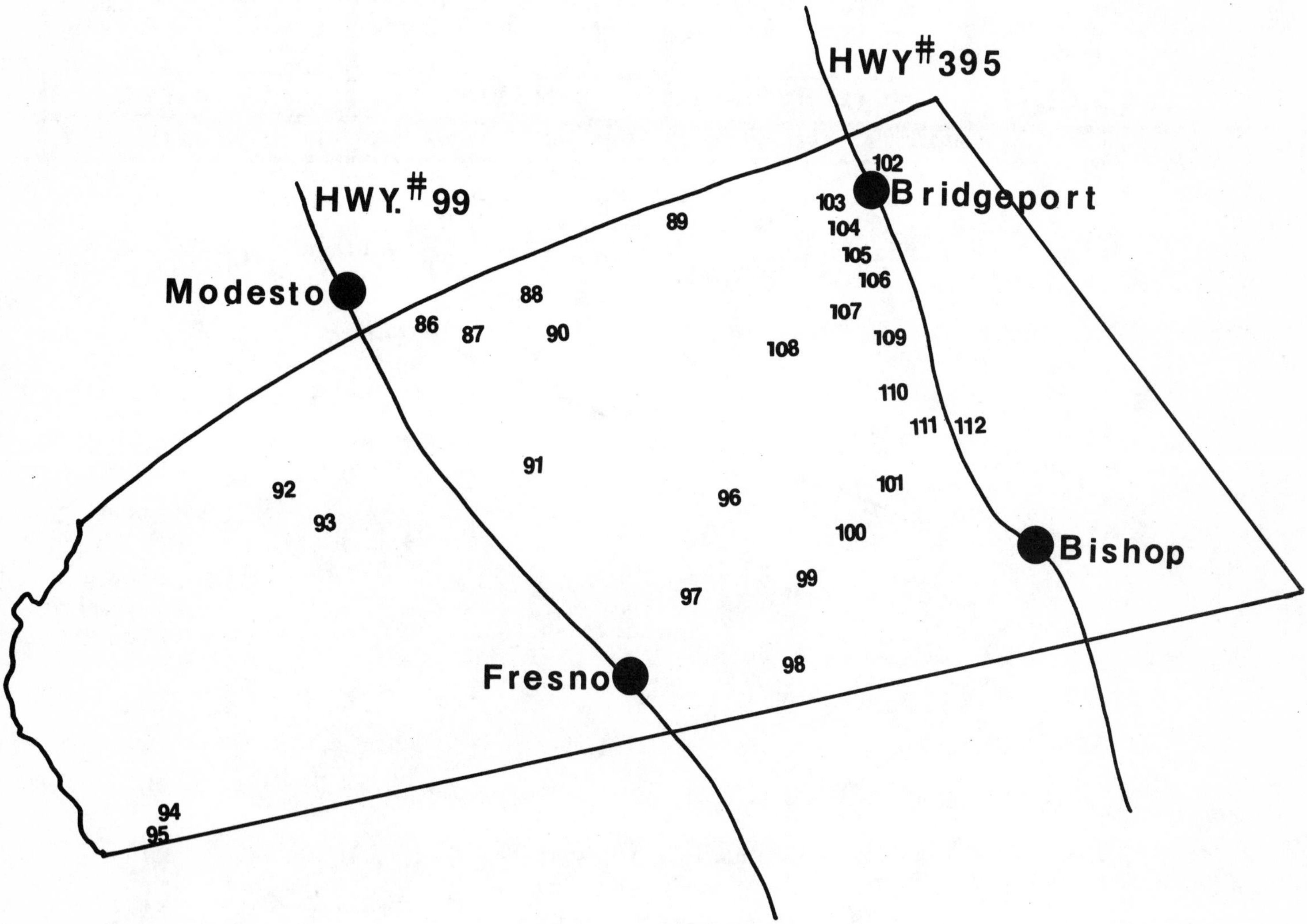
HWY#395
HWY.#99
Bridgeport
Modesto
Bishop
Fresno
102
103
104
105
106
107
108
109
110
111
112
89
88
86
87
90
91
92
93
96
101
100
99
97
98
94
95

SECTION III

SECTION III

86. MODESTO RESERVOIR
87. TURLOCK LAKE
88. DON PEDRO LAKE
89. CHERRY LAKE
90. LAKES MC CLURE & MC SWAIN
91. LAKE YOSEMITE
92. SAN LUIS RESERVOIR & O'NEILL FOREBAY
93. LOS BANOS RESERVOIR
94. SAN ANTONIO RESERVOIR
95. NACIMIENTO RESERVOIR
96. BASS LAKE
97. MILLERTON LAKE
98. PINE FLAT LAKE
99. SHAVER LAKE
100. HUNTINGTON LAKE
101. EDISON & FLORENCE LAKES
102. BRIDGEPORT RESERVOIR
103. TWIN LAKES
104. VIRGINIA LAKES
105. LUNDY LAKE
106. SADDLEBAG LAKE
107. ELLERY & TIOGA LAKES
108. TENAYA LAKE
109. JUNE LAKE LOOP
    - GRANT LAKE
    - SILVER LAKE
    - GULL LAKE
    - JUNE LAKE
110. MAMMOTH LAKES
111. CONVICT LAKE
112. CROWLEY LAKE

MODESTO RESERVOIR

Modesto Reservoir covers 2,700 acres, and the Lake water is used for irrigation of agricultural lands. Many pretty coves with trees in the water, are surrounded by rather barren hills. All types of boating are permitted and boat camping is unlimited. There are two launching ramps, a gas dock, store and snack shop. 60 campsites are located at Sierra View with tables, barbecues and drinking water. Hot showers and a dump station are also available. This can be a good Lake for sailing as the winds are westerly and the land around the Lake is fairly low. Waterskiing is very popular, and you can fish from shore or boat in the many coves.

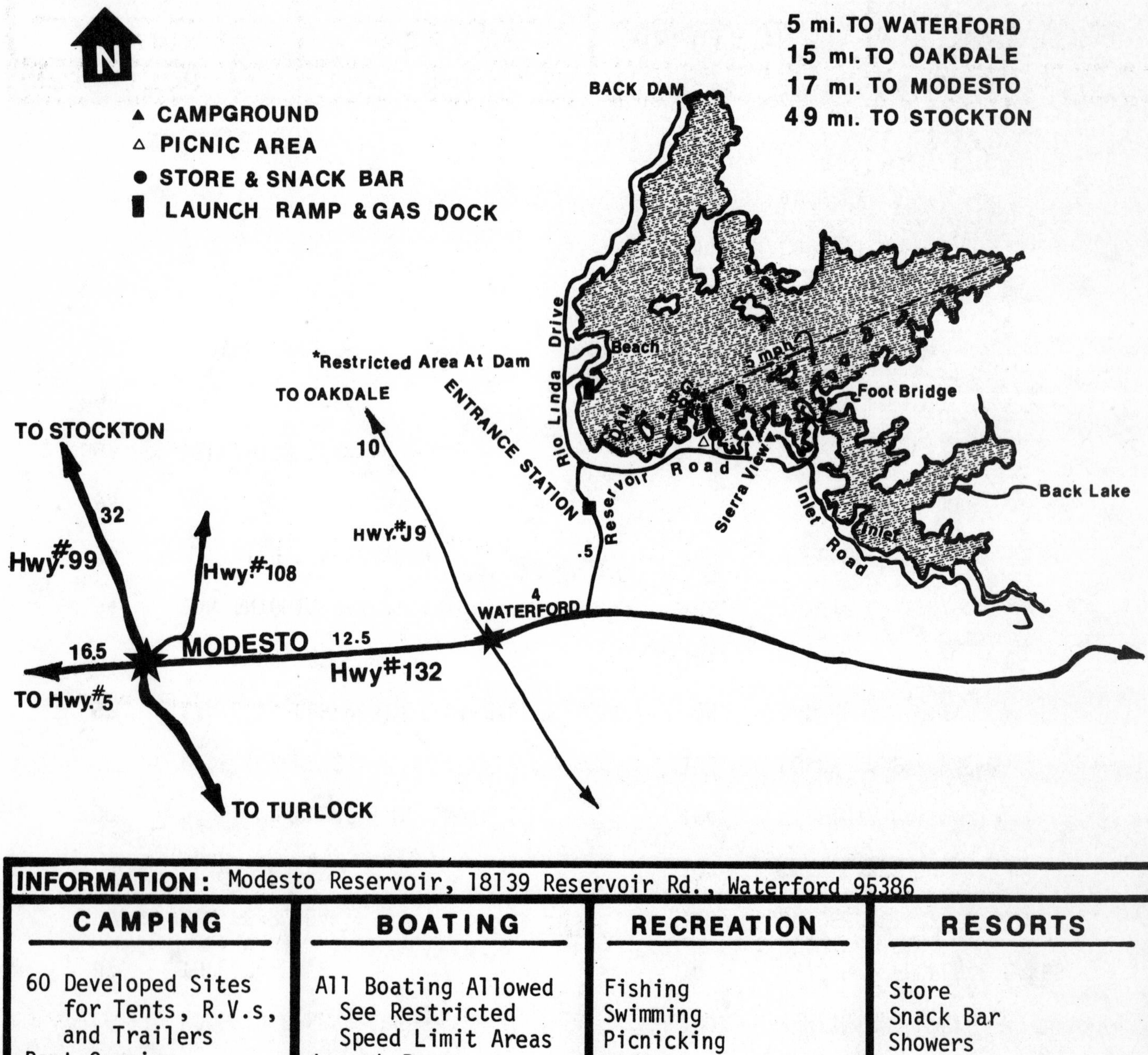
N
▲ CAMPGROUND
△ PICNIC AREA
● STORE & SNACK BAR
■ LAUNCH RAMP & GAS DOCK
5 mi. TO WATERFORD
15 mi. TO OAKDALE
17 mi. TO MODESTO
49 mi. TO STOCKTON
BACK DAM
Beach
5 mph
Foot Bridge
Back Lake
Inlet
Inlet Road
Sierra View
Reservoir Road
Rio Linda Drive
ENTRANCE STATION
*Restricted Area At Dam
TO OAKDALE
10
HWY.#J9
.5
4
WATERFORD
TO STOCKTON
32
Hwy.#99
Hwy.#108
MODESTO
12.5
16.5
Hwy#132
TO Hwy.#5
TO TURLOCK

INFORMATION: Modesto Reservoir, 18139 Reservoir Rd., Waterford 95386

CAMPING	BOATING	RECREATION	RESORTS
60 Developed Sites for Tents, R.V.s, and Trailers Boat Camping Fee: $3 - $5 a Day	All Boating Allowed See Restricted Speed Limit Areas Launch Ramps - FeeL $1.50	Fishing Swimming Picnicking Hiking Day Use Only - $1.50	Store Snack Bar Showers

TURLOCK LAKE

Turlock Lake has 3,500 surface acres, although it can drop to 1,800 acres in late summer, and 26 miles of shoreline. The elevation is 250 feet, and the weather is often hot and dry during summer days but cool at night. The Lake has two swimming beaches and a full facility Marina with launch ramp, boat dock and grocery store. All boats must be off the Lake by sunset but there are moorings near the launch ramp. 67 campsites offer tables, barbecues, drinking water, toilets and showers. Reservations are through your local Ticketron outlet or write: Ticketron, P. O. Box 26430, San Francisco 94120. There are two picnic areas with many nice shade trees and grassy areas.

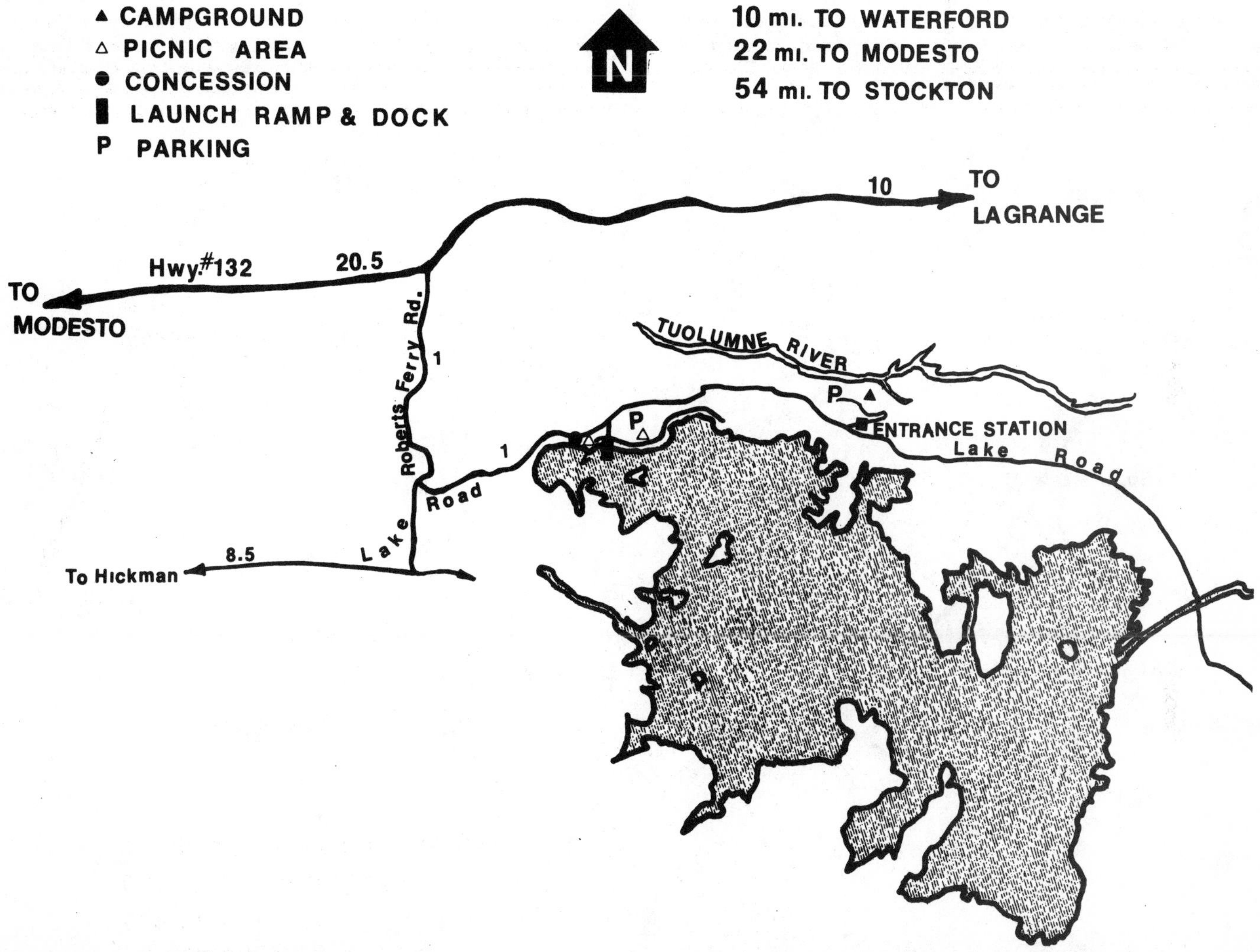
▲ CAMPGROUND
△ PICNIC AREA
● CONCESSION
▮ LAUNCH RAMP & DOCK
P PARKING
N
10 mi. TO WATERFORD
22 mi. TO MODESTO
54 mi. TO STOCKTON
10
TO LAGRANGE
Hwy.#132
20.5
TO MODESTO
Roberts Ferry Rd.
1
TUOLUMNE RIVER
P
ENTRANCE STATION
Lake Road
P
1
Road
Lake
8.5
To Hickman

INFORMATION: Turlock Lake, 22600 Lake Rd., La Grange 95329, Phone: 209-874-2008

CAMPING	BOATING	RECREATION	RESORTS
67 Developed Sites for Tents, R.V.s, and Trailers to 21 feet Fee: $5 a Day Persons 62 years and older - 1/2 price Reservations through Ticketron	All Boating Allowed Launch Ramp Dock Moorings Full Service Marina Launch Fee: $2	Fishing Swimming Picnicking Hiking Day Use Only: $2	Snack Bar Store

DON PEDRO LAKE

Don Pedro covers nearly 13,000 surface acres with a shoreline of 160 miles. Summers are warm with temperatures reaching into the 100's. There are three recreation sites along the Lake. Fleming Meadows offers 146 developed tent campsites and 90 hookup sites for trailers and R.V.s, 32 picnic units and a Group picnic unit. There is also a nice 2-acre swimming lagoon with a maximum depth of 6 feet, dressing rooms, showers and a refreshment stand. On the West shore at Mexican Gulch, there are 195 developed tent campsites. At Moccasin Point on the North end of the Lake are 53 tent campsites, 15 trailer hookup sites and 16 picnic units. All three areas have launching ramps. Full service Marinas are located at Fleming Meadows and Moccasin Point along with boat rentals, including houseboats, dry storage, a grocery and supply store and a snack bar. All boating is permitted and many sailing regattas, and fishing tournaments are held at Don Pedro. Waterskiing is also very popular.

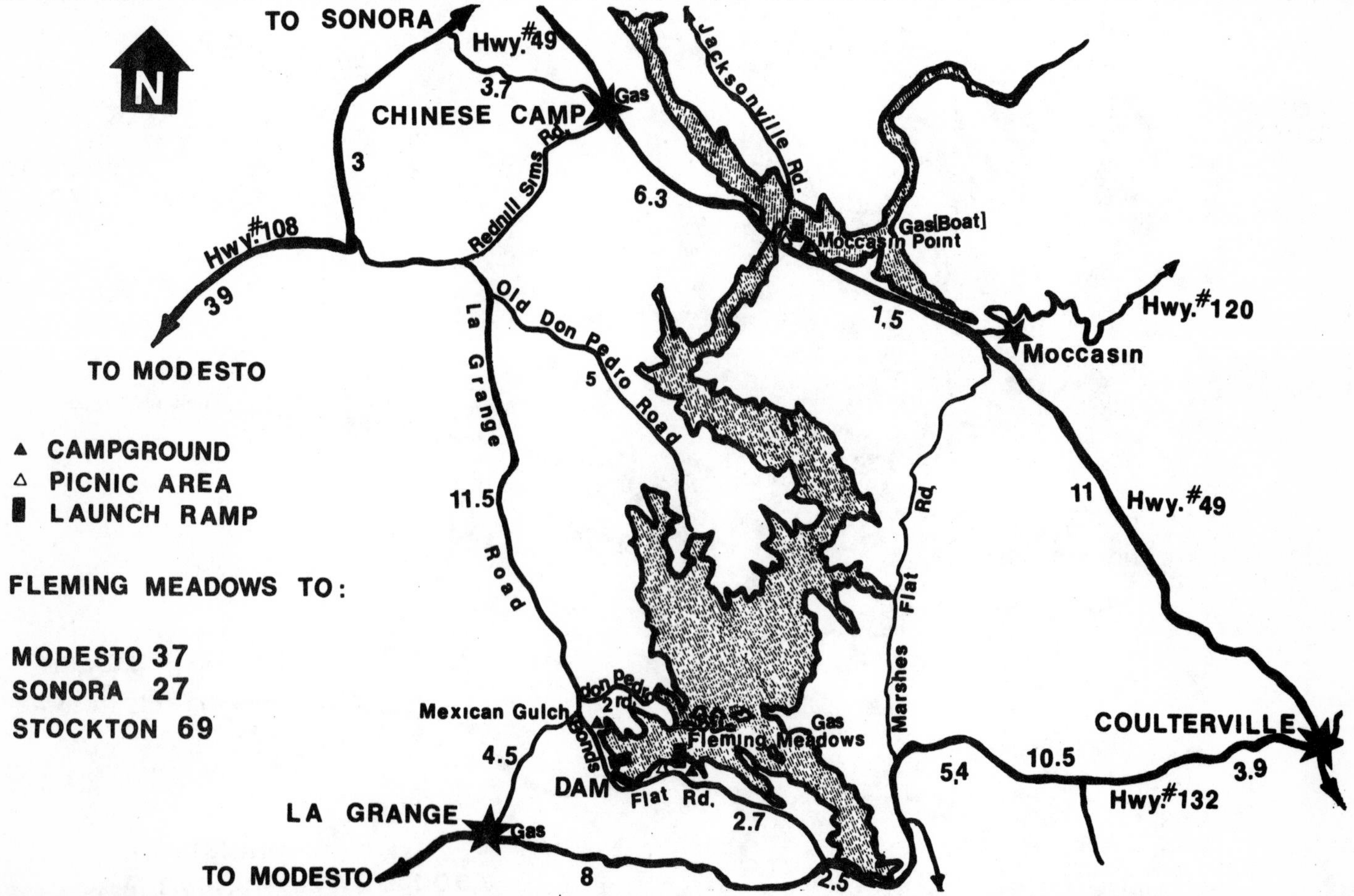

N
TO SONORA
Hwy.#49
3.7
CHINESE CAMP
Gas
Rednill Sims Rd.
3
6.3
Jacksonville Rd.
Gas[Boat]
Moccasin Point
Hwy.#108
39
TO MODESTO
Old Don Pedro Road
5
La Grange Road
1.5
Moccasin
Hwy.#120
▲ CAMPGROUND
△ PICNIC AREA
▮ LAUNCH RAMP
11.5
11
Hwy.#49
Marshes Flat Rd.
FLEMING MEADOWS TO:
MODESTO 37
SONORA 27
STOCKTON 69
Mexican Gulch
Don Pedro 2nd.
Bonds
Gas
Fleming Meadows
COULTERVILLE
4.5
DAM
Flat Rd.
5.4
10.5
3.9
Hwy.#132
LA GRANGE
Gas
2.7
TO MODESTO
8
2.5

INFORMATION: Don Pedro Recreation Agency, 31 Bonds Flat Rd., La Grange 95329

CAMPING	BOATING	RECREATION	RESORTS
394 Developed Sites for Tents 105 Hookup Sites for R.V.s and Trailers Reservations - Call: 209-852-2396	All Boating Allowed Launch Ramps Boat Rentals Dry Storage Moorings and Berths Full Service Marina Houseboat Rentals	Fishing Swimming Hiking Picnicking	Snack Bars Store Showers Laundromat

CHERRY LAKE

Cherry Lake is at 4,700 feet elevation in lovely rugged back country. A 24-mile winding road from Highway 120 takes you into the Lake. The launching ramp is rocked, and camping facilities are two miles away at Cherry Valley Campground where there are 46 units with tables, barbecues and water. The Lake is good for boating and trout fishing but the water can drop up to 50 feet by end of summer. There is also a pack station with horses and mules as well as day rides. They offer various types of pack trips ranging from an all inclusive trip with horses, pack mules, guide and food, to the use of a "walking burro" to carry supplies. Novices will even find this can be a most delightful vacation experience.

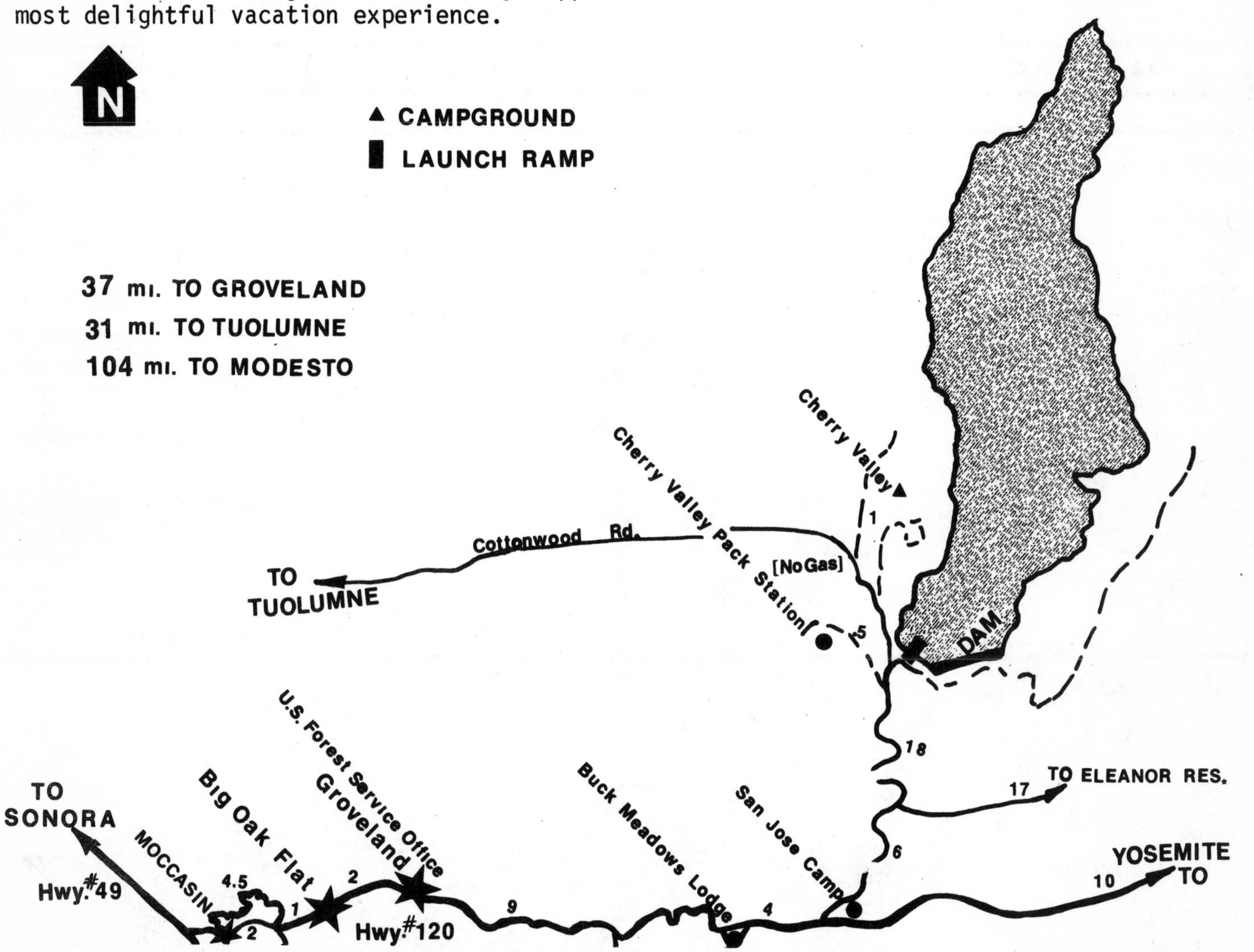
N
CAMPGROUND
LAUNCH RAMP
37 mi. TO GROVELAND
31 mi. TO TUOLUMNE
104 mi. TO MODESTO
Cherry Valley
Cherry Valley Pack Station
[No Gas]
Cottonwood Rd.
TO TUOLUMNE
DAM
TO ELEANOR RES.
YOSEMITE TO
TO SONORA
MOCCASIN
Big Oak Flat
Groveland
U.S. Forest Service Office
Buck Meadows Lodge
San Jose Camp
Hwy. #49
Hwy. #120
1
5
18
17
6
10
4
9
2
4.5
2
1

INFORMATION: U. S. Forest Service, Drawer I, Groveland 95321

CAMPING	BOATING	RECREATION	RESORTS
46 Developed Sites for Tents, R.V.s and Trailers Fee: $3 a Day - Single Family Unit. $6 a Day - Multi-Family Unit.	All Boating Allowed Rocked Launch Ramp	Fishing Hiking Swimming Horseback Riding Various Types of Pack Trips	Cherry Valley Pack Station P. O. Box 1339 Sonora 95370

LAKE MC CLURE AND LAKE MC SWAIN

Lake McClure, at 867 feet elevation, has 82 miles of shoreline and 7,100 surface acres. It is surrounded by rolling foothills and offers a good variety of vacation facilities at 5 recreation areas. All boating is allowed and waterskiing is popular as well as fishing along the many coves.

. . . Continued . . .

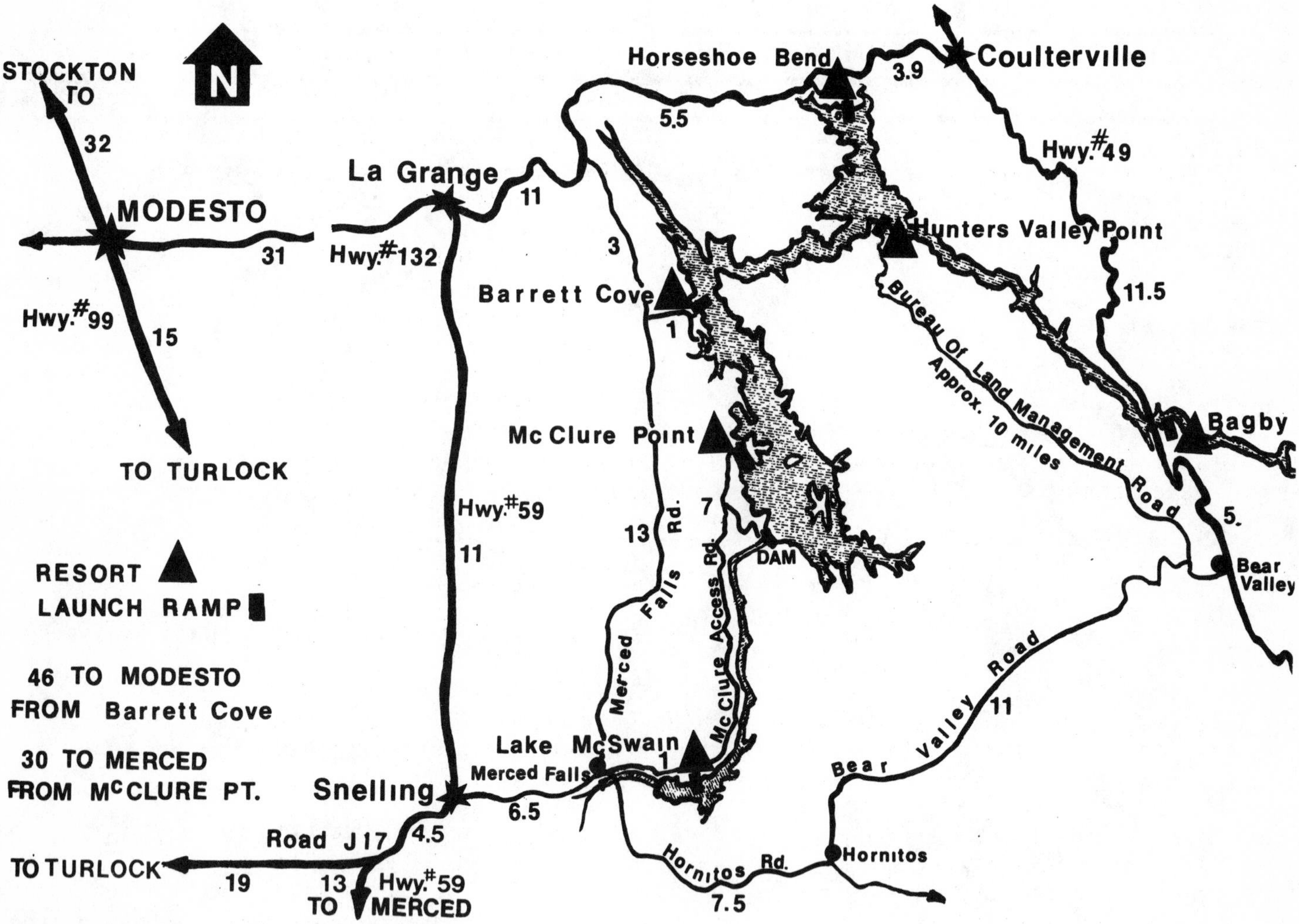
STOCKTON
TO
N
32
MODESTO
31
Hwy.#99
15
TO TURLOCK
La Grange
11
Hwy.#132
Horseshoe Bend
3.9
Coulterville
5.5
Hwy.#49
Hunters Valley Point
3
Barrett Cove
1
11.5
Bureau Of Land Management Road
Approx. 10 miles
Mc Clure Point
Bagby
Hwy.#59
11
13
Rd.
7
Merced Falls Rd.
Mc Clure Access Rd.
DAM
5.
Bear Valley
RESORT
LAUNCH RAMP
46 TO MODESTO
FROM Barrett Cove
30 TO MERCED
FROM McCLURE PT.
Bear Valley Road
11
Lake McSwain
1
Merced Falls
Snelling
6.5
Road J17
4.5
TO TURLOCK
19
13
Hwy.#59
TO MERCED
Hornitos Rd.
Hornitos
7.5

INFORMATION: See Individual Recreation Area

CAMPING	BOATING	RECREATION	RESORTS
565 Developed Sites for Tents, R.V.s and Trailers - 99 Electric and Water Hookups Fee: $5 a Day for Campsite $6 a Day with Hookup	All Boating Allowed at Lake McClure No Waterskiing at Lake McSwain Launch Ramps - $2 Full Service Marinas Boat Rentals Houseboat Rentals Moorings	Fishing Swimming Hiking Picnicking Sightseeing - Gold Rush Towns Day Use Only - $2	Stores Snack Bars Showers Laundromats Playgrounds

	Camping Information and Reservations	Marina and Boat Rentals
McClure Point	M I D Parks Department 9014 Village Drive Snelling 95369 Phone: 209-378-2521	McClure Point Marina 9561 Boat Club Road Snelling 95369 Phone: 209-378-2491

100 Developed Campsites for tents, R.V.s and trailers, 27 water and electric hookups, 64 picnic units, Full Service Marina with Chevron Gas for boats and cars, 5-lane launch ramp, boat rentals, houseboats, moorings, swimming lagoon, snack bar, store, showers, laundromat.

Barrett Cove	M I D Department Star Route La Grange 95329 Phone: 209-378-2711	Barrett Cove Marina Star Route La Grange 95329 Phone: 209-378-2441

260 Developed Campsites for tents, R.V.s and trailers, 27 water and electric hookups, 100 picnic units, Full Service Marina with gas for boats and cars, 4-lane launch ramp, boat rentals, houseboats, moorings, swimming lagoon, snack bar, store, showers, laundromat.

Horseshoe Bend	M I D Parks Department 4244 Highway 132 Coulterville 95311 Phone: 209-878-3452	Horseshoe Bend Marina Star Route La Grange 95329 Phone: 209-378-2441

90 Developed Campsites for tents, R.V.s and trailers, 15 water and electric hookups, 32 picnic units, Full Service Marina, 2-lane launch ramp, boat rentals, houseboats, moorings, swimming lagoon, snack bar, store, showers, laundromat, gas for boats.

Hunters Valley Point

Hunters Valley Marina
P. O. Box 568
Mariposa 95338

15 Developed Campsites for tents, R.V.s and trailers, 12 picnic units, Full Service Marina, gas for boats, 1-lane launch ramp, boat rentals, moorings, store.

Bagby

A.M.S. Marina
8324 Highway 49 North
Mariposa 95338

25 Developed Campsites for tents, R.V.s and trailers, 25 picnic units, Full Service Marina, 1-lane launch ramp, boat rentals, moorings, snack bar, store.

. . . Continued . . .

LAKE MC CLURE AND LAKE MC SWAIN

. . . Continued . . .

Lake McSwain, the Forebay, has very cold water which comes from the bottom of Lake McClure's Dam so it is good fishing as the water is constantly flowing. It is a small Lake with no waterskiing allowed and regular planting of trout.

Lake McSwain

Camping Information and Reservations

M I D Parks Department
9014 Village Drive
Snelling 95369
Phone: 209-378-2521

Marina and Boat Rentals

Lake McSwain Marina, Inc.
8044 Lake McClure Rd.
Snelling 95369
Phone: 209-378-2534

80 Developed Campsites for tents, R.V.s and trailers, 30 water and electric hookups, 48 picnic units, Full Service Marina, 2-lane launch ramp, boat rentals, swimming lagoon, snack bar, store, showers, laundromat.

snyder'79

Family fire wood fishing

LAKE YOSEMITE

Lake Yosemite Park is a total of 550 acres with a 25-acre Lake. The Park is for Day Use only and has a nice swimming area and Marina with rental boats. A great building that rents for $10.00 per hour accommodates up to 200 people with heating, air conditioning and barbecue and kitchen. Picnic areas can also accommodate 200 people. You need reservations for groups at this outstanding facility. The Lake is excellent for sailing and has a launch ramp with many docks. All boating is permitted, and there is a designated waterskiing area. Lake Yosemite also has its own Yacht Club. This is really a lovely Park with many beautiful trees and well-kept facilities.

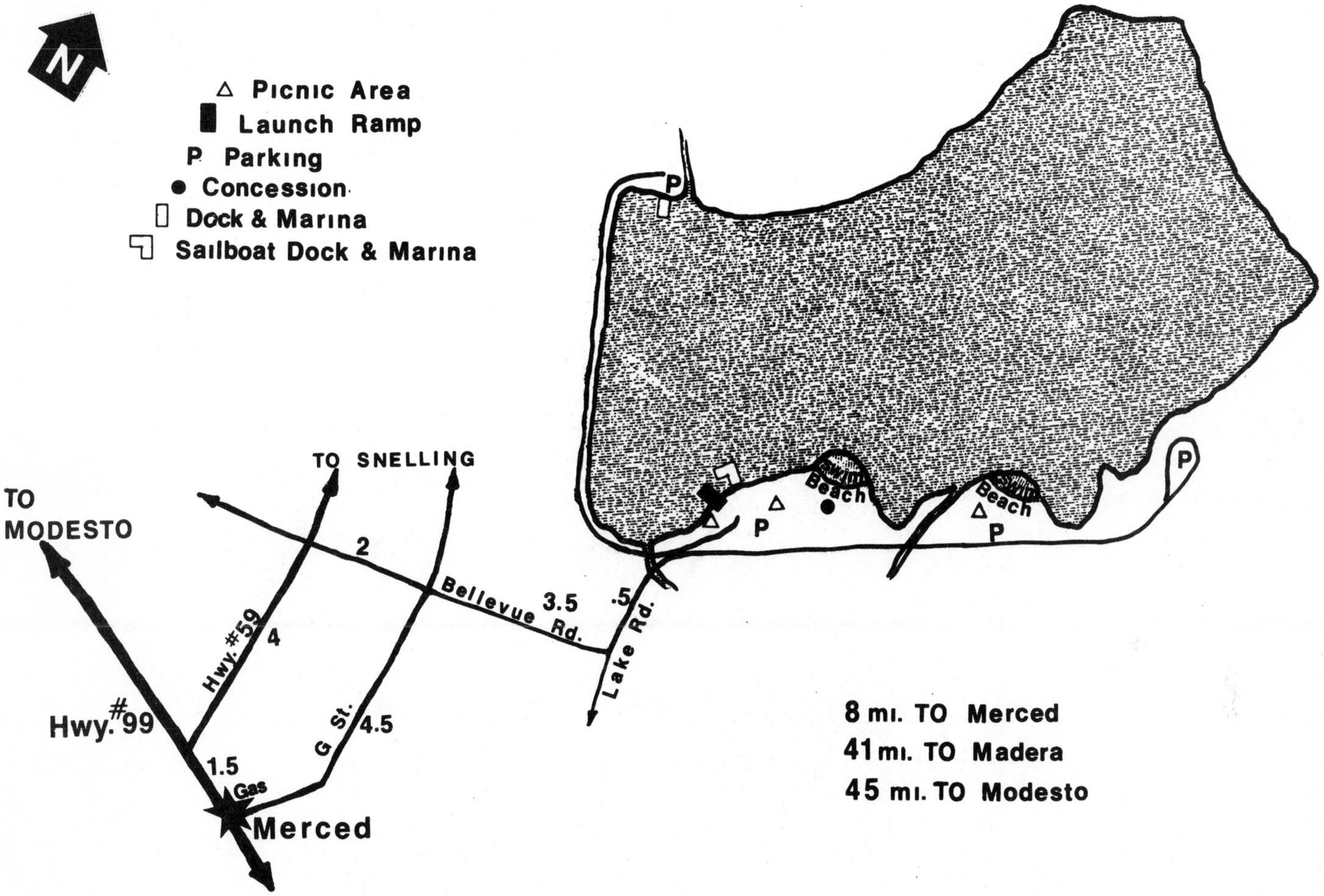

N
Picnic Area
Launch Ramp
P Parking
Concession
Dock & Marina
Sailboat Dock & Marina
TO SNELLING
TO MODESTO
2
Bellevue Rd.
3.5
.5
Lake Rd.
Hwy. #59
4
Hwy. #99
G St.
4.5
1.5
Gas
Merced
Beach
Beach
P
8 mi. TO Merced
41 mi. TO Madera
45 mi. TO Modesto

INFORMATION: Parks & Recreation Div., Merced County Courthouse, Merced 95340

CAMPING	BOATING	RECREATION	RESORTS
Day Use Only Reservations: Ph. 209-726-7426 Youth Groups	All Boating Allowed Designated Areas for Waterskiing, Sailboats, Rowboats and Powerboats. Launch Ramp Docks and Marina Merced Yacht Club Boat Rentals	Fishing Swimming - Designated Area Picnicking Group Picnic Facilities April - October 7:30 a.m.-11:30 p.m. Winter - 8:00 - 5:00	Snack Bar

SAN LUIS RESERVOIR AND O'NEILL FOREBAY

San Luis Reservoir has all recreational facilities available, although winds can limit boating activities as they can be very strong at times. There are 65 miles of shoreline and up to 13,800 surface acres. Day Use is at Dinosaur Point, which has been redone at a cost of $137,000, and provides a launch ramp and toilets. Basalt Area has 79 campsites with showers, cupboards and trailer dump station. This is a big Lake that can get very hot and dry, but trees have been planted as well as irrigated turf. The water is good for swimming and waterskiing. A Minibike trail area covers 157 acres and can be great fun for youngsters. Reservations for campsites can be made through your local Ticketron outlet or write: Ticketron, P. O. Box 26430, San Francisco 94120.

O'Neill Forebay, with 2,000 surface acres, has two facilities. The one at San Luis Creek is for Day Use. There is a launch ramp, swim beach and 482 picnic sites. The irrigated turf helps keep the area cool on hot days. Medeiros Area has 28 developed campsites, a launch ramp and swim beach. This area can hold up to 400 campers or trailers.

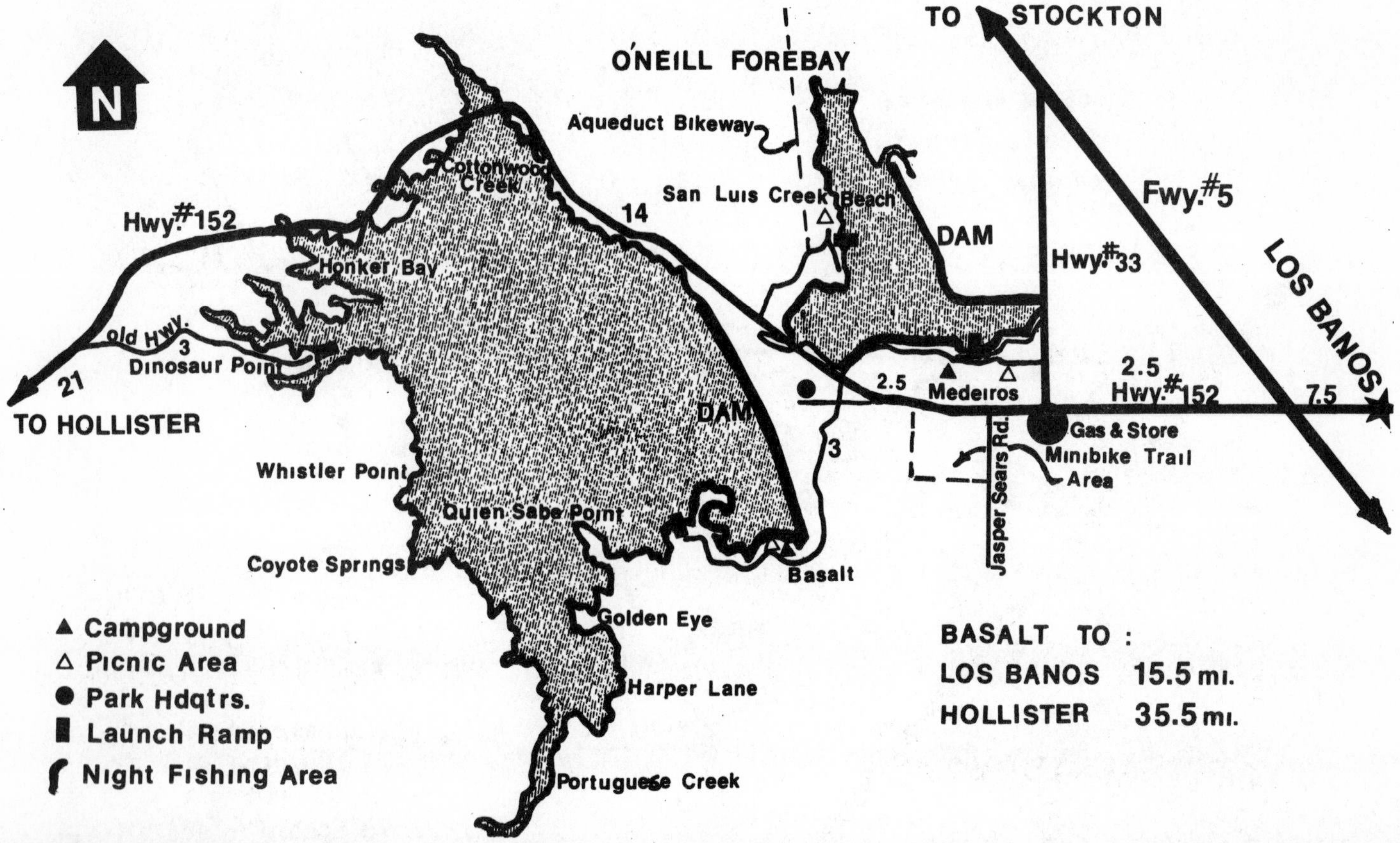
TO STOCKTON
O'NEILL FOREBAY
N
Aqueduct Bikeway
Cottonwood Creek
San Luis Creek Beach
14
Fwy. #5
Hwy. #152
DAM
Honker Bay
Hwy. #33
LOS BANOS
Old Hwy. 3
Dinosaur Point
21
2.5
Medeiros
2.5
Hwy. #152
7.5
TO HOLLISTER
DAM
3
Gas & Store
Minibike Trail Area
Whistler Point
Jasper Sears Rd.
Quien Sabe Point
Coyote Springs
Basalt
Golden Eye
Harper Lane
Portuguese Creek
▲ Campground
△ Picnic Area
● Park Hdqtrs.
Launch Ramp
Night Fishing Area
BASALT TO :
LOS BANOS 15.5 mi.
HOLLISTER 35.5 mi.

INFORMATION: Ticketron, P. O. Box 26430, San Francisco 94120

CAMPING	BOATING	RECREATION	RESORTS
79 Developed Sites for Tents, R.V.s and Trailers Fee: $5 a Day at Basalt Area 28 Developed Sites Fee: $2 a Day at Medeiros Area for 400 R.V.s	All Boating Allowed Launch Ramps - $2	Fishing Swimming Picnicking Bicycle Trails Day Use Only: $2 157 Acre Minibike Trail Area	

LOS BANOS RESERVOIR

Located 9 miles from the town of Los Banos, this Reservoir has 10 miles of shoreline and 410 surface acres. There is one facility with 20 camping and picnicking sites with shade ramadas, tables, stoves, toilets and piped drinking water. Fishing and swimming are the main activities, and there is a 5 MPH speed limit for boaters with motors 10 HP or under.

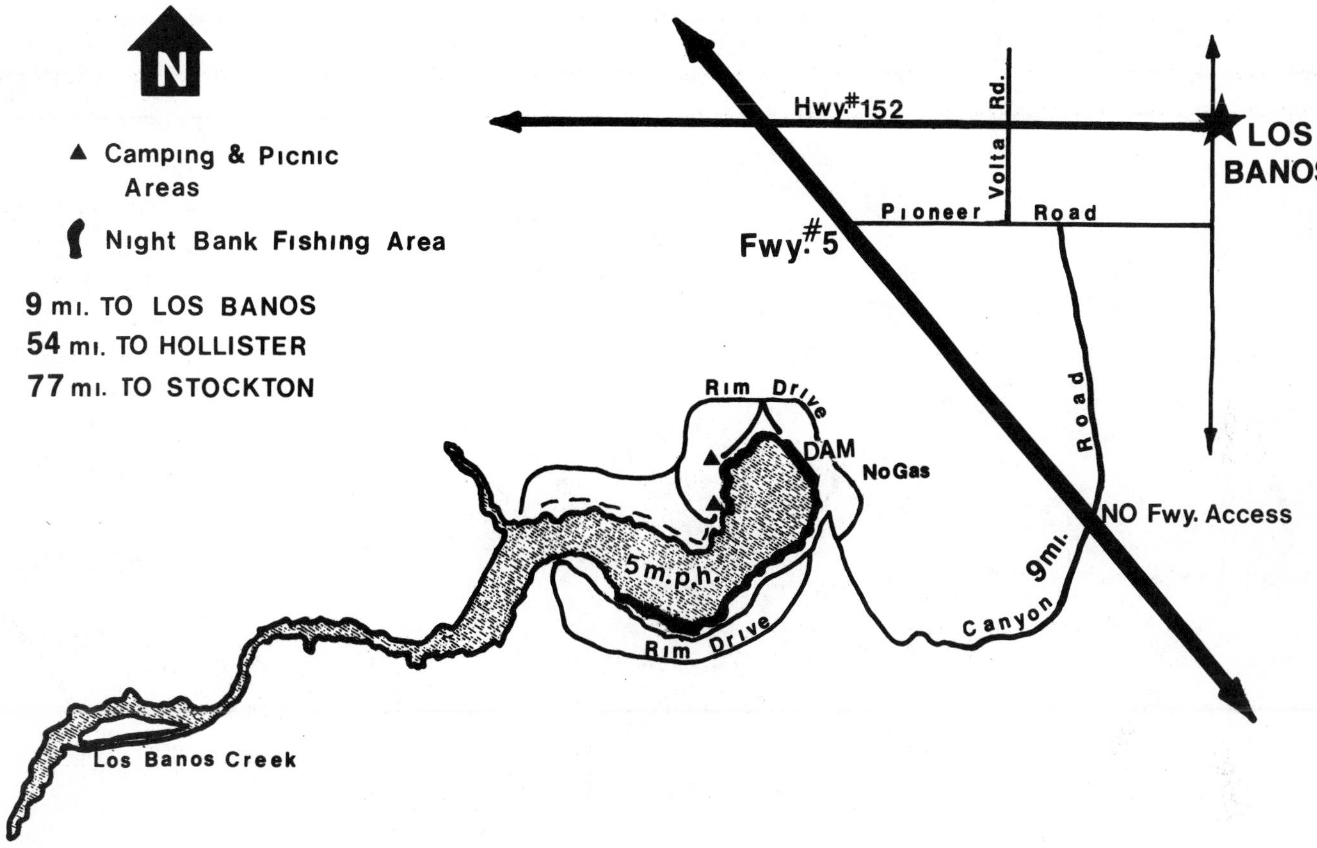
N
Camping & Picnic Areas
Night Bank Fishing Area
9 mi. TO LOS BANOS
54 mi. TO HOLLISTER
77 mi. TO STOCKTON
Hwy.#152
Volta Rd.
LOS BANOS
Pioneer Road
Fwy.#5
Rim Drive
DAM
NoGas
Road
NO Fwy. Access
9mi.
Canyon
5 m.p.h.
Rim Drive
Los Banos Creek

INFORMATION: California State Parks, P. O. Box 2390, Sacramento 95811

CAMPING	BOATING	RECREATION	RESORTS
20 Primitive Sites for Tents, R.V.s and Trailers	Boating with 5 MPH Speed Limit 10 HP Motors or under	Fishing Swimming Picnicking	

SAN ANTONIO RESERVOIR

San Antonio Reservoir, which opened in 1967, is operated by Monterey County Parks and Recreation Department. The Lake covers 5,687 surface acres and is about 16 miles long. It can be an excellent Lake for trout fishing as well as some oversized striped bass and black bass. The facilities are open all year and there are complete services for all vacation activities including camping, picnicking and waterskiing. See following page for full details.

. . . Continued . . .

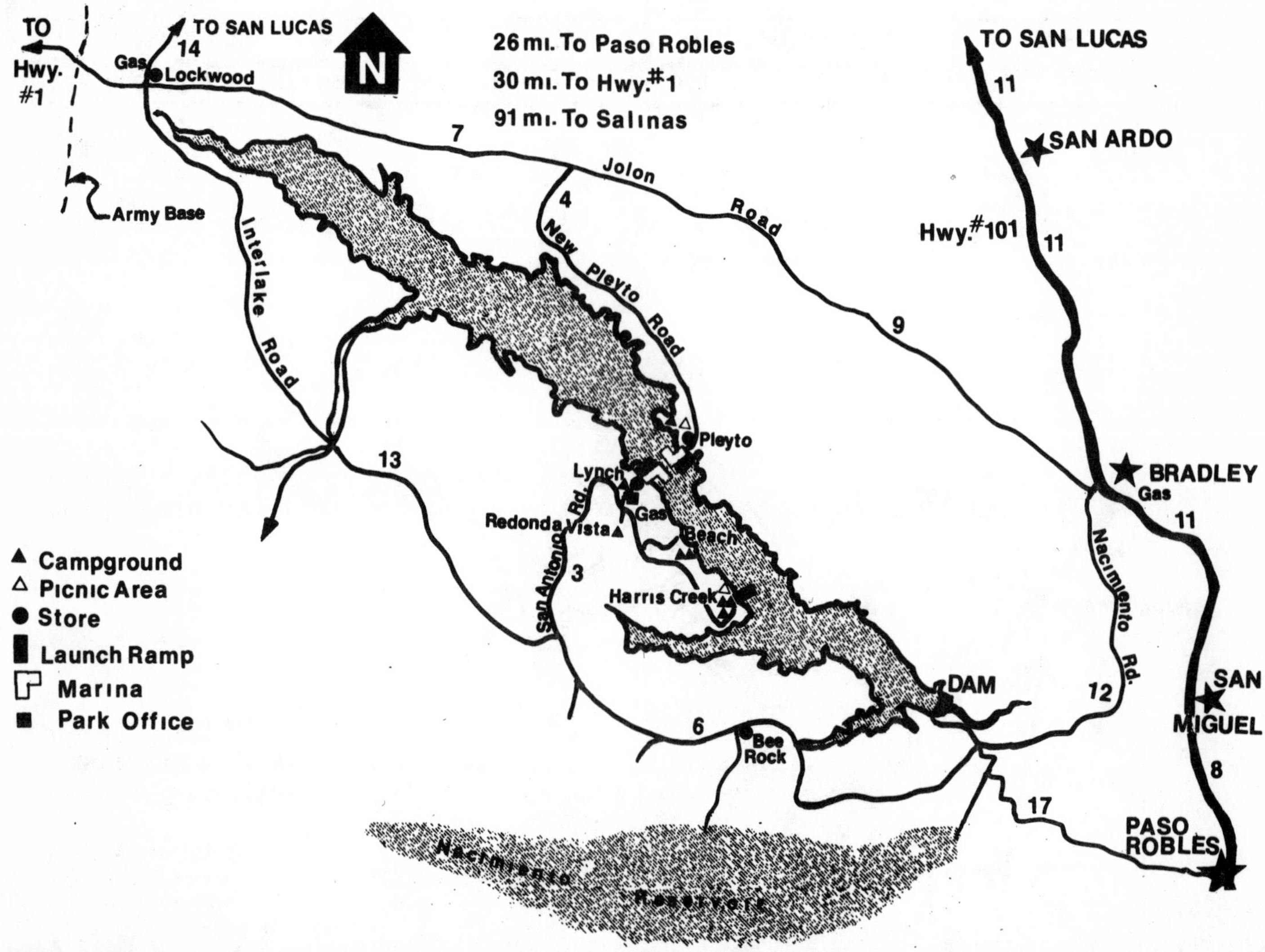

TO Hwy. #1
TO SAN LUCAS
14
Gas
Lockwood
N
26 mi. To Paso Robles
30 mi. To Hwy. #1
91 mi. To Salinas
TO SAN LUCAS
11
SAN ARDO
7
Jolon
Road
4
New Pleyto Road
Hwy. #101
11
Army Base
Interlake Road
9
Pleyto
13
Lynch
BRADLEY
Gas
11
Redonda Vista
Rd.
Gas
Beach
San Antonio
3
Nacimiento Rd.
Harris Creek
Campground
Picnic Area
Store
Launch Ramp
Marina
Park Office
DAM
12
SAN MIGUEL
6
Bee Rock
8
17
PASO ROBLES
Nacimiento
Reservoir

INFORMATION: Lake San Antonio Resort, Bradley 93426, Phone: 805-472-2313 or 472-2311			
CAMPING	**BOATING**	**RECREATION**	**RESORTS**
574 Developed Sites for Tents, R.V.s and Trailers Plus 200 with Full Hookups Fees: $5 a Day - Reg. $7 a Day - See next page for further information.	All Boating Allowed Full Service Marina Dry Storage Launch Ramps Boat Rentals: Fishing Boats, Waterskiing Boats and Pontoons Launch Fee: $2	Fishing Swimming Picnicking Hiking	Mobile Home Rentals Laundromat Game Room Restaurant

. . . Continued . . .

North Shore - Pleyto Campground

198 Regular Campsites for Tents, R.V.s and Trailers Plus 87 with Full Hookups (Further Expansion is in process). Sites have camp stoves and picnic tables with restrooms and hot showers available. There is a boat ramp, boat rentals, tackle and supply store and trailer rentals. (Phone for boat rental information: 805-472-2507)

South Shore - Lynch, Redonda Vista and Harris Creek Campgrounds

376 Regular Campsites for Tents, R.V.s and Trailers Plus 113 with Full Hookups. Sites have camp stoves and picnic tables with restrooms and hot showers available and a Disposal Station. There is a swim beach with life guard, launch ramps, large rental fleet of 65 boats for fishing and waterskiing as well as pontoon boats. Other facilities in this area include a Snack Bar, bait and tackle shop, boat slip rentals, dry storage, trailer rentals, full service Marina, gas, grocery store, laundromat, game room and restaurant.

Camping Fees: $5 a Day Regular Site and $7 a Day Full Hookup
Weekly Rates: $20 a Week Regular Site and $30 a Week Full Hookup
Winter Rates: $15 a Week Regular Site and $25 a Week Full Hookup
(From September 15 to March 15)

If you come in on motorcycle, Fees are: $3 a Day Regular Site, $5 a Day Full Hookup

Dogs - $1 a Day

Youth Group Campground: 60 People Maximum - Information and Reservations: Phone: 805-472-2311 - Located Next to Beach Area

Group Camp Sites - Reserve 5 or more at Harris Creek - Send $2 Deposit.

Mobile Home Rentals - 6 New 2 and 3 Bedroom Units - Completely Furnished Except Linens - Reservations a Must.

Boat Fees - Same as Nacimiento - Stickers and Passes good at both facilities:

Boats - $2 a Day or $8 a Month or $20 a Year

Day Use Only - $2 a Day or Tow-in Vehicle - $3 a Day

Day Use Pass - $18 a Year

LAKE NACIMIENTO

Nacimiento is nestled in a valley of pines and oaks with 165 miles of shoreline full of delightful coves. Fishing from shore or boat will usually produce both black and white bass. Crappie, bluegill and catfish are often plentiful, too. Waterskiing is excellent on the 16 mile long Lake with water temperature about 63 degrees. The Resort operates the campsites and full vacation facilities. See the following page for full details.

. . . Continued . . .

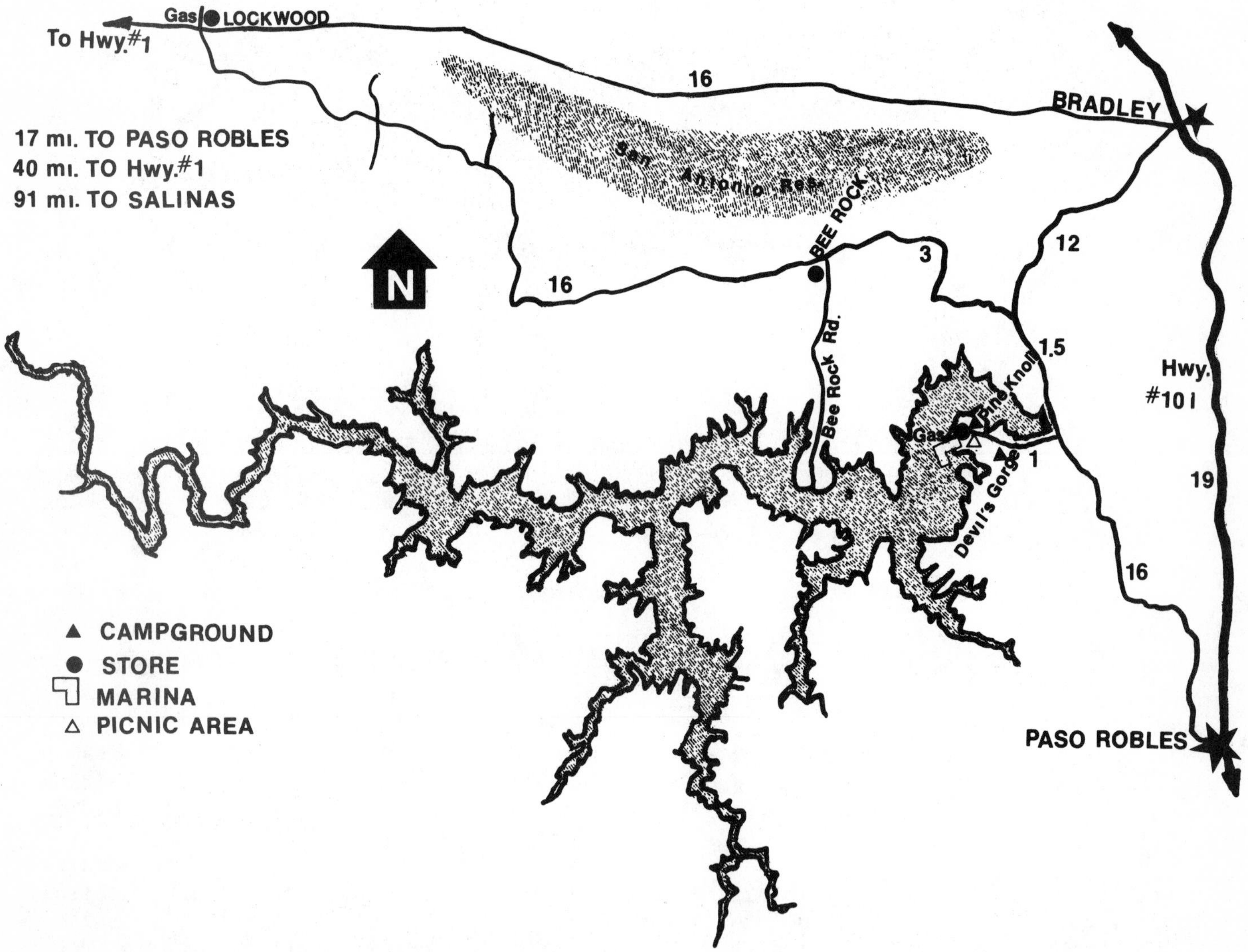

Gas LOCKWOOD
To Hwy.#1
17 mi. TO PASO ROBLES
40 mi. TO Hwy.#1
91 mi. TO SALINAS
16
BRADLEY
San Antonio Res.
BEE ROCK
3
12
16
N
Bee Rock Rd.
1.5
Hwy. #101
Pine Knoll
Gas
1
19
Devil's Gorge
16
CAMPGROUND
STORE
MARINA
PICNIC AREA
PASO ROBLES

INFORMATION: Lake Nacimiento Resort, Star Route, Bradley 93426, Ph. 805-238-3256

CAMPING	BOATING	RECREATION	RESORTS
305 Developed Sites for Tents, R.V.s and Trailers Fee: $6 a Day or $30 a Week	All Boating Allowed Full Service Marina Dry Storage Launch Ramps Boat Rentals: Fishing Boats, Bass Boats, Jet Skiis Water Use Fee: $2	Fishing Swimming Picnicking Hiking	Camp Trailer Rentals Cafe Playgrounds Swimming Pool Hot Tubs Store

Pine Knoll Campground

194 Developed Sites for Tents, R.V.s and Trailers with camp stoves and picnic tables, restrooms, showers, pool and hot tubs available. This Campground is adjacent to the Full Service Marina. Facilities include a launch ramp, dry storage, fish cleaning station, gas, propane, store, cafe and playground. Also included are boat rentals with or without motors, pontoons for bass fishing, marina supplies, ski equipment rentals, boat slips and rental trailers.

Devil's Gorge Campground

111 Developed Sites for Tents, R.V.s and Trailers with camp stoves and picnic tables, restrooms and showers available. This Campground is adjacent to a playground.

Camping Fees: $6 a Day
$30 a Week

Boat Fees - Same as San Antonio - Stickers and Passes good at both facilities.

Boats - $2 a Day or $8 a Month or $20 a Year

snyder
No Matter How you go - use Boat Safety!

BASS LAKE

Bass Lake, situated at 3,400 feet elevation in the Southern Sierra Nevada, is operated by P. G. & E. to produce hydroelectric power. Lake levels are generally maintained through Labor Day. Facilities on the West Shore are administered by the U. S. Forest Service and are described on the following page. All boating is allowed on the Lake and there are two launch ramps in addition to rental boats and swimming beaches. Fishing can be good for bass, trout, catfish and Kokanee salmon. Reservations for family campsites are available through your local Ticketron outlet or write: Ticketron, P. O. Box 26430, San Francisco 94120. Along with a Group Campground and Group Picnic Area, a Youth Campground accommodates a maximum of 135 youngsters. All Group reservations are obtained from the U. S. Forest Service, P. O. Box 355, Oakhurst 93644, Phone: 209-642-3212. Cabins and full service Trailer Parks are available at privately-owned areas.

. . . Continued . . .

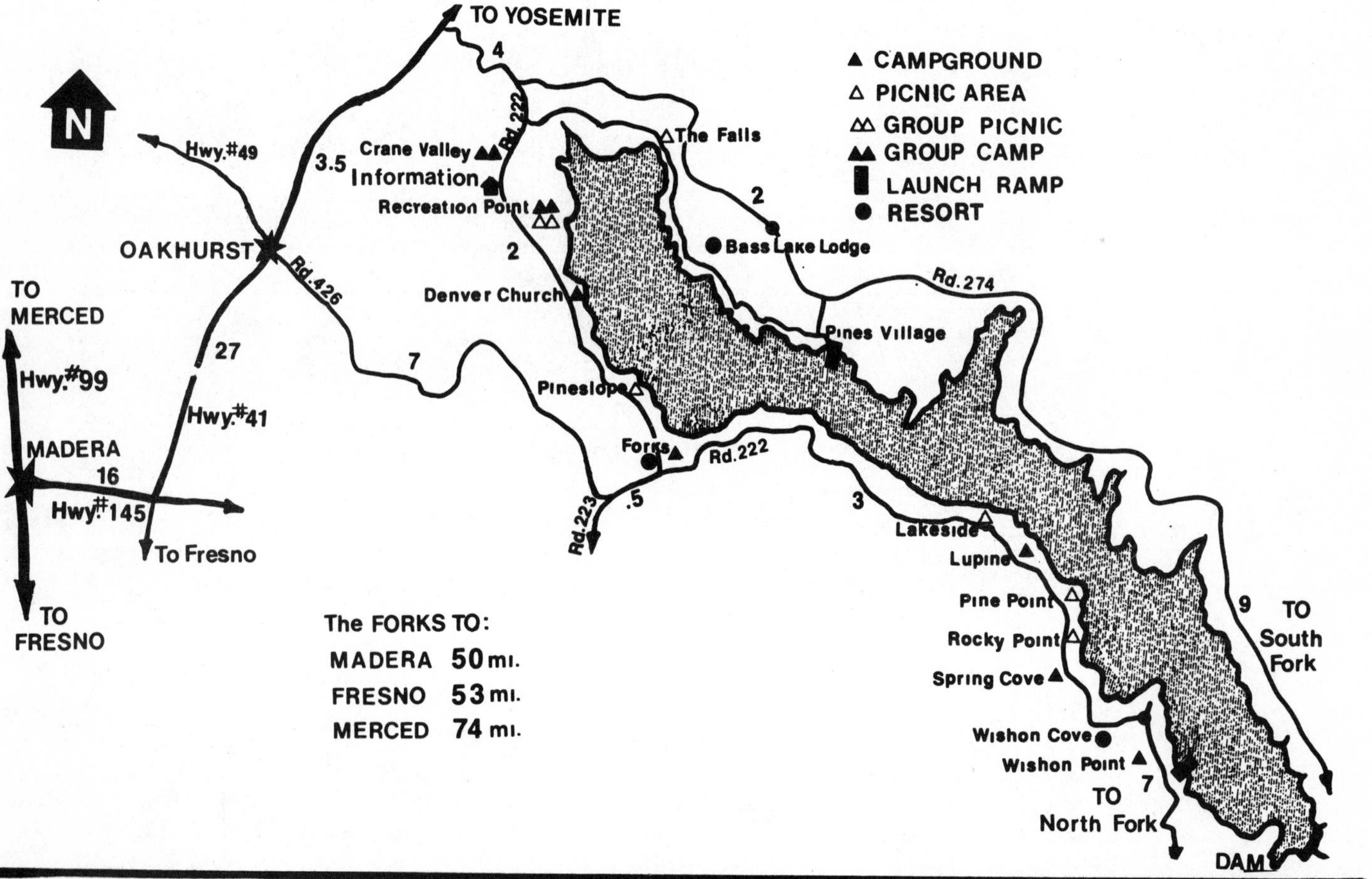

TO YOSEMITE
4
N
Hwy.#49
3.5
Crane Valley
Rd.222
Information
Recreation Point
The Falls
2
Bass Lake Lodge
OAKHURST
Rd.426
2
Denver Church
Rd.274
Pines Village
TO MERCED
27
7
Hwy.#99
Pineslope
Hwy.#41
MADERA
16
Forks
Rd.222
Hwy.#145
.5
3
Rd.223
To Fresno
Lakeside
Lupine
TO FRESNO
Pine Point
9
TO South Fork
Rocky Point
Spring Cove
Wishon Cove
Wishon Point
7
TO North Fork
DAM
CAMPGROUND
PICNIC AREA
GROUP PICNIC
GROUP CAMP
LAUNCH RAMP
RESORT
The FORKS TO:
MADERA 50 mi.
FRESNO 53 mi.
MERCED 74 mi.

INFORMATION: U.S.F.S., P.O. Box 366, Oakhurst 93644, Ph. 209-642-3212 or Ticketron

CAMPING	BOATING	RECREATION	RESORTS
232 Developed Sites for Tents, R.V.s and Trailers to 20 feet Fee: $3 a Day Reserv. - Ticketron Group Areas - Reserve through U.S.F.S. Privately owned Facilities	All Boating Allowed Launch Ramps Full Service Marina Boat Rentals	Fishing Swimming Hiking Picnicking Nature Programs	Stores Restaurants Housekeeping Cabins

. . . Continued . . .

U. S. Forest Service - Camping Facilities
Reservations through Ticketron

Wishon Point - 13 tent sites, 11 trailer/R.V. sites for single family and 13 multiple family sites for tents, R.V.s and trailers, water, toilets launch ramp.

Spring Cove - 54 tent sites, 11 trailer/R.V. sites, water, toilets.

Lupine - 42 tent sites, 19 trailer/R.V. sites, water, toilets. (Paved steep entrance).

Forks - 25 tent sites, 6 trailer/R.V. sites, water, toilets.

Denver Church - 19 tent sites, 12 trailer/R.V. sites, 7 Combination sites, water, toilets.

U. S. Forest Service - Group Campground
Reservations through U. S. Forest Service, Oakhurst

Recreation Point - 135 people maximum

Crane Valley - 125 people maximum

U. S. Forest Service - Picnic Grounds

Rocky Point - 8 Units, Rocky Beach

Pine Point - 12 Units

Lakeside - 8 Units, Sandy Beach

Pine Slope - 10 Units, Sandy Beach

The Falls - 5 Units

U. S. Forest Service - Group Picnic Grounds
Reservations through U. S. Forest Service

Recreation Point - 3 Group Picnic Areas for 300 people maximum - Game Field

Private Facilities

Fork's Resort - Cabins, restaurant, bar, grocery store, gasoline, boat rentals and marina.

The Pines Resort - Housekeeping cabins, trailer and tent sites, dormitory building, restaurant, bar, grocery store, shops, boat rentals and marina.

Wishon Cove Resort - Cabins, snack bar, grocery store, boat rentals and marina.

Yosemite Mountain-Sugar Pine Railroad - Historic train rides, gold panning, shops, picnic facilities for families or groups, snack bar.

Yosemite Trails Packstation - Horse rentals, riding lessons, packing services.

For Detailed Information Contact: The Eastern Madera County Chamber of Commerce, P. O. Box 374, Oakhurst 93644 or The North Fork Chamber of Commerce, P. O. Box 426, North Fork 93643.

Millerton Lake is 16 miles long with 43 miles of shoreline. At the Eastern end of the Lake, the surrounding hills become steeper and higher. There are a total of 94 developed sites for tents, R.V.s and trailers and 39 primitive sites at Fort Miller, Tank Hill, Rocky Point and Meadow Area. A Boat Access Only Camp is located at Temperance Flat with 25 campsites with tables, stoves and water. 2 Group Camps are available in the Meadow Area accommodating 40 people and 75 people each. Hundreds of picnic units are located around the Lake, and there is a Group Picnic Area which accommodates up to 150 people with a special shelter. Launching ramps are on both sides of the Lake and there is a nice sandy swimming beach. The Lake generally offers good boating conditions with light winds. Family and group campsites can be reserved through your local Ticketron outlet or write: Ticketron, P. O. Box 26430, San Francisco 94126.

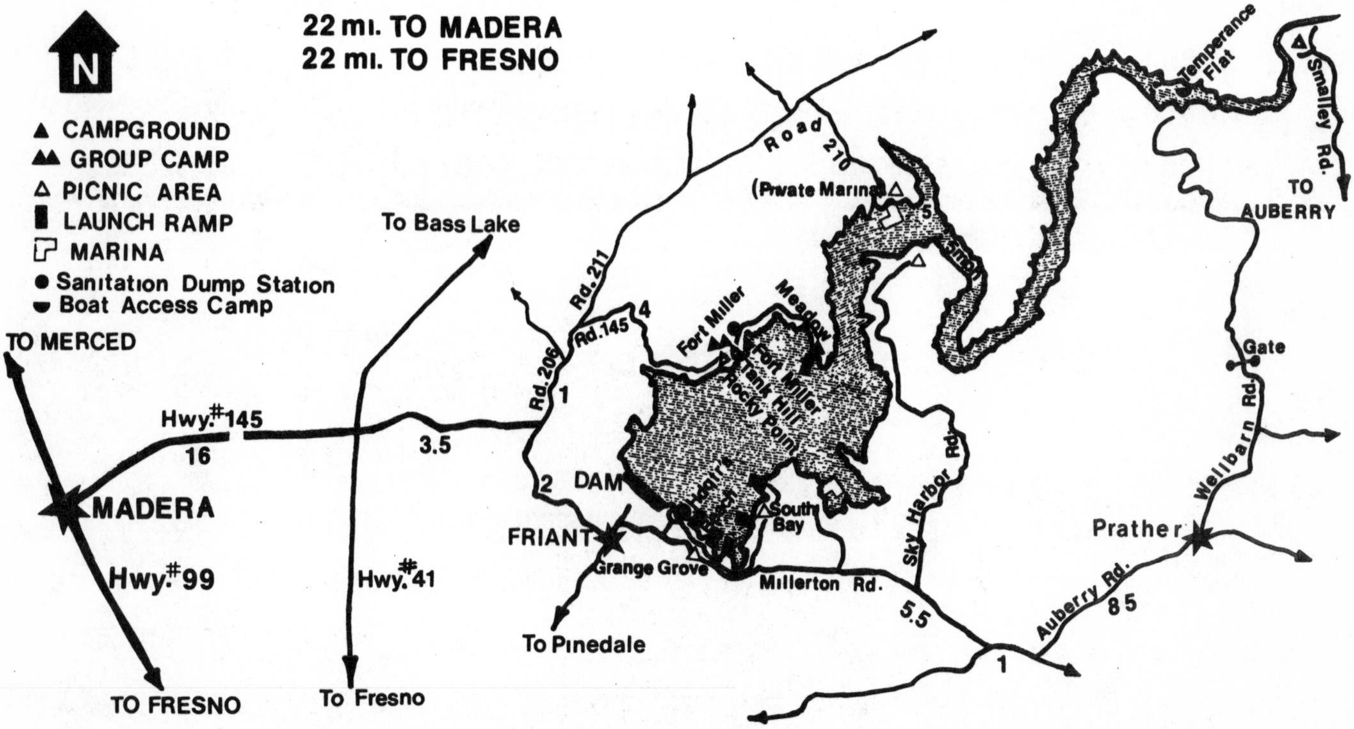
N
22 mi. TO MADERA
22 mi. TO FRESNO
CAMPGROUND
GROUP CAMP
PICNIC AREA
LAUNCH RAMP
MARINA
Sanitation Dump Station
Boat Access Camp
TO MERCED
Hwy. #145
16
3.5
MADERA
Hwy. #99
TO FRESNO
To Bass Lake
Hwy. #41
To Fresno
Rd. 211
Rd. 145
4
Rd. 206
1
2
DAM
FRIANT
Grange Grove
To Pinedale
Road 210
(Private Marina)
Fort Miller
Meadow
Tank Hill
Rocky Point
South Bay
Sky Harbor Rd.
Millerton Rd.
5.5
1
Auberry Rd.
8 5
Prather
Wellbarn Rd.
Gate
TO AUBERRY
Smalley Rd.
Temperance Flat

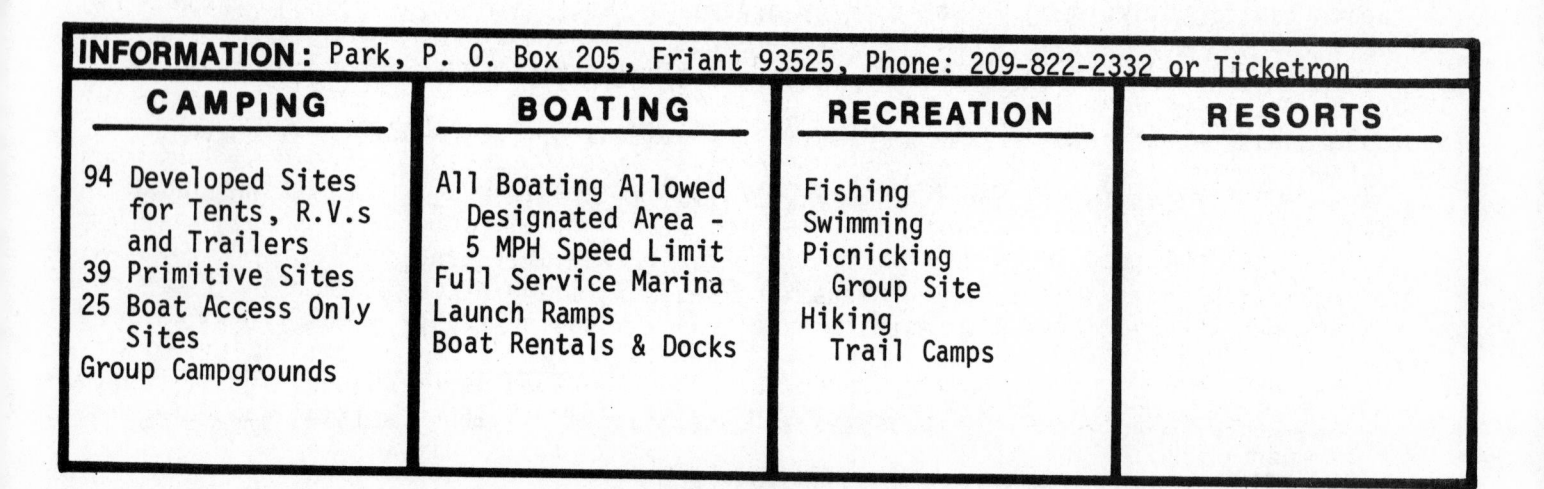

INFORMATION: Park, P. O. Box 205, Friant 93525, Phone: 209-822-2332 or Ticketron

CAMPING	BOATING	RECREATION	RESORTS
94 Developed Sites for Tents, R.V.s and Trailers 39 Primitive Sites 25 Boat Access Only Sites Group Campgrounds	All Boating Allowed Designated Area - 5 MPH Speed Limit Full Service Marina Launch Ramps Boat Rentals & Docks	Fishing Swimming Picnicking Group Site Hiking Trail Camps	

PINE FLAT LAKE

Pine Flat Lake is a U. S. Army Corps of Engineers flood control project. It is 21 miles long and has 67 miles of shoreline. The water is used for irrigation and Lake levels can fluctuate from April to October. The U. S. Forest Service operates facilities East of Trimmer. 24 sites for tents, R.V.s and trailers with water and toilets are located at Sycamore Campground #1. At Sycamore Campground #2, there are 30 sites for tents, R.V.s and trailers, also with water and toilets. At Kirch Flat there are 15 sites for tents, R.V.s and trailers with toilets. At Lakeview, next to Sycamore, there are 20 picnic units. The West end of the Lake is operated by the U. S. Army Corps of Engineers with over 75 campsites with toilets and showers. An overflow area is available at Island Park and Trimmer. A trailer dump station is available at Island Park. A private development at Lake View also has overnight facilities. There are 4 launch ramps, 3 full service Marinas and 6 boat access sites for camping or picnicking. The water is warm for swimming and the climate can be hot in the summer. There are some small trees, but generally the shoreline is in the open and waterskiing is quite popular.

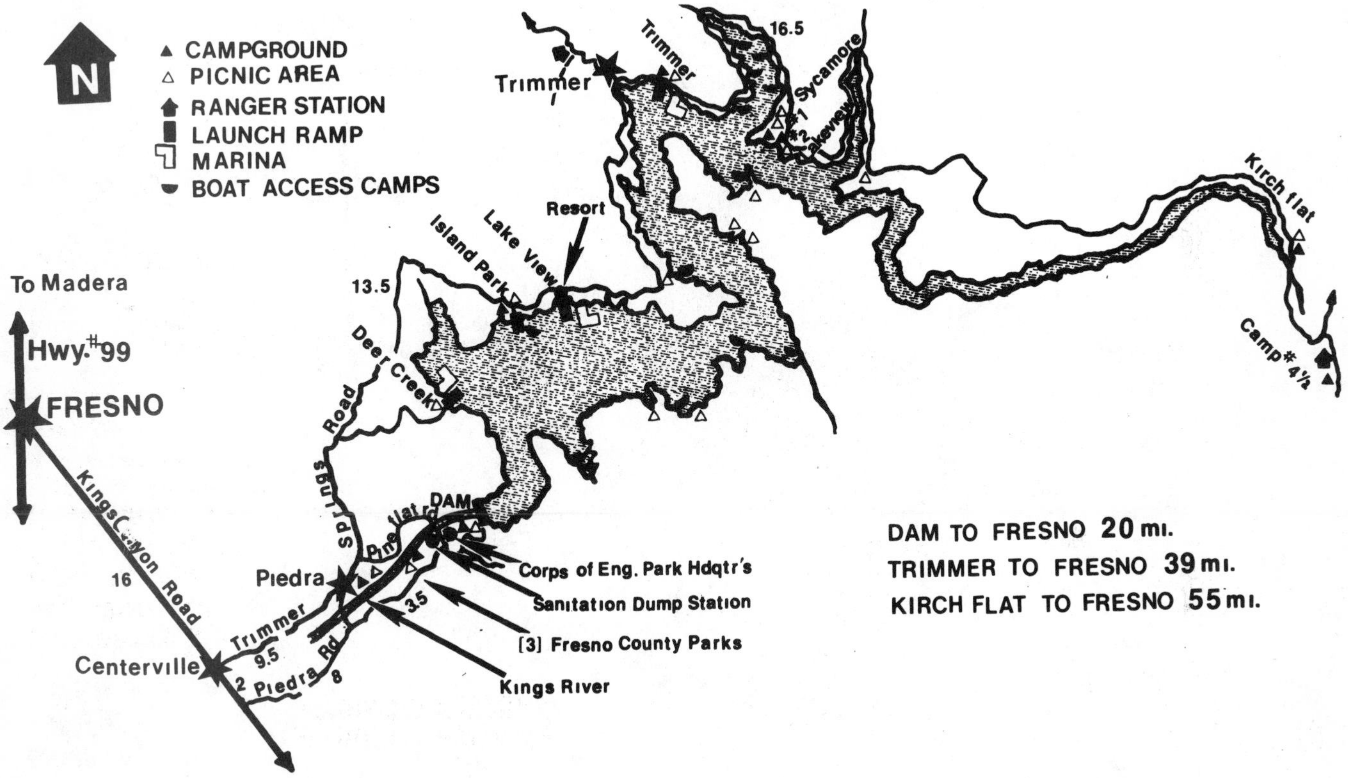
N
CAMPGROUND
PICNIC AREA
RANGER STATION
LAUNCH RAMP
MARINA
BOAT ACCESS CAMPS
Trimmer
Trimmer
16.5
Sycamore
Lakeview
Kirch flat
Camp # 4½
Resort
Lake View
Island Park
13.5
To Madera
Hwy. # 99
FRESNO
Deer Creek
Springs Road
Pine flat Rd
DAM
Corps of Eng. Park Hdqtr's
Sanitation Dump Station
[3] Fresno County Parks
Kings River
Piedra
Trimmer
9.5
3.5
16
Centerville
2
Piedra Rd
8
DAM TO FRESNO 20 mi.
TRIMMER TO FRESNO 39 mi.
KIRCH FLAT TO FRESNO 55 mi.

INFORMATION: Park Manager, P. O. Box 117, Piedra 93649, Phone: 209-787-2589

CAMPING	BOATING	RECREATION	RESORTS
100 Plus Developed Sites for Tents, R.V.s and Trailers No Reservations Fee: $2 a Day April through September	All Boating Allowed Launch Ramps Full Service Marinas Boat Rentals	Fishing Swimming Picnicking Boat Access Sites - Day Use	Stores Restaurants Showers Full Accommodations at Piedra

SHAVER LAKE

Shaver Lake is about 5,500 feet in elevation and has lovely campgrounds near the water. Dorabelle, operated by the U. S. Forest Service, is 1/2 mile from town and has 67 developed sites with water, toilets and barbecues, and a swim beach. Naturalist programs are offered in July and August. There are also 14 undeveloped sites at Swanson Meadow. Camp Edison, operated by Southern California Edison Company, is about 3 miles Northeast of town. It has 68 campsites with electric and water hookups, dump station, a group picnic area and recreation facilities. This area is on a first-come basis and offers a launch ramp and swim beach. Fees for these sites are $5 a Day, $1 per dog, and $1 for boat launching. Marinas are available at the public ramp at the Northern tip of the Lake and at Shaver Lodge. The Lake has trees along the shoreline with large granite boulders and crystal clear water.

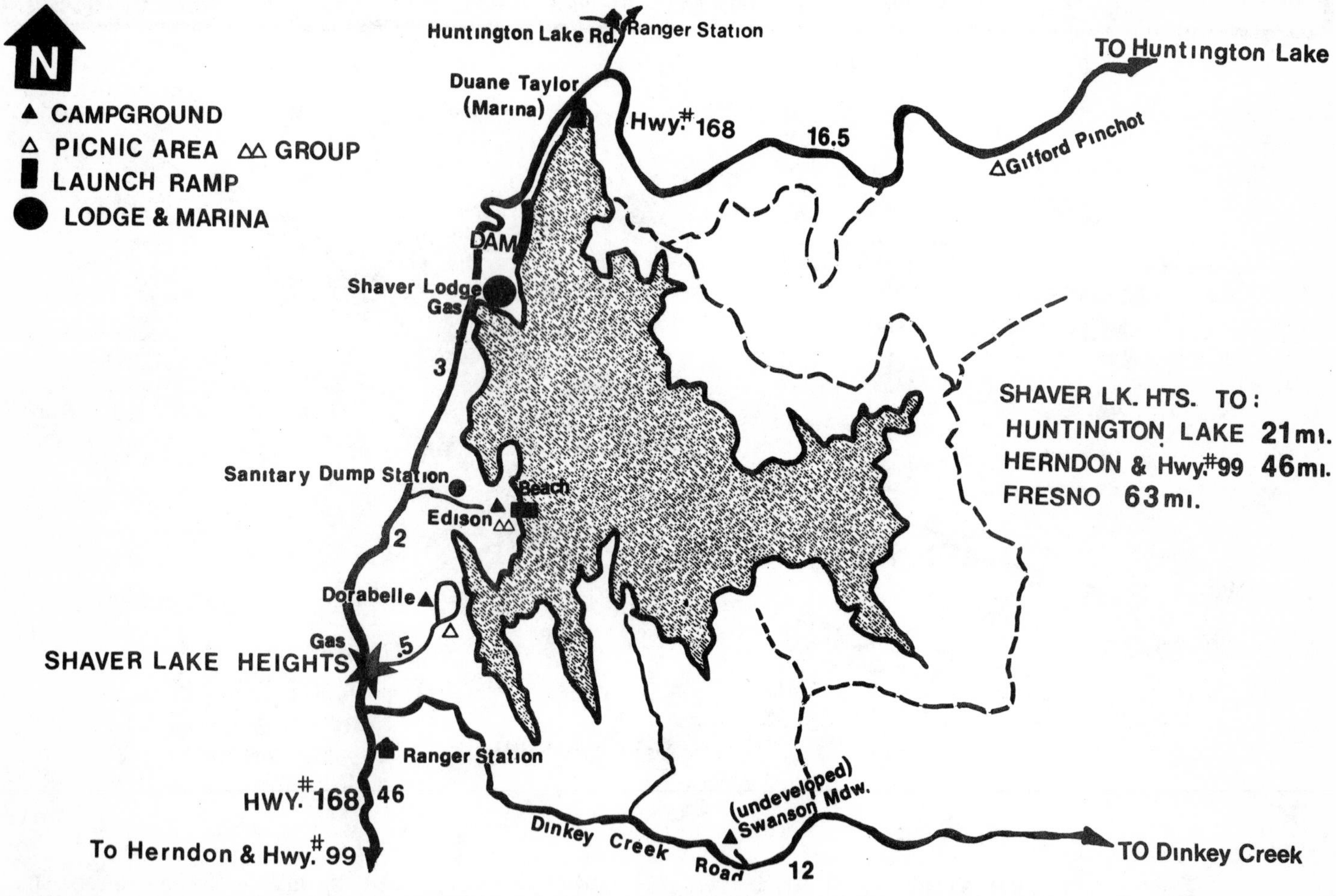
N
CAMPGROUND
PICNIC AREA
GROUP
LAUNCH RAMP
LODGE & MARINA
Huntington Lake Rd.
Ranger Station
TO Huntington Lake
Duane Taylor
(Marina)
Hwy.# 168
16.5
Gifford Pinchot
DAM
Shaver Lodge
Gas
3
SHAVER LK. HTS. TO:
HUNTINGTON LAKE 21 mi.
HERNDON & Hwy.#99 46 mi.
FRESNO 63 mi.
Sanitary Dump Station
Beach
Edison
2
Dorabelle
Gas
.5
SHAVER LAKE HEIGHTS
Ranger Station
HWY.# 168
46
To Herndon & Hwy.# 99
Dinkey Creek Road
(undeveloped)
Swanson Mdw.
12
TO Dinkey Creek

INFORMATION: U.S.F.S., Pineridge Ranger District, P. O. Box 300, Shaver Lake 93664

CAMPING	BOATING	RECREATION	RESORTS
67 U.S.F.S. Developed Sites for Tents, R.V.s and Trailers Fee: $3 a Day 14 Undeveloped Sites So. Cal. Edison 68 Developed Sites	All Boating Allowed Launch Ramps Full Service Marinas Rental Boats	Fishing Swimming Hiking Picnicking	Shaver Lodge Stores Restaurants Sierra Outpost Motel Eckerts Lodge

Huntington Lake has 7 U. S. Forest Service Campgrounds with hundreds of units available for tents, R.V.s and trailers. Details on the sites are shown on the following page. There are many commercial facilities that are under special use permit to the U. S. Forest Service which include Lakeshore Village on the Northeast end close to the launch ramp offering cabins, grocery store, fishing tackle, bar, restaurant and laundry. Cedar Crest Resort is about two miles further up the road and has very lovely accommodations as well as rental boats. Huntington Lake Resort is on the Northwest corner of the Lake with a marina and sandy beach. Motel units and housekeeping cabins are available and there is a launching ramp. Hiking trails surround the Lake with many very scenic views and waterfalls. Check at the Visitor Center to obtain permits, maps and information. Naturalist Programs are scheduled from Tuesday through Saturday, June 15 to September 8. There are good winds in the early afternoon from the West running the length of the Lake, and sailing regattas are held through the summer.

. . . Continued . . .

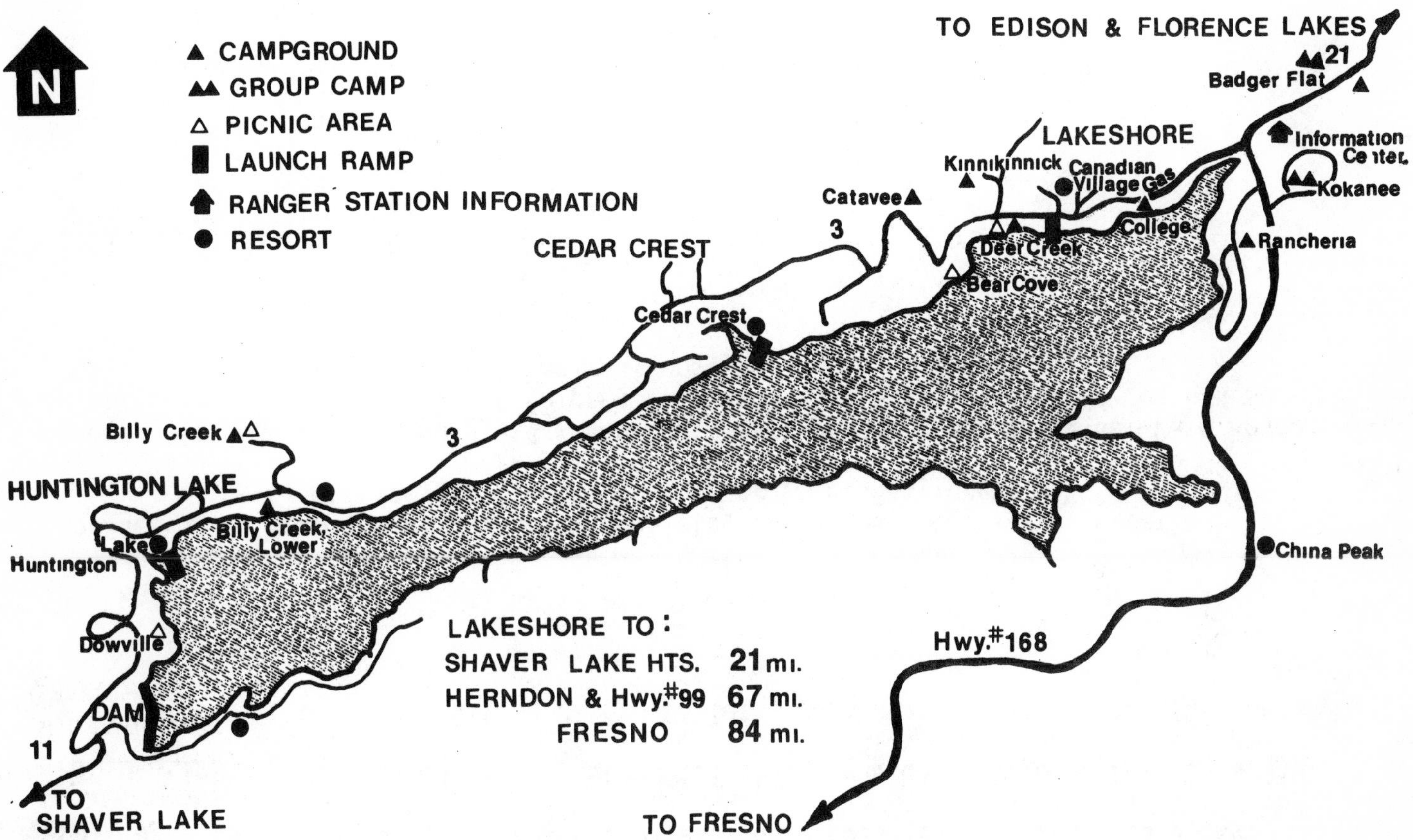
N
CAMPGROUND
GROUP CAMP
PICNIC AREA
LAUNCH RAMP
RANGER STATION INFORMATION
RESORT
TO EDISON & FLORENCE LAKES
21
Badger Flat
LAKESHORE
Information Center
Kinnikinnick
Canadian
Village Gas
Kokanee
Catavee
College
Rancheria
3
Deer Creek
Bear Cove
CEDAR CREST
Cedar Crest
Billy Creek
3
HUNTINGTON LAKE
Billy Creek, Lower
Lake
Huntington
Dowville
DAM
11
TO SHAVER LAKE
LAKESHORE TO:
SHAVER LAKE HTS. 21 mi.
HERNDON & Hwy.#99 67 mi.
FRESNO 84 mi.
Hwy.#168
China Peak
TO FRESNO

INFORMATION: U.S.F.S., Pineridge Ranger District, P. O. Box 300, Shaver Lake 93664

CAMPING	BOATING	RECREATION	RESORTS
334 Developed Sites for Tents, R.V.s and Trailers Fee: $2-$3 a Day Group Campgrounds for 200 people and 45 people	All Boating Allowed Launch Ramps Full Service Marinas Boat Rentals	Fishing Swimming Picnicking Hiking Backpacking - Wilderness Area Horseback Riding	Motels Housekeeping Cabins Stores Restaurants Full Vacation Facilities

. . . Continued . . .

U. S. Forest Service - Camping Facilities

Billy Creek - 45 Developed Sites, water, toilets, barbecues, tables. Fee: $2 a Day.

Billy Creek - Lower - 13 Developed Sites, water, toilets, barbecues, tables. Fee: $3 a Day

Catavee - 26 Developed Sites, water, toilets, barbecues, tables. Fee: $2 a Day.

Kinnikinnick - 32 Developed Sites, water, toilets, barbecues, tables. Fee: $2 a Day.

Deer Creek - 38 Developed Sites, water, toilets, barbecues, tables. Fee: $3 a Day.

College - 24 Developed Sites, water, toilets, barbecues, tables. Fee: $3 a Day.

Badger Flat - 10 Developed Sites, water, toilets, barbecues, tables. Fee: $3 a Day.

Rancheria - 146 Developed Sites, water, toilets, barbecues, tables. Fee: $3 a Day.

Group Campgrounds

Kokanee - 200 people maximum, water, toilets, barbecues, tables. Reservations: U. S. Forest Service, P. O. Box 300, Shaver Lake, California 93664.

Badger Flat Group Campground - 4 miles Northeast of Huntington on Kaiser Pass Road. 45 people maximum, toilets, tables. No fee and no reservations.

Picnic Grounds

Dowville - 3 Units

Billy Creek - 7 Units

Bear Cove - 17 Units

Deer Creek - 5 Units

EDISON LAKE
and
FLORENCE LAKE

Edison is a beautiful Lake in the high altitude of 7,643 feet. Granite boulders and sandy beaches around the shoreline make a lovely setting. The water is too cold for swimming at about 40 degrees. All boating is allowed with a 15 MPH speed limit. The U. S. Forest Service operates the following: Portal Forebay with 9 sites, Bolsillo with 4 sites, Mono Hot Springs with 31 sites, Mono Creek with 18 sites, Vermillion with 30 sites, Ward Lake with 6 sites, Florence Lake with 14 sites, and Jackass Meadow with 15 sites. There is a very narrow road for 20 miles leading into this quiet area with some of the campsites along the way. Recreation Vehicles and trailers are not advised to attempt this road. There is a dirt launch ramp and the fishing for trout is good. Florence Lake is similar to Edison also with a dirt launch ramp. There is a small store with limited supplies. A Resort with store, cabins, gas, restaurant and hot mineral baths is also located at Mono Hot Springs. Portal Forebay is a very small Lake but the fishing is good night and morning. This entire area is a delightfully peaceful vacation spot for those who want to get away from the busy life.

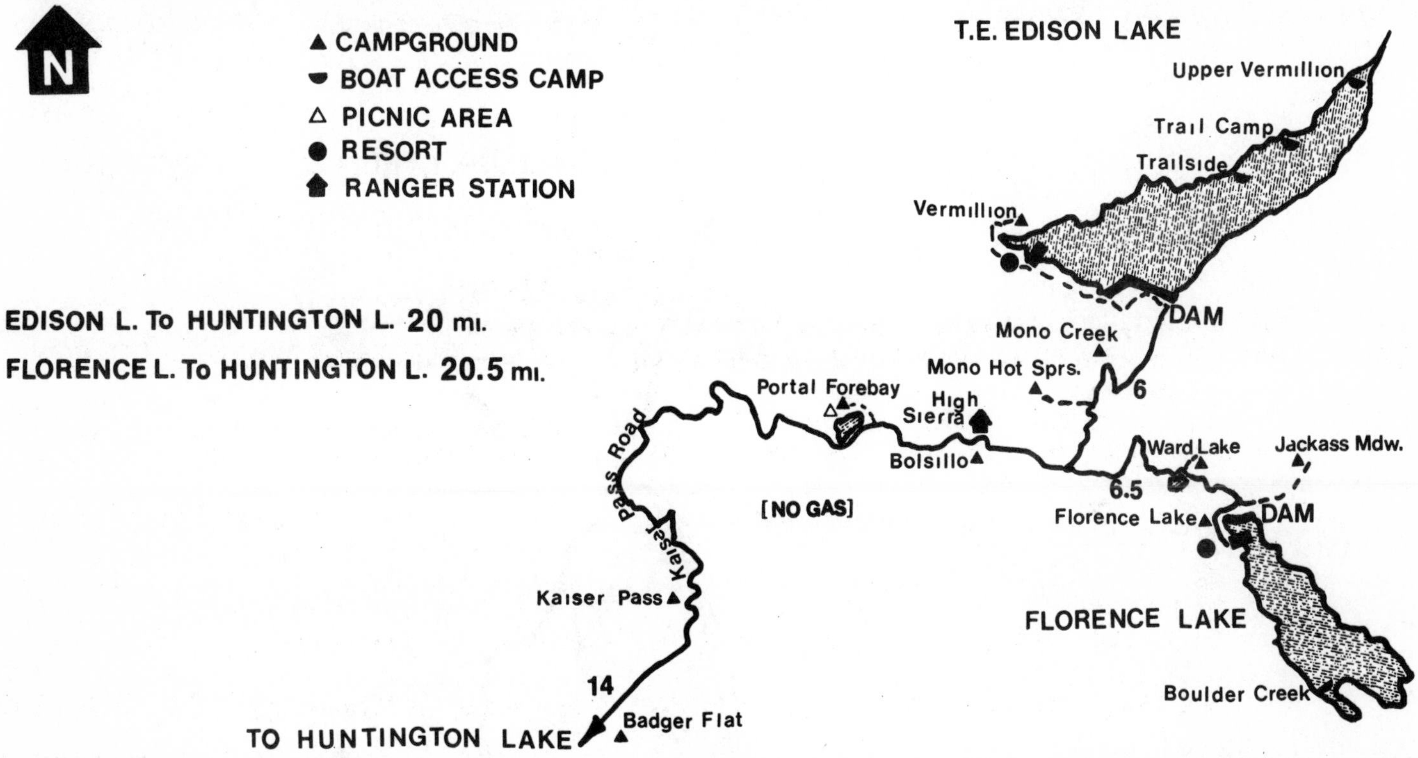

N
▲ CAMPGROUND
BOAT ACCESS CAMP
△ PICNIC AREA
● RESORT
RANGER STATION
T.E. EDISON LAKE
Upper Vermillion
Trail Camp
Trailside
Vermillion
DAM
Mono Creek
Mono Hot Sprs.
6
Portal Forebay
High Sierra
Bolsillo
Ward Lake
Jackass Mdw.
6.5
Florence Lake
DAM
[NO GAS]
Kaiser Pass Road
Kaiser Pass
FLORENCE LAKE
Boulder Creek
14
Badger Flat
TO HUNTINGTON LAKE
EDISON L. To HUNTINGTON L. 20 mi.
FLORENCE L. To HUNTINGTON L. 20.5 mi.

INFORMATION: U. S. Forest Service, P.O. Box 300, Shaver Lake 93664

CAMPING	BOATING	RECREATION	RESORTS
127 Sites for Tents R.V.s and Trailers are not recommended due to narrow one-lane winding road.	All Boating Allowed No Waterskiing 15 MPH Speed Limit Dirt Launch Ramps	Fishing Picnicking Hiking	Cabins Stores Restaurant

LAKES ON Hwy.#395 From Bridgeport To Bishop

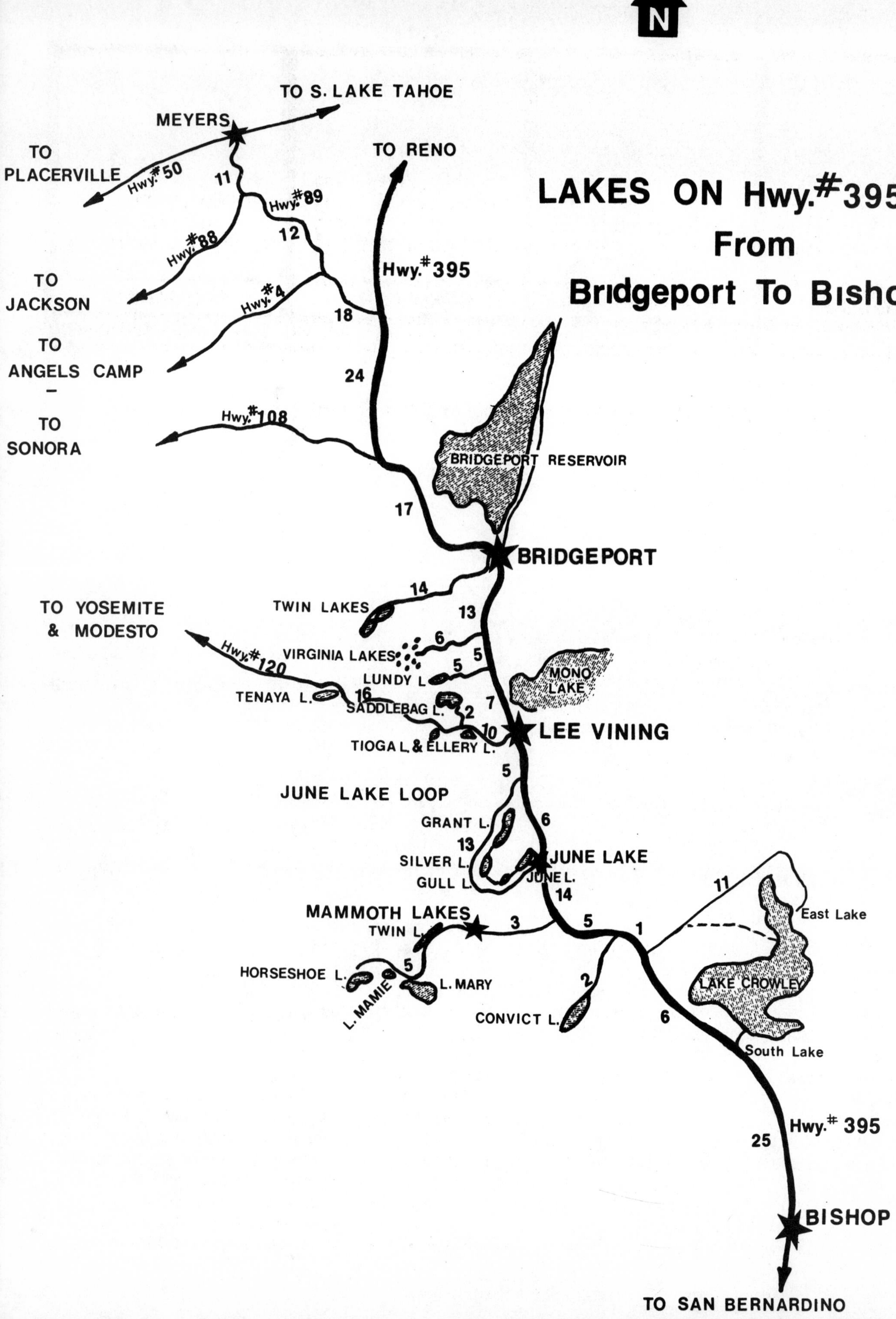
N
TO S. LAKE TAHOE
MEYERS
TO PLACERVILLE
Hwy.#50
11
Hwy.#89
12
Hwy.#88
TO JACKSON
Hwy.#4
18
TO ANGELS CAMP
–
TO SONORA
Hwy.#108
TO RENO
Hwy.#395
24
BRIDGEPORT RESERVOIR
17
BRIDGEPORT
14
TWIN LAKES
13
TO YOSEMITE & MODESTO
Hwy.#120
6
VIRGINIA LAKES
5
LUNDY L.
5
MONO LAKE
TENAYA L.
16
SADDLEBAG L.
2
7
10
LEE VINING
TIOGA L. & ELLERY L.
5
JUNE LAKE LOOP
GRANT L.
6
13
SILVER L.
GULL L.
JUNE LAKE
JUNE L.
14
MAMMOTH LAKES
TWIN L.
3
5
1
11
East Lake
HORSESHOE L.
5
L. MARY
L. MAMIE
2
CONVICT L.
LAKE CROWLEY
6
South Lake
Hwy.# 395
25
BISHOP
TO SAN BERNARDINO

BRIDGEPORT RESERVOIR

Bridgeport Reservoir is 5-1/2 miles long at an elevation of 6,500 feet with 23 miles of shoreline. The Lake water is used for irrigation with the season from May to November. Falling Rock Marina has 19 spaces for trailers with full hookups, snack bar, boat and motor rentals and fishing gear. Boat slips are also available. The U. S. Forest Service and Mono County Park Department operate campgrounds in this area. The Lake is surrounded by barren land so there can be strong winds in the afternoon. This is a popular fishing Lake, and you can catch some good-sized German Brown Trout.

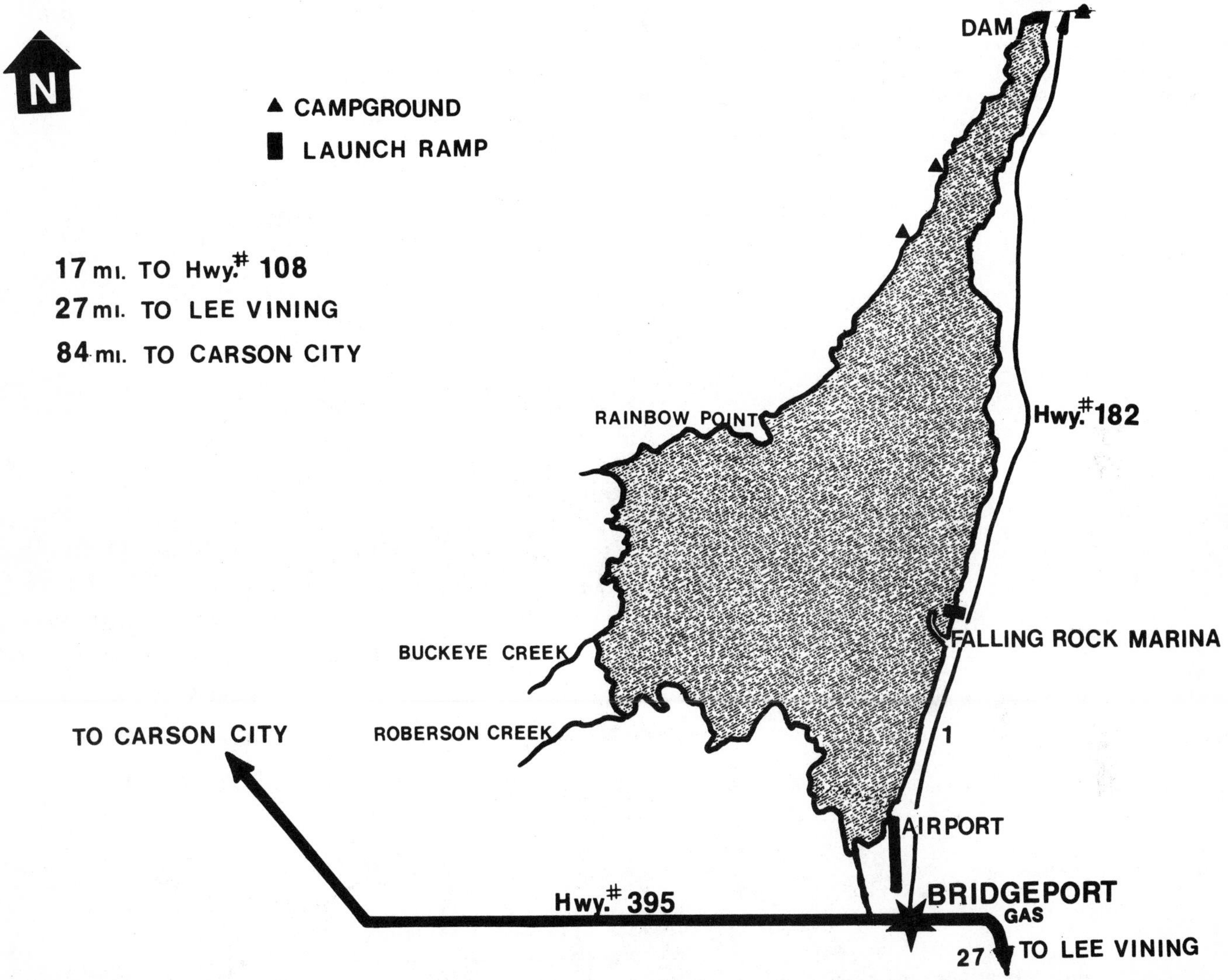
N
CAMPGROUND
LAUNCH RAMP
17 mi. TO Hwy.# 108
27 mi. TO LEE VINING
84 mi. TO CARSON CITY
DAM
RAINBOW POINT
Hwy.# 182
FALLING ROCK MARINA
BUCKEYE CREEK
ROBERSON CREEK
TO CARSON CITY
1
AIRPORT
Hwy.# 395
BRIDGEPORT
GAS
27
TO LEE VINING

INFORMATION: Falling Rock Marina, P. O. Box 338, Bridgeport 93517

CAMPING	BOATING	RECREATION	RESORTS
19 Spaces for R.V.s and Trailers with Full Hookups	All Boating Allowed Launch Ramp Full Service Marina Boat Rentals	Fishing Visit Ghost Town of Bodie	Store Snack Bar Full Facilities in Bridgeport

The Twin Lakes are at an elevation of 7,000 feet and the season is from May to October. About 75,000 trout are planted annually and September and October are often the best months for fishing. Within a radius of 15 miles of Bridgeport-Twin Lakes, there are 35 lakes and 17 streams.

The Upper Lake facility is Mono Village which has cabins, motel units, camp and trailer sites, grocery store, fishing tackle, bar and restaurant. There is a big Marina with a breakwater, boat dock and launch ramp at the end of the paved road. Boat rentals are also available. Write: Mono Village, P. O. Box 455, Bridgeport 93517 or Phone: 714-932-7071.

The Lower Lake facility is the Lower Twin Lakes Resort, Bridgeport 93517. They have cottages for rent, grocery store and fishing tackle, restaurant, boat rentals and a small paved launch ramp with a breakwater. All boating is allowed on the Lakes and the water is cold at about 40 degrees. The shoreline is rocky and steep in many areas with trees down to water's edge. There are usually strong afternoon breezes.

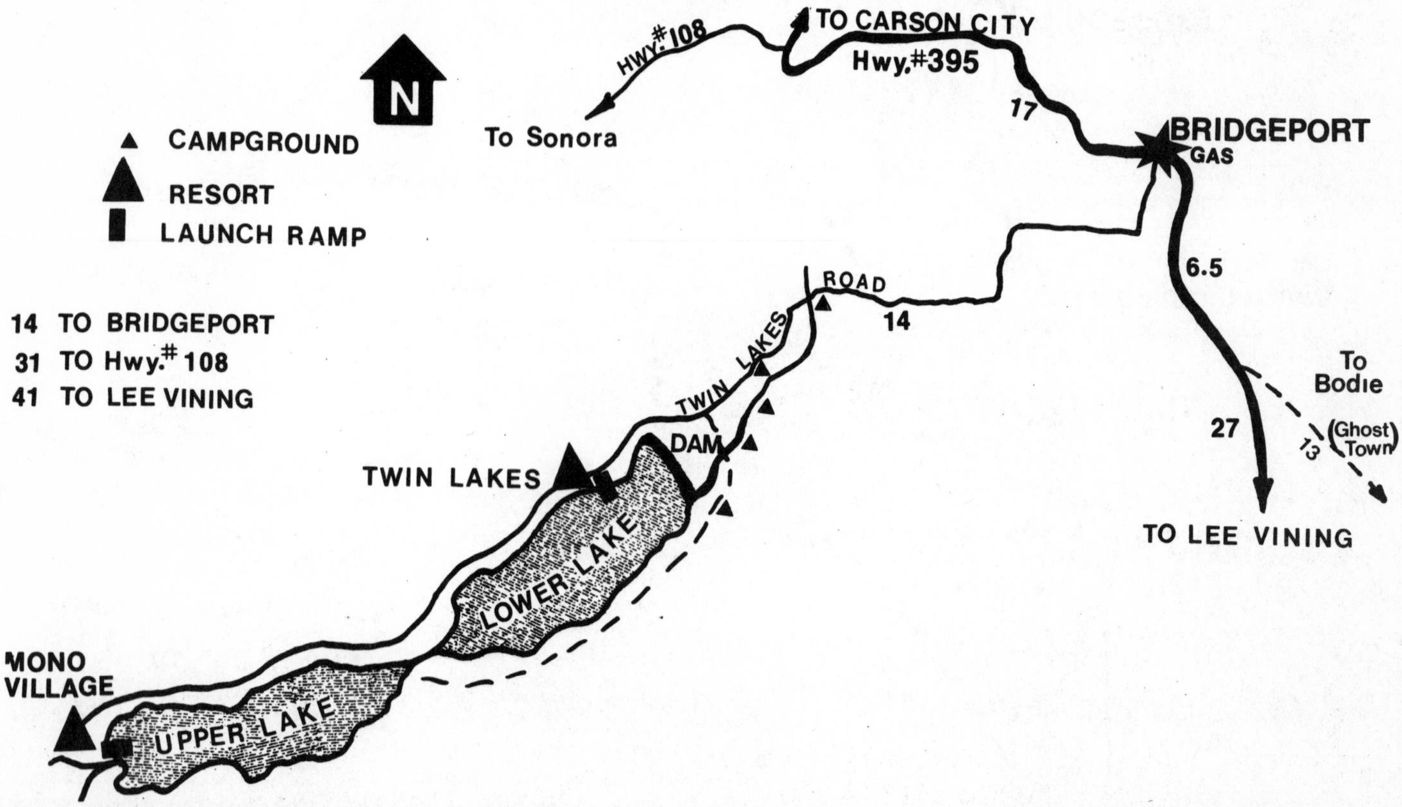
TO CARSON CITY
Hwy.#395
HWY.#108
N
To Sonora
17
BRIDGEPORT
GAS
CAMPGROUND
RESORT
LAUNCH RAMP
ROAD
14
6.5
14 TO BRIDGEPORT
31 TO Hwy.# 108
41 TO LEE VINING
TWIN LAKES
To Bodie
(Ghost Town)
13
27
DAM
TWIN LAKES
TO LEE VINING
LOWER LAKE
MONO VILLAGE
UPPER LAKE

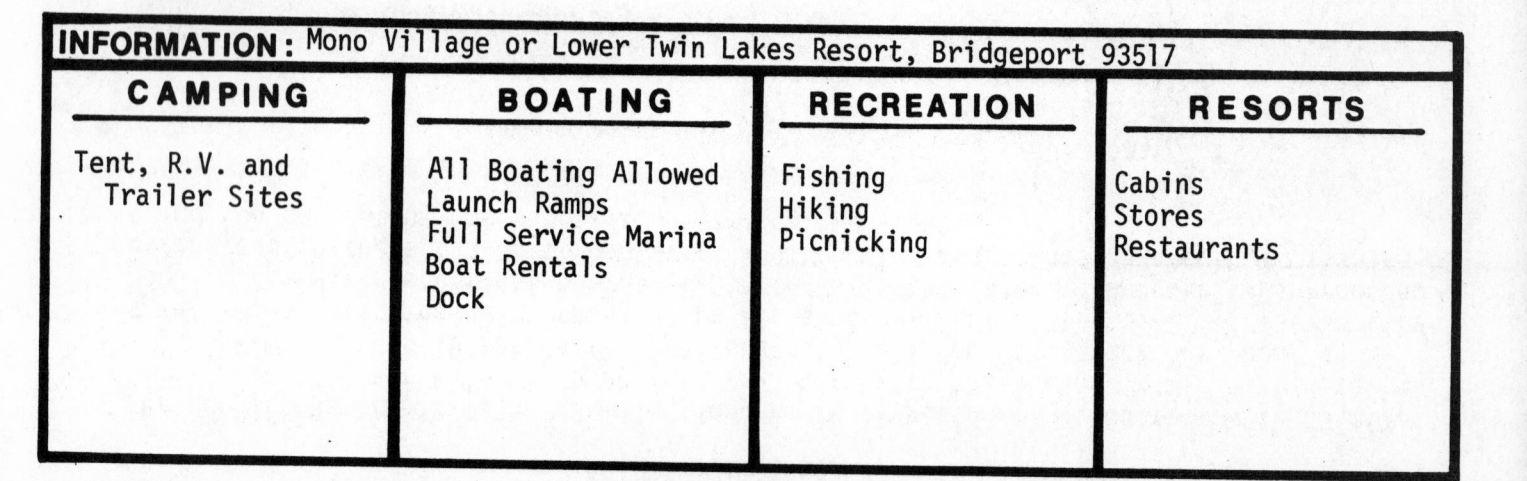

INFORMATION: Mono Village or Lower Twin Lakes Resort, Bridgeport 93517

CAMPING	BOATING	RECREATION	RESORTS
Tent, R.V. and Trailer Sites	All Boating Allowed Launch Ramps Full Service Marina Boat Rentals Dock	Fishing Hiking Picnicking	Cabins Stores Restaurants

VIRGINIA LAKES

The Virginia Lakes are 10 small Lakes at 9,000 feet elevation located 6 miles West of Highway 395. No swimming is allowed in the Lakes. Virginia Lake Resort has 18 cabins, a grocery store, fishing supplies and restaurant. The U. S. Forest Service operates 60 sites for tents, R.V.s and trailers. There is a pack station below the Lodge with horses for rent. You can rent rowboats with electric motors also. The season is from Memorial Day to mid-October. This is truly a fisherman's paradise as the 10 Lakes are within 1-1/2 miles of the Lodge and there are miles of streams.

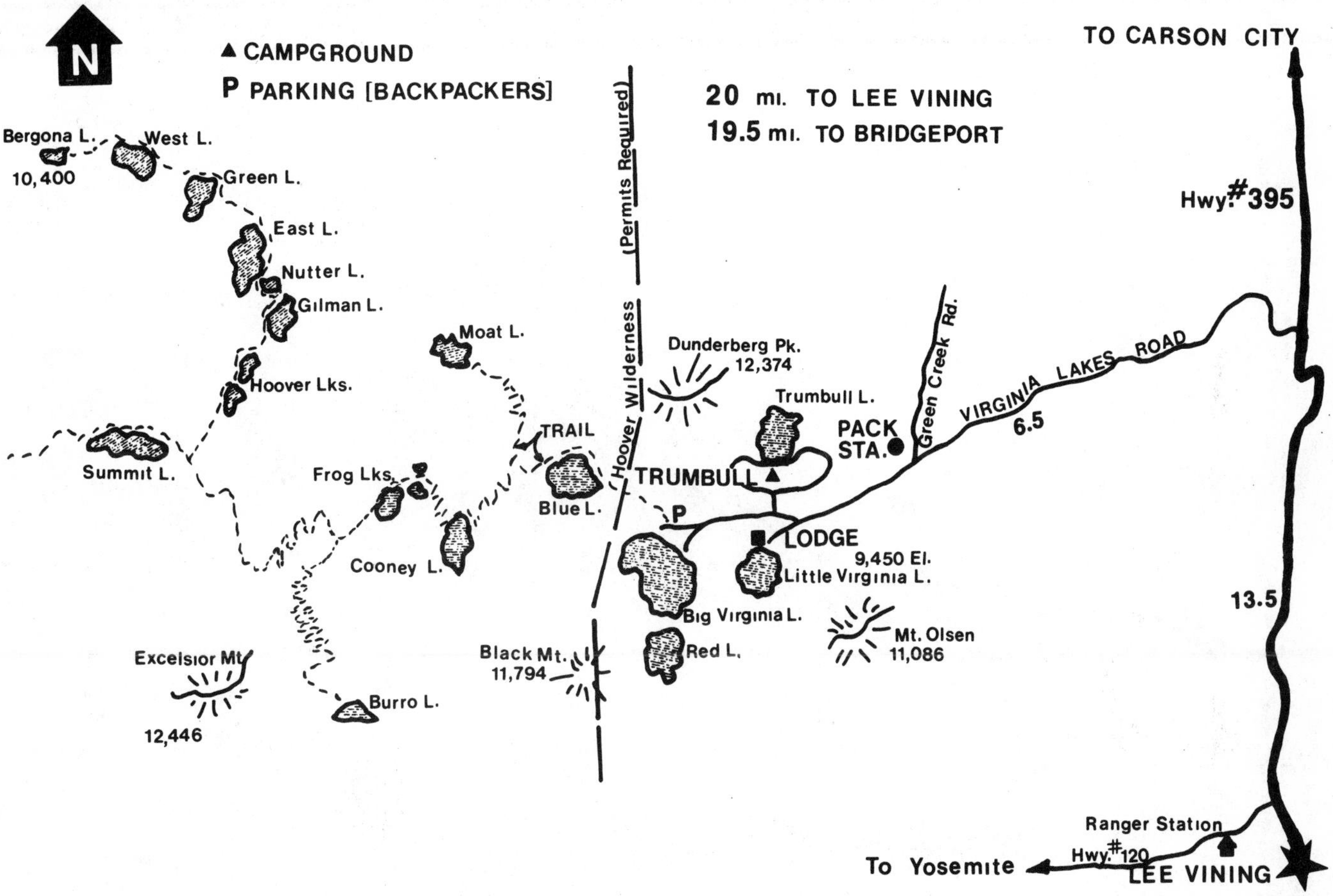
N
▲ CAMPGROUND
P PARKING [BACKPACKERS]
20 mi. TO LEE VINING
19.5 mi. TO BRIDGEPORT
TO CARSON CITY
Hwy.#395
Bergona L.
10,400
West L.
Green L.
East L.
Nutter L.
Gilman L.
Hoover Lks.
Summit L.
Moat L.
Frog Lks.
Cooney L.
TRAIL
Blue L.
(Permits Required)
Hoover Wilderness
Dunderberg Pk.
12,374
Trumbull L.
TRUMBULL
PACK STA.
Green Creek Rd.
VIRGINIA LAKES ROAD
6.5
P
LODGE
9,450 El.
Little Virginia L.
Big Virginia L.
Red L.
Mt. Olsen
11,086
Black Mt.
11,794
Excelsior Mt.
12,446
Burro L.
13.5
Ranger Station
Hwy.#120
To Yosemite
LEE VINING

INFORMATION: Virginia Lakes Resort, Conway Summit, Bridgeport 93517			
CAMPING	**BOATING**	**RECREATION**	**RESORTS**
60 Developed Sites for Tents, R.V.s and Trailers - U.S.F.S.	Rentals - Rowboats and Electric Motors	Fishing Hiking Pack Station	Cabins Store Restaurant

LUNDY LAKE

Lundy Lake, at 7,800 feet elevation, is nestled down in a valley that is open to the West. High majestic mountains to the North and South and a rocky shoreline provide for most spectacular scenery. The Lake water is very clear and cold, and the fishing can be excellent. Lundy Lake Resort has full housekeeping cabins, mobile homes and rustic housekeeping cabins with cold water only. There are trailer sites with hookups as well as tent campgrounds. There is a small launching ramp for boats under 16 feet and rental boats are also available. A nice addition to this Resort are its Camp Huts which provide a shelter, electricity and gas hot plates. This is a delightful spot for the fisherman and photographer as well.

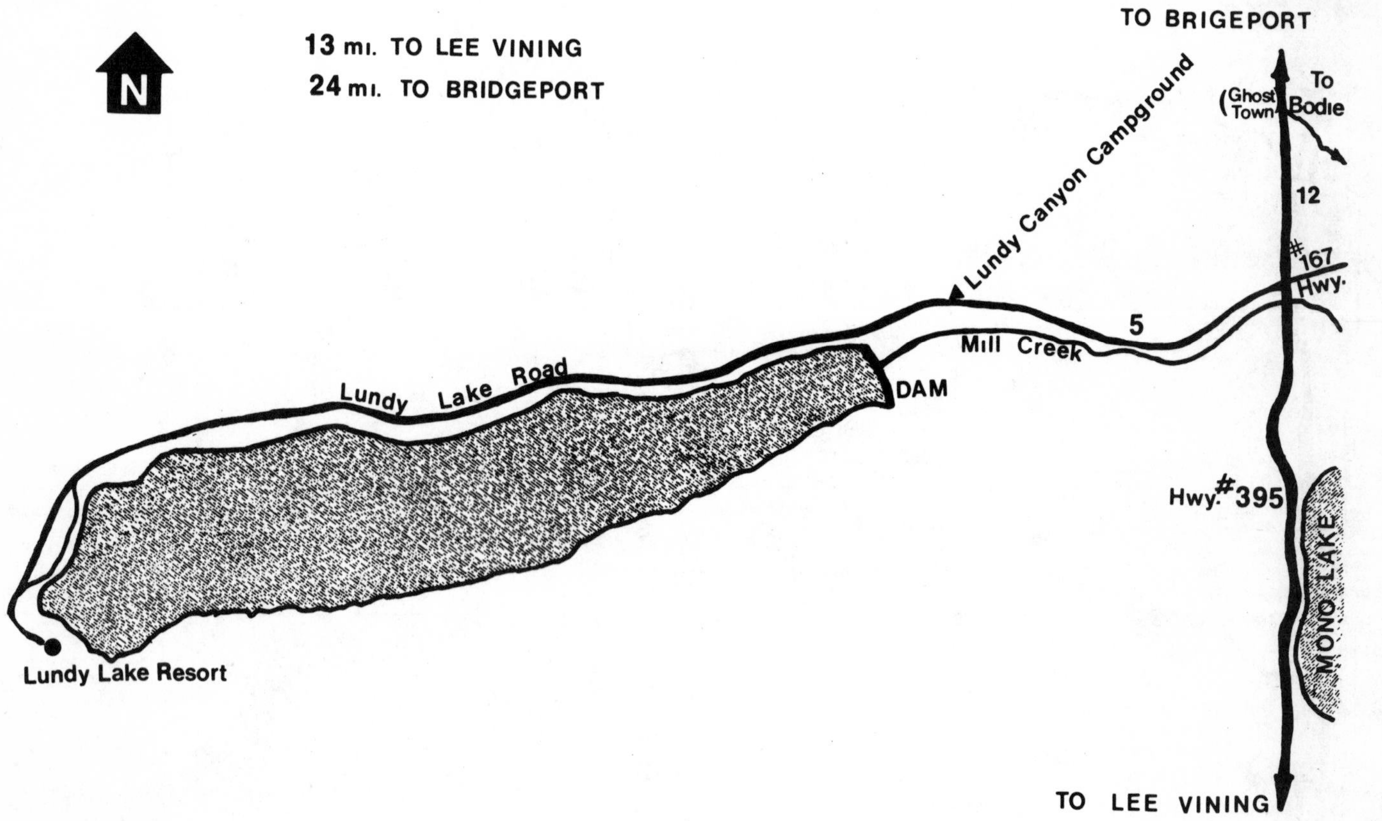
N
13 mi. TO LEE VINING
24 mi. TO BRIDGEPORT
TO BRIGEPORT
To Bodie (Ghost Town)
12
Lundy Canyon Campground
#167 Hwy.
5
Mill Creek
Lundy Lake Road
DAM
Hwy. #395
MONO LAKE
Lundy Lake Resort
TO LEE VINING

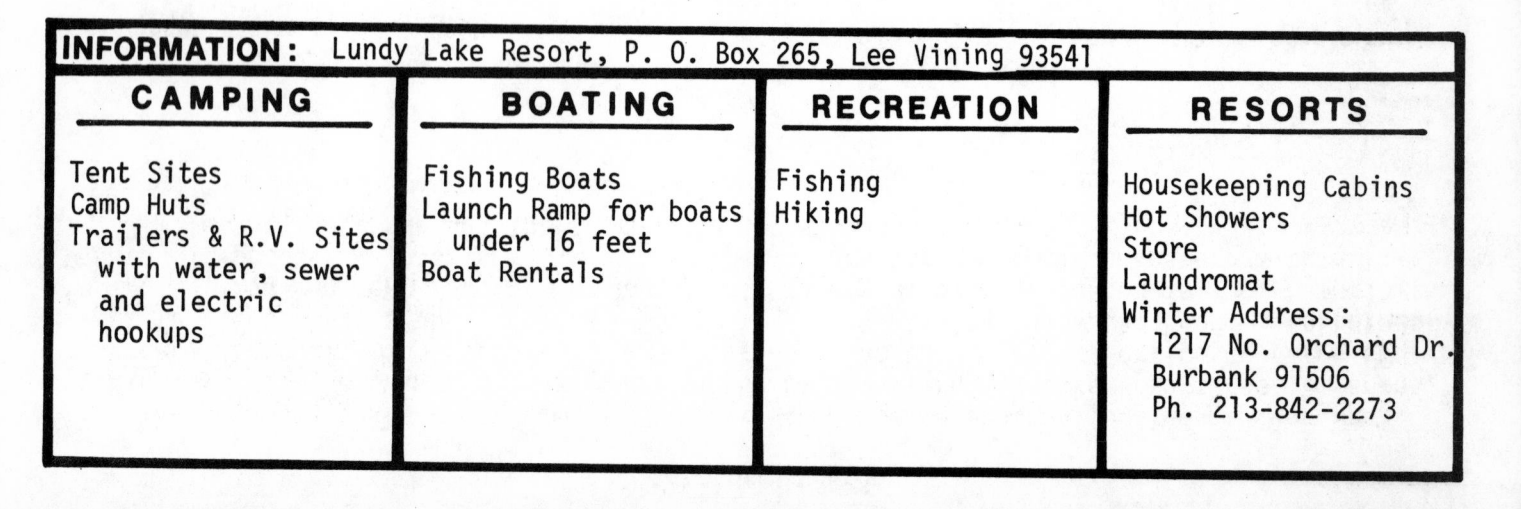

INFORMATION: Lundy Lake Resort, P. O. Box 265, Lee Vining 93541

CAMPING	BOATING	RECREATION	RESORTS
Tent Sites Camp Huts Trailers & R.V. Sites with water, sewer and electric hookups	Fishing Boats Launch Ramp for boats under 16 feet Boat Rentals	Fishing Hiking	Housekeeping Cabins Hot Showers Store Laundromat Winter Address: 1217 No. Orchard Dr. Burbank 91506 Ph. 213-842-2273

SADDLEBAG LAKE

Saddlebag Lake is a pretty Lake in very rugged country just before the Northeast entrance to Yosemite Park. There is a rocked road 2-1/2 miles in from Highway 120. The rocky shoreline is quite rough and the elevation is over 10,000 feet. The U. S. Forest Service has a small campground with 20 sites with toilets and barbecues. There are miles of trails into the Wilderness Area, permit required, for the experienced hiker. The Resort has a launch ramp for boats not over 16 feet as well as a store, cafe, rental boats and a water taxi which is a good way to sightsee or come closer to the Twenty Lake Basin for backpackers. The water is extremely cold and the fishing is good.

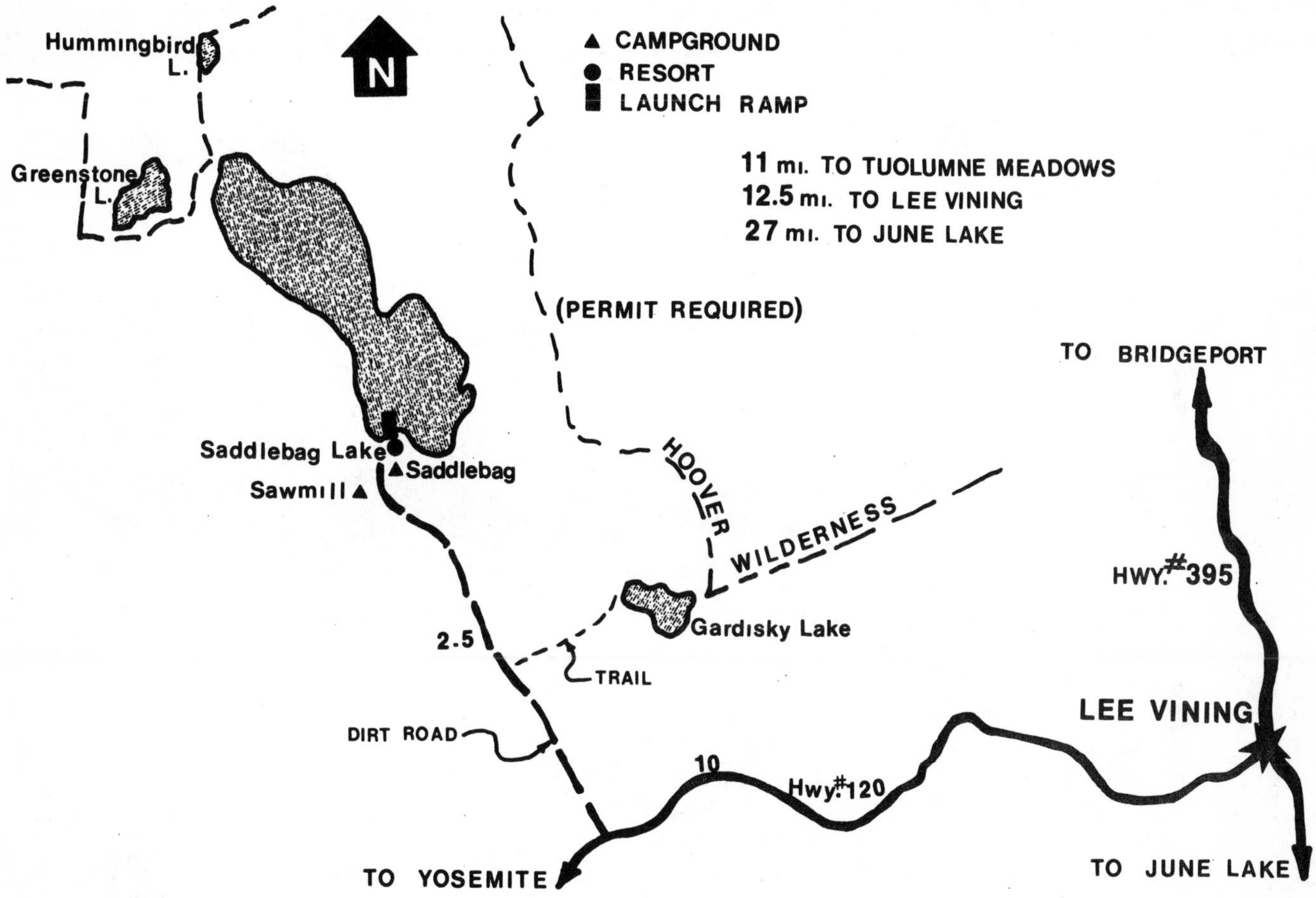
Hummingbird L.
N
CAMPGROUND
RESORT
LAUNCH RAMP
11 mi. TO TUOLUMNE MEADOWS
12.5 mi. TO LEE VINING
27 mi. TO JUNE LAKE
Greenstone L.
(PERMIT REQUIRED)
TO BRIDGEPORT
Saddlebag Lake
Saddlebag
Sawmill
HOOVER
WILDERNESS
HWY.#395
Gardisky Lake
2.5
TRAIL
LEE VINING
DIRT ROAD
10
Hwy.#120
TO YOSEMITE
TO JUNE LAKE

INFORMATION: Saddlebag Lake Resort, P. O. Box 36, Lee Vining 93541

CAMPING	BOATING	RECREATION	RESORTS
20 Sites for Tents, Small R.V.s and Trailers due to road condition U. S. Forest Service Fee: $2 a Day	Fishing Boats Launch Ramp for Boats to 16 feet Boat Rentals Water Taxi	Fishing Hiking Backpacking - Wilderness Permit Required	Store Cafe Winter Address: Saddlebag Lake Resort 389 O'Connor St. Palo Alto 94303

ELLERY LAKE
and
TIOGA LAKE

Ellery and Tioga Lakes, at about 10,000 feet elevation, are open from approximately May 20 to October 15. The water is cold and trout fishing is excellent both at these Lakes and the numerous streams and other Lakes in this area. There are 13 campsites at each Lake with water, toilets and fire pits. Cartop boats only can be launched as there is no ramp. These are lovely Lakes in a spectacular mountain setting. Tioga Pass Resort offers housekeeping cabins, a store and restaurant along with rental boats. It is located just two miles from the East entrance to Yosemite National Park.

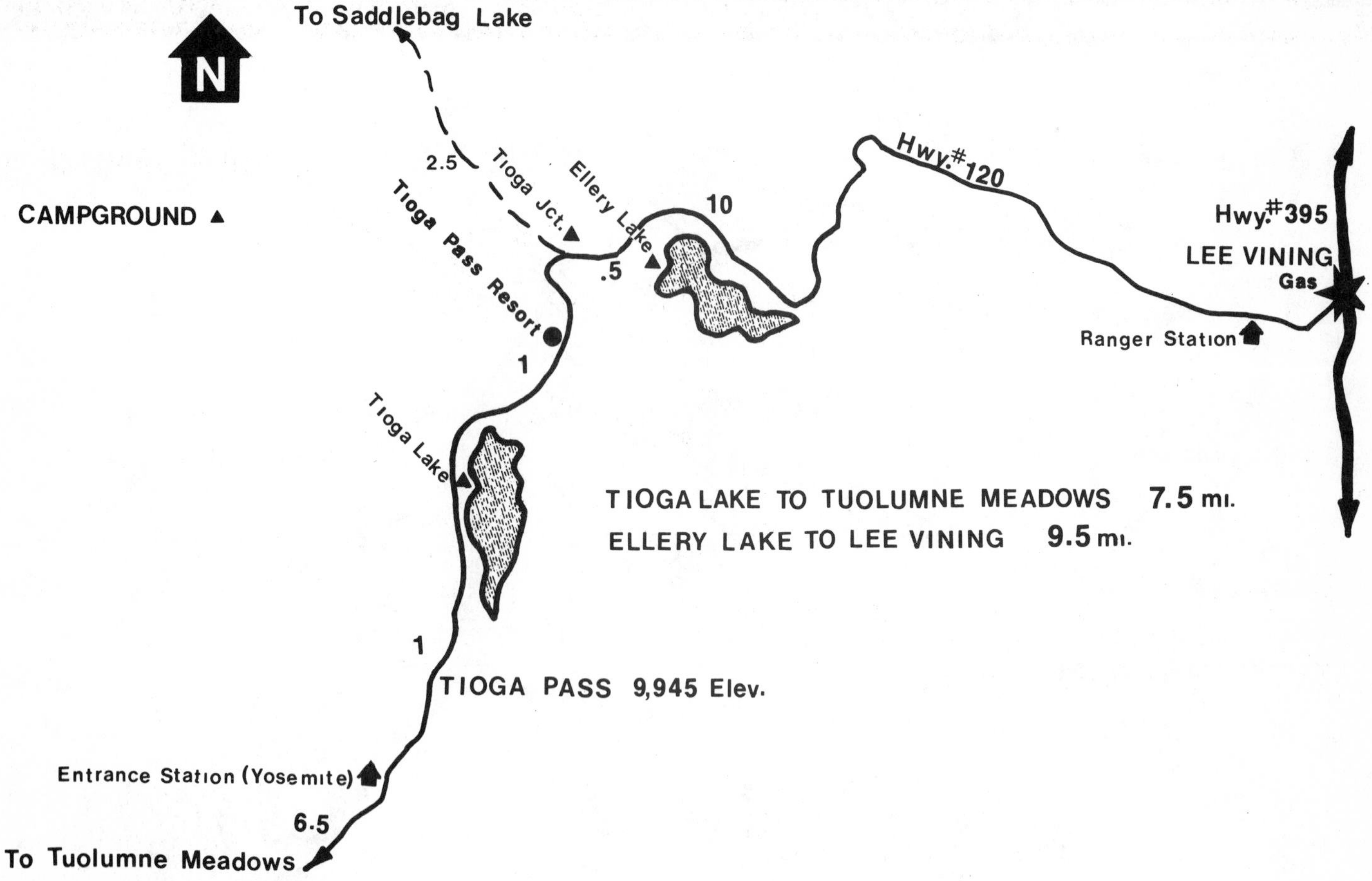
To Saddlebag Lake
N
2.5
Tioga Jct.
Ellery Lake
Tioga Pass Resort
CAMPGROUND ▲
10
Hwy.#120
Hwy.#395
LEE VINING
Gas
.5
Ranger Station
1
Tioga Lake
TIOGA LAKE TO TUOLUMNE MEADOWS 7.5 mi.
ELLERY LAKE TO LEE VINING 9.5 mi.
1
TIOGA PASS 9,945 Elev.
Entrance Station (Yosemite)
6.5
To Tuolumne Meadows

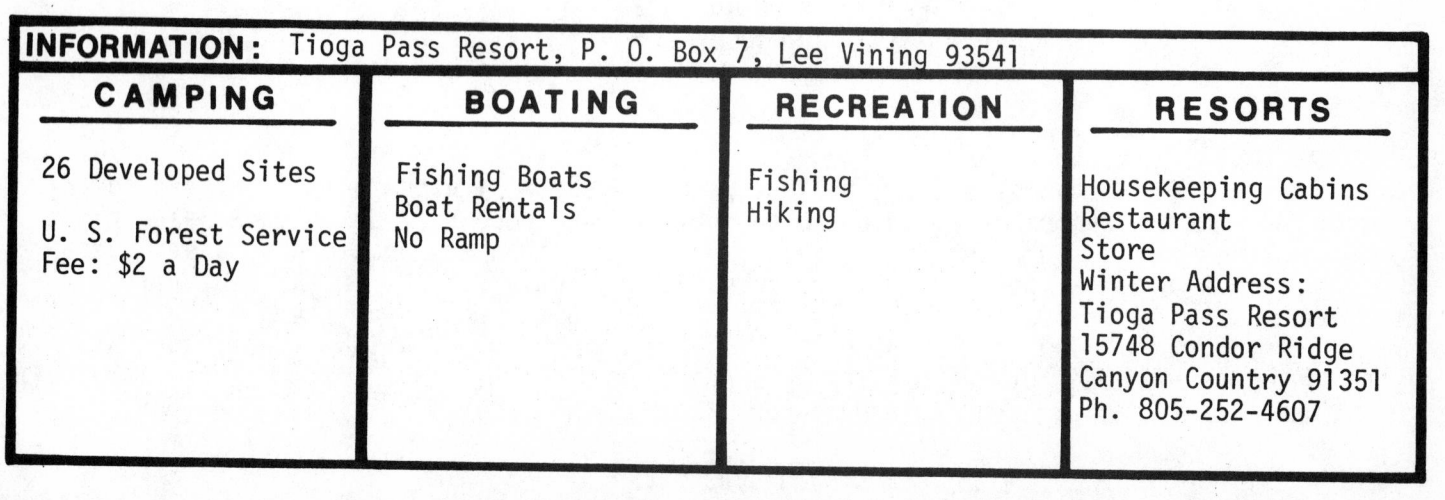

INFORMATION: Tioga Pass Resort, P. O. Box 7, Lee Vining 93541

CAMPING	BOATING	RECREATION	RESORTS
26 Developed Sites U. S. Forest Service Fee: $2 a Day	Fishing Boats Boat Rentals No Ramp	Fishing Hiking	Housekeeping Cabins Restaurant Store Winter Address: Tioga Pass Resort 15748 Condor Ridge Canyon Country 91351 Ph. 805-252-4607

TENAYA LAKE

Tenaya Lake in Yosemite National Park has 50 walk-in campsites at the West end of the Lake. The elevation is about 8,000 feet. The parking lot is above the campsites and motorhomes are not permitted. Powerboats are not allowed on the Lake, and there is no ramp so cartop boats only can be launched. Picnic areas are on the East end of the Lake and make for a pleasant stop if you are traveling through Yosemite.

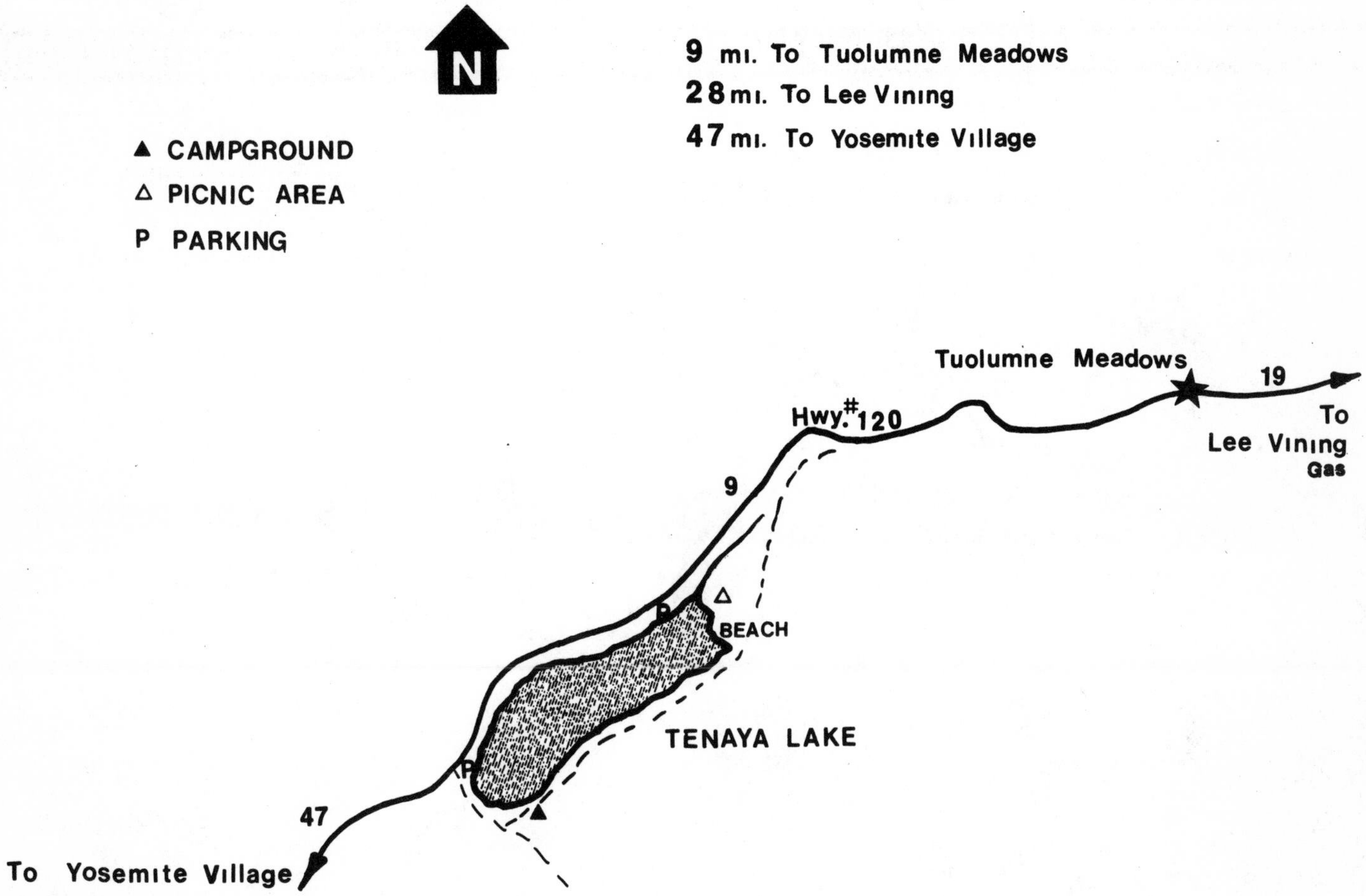
N
9 mi. To Tuolumne Meadows
28 mi. To Lee Vining
47 mi. To Yosemite Village
▲ CAMPGROUND
△ PICNIC AREA
P PARKING
Tuolumne Meadows
19
To
Lee Vining
Gas
Hwy.# 120
9
P
BEACH
TENAYA LAKE
P
47
To Yosemite Village

INFORMATION: Superintendent, Yosemite National Park 95389

CAMPING	BOATING	RECREATION	RESORTS
50 Walk-in Sites	No Powerboats No Ramp	Fishing Hiking Picnicking	

JUNE LAKE LOOP

June Lake Loop consists of 4 Lakes off Highway 395. Grant Lake is the largest with 1,100 acres. Silver Lake has 80 acres. Gull Lake, the smallest, has 64 acres, and June Lake has 160 acres, all interlocked by mountain streams. Full vacation facilities offer all types of accommodations and recreation as shown on the following page.

. . . Continued . . .

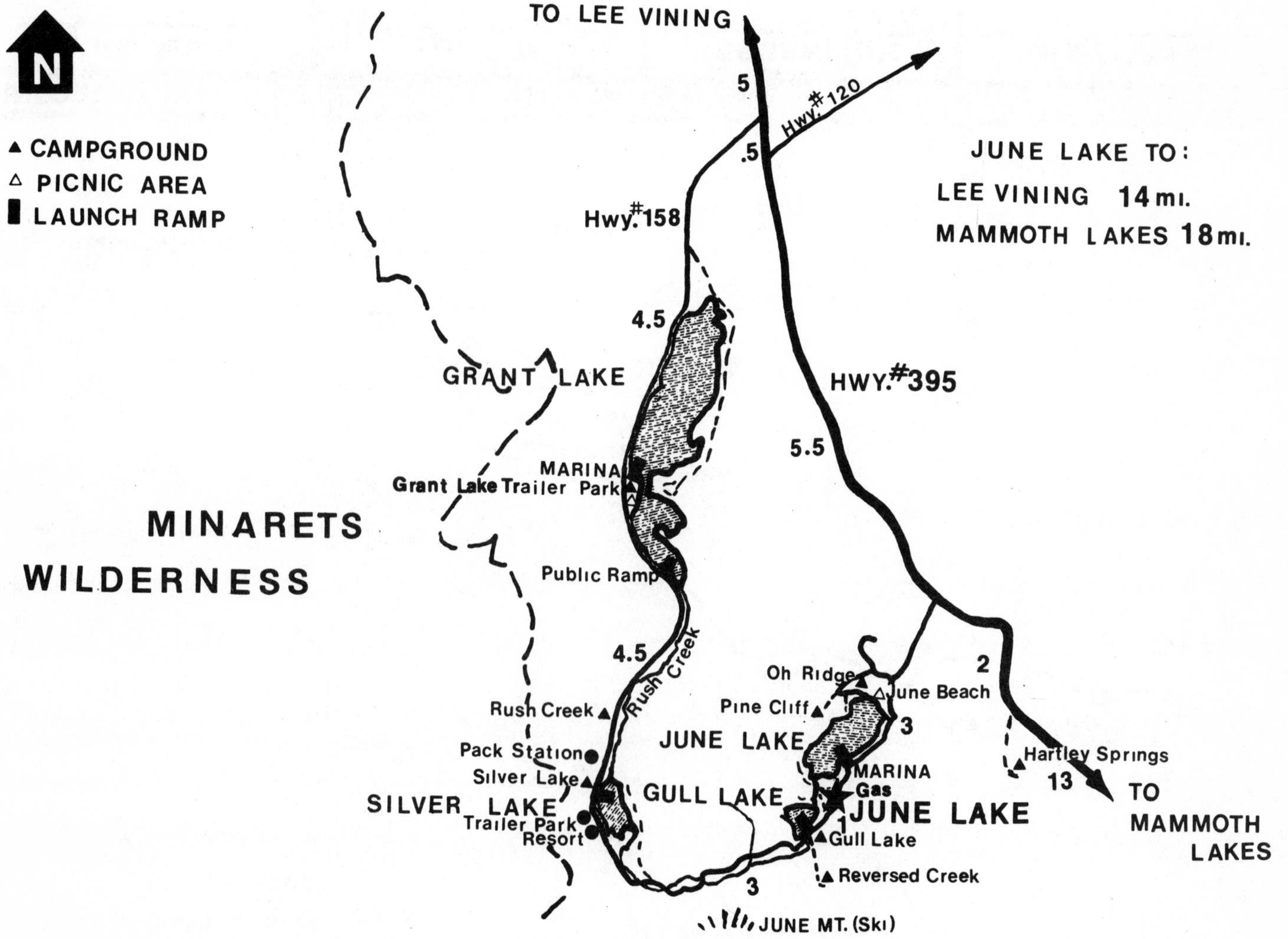
TO LEE VINING
N
▲ CAMPGROUND
△ PICNIC AREA
▮ LAUNCH RAMP
5
Hwy. #120
.5
Hwy. #158
JUNE LAKE TO:
LEE VINING 14 mi.
MAMMOTH LAKES 18 mi.
4.5
GRANT LAKE
HWY. #395
5.5
MARINA
Grant Lake Trailer Park
MINARETS
WILDERNESS
Public Ramp
4.5
Rush Creek
Oh Ridge
2
June Beach
Rush Creek
Pine Cliff
3
JUNE LAKE
Pack Station
Hartley Springs
Silver Lake
MARINA
13
Gas
TO
SILVER LAKE
GULL LAKE
JUNE LAKE
MAMMOTH
Trailer Park
Resort
1
Gull Lake
LAKES
Reversed Creek
3
JUNE MT. (Ski)

INFORMATION: U. S. Forest Service and Individual Resorts

CAMPING	BOATING	RECREATION	RESORTS
Over 300 Developed Sites for Tents, R.V.s and Trailers U. S. Forest Service Privately Owned Facilities	Small Boats Restricted Speeds Full Service Marina Launch Ramps Rental Boats	Fishing Picnicking Hiking Horseback Riding Swimming (June Lake)	Housekeeping Cabins Motels Restaurants Stores Laundromats

GRANT LAKE

Campgrounds - Grant Lake Marina
Star Route No. 3, Box 19
June Lake 93529

70 Developed Sites for tents, R.V.s and trailers, water, toilets, barbecues, hot showers, dump station, restaurant, boat rentals, picnicking, hiking, bicycle and motorbike trails - No Swimming.

SILVER LAKE

Campgrounds - U. S. Forest Service
65 Developed Sites for tents, R.V.s and trailers, water, toilets, barbecues.

Resort - Silver Lake Resort and Trailer Park
Box 116
June Lake 93529

Resort Phone: 714-648-7525
Trailer Park: 714-648-7355

Full Housekeeping Cabins, store, restaurant, gas station, pump station, hot showers, launch ramp, rental boats and a 75-Unit Trailer Park with full hookups. No Swimming, 10 MPH Speed Limit on Lake.

GULL LAKE

Campgrounds - U. S. Forest Service
Gull Lake - 13 Tent Sites, water, toilets, barbecues.
Reversed Creek - 17 Trailer Sites, water, toilets, barbecues.

Gull Lake Boat Landing - P. O. Box 65, June Lake 93529
Full Service Marina, 30 Rental Boats and Motors, launch ramp.
No Swimming.

JUNE LAKE

Campgrounds - U. S. Forest Service
Oh Ridge - 111 Developed sites for tents, R.V.s and trailers, water, toilets, barbecues.
June Lake - 22 Developed sites for tents, R.V.s and trailers, water, toilets, barbecues.
Hartley Springs (South on Highway 395) - 20 Developed sites for tents, R.V.s and trailers, toilets, barbecues.

Some Resorts - Pine Cliff Trailer Park - 75 Trailer sites, water, toilets, showers.
Golden Pine - Trailer rentals for 4 to 6 people.
Village Motel - Housekeeping Units
Lake Front Cabins - Housekeeping Units
Fern Creek Lodge - Units from 2 people to 17 people

Full Service Marina, launch ramps, picnic areas, swim beach, full vacation facilities.

MAMMOTH LAKES

The Mammoth Area is the doorway to magnificent High Sierra wilderness country. Twin Lakes (different from Lake No. 103), Lake Mary, Lake Mamie and Horseshoe Lake are four of the Lakes that have paved road access, but there are many others within easy hiking distance. The Lakes are small with Lake Mary being the largest. The water is cold and the fishing can be excellent. Further information on facilities are on the following page. The resort town of Mammoth Lakes, a popular ski resort in the winter, has many motels, housekeeping cabins, restaurants and stores as well as U. S. Forest Service campgrounds.

. . . Continued . . .

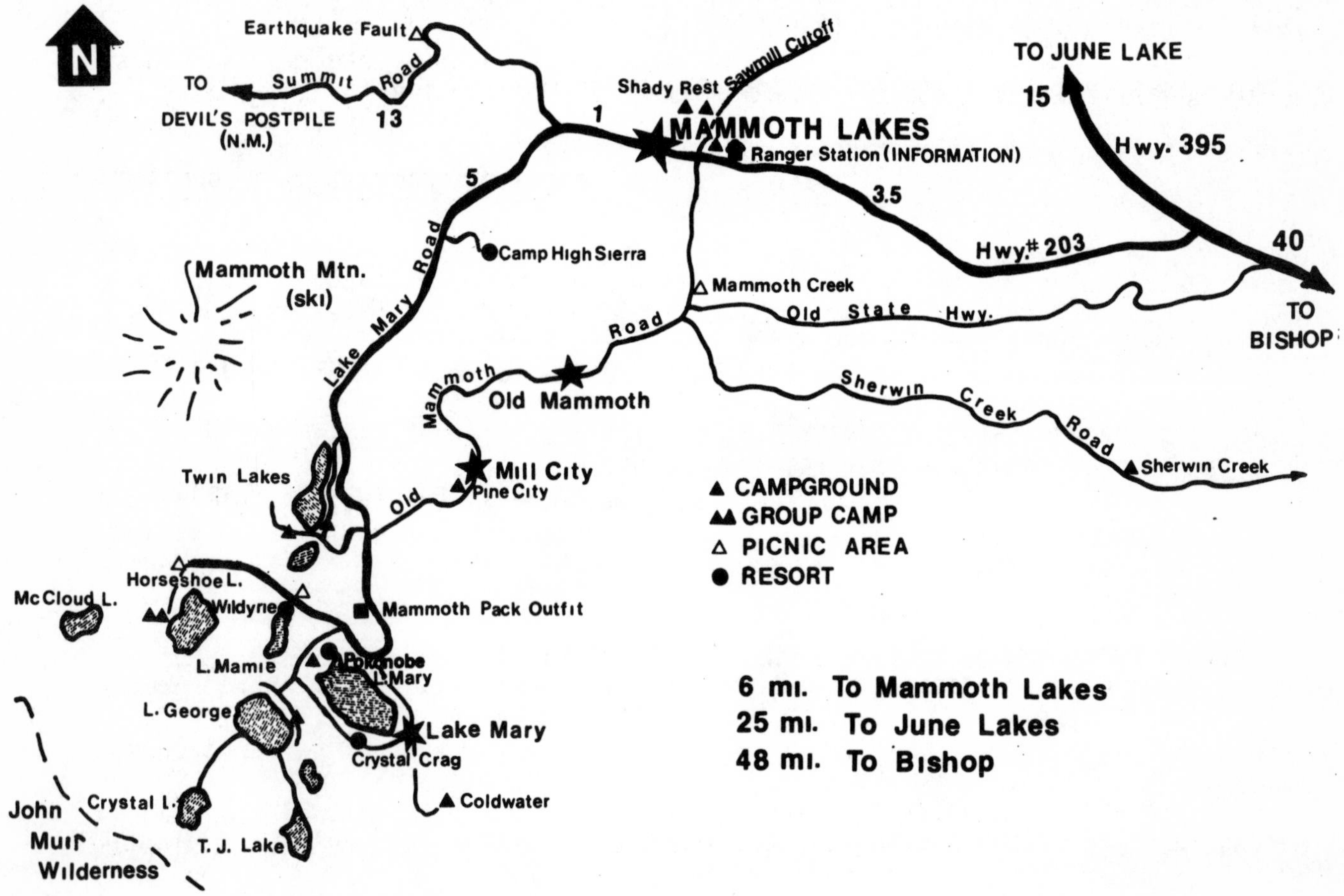
N
Earthquake Fault
TO DEVIL'S POSTPILE (N.M.)
Summit Road
13
Shady Rest
Sawmill Cutoff
1
MAMMOTH LAKES
Ranger Station (INFORMATION)
TO JUNE LAKE
15
Hwy. 395
3.5
5
Hwy.# 203
40
TO BISHOP
Camp High Sierra
Mammoth Mtn. (ski)
Mammoth Creek
Old State Hwy.
Lake Mary Road
Mammoth Road
Old Mammoth
Sherwin Creek Road
Sherwin Creek
Twin Lakes
Mill City
Pine City
Old
Horseshoe L.
McCloud L.
Wildyne
Mammoth Pack Outfit
L. Mamie
Pokonobe
L. Mary
L. George
Lake Mary
Crystal Crag
Coldwater
Crystal L.
T. J. Lake
John Muir Wilderness
▲ CAMPGROUND
▲▲ GROUP CAMP
△ PICNIC AREA
● RESORT
6 mi. To Mammoth Lakes
25 mi. To June Lakes
48 mi. To Bishop

INFORMATION: U. S. Forest Service - See following page

CAMPING	BOATING	RECREATION	RESORTS
Developed Sites for Tents, R.V.s and Trailers See Individual Lake Group Campground - 385 People Maximum Handicapped Facilities	Fishing Boats Primarily Launch Ramps Boat and Motor Rental	Fishing Hiking Picnicking Wilderness Backpack Horseback Riding Pack Stations Sightseeing	Motels Housekeeping Cabins Restaurants Stores

TWIN LAKES

U. S. Forest Service Campground - 97 Developed Sites (23 tents/74 trailers), water, toilets, barbecues. Fee: $3 a Day.
Hot showers, store, cafe, launch ramp, rental boats.

LAKE MARY

U. S. Forest Service Campground - 77 Developed Sites for tents, water, toilets, barbecues. Fee: $3 a Day.

Private Resorts

Crystal Crag Lodge P. O. Box 21 Mammoth Lakes 93546 Phone: 714-934-2436	Housekeeping Cabins Store Boat and Motor Rentals Bicycle Rentals	Open - May 25 to October 1
Pokonobe Resort P. O. Box 72 Mammoth Lakes 93546	Camp Sites Boat Rentals Store	

LAKE MAMIE

Wildyrie Lodge Mammoth Lakes 93546 Phone: 714-934-2444	Housekeeping Cabins Store Coffee Shop Boat and Bicycle Rentals	Open - May 25 October 1

HORSESHOE LAKE

U. S. Forest Service Group Campground - 6 Group Sites - 385 people maximum - Tents, R.V.s and Trailers, water, toilets, barbecues - $10 Minimum a Day - Reservations: Your local Ticketron outlet or write: Ticketron, P. O. Box 26430, San Francisco 94120.

OTHER U. S. FOREST SERVICE FACILITIES

Mammoth Lakes Town -
New Shady Rest - 96 Developed Sites for Tents, R.V.s and Trailers - water, toilets, barbecues, disposal station. Fee: $3 a Day.

Old Shady Rest - 67 Developed Sites for Tents, R.V.s and Trailers - water, toilets, barbecues, disposal station. Fee: $3 a Day.

Pine Glen - 18 Developed Sites, Single Family and 3 Developed Sites, Multiple Families, for Tents, R.V.s and Trailers, Handicapped Facilities, water, toilets, barbecues. Fee: $3 a Day.

Coldwater Campground - Trail Head into John Muir Wilderness - 79 Developed Sites for Tents, R.V.s and Trailers, water, toilets, barbecues. Fee: $3 a Day.

Lake George Campground - 40 Developed Sites (12 tents only, 28 tents, R.V.s and trailers), water, toilets, barbecues, store, boat rentals, boat launch.

CONVICT LAKE

Convict Lake, at 7,583 feet elevation, has to be one of the most beautiful Lakes in the Sierras. The water is crystal clear, and it is nestled in a steep canyon where the mountains seem to touch the sky. The U. S. Forest Service operates a campground with 92 units (21 tents, 62 trailers) with water, toilets and barbecues, open from May to October. Convict Lake Resort has housekeeping cabins, restaurant, bar, general store and boat and motor rentals. There is a launching ramp with breakwater. A Pack Station with horses for rent is also available. This is also one of the best fishing Lakes in the area.

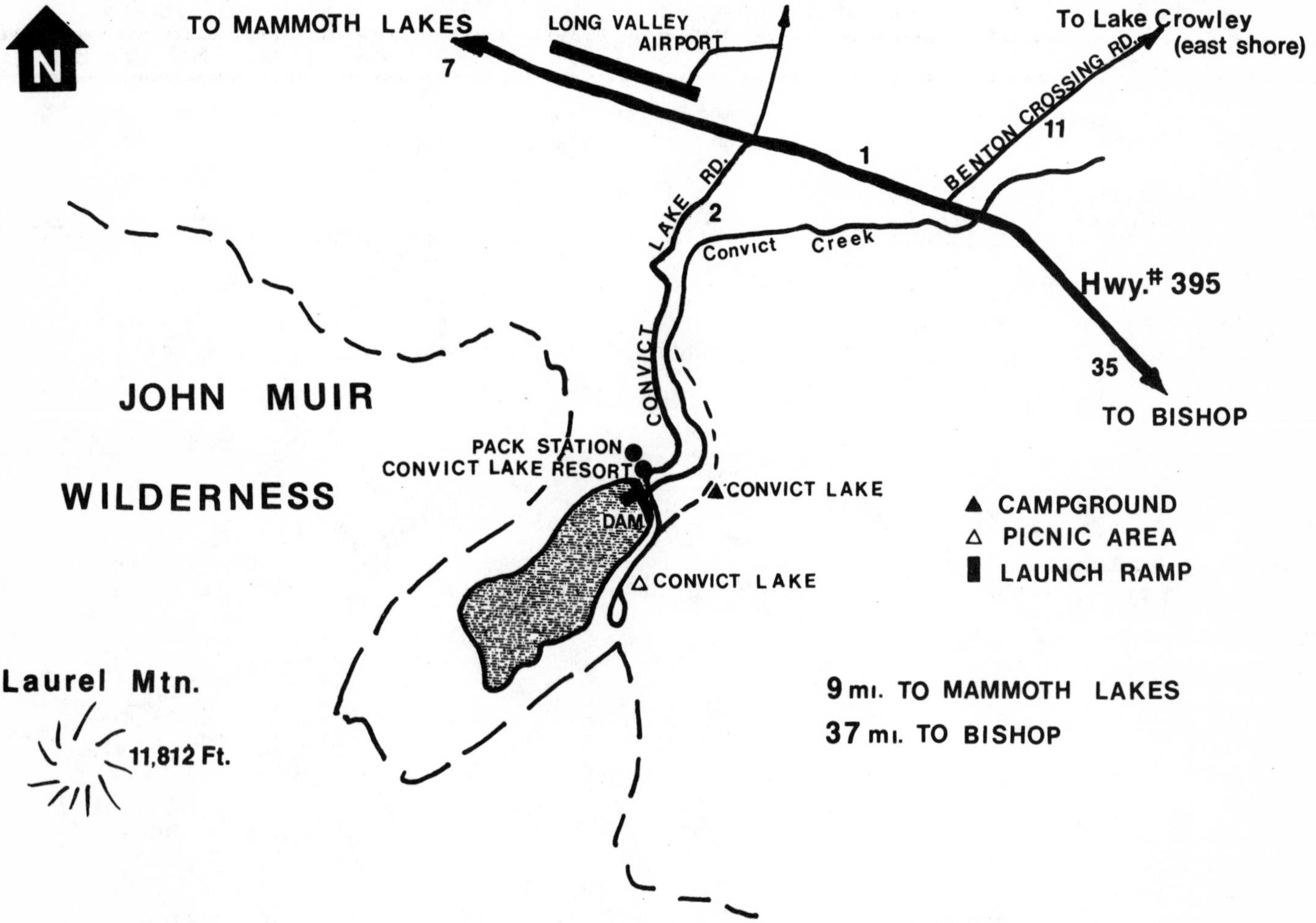
N
TO MAMMOTH LAKES
7
LONG VALLEY
AIRPORT
To Lake Crowley
(east shore)
BENTON CROSSING RD.
11
1
LAKE RD.
2
Convict Creek
Hwy.# 395
35
TO BISHOP
CONVICT
JOHN MUIR
WILDERNESS
PACK STATION
CONVICT LAKE RESORT
DAM
CONVICT LAKE
CONVICT LAKE
CAMPGROUND
PICNIC AREA
LAUNCH RAMP
Laurel Mtn.
11,812 Ft.
9 mi. TO MAMMOTH LAKES
37 mi. TO BISHOP

INFORMATION: Convict Lake Resort, Route 1, Box 204, Mammoth Lakes 93546, Ph.714-935-4213

CAMPING	BOATING	RECREATION	RESORTS
92 Developed Sites for Tents, R.V.s and Trailers U. S. Forest Service Fee: $4 a Day	Fishing Boats Launch Ramp Boat & Motor Rentals	Fishing Hiking Picnicking Horseback Riding Pack Station	Housekeeping Cabins Restaurant Snack Bar Store

CROWLEY LAKE

This huge man-made Reservoir is 12 miles long and open to fishermen from May through July. A special season for fly fishing only is from September 15 to October 31. Swimming is not permitted as Crowley Lake is the key to the domestic water supply for Los Angeles. Boats must be 12 feet in length minimum and must pass inspection prior to launching. There are numerous camping and resort areas nearby.

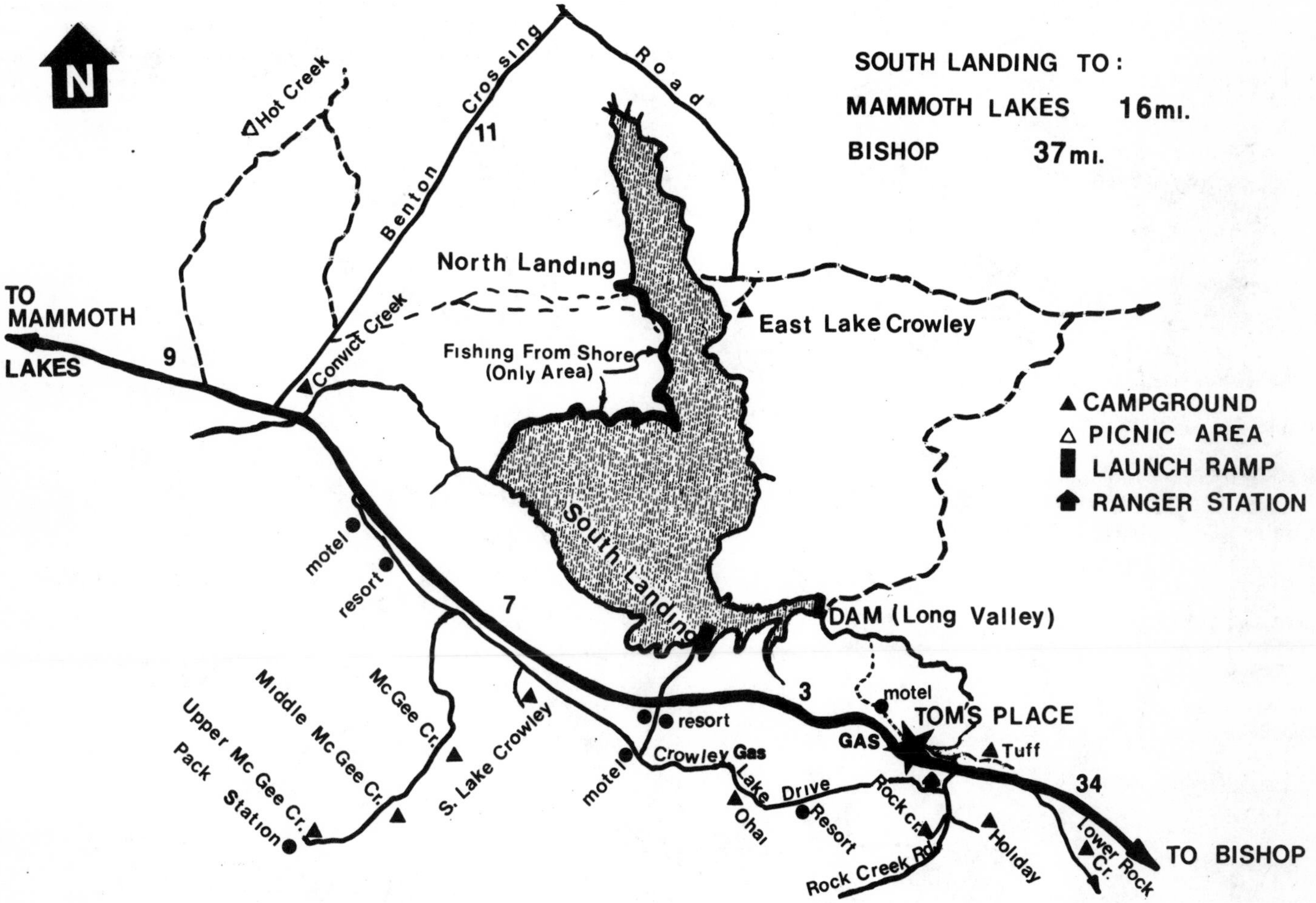

N
Hot Creek
Benton Crossing Road
11
SOUTH LANDING TO:
MAMMOTH LAKES 16mi.
BISHOP 37mi.
North Landing
TO MAMMOTH LAKES
9
Convict Creek
East Lake Crowley
Fishing From Shore (Only Area)
CAMPGROUND
PICNIC AREA
LAUNCH RAMP
RANGER STATION
motel
resort
South Landing
7
DAM (Long Valley)
Middle Mc Gee Cr.
Mc Gee Cr.
Upper Mc Gee Cr.
Pack Station
S. Lake Crowley
3
motel
resort
TOM'S PLACE
GAS
Tuff
motel
Crowley Gas
Lake Drive
Ohai
Resort
Rock cr.
34
Holiday
Lower Rock Cr.
TO BISHOP
Rock Creek Rd.

INFORMATION: South Landing, Crowley Lake 93514

CAMPING	BOATING	RECREATION	RESORTS
Privately Owned Campgrounds and Trailer Parks	Fishing Boats Launch Ramp - Inspection Permit Required Rental Boats & Motors Docks	Fishing	Crowley Lake Store Full Facilities adjacent to Highway 395

At the end of the day-up the ramp....

.....and home to supper of fresh pan fried fish
COD of INDIA
Snyder '79

TO: SAIL SALES
P. O. BOX 1028
APTOS, CA. 95003

ORDER BLANK

SEND RECREATION LAKES OF CENTRAL CALIFORNIA

5.95	BOOK
.39	SALES TAX
.66	POSTAGE
$ 7.00	CHECK ENCOSED

NAME: ______________________________

ADDRESS: ______________________________

TO: SAIL SALES
P. O. BOX 1028
APTOS, CA. 95003

ORDER BLANK

SEND RECREATION LAKES OF CENTRAL CALIFORNIA

5.95	BOOK
.39	SALES TAX
.66	POSTAGE
$ 7.00	CHECK ENCLOSED

NAME: ______________________________

ADDRESS: ______________________________

TO: SAIL SALES
P. O. BOX 1028
APTOS, CA. 95003

ORDER BLANK

SEND RECREATION LAKES OF CENTRAL CALIFORNIA

5.95	BOOK
.39	SALES TAX
.66	POSTAGE
$ 7.00	CHECK ENCLOSED

NAME: ______________________________

ADDRESS: ______________________________